PRIVACY AS VIRTUE

School of Human Rights Research Series, Volume 81.

The titles published in this series are listed at the end of this volume.

PRIVACY AS VIRTUE

Moving Beyond the Individual in the Age of Big Data

Bart van der Sloot

Cambridge – Antwerp – Portland

Intersentia Ltd
Sheraton House | Castle Park
Cambridge | CB3 0AX | United Kingdom
Tel.: +44 1223 370 170 | Fax: +44 1223 370 169
Email: mail@intersentia.co.uk
www.intersentia.com | www.intersentia.co.uk

Distribution for the UK and Ireland:
NBN International
Airport Business Centre, 10 Thornbury Road
Plymouth, PL6 7 PP
United Kingdom
Tel.: +44 1752 202 301 | Fax: +44 1752 202 331
Email: orders@nbninternational.com

Distribution for Europe and all other countries:
Intersentia Publishing nv
Groenstraat 31
2640 Mortsel
Belgium
Tel.: +32 3 680 15 50 | Fax: +32 3 658 71 21
Email: mail@intersentia.be

Distribution for the USA and Canada:
International Specialized Book Services
920 NE 58th Ave. Suite 300
Portland, OR 97213
USA
Tel.: +1 800 944 6190 (toll free) | Fax: +1 503 280 8832
Email: info@isbs.com

Privacy as Virtue: Moving Beyond the Individual in the Age of Big Data
© Bart van der Sloot 2017

Cover image: Allégorie des Vertus, Allegri Antonio (1489-1534) © RMN-Grand Palais (musée du Louvre) / Hervé Lewandowski

The editor and contributors have asserted the right under the Copyright, Designs and Patents Act 1988, to be identified as authors of this work.

No part of this book may be reproduced, stored in a retrieval system, or transmitted, in any form, or by any means, without prior written permission from Intersentia, or as expressly permitted by law or under the terms agreed with the appropriate reprographic rights organisation. Enquiries concerning reproduction which may not be covered by the above should be addressed to Intersentia at the address above.

ISBN 978-1-78068-505-2
D/2017/7849/61
NUR 828

British Library Cataloguing in Publication Data. A catalogue record for this book is available from the British Library.

CONTENTS

Chapter I
Introduction... 1

Chapter II
The Transformation of the Right to Privacy and the Right to Data Protection..... 11

1. Introduction.. 11
2. The right to privacy.. 13
   2.1. Right to complain..................................... 17
   2.2. Interests... 23
   2.3. Assessments.. 29
   2.4. Enforcement.. 35
3. Data Protection.. 39
   3.1. Obligations of the data processor..................... 48
   3.2. Rights of the data subject............................ 52
   3.3. Assessments.. 55
   3.4. Enforcement.. 65
4. Conclusion... 69

Chapter III
The Challenges for and Alternatives to the Current Privacy Paradigm........... 71

1. Introduction... 71
2. The challenges Big Data poses to the current legal paradigm................ 71
   2.1. Big Data and Data Protection......................... 72
   2.2. Focus on the individual............................... 75
   2.3. Regulation through legal means....................... 76
3. How the ECtHR is gradually moving beyond the individualized privacy paradigm... 81
   3.1. Reasonable likelihood (hypothetical harm)............. 82
   3.2. Chilling effect (future harm)......................... 85
   3.3. *In abstracto* claims (no individual harm)............ 88
   3.4. Conventionality...................................... 92
4. Alternatives for the current privacy paradigm in the scholarly literature....... 96
   4.1. Constitutive interests................................ 97
   4.2. Group and collective interests........................ 99

	4.3.	Potential harm 101
	4.4.	Agent-based theories... 103
5.	Analysis.. 105	

Chapter IV
Developing an Alternative Privacy Paradigm through Virtue Ethics 107

1. Introduction 107
2. Virtue ethics and legal regulation..................................... 108
   - 2.1. Virtue ethics.. 108
   - 2.2. Virtue ethical approach to the legal realm 114
   - 2.3. Building blocks for an alternative privacy paradigm............. 127
3. Counterarguments against adopting a virtue ethical approach to privacy 129
   - 3.1. The correlation of rights and duties 130
   - 3.2. Is-ought fallacy... 135
   - 3.3. Action guidance... 140
4. Conclusion 143

Chapter V
Embedding a Virtue-based Approach in Privacy Regulation 145

1. Introduction 145
2. Minimum requirements.. 147
   - 2.1. Regulating 'data' 148
   - 2.2. Applying the rule of law test in abstracto 156
   - 2.3. Regulating the analysis phase 160
3. Aspirations 167
   - 3.1. The limits of aspirations overriding privacy interests 168
   - 3.2. Aspirations directed at promoting human freedom 172
   - 3.3. How to embed aspirations in a juridical framework 177
4. Analysis... 181

Chapter VI
Conclusion 187

1. Main argument 187
2. Outline of this book... 192
3. Conclusions... 196

Bibliography 201

CHAPTER I
INTRODUCTION

There seems to be an increasingly wide chasm between technological developments and the juridical paradigm. The juridical paradigm is focused on individual, subjective rights and personal interests, while new technological applications such as Big Data and mass surveillance do not revolve around the individual per se. The individual and individual interests are only incidental to these types of data analytics. These processes thrive on data sets about large groups of unidentified persons, from which statistical correlations and patterns are distilled. They can serve as a basis for data controllers to develop general policies and make decisions which have a significant impact on society.[1]

This book will show that the legal privacy paradigm did not always focus on subjective rights and individual interests to the extent that it currently does. Rather, the focus was on duties of care for data controllers and states not to abuse their power, and on protecting general, societal interests. The turn to subjective rights and individual interests, a turn which is by no means exclusive to privacy and data protection, was seen as a sign of progress. Individuals could invoke rights themselves before a court of law if they were under the impression that their interests had been harmed. The shift from general obligations for data controllers to subjective rights for natural persons, and from a focus on general, societal interests to a focus on personal interests, was aimed at strengthening the position of the individual. The paradox, however, is that it is precisely due to the focus on subjective rights and personal interests that the position of the individual and her interests are no longer adequately protected in the current technological paradigm. That is why this book will argue for a renewed emphasis on duties of care and general, societal interests, and develop an additional approach to privacy regulation by turning to virtue ethics.

The first signs of such a shift may already be witnessed in recent developments in the various juridical privacy and data protection frameworks. This book will signal and explain those trends. Furthermore, it will develop a normative framework for this shift and the additional approach to privacy and data protection regulation that arises from that shift. This will be done by turning to virtue ethics, for which building blocks will be found by studying the work of Lon L. Fuller. A virtue ethical approach to privacy and

---

[1] This introduction is based in part on: B. van der Sloot, 'Do groups have a right to privacy and should they?', in: L. Taylor, L. Floridi & B. van der Sloot (eds.), 'Group Privacy: New Challenges of Data Technologies', Springer, Dordrecht, 2017.

data protection regulation complements the current legal paradigm in two ways. First, it focuses on rule of law principles – safeguards against the abuse of power that need to be respected even if no individual rights or personal interests are at stake. Second, it specifies duties of care for data controllers – goals and aspirations which they must strive to achieve, but which do not correlate directly with subjective, individual rights. Just as a doctor is not merely under the legal duty to avoid medical errors, but also to aspire to be a good doctor, and a parent is not merely under a legal obligation to avoid physical or mental harm to its child, so the state may be under the legal obligation not merely to prevent harm or to refrain from abusing its powers, but also to be a good state – a state that uses its powers in the best way. In this binary way, the gap between the current legal paradigm, with its goal of protecting subjective rights and individual interests, and the current technological paradigm, which paradoxically ensures that this focus no longer suffices to protect the individual and her interests, can be closed.

The right to privacy is perhaps the legal concept where this divide is most visible. In short, the current privacy paradigm grants a natural person a subjective right to claim her right to privacy. This right protects her legitimate interests to human dignity, personal autonomy or individual freedom. In concrete cases, these private interests are balanced against the common interest to which the privacy violation is said to be instrumental, for example national security. This focus on individual rights and individual interests of natural persons no longer holds in an age of Big Data, or whatever other term is used to capture the capacity to collect, store, analyze and use massive amounts of data for all kinds of purposes. Of course, subjective rights and individual interests will always remain of (the greatest) importance – if nude pictures leak, if a person is spied upon for years, if her house is entered by her neighbors without permission, if she is denied a loan or a health insurance on the basis of her race – a person should always have a subjective right to protect her individual interests. The current legal paradigm is relatively fit for addressing these types of problems, although it may require some dusting here and there. What is essential to the new technological developments is, however, that they do not revolve around the individual and her specific interests as such.

Big Data may be defined as gathering massive amounts of data about an undefined number of people without a pre-established goal or purpose. These data are then processed on an aggregated or group level through the use of statistical correlations. The essence is thus that the individual element is mostly lost. Data are not gathered about a specific person or group (for example those suspected of having committed a particular crime). Rather, they are gathered about an undefined number of people during an undefined period of time, often without a pre-established reason. The potential value of the gathered data becomes clear only after they are subjected to analysis by computer algorithms, not beforehand. These data, even if they are originally linked to specific persons, are subsequently mainly processed on an aggregated level by finding statistical correlations. It may appear that the data string 'Muslim + vacation to Yemen + visit to website X' signals an increased risk of a person being a terrorist.

The data are not based on personal data of specific individuals, but processed on an aggregated level. The profiles revolve around groups and categories.[2] (Note: if a specific individual is discriminated against on the basis of a general profile, this has an impact on her individual interests and subjective rights – but the problem of the creation of the profile itself and the fact that policies are based on such profiles remains unaddressed. This becomes even more urgent when these profiles are not based on sensitive data nor lead to severe restrictions, but are based on general data, zipcodes for example, and are used to develop social and economic policies. This might be problematic because people are judged and treated on pre-established profiles and pre-established character traits, but the harm to the specific individual is difficult to demonstrate).

Under these circumstances, it becomes more and more difficult for an individual to establish specific personal interests and personal harms. It should be acknowledged that in the field of privacy, the notion of harm has always been problematic as it is often difficult to substantiate the harm done by a particular violation. For example, what harm follows from entering a home when no property is stolen, or from eavesdropping on a telephone conversation when no private information is disclosed to third parties? Even so, the more conventional privacy violations (house searches, telephone taps, etc.) are clearly demarcated in time, place and person and the effects are therefore relatively easy to define. In the current technological environment, however, the individual is often simply unaware that her personal data are gathered by either her fellow citizens (e.g. through the use of their smartphones), by companies (e.g. by tracking cookies) or by governments (e.g. through covert surveillance). Obviously, people unaware of the fact that their data are gathered will not invoke their right to privacy in court.

But even if a person would be aware of these data collections, given the fact that data gathering and processing is currently so widespread and omnipresent, and will become even more so in the future, it will quite likely be impossible for her to keep track of every data processing which includes (or might include) her data, to assess whether the data controller abides by the legal standards applicable, and if not, to file a legal complaint. And if an individual does go to court to defend her rights, she has to demonstrate a personal interest, i.e. personal harm, which is a particularly problematic notion in Big Data processes. For example, what concrete harm has the data gathering by the NSA done to an ordinary American or European citizen?

Finally, Big Data processing can also undermine the standard way in which a court usually deals with cases in substance, namely by balancing the different interests at stake. In a concrete matter, the societal interests served with the data gathering, for example wire-tapping a person's telephone because she is suspected of committing a murder, is weighed against the harm the data gathering does to her personal autonomy, freedom or dignity. However, the balancing of interests becomes increasingly difficult in the age of Big Data, not only because the individual interest involved with a particular

---

[2] WRR, 'Big Data in een vrije en veilige samenleving', Amsterdam University Press, Amsterdam, 2016. B. van der Sloot, D. Broeders & E. Schrijvers (eds.), 'Exploring the boundaries of Big Data', Amsterdam University Press, Amsterdam, 2016.

case is difficult to substantiate, but also because the societal interest at the other end is also increasingly difficult to specify. For example, it is mostly unclear to what extent the large data collections by intelligence services have actually prevented or forestalled concrete terrorist attacks. This assessment becomes even more problematic if conducted at an individual level, i.e. how the gathering and processing of personal data of a specific complainant has benefitted society or societal interests.

In these types of cases, the problem is not that any particular person has been affected, or that her specific interests have been harmed, but that large groups or society as a whole are affected and that their interests are undermined. For example, the problem with the NSA revelations or with hanging CCTV cameras on the corner of every street is not that specific individuals are affected, but rather that such initiatives trigger the structural question of how power is used (or perhaps better, abused). These large data gathering systems and mass surveillance activities by states undermine trust in governmental institutions and, perhaps more importantly, undermine the basic preconditions for the legitimate use of power: the rule of law. Using the state's power to surveil so many people, at so many places, over so many years and without a clear and concrete reason, simply verges on the abuse of power. Principles prohibiting the abuse of power, in contrast to individual rights, are not conceived as relative interests which can be weighed and balanced against other interests, but rather must be seen as absolute interests, minimum conditions which may never be trespassed and which cannot be limited with reference to, for example, a national security interest. (Note: these types of duties do not correlate with specific rights of others; these duties correlate with having a certain type of power and/or freedom which may be exercised only in a careful and responsible manner).

As stated above, the right to privacy is perhaps the right where the tension between the technological developments and the current legal paradigm is most visible. But other rights face a similar problem, perhaps most prominently the right to data protection. This right too is (increasingly) based on the idea of individual rights to control data (through doctrines such as informed consent, the right to be forgotten and the right to data portability) and to seek legal remedy by invoking subjective rights. And similar to privacy, data protection increasingly aims at protecting individual interests; the scope of data protection instruments is determined by the term 'personal data', which is defined as any data that can be used to identify a person. But here too, the problem is that the data that are processed in Big Data initiatives often do not directly identify a person, but are gathered, assessed and used on a general, aggregated or group level. For example, they may be used to adopt policies on the basis of zip codes, income levels, or any other general criterion. Thus, these data do not directly identify a person, and consequently fall outside the scope of the data protection regulations, even though they may affect the data subject as being part of a specific group. (Please note: of course one could focus on the initial moment, when personal data are gathered and not yet aggregated, but this may only concern the split second which it takes to aggregate data. The same goes for the moment at which group profiles are applied and used to affect a specific person (if this can be determined). The use of dataonly concerns the very end of the data process. By focusing on the individual, her interests and her rights, one loses from sight the larger part of the data processing scheme and the general issues concerned with it).

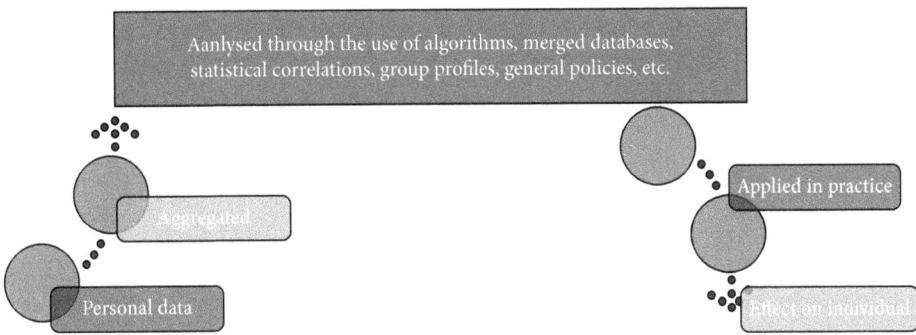

Trends such as Big Data analytics and mass surveillance have an effect on other human rights too, for example the right to be free from discrimination. Of there may be a direct effect on the level of the individual. If a person is denied a loan because a bank has calculated that her neighborhood correlates with an increased risk of default, this clearly affects her (especially if done through the technique known as red-lining[3]). The same goes for a health insurer who demands a higher monthly payment because a person is part of a group (for example lower educated, male, living in a low income neighborhood) which is more likely to have an unhealthy lifestyle. It also applies to states, secret service agencies or police authorities who decide to follow a person on the basis of the fact that she is a Muslim, traveled to Yemen recently and visits a mosque now and then. As has been said, the effect on the individual was, is and will remain of the greatest importance. But the current legal paradigm is relatively well-suited to address these kinds of problems, because it grants people an individual right not to be discriminated against and to go to court if their specific interests have been harmed.

But the more general problem is difficult to address through the existing paradigm. The increased importance of group profiles, statistical correlations and data patterns raises concerns of an increased division between the rich and the poor, as these types of systems tend to benefit those in 'good' groups, while avoiding or limiting the claims of 'bad' groups (this is also called the 'Matthew effect'). This negative effect can of course be brought down to the level of the individual, but in reality the problem is societal. It concerns the general issue of a stratified society, which may be detrimental not only to individual persons but to society as a whole. (It may also create societal unrest. This also brings up the following problem: is this still a legal issue, or is it in reality a political/ethical dilemma?).

To provide a final example, freedom rights such as the freedom of expression, the freedom of religion, the freedom of assembly and the freedom of movement, are

---

[3] B. Custers, T. Calders, B. Schermer & T. Zarsky (eds.), 'Discrimination and Privacy in the Information Society. Data Mining and Profiling in Large Databases', Springer, Heidelberg, 2012.

formulated at the individual level, while the restriction on the freedom and autonomy of citizens is increasingly taking place on a group and general level. This is the case, for example, with city planning based on Big Data processes ('smart cities'), which affects the environment in which people live without them being aware that certain tacit choices are made to affect their behavior. This relates to the debate about nudging; the state often has legitimate reasons to persuade people towards certain behaviors – to live healthily, for example – and it has always done so, *inter alia* through taxes on cigarettes, alcohol, etc. But it is becoming increasingly unclear for citizens/consumers which of their choices are actually affected and in what way. For example, there are now plans to incorporate models predicting public health risks into city design; if a certain neighborhood is expected to see an increased risk of obesity in twenty years' time, squares can be designed so as to motivate people to walk rather than to take the car, and stairs can be given a more prominent and convenient location than elevators, etc. Here again, it is very difficult to point to a specific individual interest being at stake, a specific form of autonomy being undermined – what harm does it do when a person is motivated to take the stairs rather than the elevator? Likewise, the same question can be asked with regard to the fact that some cities are experimenting with spraying tangerine scents in streets to reduce aggressive behaviour at night. But these examples do point to a more general concern and interest: we seem to be moving towards a world in which citizens are constantly and systemically nudged, not only by states and governmental institutions, but also by businesses and perhaps in future even by fellow citizens. This creates a society in which the very idea of individual autonomy will have a substantially different meaning.

To summarize, there is a constant tension between the level on which the violation takes places and the level at which the legal remedies are provided. The potential violation takes place at a general and group level and while it can be connected to individual concerns, this is increasingly besides the point. Individual interests are only incidentally connected to the problems at the heart of current developments. The legal paradigm could maintain its focus on individual rights and personal interests to address cases in which these are at stake. However, if it wants to address the more general concerns that are increasingly at stake in these types of processes, an additional approach is necessary.

Turning to virtue ethics can prove helpful. Virtue ethics does not look to the 'patient' (the one being acted upon, the one bearing the consequences of the acts, such as the data subject) but to the 'agent' (the actor, such as the data controller). It lays down obligations on the agents and these obligations do not (necessarily) correlate with the rights of the patients. Therefore, the focus on individual interests and harm and on subjective rights is complemented with duties that an agent has to comply with irrespective of others' rights to compel her to do so. This means, for example, that rules can be developed for handling nonpersonal data, metadata and statistical data. Also, rules can be developed on the abuse of power by data controllers in order to affirm the principles of the rule of law. In addition to such minimum requirements, virtue ethics also involves on aspirations and goals: those aims that an agent must attempt to achieve. Accordingly, the regulation of privacy and data protection could not only aim at preventing abuse of power by states and companies, but also at stimulating the good use of power in relation to data processing. These are rules that build on open norms and ethical principles, rather than on black letter law principles.

This book will focus primarily on privacy, to a lesser extent on data protection, and only marginally on other individual rights such as the freedom from discrimination. Still, it has to be stressed that these interests are increasingly intertwined and difficult to separate from each other, so that a discussion of privacy interests necessarily includes a discussion of other interests. It must also be underlined that this book will treat privacy and data protection as two separate doctrines, with one of the main differences lying in the material scope (as will be explained in more detail in Chapter II of this book). Furthermore, this book will take as prime example the infringement of privacy for the promotion of public order and national security and the relationship between the state and citizens, but will occasionally also discuss other matters including the relationship between businesses and consumers.

It should also be underlined that this book will focus on the legal situation in Europe, while much of the relevant scholarly literature is American. In Europe, it is important to distinguish between two European institutions: the European Union (EU) and the Council of Europe (CoE). With regard to privacy, the case law on Article 8 of the European Convention on Human Rights (ECHR) of the CoE will be central to the discussion. With regard to data protection, the EU's Data Protection Directive and the General Data Protection Regulation, which will replace the Directive, will function as the primary (though not exclusive) points of reference. It has to be stressed that the Directive is to a large extent inspired by the CoE's Convention for the Protection of Individuals with regard to Automatic Processing of Personal Data and that the ECtHR often refers to the EU's Charter of Fundamental Rights when delivering its decisions.[4] Consequently, the instruments of both organizations are increasingly intertwined and interrelated and can (and perhaps need to) be studied in connection to each other. Finally, it is important to note that this book does not aim at giving a final interpretation of these instruments nor at an in depth discussion of specific legal cases or instruments. Rather, it takes a bird's eye view and points to general trends in the jurisprudential and legislative development. That is why this book often refers to human rights, fundamental rights, Directives, non-binding Conventions and case law of various courts on an ad hoc basis – they serve as examples of a general trend rather than as objects of study in their own right.

In essence, this book will argue that the right to privacy is currently based on the individual and her interests in a threefold manner: (1) It provides the individual with a right to submit a complaint about a violation of her privacy. (2) It provides her with protection of her personal interests, related to human dignity, personal autonomy and

---

[4] See for example: ECtHR, Christine Goodwin v. the United Kingdom, application no. 28957/95, 11 July 2002. ECtHR, I. v. the United Kingdom, application no. 25680/94, 11 July 2002.

individual freedom. (3) In concrete cases, a privacy infringement will be judged on its legitimacy by balancing the individual with a societal interest, for example national security. It is important to add a fourth component, namely (4) the focus on juridical and legal solutions instead of, for instance, soft law or codes of conduct.

The new developments of Big Data leads to the following outcome: (1) it is increasingly difficult to demonstrate personal damage and to claim an individual right, (2) the value at stake in these types of processes often transcend the individual, (3) the balance of different interests no longer provides an adequate test to determine the outcome of cases, as both the individual and the societal interest involved are particularly vague and (4) it is increasingly difficult to regulate Big Data processes and their consequences through legal and juridical doctrines. This book will suggest a possible solution for overcoming this discrepancy by turning to virtue ethics.

This book has the following structure. Chapter II will discuss in more detail the transition from the original to the current privacy paradigm. Chapter III will discuss on which points the current privacy paradigm fails when applied to Big Data processes and analyses what alternatives have already been adopted and proposed to overcome the challenges signaled. Chapter IV will develop a virtue ethical approach to privacy regulation and explain how this approach might help to overcome the problems the current privacy paradigm faces. Chapter V will discuss in more detail how such an ethical paradigm could be implemented in the legal realm and on which points it would have an additional value over the current privacy paradigm. Finally, the conclusion will provide a wrap-up of the arguments previously made, further redefine the principles of privacy as virtue and make suggestions for further research.

In further detail, the chapters will be structured as follows. Chapter II will take an extensive look at the privacy paradigm under the European Convention on Human Rights, Article 8 ECHR and the data protection rules in Europe. It will argue that under both regimes, four shifts can be seen. First, that privacy/data protection has changed from a duty of the government/data controller to a right of the individual/data subject. Second, that the original privacy/data protection paradigm primarily focused on societal interests, while the current paradigm primarily focuses on individual interests. Third, that this affects the way in which courts address privacy/data protection violations. Originally, the question was simply whether certain infringements were necessary or not. Now, the trend is to balance different societal and individual interests against each other. Fourth, that there has been a trend of juridification, with an expanding material scope of both doctrines and an increased focus on juridical enforcement mechanisms. All four trends (especially the last one) are not unique to privacy/data protection, but are part of a broader development.

Chapter III will argue that the current paradigm cannot adequately address many of the current and upcoming privacy challenges following from Big Data processes. This chapter will take a somewhat broader view and address the legal challenges posed by Big Data processes in general. It will furthermore be argued that in order to address cases following from mass surveillance and Big Data processes, the European Court of

Human Rights, which will be taken as an example, has been forced to let go of the victim requirement, has opened up the right to petition about a violation of Article 8 ECHR to, *inter alia*, class actions, has been pushed to focus on general, societal interests instead of individual interests, and is unable to balance different interests, because neither the individual nor the societal interests are particularly clear in these types of cases. In fact, it seems that it needs to move beyond the parameters of the human rights framework the ECtHR has itself developed. Finally, this chapter will analyze which alternatives to the current privacy paradigm have been developed in scholarly literature and suggest that virtue-type alternatives seem most promising for tackling the problems involved with the current focus on individual interests and subjective rights.

Chapter IV will develop a virtue ethical perspective on privacy regulation. It will assess the nature of the legal regime and discuss to what extent legal regimes can include a focus on the character of agents, as virtue ethics proposes. It will argue that it might be worthwhile to assess the character of the state, especially with respect to privacy related matters in Big Data processes. Consequently, it will be argued, a virtue ethical approach to privacy regulation could be included in the legal realm, and would have an additional value when compared to the current privacy paradigm. Virtue ethics revolves around three central concepts: 'virtue', 'human flourishing' and 'prudence' or 'practical wisdom'. These concepts will be explained and special attention will be paid to a number of potential pitfalls for implementing a virtue ethical approach to privacy regulation in law. As an example, one specific author will be discussed who used the virtue ethical paradigm to interpret the nature of the legal realm, namely Lon L. Fuller. Doing so, building blocks for developing a virtue ethical privacy paradigm will be gathered.

Chapter V develops the minimum standards and the goals or aspirations for virtuous states with respect to data processing. Regarding the minimum standards, it will be argued that regulation should apply to 'data' independent of whether they are personal, private or sensitive; it is suggested that there are a number of intrinsic qualities of laws and policies that could be assessed irrespectively of whether personal interests have been harmed; and several minimum conditions for analyzing data are developed. Likewise, suggestions are put forwards which goals and aspirations virtuous states might embrace in relation to data processing and what these principles might entail in practice. It is also discussed how such an approach might be implemented in and connected to the current legal privacy paradigm.

This book uses parts of articles and chapters that have already been published elsewhere:

- B. van der Sloot, 'Privacy in the Post-NSA Era: Time for a Fundamental Revision?', JIPITEC, 2014–1.
- B. van der Sloot, 'Privacy as human flourishing: could a shift towards virtue ethics strengthen privacy protection in the age of Big Data?', JIPITEC 2014–3.

- B. van der Sloot, 'Do data protection rules protect the individual and should they? An assessment of the proposed General Data Protection Regulation', International Data Privacy Law, 2014-3.
- B. van der Sloot, 'How to assess privacy violations in the age of Big Data? Analysing the three different tests developed by the ECtHR and adding for a fourth one', ICTL, 2015.
- B. van der Sloot, 'Privacy as Personality Right: Why the ECtHR's Focus on Ulterior Interests Might Prove Indispensable in the Age of "Big Data"', Utrecht Journal of International and European Law, 2015-80.
- B. van der Sloot, 'Do privacy and data protection rules apply to legal persons and should they? A proposal for a two-tiered system', Computer Law & Security Review, 2015-1.
- B. van der Sloot, 'Is the Human Rights Framework Still Fit for the Big Data Era? A Discussion of the ECtHR's Case Law on Privacy Violations Arising from Surveillance Activities', IN: S. Gutwirth, R. Leenes & P. De Hert (eds.), 'Data Protection on the Move', Springer, Dordrecht, 2016.
- B. van der Sloot, 'The Individual in the Big Data Era: Moving towards an Agent-Based Privacy Paradigm', in: B. van der Sloot & D. Broeders & E. Schrijvers (eds.), 'Exploring the boundaries of Big Data', Amsterdam University Press, Amsterdam 2016.
- B. van der Sloot & S. van Schendel, 'International and comparative legal study on Big Data', WRR-rapport, working paper 20, <www.wrr.nl/publicaties/publicatie/article/international-and-comparative-legal-study-on-big-data/ >.
- B. van der Sloot, 'The Practical and Theoretical Problems with 'balancing': Delfi, Coty and the redundancy of the human rights framework', Maastricht Journal of European and Comparative Law, 2016-3.
- B. van der Sloot, 'Do groups have a right to privacy and should they?', in: L. Taylor, L. Floridi & B. van der Sloot (eds.), 'Group Privacy: New Challenges of Data Technologies', Springer, Dordrecht, 2017.
- B. van der Sloot, 'Privacy as virtue: searching for a new privacy paradigm in the age of Big Data', in: E. Beyvers, P. Helm, M. Hennig, C. Keckeis, I. Kreknin & F. Püschel (eds.), 'Räume und Kulturen des Privaten', Springer, Heidelberg, 2016.
- B. van der Sloot, 'Legal fundamentalism: is data protection really a fundamental right?', in: S. Gutwirth, R. Leenes & P. De Hert (eds.), 'Data Protection and Privacy: (In)visibilities and Infrastructure', Springer, Dordrecht, 2017 (forthcoming).

CHAPTER II
THE TRANSFORMATION OF THE RIGHT TO PRIVACY AND THE RIGHT TO DATA PROTECTION

1. INTRODUCTION

This chapter introduces the European approach to privacy and data protection. Two things are important to point out from the start. First, there are differences between the right to privacy and the right to data protection, which will be described in more detail below. Perhaps the most prominent difference lies in the material scope. The right to privacy usually does not extend to the collection of nonprivate and non-privacy-sensitive data,[5] whereas the term 'personal data', central to most data protection documents, is not limited to private or sensitive information, but extents to any data with which someone could potentially be identified. 'Even ancillary information, such as "the man wearing a black suit" may identify someone out of the passers-by standing at a traffic light.'[6]

Second, this study will primarily discuss the European perspective and in doing so will refer to documents of both the European Union (EU) and the Council of Europe (CoE). For privacy, the case law by the European Court of Human Rights (ECtHR) on Article 8 of the European Convention on Human Rights (ECHR) will be central and with regard to data protection, the EU's Data Protection Directive[7] and the General Data Protection Regulation,[8] which will replace the Directive over time, will function as the primary (though not exclusive) points of reference.

---

[5] J. Kokott & C. Sobotta, 'The Distinction between privacy and data protection in the jurisprudence of the CJEU and the ECtHR', in: H. Hijmans & H. Kranenborg (eds.), 'Data Protection anno 2014: How to Restore Trust? Contributions in honour of Peter Hustinx, European Data Protection Supervisor (2004–2014)', Intersentia, Cambridge, 2014. See in the same book also: C. Docksey, 'The European Court of Justice and the Decade of surveillance'. In: H. Hijmans & H. Kranenborg (eds.), 'Data Protection anno 2014: How to Restore Trust? Contributions in honour of Peter Hustinx, European Data Protection Supervisor (2004–2014)', Intersentia, Cambridge, 2014.

[6] Article 29 Working Party, 'Opinion 4/2007 on the concept of personal data', 01248/07/EN, WP 136, 20 June 2007, Brussels, p. 13.

[7] Directive 95/46/EC of the European Parliament and of the Council of 24 October 1995 on the protection of individuals with regard to the processing of personal data and on the free movement of such data.

[8] Regulation (EU) 2016/679 of the European Parliament and of the Council of 27 April 2016 on the protection of natural persons with regard to the processing of personal data and on the free movement of such data, and repealing Directive 95/46/EC (General Data Protection Regulation).

Article 8 ECHR grants a right to respect for private and family life, home and correspondence:

1. Everyone has the right to respect for his private and family life, his home and his correspondence.
2. There shall be no interference by a public authority with the exercise of this right except such as is in accordance with the law and is necessary in a democratic society in the interests of national security, public safety or the economic wellbeing of the country, for the prevention of disorder or crime, for the protection of health or morals, or for the protection of the rights and freedoms of others.

The right to data protection is currently protected by the Data Protection Directive, which contains rules for data controllers such as: store data only when necessary, store data safely, process personal data with a legitimate aim, be transparent about the processing activities, etc. It also contains some rights for data subjects, such as the right to have access to personal data, to correct inaccurate data and to object to certain types of data processing. Finally, the Directive provides rules on enforcement and territoriality. The European Court of Justice (ECJ or CoJ or CJEU) oversees the implementation of the Directive.

The EU's European Charter of Fundamental Rights (from 2000) contains a right to data protection separate from the right to privacy, in contrast to the CoE's ECHR (from 1950), which only contains a provision on the protection of privacy. Article 7 of the Charter concerning the respect for private and family life holds: 'Everyone has the right to respect for his or her private and family life, home and communications.' Article 8 regarding the protection of personal data specifies:

1. Everyone has the right to the protection of personal data concerning him or her.
2. Such data must be processed fairly for specified purposes and on the basis of the consent of the person concerned or some other legitimate basis laid down by law. Everyone has the right of access to data which has been collected concerning him or her, and the right to have it rectified.
3. Compliance with these rules shall be subject to control by an independent authority.

The fact that there are now two articles signals a trend in which the right to data protection is increasingly disconnected from the right to privacy.[9] This trend will be discussed in more detail in the following sections.

This chapter will introduce the notions of privacy and data protection in Europe. It will explain the core characteristics of the legal instruments; consequently, it will focus primarily on laws, directives and case-law and to a lesser extent on scholarly literature. This chapter will discuss in detail how the regulation of privacy and data protection has developed over time. It will make four arguments. First, both doctrines were first

---

[9] See to the contrary: H. Hijmans, 'The European Union as Guardian of Internet Privacy: The Story of Art 16 TFEU', Dordrecht, Springer International Publishing, 2016.

primarily conceived as laying down duties of care and general obligations for states and data controllers. Gradually, however, they have been interpreted mainly as subjective rights of natural persons. Second, this has meant a great deal for the type of interests that are protected by both doctrines. Although originally the prime focus was on the protection of general and societal interests, related for example to the prevention of the abuse of power, currently, the core interests that are protected are personal and individual values, such as human dignity, personal autonomy and individual freedom.

Third, this has had an influence on the way judges and courts assess and address privacy and data protection issues. The original paradigm embraced a binary necessity test. If a privacy infringement was necessary, it was deemed legitimate. If a privacy infringement was unnecessary, arbitrary or untimely, it was considered illegitimate. Although this approach is still applied occasionally, it has been moved to the background and replaced by a balancing test. Under this approach, almost all interests are taken into account, both those of the individual and those of the state or the data controller. In concrete cases, these interests are weighed and balanced against each other to determine the legitimacy of the privacy/data protection infringement. Finally, there has been a juridification of both doctrines. This is partly due to the fact that the material scope of both the right to privacy and the right to data protection has been broadened considerably. Also, while the original instruments were conceived only partially as juridical doctrines and primarily as ethical guidelines and codes of conduct, the trend has been to focus more and more on juridical rules and the enforcement of those rules through legal means.

2. THE RIGHT TO PRIVACY

There has always been a troubled marriage between privacy and personality rights.[10] Perhaps one of the first to make a sharp distinction between these two types of rights was Stig Strömholm in 1967 when he wrote *Rights of privacy and rights of the personality: a comparative survey*.[11] Since then, many have argued that the right to privacy is a predominantly American concept, coined first by Cooley[12] and made famous by Warren and Brandeis' article 'The right to privacy'[13] from 1890. Personality rights, in contrast, were the key notion used in the European context, having a long history in the legal systems of countries like Germany and France. Although a large overlap exists between the two types of rights, scholars have also signaled important differences. In short, the right to privacy is primarily conceived as a negative right,

---

[10] This section is based in part on: B. van der Sloot, 'Privacy as Personality Right: Why the ECtHR's Focus on Ulterior Interests Might Prove Indispensable in the Age of "Big Data"', Utrecht Journal of International and European Law, 2015-80.
[11] S. Strömholm, 'Right of privacy and rights of the personality: a comparative survey', Nordic Conference on Privacy organized by the International Commission of Jurists, Stockholm, 1967.
[12] T. M. Cooley, 'A Treatise on the Law of Torts', Callaghan, Chicago, 1888.
[13] S. D. Warren & L. D. Brandeis, 'The Right to Privacy', 4 Harvard Law Review No. 5, 1890.

which protects a person's right to be let alone, placing duties on others to restrict their behavior, while personality rights also include a person's interest to represent herself in a public context and develop her identity and personality.

The supposed difference between the American and European approach has remained a field of interest. For example, James Q. Whitman has stressed that American privacy laws have as basic rationale the respect for (negative) liberty, while the European approach (distilled from French and German law) focuses on the protection of dignity.[14] This difference regarding the underlying rationales, he argues, also has a considerable impact on the material scope of the respective rights, with the American privacy laws being quite delimited and, from a European perspective, rather minimalistic and the European privacy framework being quite broad and, from an American point of view, almost all-encompassing.[15] Another difference which is often coined is that America's tort law is the primary source for privacy protection, while in Europe privacy is primarily regarded as a constitutional guarantee.[16]

However, in reality, this contrast does not seem so sharp. Europeans have for centuries acknowledged the rights of citizens to be protected against arbitrary interferences by governments with their bodily integrity, the privacy of their home and the secrecy of their correspondence. Likewise, American scholars have often argued that there is a need for a stronger focus on dignity as the underlying rationale of privacy protection[17] and for the introduction of personality rights in their legal discourse.[18] Even Warren and Brandeis, hailed as the founders of the American approach, formulated the right to privacy as the right to 'an inviolate personality' and viewed 'the right to privacy, as a part of the more general right to the immunity of the person, – the right to one's personality'. Finally, the American Bill of Rights is becoming increasingly important in America's legal privacy discourse,[19] while the Europeans have numerous non-constitutional frameworks for protecting privacy in horizontal relationships. Thus, in reality, the difference between the European and the American approach is blurry and indistinct.

Although the transatlantic divide seems not so evident, the distinction between privacy and personality rights remains a potent one. Privacy rights protect a person against arbitrary interference with personal matters, her private and family life, her body, her home and the secrecy of her correspondence. In essence, privacy is about retracting matters from the public sphere – the word comes from the Latin *privare*, taking something out of the public domain, and is thus the exact opposite of *publicare*,

---

[14] J. Q. Whitman, 'The Two Western Cultures of Privacy: Dignity versus Liberty', 113 Yale Law Journal 1151, 2004.
[15] See further: E. J. Eberle, 'Human Dignity, Privacy, and Personality in German and American Constitutional Law', Utah Law Review 963, 1997.
[16] P. M. Schwartz & K.-N. Peifer, 'Prosser's Privacy and the German Right of Personality: Are Four Privacy Torts Better than One Unitary Concept?', 98 California Law Review 1925, 2010.
[17] E. J. Bloustein, 'Privacy as an Aspect of Human Dignity: An Answer to Dean Prosser', 39 New York University Law Review 962, 1964.
[18] See further: R. Pound, 'Interests of Personality', 28 Harvard Law Review No. 4, 1915.
[19] Supreme Court of the United States, Riley v. California, No. 13-132. Argued April 29, 2014 – Decided June 25, 2014.

taking something from the private to the public domain.[20] The core rationale underlying the right to privacy is the protection from – it is a negative right to be free from arbitrary interference. Such interference might be initiated by citizens, businesses and states alike (still, this chapter will focus primarily on governmental interferences). Privacy thus protects the negative freedom of the citizen and entails a negative obligation for the state, i.e. to abstain from abusing its powers, such as by interfering unjustly or arbitrarily with the privacy of its citizens. It is thus primarily conceived as a duty of the state.

Personality rights, by contrast, are not only about negative freedom, 'because personality both presents the self to the world and protects the self from the world. The ambivalence is evident in the ambiguity of the term from which the word personality is derived, the "persona".'[21] Stemming from *per + sonare*, or sounding through, a persona signifies the mask worn by actors when entering the stage and thus relates to both the act of concealing and of revealing. In addition to privacy rights, personality rights also contain an element of control over one's public image and over personal information. Consequently, the protection of reputation and honor, the right to data protection and the right to (intellectual) property often fall under the material scope of personality rights, but the scope is often described as even wider. Reference is frequently made to the German Constitution, in which Article 2 Paragraph 1 specifies: 'Everyone has the right to the free development of his personality insofar as he does not violate the rights of others or offend against the constitutional order or the moral code.'[22] This means that potentially every aspect of one's personal development may be protected, provided that it does not violate the rights of others.

Whitman also explicitly refers to the notion of the development and fulfillment of one's personality as a core principle of the German privacy approach:

> The protection of privacy in the German tradition is regarded as an aspect of the protection of one of the most baffling of German juristic creations: "personality." Personality is a characteristically dense German concept, with roots in the philosophies of Kant, Humboldt, and Hegel.[23]

Whitman holds that the German legal tradition is 'most especially [focused] on the unfettered creation of the self, on the fashioning of one's image and the realization of one's potentialities.'[24] The underlying rationale of personality rights is thus not only negative freedom, as with privacy rights, but rather, or also, positive freedom; the focus is on the capacity of the individual to develop her identity, create her persona and develop as a unique individual (for which negative liberty may be a prerequisite). Consequently,

---

[20] P. Aries & G. Duby, 'A History of Private Life: Revelations of the Medieval World', Belknap, Harvard, 1988.
[21] J. Malkan, 'Stolen Photographs: Personality, Publicity, and Privacy', 75 Texas Law Review 779, 1997.
[22] Grundgesetz Article 2.1.
[23] J. Q. Whitman, 'The Two Western Cultures of Privacy: Dignity versus Liberty', 113 Yale Law Journal 1151, 2004, p. 1180.
[24] Ibid. p. 1182.

personality rights, in contrast to privacy rights, not only entail negative obligations for the state, but also a positive obligation, to facilitate the full development of its citizens.

This section will argue that Article 8 of the European Convention on Human Rights was originally adopted as a classic privacy right, but has gradually been interpreted by the European Court of Human Rights as a personality right. This has had a number of consequences. Section 2.1 will argue that the right to privacy was first conceived as a duty of the state not to abuse its powers. In contrast, under the current approach of the ECtHR, it is viewed first and foremost as the subjective right of a natural person, which she can invoke if her personal interests have been harmed. Section 2.2 will follow up by explaining that originally, the right to privacy was meant to protect general and societal interests, related to the abuse of power by governments. For example, they were only allowed to enter a home, to wiretap telecommunications or to execute a body cavity search if this was necessary in a democratic society. Article 8 ECHR was conceived primarily as entailing obligations for states not to abuse their powers and to provide negative freedom to its citizens. Currently, however, the core focus is on individual interests and Article 8 ECHR has been interpreted to allow the individual to develop her personality to the fullest and to develop as a unique individual.

Section 2.3 explains that the Convention as a whole was focused on laying down minimum duties for the state. It contains a prohibition on the abuse of power, a prohibition on torture, a prohibition on retrospective legislation, prohibition on discrimination, etc. It also contains a number of procedural safeguards, such as the right to petition, the right to a fair trial, the right to be deprived of one's liberty only in accordance with a procedure prescribed by law, etc. Finally, there are also conditional obligations, which specify that the government may use its powers only under certain conditions, namely if it is prescribed by law and necessary in a democratic society. Gradually, however, the Court has approached the Convention as providing a number of relative rights to natural persons. In concrete cases, it weighs the individual against the societal interests involved to determine the legitimacy of a privacy infringement. Finally, Section 2.4 will briefly point out that there has been a trend of juridification of the right to privacy. This has been both due to the expansion in the material scope of the right to privacy and because several changes have been made in the way the rules contained in the Convention are protected and enforced.

It has to be stressed that there are exceptions to each of the four trends. It is impossible to discuss every nuance and detail; the points made here show the dominant approach of the European Court of Human Rights when interpreting the European Convention on Human Rights in general and the right to privacy in particular. It is true that in its more recent jurisprudence, it has been forced to make exceptions to each of these points, especially in cases revolving around Big Data and mass surveillance. These cases and examples, and their significance, will be discussed in detail in the next chapter of this book. That chapter deals with the question of how the current privacy paradigm can be applied to Big Data and mass surveillance cases, which problems are involved and which solutions or alternatives have been proposed so far to overcome these problems.

Chapter II. The Transformation of the Right to Privacy and the Right to Data Protection

2.1. RIGHT TO COMPLAIN

When the Convention was drafted, there existed very few international courts.[25] One of the most prominent examples, to which the authors of the Convention often looked for inspiration, was the International Court of Justice (ICJ) in The Hague. The statute of the ICJ does not allow individuals to bring forward a case, but only provides that national governments may submit an inter-state complaint. A number of representatives favored such a model for the European Convention. They pointed out, first, that individuals might abuse their right to petition and submit claims which are totally false and unfounded. Second, some representatives dreaded that communists and communist groups would use this right for political and subversive propaganda. If their (false) claims would be denied by the Commission or the Court, this would give them only more ammunition in their political campaign.[26] Third and finally, the proponents of a model of inter-state complaints foresaw large numbers of complaints being made by individuals invoking their right to individual petition, which would paralyze the Commission and the Court. 'I foresee shoals of applications being made by individuals who imagine that they have a complaint of one kind or another against the country.'[27]

Proponents of an individual right to petition, however, argued that, first, a Convention without a right to petition would be a farce or worse, because it would provide individuals with the illusion that their rights would be protected, while in fact they remained powerless against violations of their fundamental freedoms. Furthermore, they rejected the fear for communist propaganda, pointing out that their claims might either be correct, in which case they rightly invoked their right to petition, or be false, in which case the Commission would simply reject their claims as manifestly ill-founded. Finally, they denounced the fear for shoals of complaints as unrealistic and unfounded:

> I wish to deal for one moment with the argument (...) that there would be shoals of complaints. I have never known legislation of any kind which gave to the individual a further change to establish his rights about which the same prophecy has not been made, and in the 30 years in which I have practiced law I have never seen that prophecy come true.[28]

---

[25] This section is partly based on: B. van der Sloot, 'Privacy in the Post-NSA Era: Time for a Fundamental Revision?', JIPITEC, 2014-1. B. van der Sloot, 'Privacy as virtue: searching for a new privacy paradigm in the age of Big Data', in: E. Beyvers, P. Helm, M. Hennig, C. Keckeis, I. Kreknin & F. Püschel (eds.), 'Räume und Kulturen des Privaten', Springer, Heidelberg, 2016.

[26] A. H. Robertson, 'Collected edition of the 'travaux prépar atoires' of the European Convention on Human Rights = Recueil des travaux préparatoires de la Convention Européenne des Droits de l'Homme; Council of Europe. Vol. 2 Consultative Assembly, second session of the Committee of Ministers, Standing Committee of the Assembly, 10 August-18 November 1949', Nijhoff, The Hague, 1975, p. 192.

[27] Ibid., p. 188.

[28] Robertson, vol. 2, p. 198.

Obviously, a compromise had to be found between these two groups. What the second group won is that it was accepted that there were two types of complaints which could be made: inter-state complaints and individual complaints.[29] However, it must be kept in mind that although the opponents of a system of individual petition finally surrendered their opposition, they did so only because they hoped that the system of inter-state complaints would be the most prominent and commonly used model of application.[30] It was accepted that the Convention supervision consisted of a two-tiered system. First, the European Commission on Human Rights (ECmHR) would decide on the admissibility of cases and function as a mere filtering system. It would not provide a substantial review of cases, but would only reject cases that were clearly unfounded, submitted out of time, fell outside the competence of the Court, etc. It was only with the Commission that the mechanism of individual complaints exists. Even if a case was brought before the Commission by an individual complainant and even if the Commission declared the application admissible, the individual had no right to submit it for review to the Court. The Court is the second tier; it deals with the cases in substance, and decides on the question of whether the Convention has been violated or not.

Article 25 of the original ECHR held:

> (1) The Commission may receive petitions addressed to the Secretary-General of the Council of Europe from any person, non-governmental organization or group of individuals claiming to be the victim of a violation by one of the High Contracting Parties of the rights set forth in this Convention, provided that the High Contracting Party against which the complaint has been lodged has declared that it recognizes the competence of the Commission to receive such petitions. Those of the High Contracting Parties who have made such a declaration undertake not to hinder in any way the effective exercise of this right.

Individual complainants did not have the right to petition the European Court of Human Rights, even if the Commission had declared their complaint admissible. The original text of the Convention held that four bodies could bring a case before the Court: the Commission, the state whose national is alleged to be a victim, the state which referred the case to the Commission and the state against which the complaint has been lodged.[31] The individual was explicitly excluded from this list. Consequently, the individual applicant was always 'represented' before the Court by the Commission or by a state.[32]

Although, consequently, the Convention contains the right of a natural person to petition, this represented but a segment of the European supervisory system as a whole.

---

[29] See article 45–46 of the original Convention.
[30] Article 15 ECHR.
[31] Article 48 original ECHR. <www.echr.coe.int/library/annexes/CEDH1950ENG.pdf>. Article 44 provides: 'Only the High Contracting Parties and the Commission shall have the right to bring a case before the Court'.
[32] Robertson, vol. 2, p. 156. A. H. Robertson, 'Collected edition of the 'travaux préparatoires' of the European Convention on Human Rights = Recueil des travaux préparatoires de la Convention Européenne des Droits de l'Homme; Council of Europe. Vol. 4 Committee of Experts, Committee of Ministers, Conference of Senior Officials, 30 March-June 1950', Nijhoff, The Hague, 1975, p. 44.

First it must be kept in mind that there are two different systems of petition under the Convention: individual applications and inter-state complaints.[33] In this respect, it should be noted that an inter-state complaint is not so much concerned with personal harm suffered by one or more natural persons, but rather focuses on general governmental policies or systematic abuse of state powers. For example, if a government invokes the state of emergency and derogates from the rights and freedoms under the Convention, other states may question the legitimacy or necessity of these actions before the Court.[34]

Second, the right to individual petition is open to three types of complainants: individuals, non-governmental organizations and groups of individuals. Consequently, not only can a natural person complain about a violation, a legal body may also claim to be the victim of an interference with its rights. Such an infringement is non-subjective in the sense that a church might, for example, complain about a violation of its freedom of religion when it is prevented from ringing the church bells in the morning. It is not so much that the church has suffered from harm, but that it is prevented from or hindered in executing its statutory objectives. Moreover, although earlier drafts of the Convention only referred to the right of natural and legal persons to petition, a third category was added, namely any 'group of individuals'. The right to petition of a group of individuals was inserted to broaden the width of the right to petition and to ensure that no one was excluded from access to the Commission.[35] The term 'group of individuals' referred specifically to minority groups, which must be interpreted against the background of the Second World War, in which such groups were stigmatized, discriminated or worse.[36] Thus, the Convention authors allowed such groups as a whole or a number of individuals member to such groups to submit a complaint before the Commission. Again, such application is not so much concerned with their specific personal and subjective interests, since they do not claim to have suffered themselves specifically and individually from a certain governmental practice which is already covered by the right of individual petition by natural persons. Rather, a group of individuals has the opportunity to represent the common interests of the minority group as such.

The reason for granting states, legal persons, groups and individuals a right to complaint was that the core focus of the Convention was not on individual rights (of natural persons) but on duties of the government. The reason for only allowing states and the Commission to pursue the complaints of individual applicants was that the Convention was focused on general and societal interests. The human rights violations in the fascist and communist regimes that took place at that time were not so much focused on specific individuals. Rather, large groups in society were denied their most basic rights and freedoms. This not only regarded groups such as Jews, gays and gypsies,

---

[33] Article 33 ECHR.
[34] Article 15 ECHR.
[35] Robertson, vol. 2, p. 270.
[36] A.H. Robertson, 'Collected edition of the 'travaux préparatoires' of the European Convention on Human Rights = Recueil des travaux préparatoires de la Convention Européenne des Droits de l'Homme. Vol. 1 Preparatory Commission of the Council of Europe Committee of Ministers, Consultative Assembly, 11 May-8 September 1949', Nijhoff, The Hague, 1975, p. 160–162.

who were the target of abusive practices. Other human rights violations affected larger groups in society as well. For example, the problem with secret services such as the Stasi was not so much that the privacy of specific individuals was infringed, but rather that it collected data on about everybody living in the DDR.[37] Likewise, the freedom of speech, association, religion, education, fair trial and property were violated on mass scale. Consequently, the focus of the ECHR was not on preventing specific infringements on the particular rights of individual complainants, but on large-scale abusive practices. The authors of the Convention believed that the Commission and the state would only pursue those complaints which transcended the individual level and had a broader significance for a group or society as a whole.

Over time, however, the Convention has been revised on a number of points so that, *inter alia*, individual complainants (individuals, groups and legal persons) have direct access to the Court to complain about a violation of their privacy (the task of the Commission being reassigned to a separate chamber of the Court – the two-tiered system still exists).[38] The Court has also made some major steps to revise the meaning and interpretation of the right to privacy under the Convention. Among other matters, it has accepted that Article 8 ECHR not only protects the negative freedom of citizens, but also the right to develop one's personality to the fullest, and has stressed that states may not only have a negative duty not to abuse its powers, but also a positive duty to use its powers to protect its citizens and to facilitate their quest for full personal development (see in further detail Section 2.2).[39]

Moreover, over time, the Court has strongly emphasized individual interests and personal harm when it assesses a case regarding a potential violation of Article 8 ECHR. This is linked to the doctrine of *ratione personae*, the question whether the claimant has individually and substantially suffered from a privacy violation, and in part to that of *ratione materiae*, the question whether the interest said to be interfered with falls under the protective scope of the right to privacy. This focus on individual harm and individual interests brings with it that certain types of complaints are declared inadmissible by the European Court of Human Rights, which means that the cases will not be dealt with in substance.[40]

So-called *in abstracto* claims are as a rule inadmissible. These are claims that regard the mere existence of a law or a policy, without them having any concrete or practical effect on the claimant. In the words of the ECtHR:

---

[37] Deutsche Demokratische Republik.
[38] Protocol No. 9 to the Convention for the Protection of Human Rights and Fundamental Freedoms Rome, 6.XI.1990. This Protocol has been repealed as from the date of entry into force of Protocol No. 11 (ETS No. 155) on 1 November 1998. Protocol No. 11 to the Convention for the Protection of Human Rights and Fundamental Freedoms, restructuring the control machinery established thereby. Strasbourg, 11.V.1994. Since its entry into force on 1 November 1998, this Protocol forms an integral part of the Convention (ETS No. 5).
[39] B. van der Sloot, 'Privacy as human flourishing: could a shift towards virtue ethics strengthen privacy protection in the age of Big Data?', JIPITEC, 2014-3.
[40] See about the focus on individual rights and individual interests with respect to data protection: B. van der Sloot, 'Do data protection rules protect the individual and should they? An assessment of the proposed General Data Protection Regulation', International Data Privacy Law, 2014-4.

Insofar as the applicant complains in general of the legislative situation, the Commission recalls that it must confine itself to an examination of the concrete case before it and may not review the aforesaid law *in abstracto*. The Commission therefore may only examine the applicant's complaints insofar as the system of which he complains has been applied against him.[41]

A priori claims are rejected as well, as the Court will usually only receive complaints about injury which has already materialized. Claims about future damage will in principle not be considered.

It can be observed from the terms 'victim' and 'violation' and from the philosophy underlying the obligation to exhaust domestic remedies provided for in Article 26 that in the system for the protection of human rights conceived by the authors of the Convention, the exercise of the right of individual petition cannot be used to prevent a potential violation of the Convention: in theory, the organs designated by Article 19 to ensure the observance of the engagements undertaken by the Contracting Parties in the Convention cannot examine – or, if applicable, find – a violation other than *a posteriori*, once that violation has occurred. Similarly, the award of just satisfaction, i.e. compensation, under Article 50 of the Convention is limited to cases in which the internal law allows only partial reparation to be made, not for the violation itself, but for the consequences of the decision or measure in question which has been held to breach the obligations laid down in the Convention.[42]

Hypothetical claims regard damage which might have materialized, but about which the claimant is unsure. The Court usually rejects such claims because it is unwilling to provide a ruling on the basis of presumed facts. The applicant must be able to substantiate her claim with concrete facts, not with beliefs and suppositions. The ECtHR will in principle also not receive an *actio popularis*, a case brought up by a claimant or a group of claimants, not to protect their own interests, but that of others or society as a whole. A well-known example of the *actio popularis* is the so-called class action:

The Court reiterates in that connection that the Convention does not allow an *actio popularis* but requires as a condition for exercise of the right of individual petition that an applicant must be able to claim on arguable grounds that he himself has been a direct or indirect victim of a violation of the Convention resulting from an act or omission which can be attributed to a Contracting State.[43]

Then there is the material scope of the right to privacy, Article 8 ECHR. In principle, it only protects the private life, family life, correspondence and home of an applicant. However, the Court has been willing to give a broader interpretation. For example, it has held that it also protects the personal development of an individual, that it includes

---

[41] ECtHR, Lawlor v. The United Kingdom, application no. 12763/87, 14 July 1988.
[42] ECmHR, Tauira and others v. France, application no. 28204/95, 04 December 1995.
[43] ECtHR, Asselbourg and 78 others and Greenpeace Association-Luxembourg v. Luxembourg, application no. 29121/95, 29 June 1999.

protection from environmental pollution and that it may extend to data protection issues. Still, what distinguishes the right to privacy, under the interpretation of the ECtHR, from other rights under the Convention, such as the freedom of expression, is that it in principle only provides protection to individual interests. While the freedom of expression is linked to personal expression and development, it also connected to societal interests, such as the search for truth through the market place of ideas and the well-functioning of the press, a precondition for every liberal democracy.[44] By contrast, Article 8 ECHR only protects individual interests such as autonomy, dignity and personal development. Cases that do not regard such matters are rejected by the Court.[45]

This focus on individual interests has also had an important effect on the types of applicants that are able to submit a complaint about the right to privacy. The Convention, in principle, allows natural persons, groups of persons and legal persons to complain about an interference with their rights under the Convention. Indeed, the Court has accepted that churches may invoke the freedom of religion (Article 9 ECHR) and that press organizations may rely on the freedom of expression (Article 10 ECHR). However, because Article 8 ECHR only protects individual interests, the Court has said that in principle, only natural persons can invoke a right to privacy. For example, when a church complained about a violation of its privacy by the police in relation to criminal proceedings, the Commission found:

> [T]he extent to which a non-governmental organization can invoke such a right must be determined in the light of the specific nature of this right. It is true that under Article 9 of the Convention a church is capable of possessing and exercising the right to freedom of religion in its own capacity as a representative of its members and the entire functioning of churches depends on respect for this right. However, unlike Article 9, Article 8 of the Convention has more an individual than a collective character(…).[46]

Accordingly, the Commission declared the complaint inadmissible. This position is still embraced by the Court; it is willing to accept legal persons as complainants only in exceptional circumstances.[47] In similar fashion, the Court has rejected the capacity of groups to complain about a violation of human rights. Contrary to the intention of the authors of the Convention, it has stressed that only individuals who have been harmed personally and significantly by a specific violation or infringement can bundle their claims. They are approached as a collective, rather than as a group. Consequently, Article 8 ECHR has been interpreted by the Court such that it primarily aims at protecting individual interests by granting individuals a right to complain.

---

[44] Media-diversity is another classic example.
[45] See for one of the first cases focusing on positive freedom and personal development: ECmHR, X. v. Iceland, application no. 6825/74, 18 May 1976. See about the widened scope of Article 8 ECHR: B. van der Sloot, 'Privacy as personality right: why the ECtHR's focus on ulterior interests might prove indispensable in the age of Big Data', Utrecht Journal of International and European Law, 2015.
[46] ECmHR, Church of Scientology of Paris v. France, application no. 19509/92, 09 January 1995.
[47] There are very few cases in which the Court is willing to relax this point. See: B. van der Sloot, 'Do privacy and data protection rules apply to legal persons and should they? A proposal for a two-tiered system', Computer Law & Security Review, 2015-1.

Finally, the last non-individual mode of complaint under the Convention, the possibility of inter-state complaints, has had almost no significance under the Convention's supervisory mechanism. In 2006, when the Court had delivered more than 15.000 judgments,[48] it was signaled that:

> [A] total of 19 applications had been lodged by States. Even this very low number provides a distorted picture. In fact only six situations in different States have been put forward in Strasbourg by means of an inter-State application. (…) Given the number of violations that have occurred during the more than 50 years that the Convention has been in force, it is evident that the right of complaint of States has not proved to be a very effective supervisory tool.[49]

With only one inter-state complaint in 2009 and another one in 2011 regarding the same matter, this trend seems to have continued after 2006.[50] Consequently, the natural person is in practice the only actor who invokes the right to privacy – and she can do so only when her individual interests are at stake.

2.2. INTERESTS

The European Convention on Human Rights was adopted in 1950 and in many respects arose from the ashes of the Second World War.[51]

> [The ECHR] is a product of the period shortly after the Second World War, when the issue of international protection of human rights attracted a great deal of attention. These rights had been crushed by the atrocities of National Socialism, and the guarantee of their protection at the national level had proved completely inadequate.[52]

Like the Universal Declaration on Human Rights, to which the European Convention makes explicit reference in its preamble[53] and on which it is based to a large extent,[54] the

---

[48] <www.echr.coe.int/NR/rdonlyres/E58E405A-71CF-4863-91EE-779C34FD18B2/0/APERCU_19592011_EN.pdf>.
[49] P. van Dijk, F. van Hoof, A. van Rijk & L. Zwaak (eds.), 'Theory and Practice of the European Convention on Human Rights', Intersentia, Antwerpen, 2006, p. 50.
[50] ECtHR, Georgia v. Russia (I), application no. 13255/07, 30 June 2009. ECtHR, Georgia v. Russia (II), application no. 38263/08, 13 December 2011.
[51] This section is partly based on: B. van der Sloot, 'Privacy as human flourishing: could a shift towards virtue ethics strengthen privacy protection in the age of Big Data?', JIPITEC 2014-3. See further: G. L. Weil, 'The European Convention on Human Rights: background, development and prospects', Leyden, Sijthoff, 1963.
[52] L. Zwaak, 'General survey of the European Convention', p. 3. In: P. van Dijk et al. (eds.), 'Theory and practice of the European Convention on Human Rights', Intersentia, Antwerpen, 2006.
[53] It specifies: 'Considering the Universal Declaration of Human Rights proclaimed by the General Assembly of the United Nations on 10th December 1948; Considering that this Declaration aims at securing the universal and effective recognition and observance of the Rights therein declared.'
[54] The authors of the Convention began their deliberation on the basis of a 'short list' of the rights and freedoms contained in the Declaration. A. H. Robertson, 'Collected edition of the 'travaux préparatoires'

Convention was primarily concerned with curtailing the powers of totalitarian states and fascist regimes. Not surprisingly, the *travaux préparatoires* of both documents, reflecting the discussions of the authors of both texts, are full of references to the atrocities of the holocaust and the other horrors of the past decades.[55]

For example, when discussion arose whether or not to include a right to marry and found a family, several delegates were outraged by the suggestion to delete this freedom from the Convention:

> [The] majority of the Committee thought that the racial restrictions on the right of marriage made by the totalitarian regimes, as also the forced regimentation of children and young persons organized by these regimes, should be absolutely prohibited.[56]

Later, when these doubts were raised once more, this line was confirmed:

> The outstanding feature of the totalitarian regimes was the ruthless and savage way in which they endeavored to wipe out the concept of the family as the natural unit of society. If we delete paragraphs 10 and 11, I submit that we are accepting the validity of that philosophy. We are declaring that the Nazis were justified in everything they did to prevent some human beings from perpetuating their race and name.[57]

The principle concern of both the Declaration and the Convention was to protect individuals from the arbitrary interference with their rights and freedoms by intrusive governments. This rationale is even more prominent in the Convention than in the Declaration, because the former document only embodies so called 'first generation' human rights.[58] While first generation or civil and political rights require states not to interfere with certain rights and freedoms of their citizens in an arbitrary way, socioeconomic rights such as the right to education, to property and to a standard of

---

[55] of the European Convention on Human Rights = Recueil des travaux préparatoires de la Convention Européenne des Droits de l'Homme. Vol. 1 Preparatory Commission of the Council of Europe Committee of Ministers, Consultative Assembly, 11 May-8 September 1949', Nijhoff, The Hague, 1975.
See regarding the origins of the Universal Declaration among others: M. G Johnson & J. Symonides, 'The Universal Declaration of Human Rights: a history of its creation and implementation, 1948–1998', Unesco, Paris, 1998. A. Eide & T. Swinehart, 'The Universal Declaration of Human Rights: a commentary', Scandinavian University Press, Oslo, 1992. A. Verdoodt, 'Naissance et signification de la Déclaration Universelle des droits de L'Homme', Louvain, Warny, 1964. N. Robinson, 'The Universal Declaration of Human Rights: its origin, significance, application, and interpretation', World Jewish Congress, New York, 1958.

[56] A. H. Robertson, 'Collected edition of the 'travaux préparatoires' of the European Convention on Human Rights = Recueil des travaux préparatoires de la Convention Européenne des Droits de l'Homme; Council of Europe. Vol. 2 Consultative Assembly, second session of the Committee of Ministers, Standing Committee of the Assembly, 10 August-18 November 1949', Nijhoff, The Hague, 1975, p. 220.

[57] Robertson, vol 2., p. 90.

[58] K. Vasak, 'Human Rights: A Thirty-Year Struggle: the Sustained Efforts to give Force of law to the Universal Declaration of Human Rights', UNESCO Courier 30:11, Paris: United Nations Educational, Scientific, and Cultural Organization, November 1977.

living require states not to abstain from action, but to actively pursue and impose such freedoms by adopting legal measures or by taking active steps.[59]

Consequently, the original rationale for the Convention as a whole was laying down negative obligations for nation states and granting negative freedom to citizens. Of all articles contained in the Convention, these rationales are most prominent in the right to privacy under Article 8 ECHR. Already under the Declaration, it was this Article that was originally plainly titled 'Freedom from wrongful interference'.[60] Likewise under the Convention, the right to privacy is only concerned with negative liberty, contrasting with other qualified rights in which positive freedoms are implicit, such as a person's freedom to manifest her religion or beliefs (Article 9), the freedom of expression (Article 10) and the freedom of association with others (Article 11). In addition, the wording of Article 8 ECHR does not contain any explicit positive obligation, such as is the case, for example, in Article 2, the obligation to protect the right to life, in Article 5, to inform an arrested person of the reason for arrest and to bring him or her promptly before a judge, in Article 6, the obligation to ensure an impartial and effective judicial system, and in Article 3 of the First Protocol, the obligation to hold free elections.[61]

The original rationale behind the right to privacy was granting the citizen negative freedom in vertical relations; that is, the right to be free from arbitrary interferences by the state. In this line, the Court still holds that the 'essential object of Article 8 is to protect the individual against arbitrary action by the public authorities'.[62] However, the Court has gradually diverged from the original approach of the Convention authors by accepting both positive obligations for national states and granting a right to positive freedom to individuals under the right to privacy. The element of positive liberty was adopted quite early in a case from 1976:

> For numerous anglo-saxon and French authors the right to respect for 'private life' is the right to privacy, the right to live, as far as one wishes, protected from publicity. [H]owever, the right to respect for private life does not end there. It comprises also, to a certain degree, the right to establish and to develop relationships with other human beings, especially in the emotional field for the development and fulfillment of one's own personality.[63]

Likewise, from very early on, the Court has broken with the strictly limited focus of the authors of the Convention on negative obligations and has accepted that states may

---

[59] See regarding the right to property protected under the First Protocol: C. B. Schutte, 'The European fundamental right of property: article 1 of Protocol no. 1 to the European Convention on Human Rights: its origins, its working and its impact on national legal orders', Kluwer, Deventer, 2004.
[60] UN documents: E/HR/3.
[61] H. Tomlinson, 'Positive obligations under the European Convention on Human Rights', <http://bit.ly/17U9TDa>, p. 2.
[62] See among others: ECtHR, Arvelo Apont v. the Netherlands, application no. 28770/05, 3 November 2011, §53.
[63] ECmHR, X. v. Iceland, application no. 6825/74, 18 May 1976.

under certain circumstances be under a positive obligation to ensure respect for the Convention.[64]

This has had an enormous impact on both the underlying rationales and the material scope of the right to privacy under the European Convention on Human Rights. It goes too far to discuss these matters in detail, but in general it can be established that the underlying rationale has moved from obligations on states not to abuse their power, to individual and subjective rights of natural persons to protect their individual autonomy, their human dignity and their personal freedom. This has had a dual effect. On the one hand, all matters with a non-personal/general character have generally been dismissed by the European Court of Human Rights because it argues that Article 8 ECHR in principle only protects personal interests. On the other hand, almost everything that is even only remotely connected to personal interests is accepted under the material scope of the right to privacy. This has meant that many of the other articles in the Convention are overshadowed by Article 8 ECHR, that rights and interests explicitly left out of the Convention have been reintroduced by the ECtHR via the right to privacy and that new rights have been accepted under the scope of Article 8 ECHR.[65]

To give a few examples, the right to privacy has overshadowed a number of other provisions in the Convention. Article 12 ECHR protects the right to marry and found a family. However, because this provision has been interpreted very restrictively by the Court and because Article 8 ECHR has been granted a very wide scope, most issues relating to gay marriage, artificial insemination, adoption and other non-traditional forms of marriage and procreation are dealt with under the scope of the right to privacy. On a similar line, the right to a fair trial is guaranteed under the Convention by Articles 5, 6 and 13 in particular. However, the Court has decided to deal with elements of a right to a fair process directly under Article 8 ECHR. 'It is true that Article 8 (art. 8) contains no explicit procedural requirements, but this is not conclusive of the matter. The local authority's decision-making process clearly cannot be devoid of influence on the substance of the decision, notably by ensuring that it is based on the relevant considerations and is not one-sided and, hence, neither is nor appears to be arbitrary. Accordingly, the Court is entitled to have regard to that process to determine whether it has been conducted in a manner that, in all the circumstances, is fair and affords due respect to the interests protected by Article 8 (art. 8). (…) The decision-making process must therefore, in the Court's view, be such as to secure that their views and interests are made known to and duly taken into account by the local authority and that they are able to exercise in due time any remedies available

---

[64] A. R. Mowbray, 'The development of positive obligations under the European Convention on Human Rights by the European Court of Human Rights', Portland, Oxford, 2004. ECtHR, Case "Relating to certain aspects of the Laws on the Use of Languages in Education in Belgium " v. Belgium, application nos. 1474/62, 1677/62, 1691/62, 1769/63, 1994/63 and 2126/64, 23 July 1968. ECtHR, Marckx v. Belgium, application no. 6833/74, 13 June 1979. ECtHR, Marzari v. Italy, application no. 36448/97, 4 May 1999. ECtHR, Monory v. Hungary, application no. 71099/01, 05 April 2005.

[65] These examples are taken from: B. van der Sloot, 'Privacy as Personality Right: Why the ECtHR's Focus on Ulterior Interests Might Prove Indispensable in the Age of "Big Data"', Utrecht Journal of International and European Law, 2015–80.

to them.'⁶⁶ A third example may be found in the protection of honor and reputation. Article 8 ECHR is built on Article 12 of the Universal Declaration of Human Rights, which holds: 'No one shall be subjected to arbitrary interference with his privacy, family, home or correspondence, nor to attacks upon his honor and reputation.' All elements have been transferred to Article 8 ECHR, except for the protection of honor and reputation, which was referred to the second paragraph of Article 10 ECHR, containing the grounds on the basis of which states could legitimate their decision to curtail the right to freedom of expression, as enshrined in Article 10 ECHR. It was thus the explicit choice of the authors of the Convention not to include a subjective right to the protection of honor and reputation. Although for a long time, the ECtHR has respected this choice, from 2007 onwards, it has revised its stance and stressed that Article 8 ECHR does provide natural persons with a subjective right to the protection of their honor and reputation.⁶⁷

Similarly, the right to privacy has, over time, been used to bring back matters under the protective scope of the Convention that were explicitly omitted by the authors of the Convention. For example, although the UDHR contains several provisions that refer to the protection of personality,⁶⁸ the Convention does not. The Court has gradually diverged from the intention of the authors. According to the ECtHR, states are under an obligation, *inter alia*, to allow individuals to receive the information necessary to know and to understand their childhood and early development as this is held to be of importance because of 'its formative implications for one's personality'. With regard to the development and fulfillment of one's identity in the external sphere, among others, the Court has not only protected (the creation of) the family sphere, it has also accepted that Article 8 ECHR 'protects a right to personal development, and the right to establish and develop relationships with other human beings and the outside world'.⁶⁹ As another example, the right to property has not only been rejected from the scope of the Convention as a whole, it has also been rejected from the right to privacy specifically. When drafting the documents, the question was posed a number of times whether or not Article 12 UDHR and Article 8 ECHR should include, besides the concepts already contained therein, a reference to the inviolability of private property. Although the authors of the Convention decided to protect the right to property in an optional Protocol to the Convention, from the start, the European Court of Human Rights has been willing to deal with many issues that relate primarily to the economic positions of the claimants, such as loss or destruction of property (such as homes), family property and inheritance matters, and demission and the right to work.⁷⁰ To provide a final

---

66　ECtHR, B. v. the United Kingdom, Application no. 9840/82, 8 July 1987, §63–64. See similarly: ECtHR, R. v. the United Kingdom, Application no. 10496/83, 8 July 1987. ECtHR, W. v. the United Kingdom, application no. 9749/82, 8 July 1987. ECtHR, Diamante and Pelliccioni v. San Marino, application no. 32250/08, 27 September 2011.
67　ECtHR, Pfeifer v. Austria, Application no. 12556/03, 15 November 2007.
68　22 UDHR, 26 UDHR and 29 UDHR.
69　ECtHR, Pretty v. the United Kingdom, application no. 2346/02, 29 April 2002, §61.
70　ECtHR, Oleksandr Volkov v. Ukraine, application no. 21722/11, 09 January 2013.

example, the Universal Declaration also contains a right to nationality.[71] The principled rejection of such a right under the Convention has been gradually overturned by the Court. It has held, for example, that the concept of private life alone, without reference to the interests of family members, can legitimise a claim for a residence permit or an objection to being extradited if a person's private life is so intrinsically connected to a specific country, among others in relation to language, work, friends, other social contacts, the possibility to develop her personality and explore her identity, the fact that that person's quality of life would be severely diminished by her exclusion from that country's territory, etc.[72]

Article 8 ECHR has also been one of the primary points of reference with respect to the living instrument doctrine, which the ECtHR uses to provide protection to new rights under the Convention. For example, data protection is not mentioned as such in the Convention. In the beginning, the Court was willing to provide personal data protection under the ECHR with reference to a number of provisions, such as Article 5, 6, 8, 9, 10 and 13,[73] but in later years it has referred almost exclusively the right to privacy when dealing with these cases. Likewise, the Convention contains no minority rights. It is article 8 ECHR that is referred to by the ECtHR when dealing with matters that revolve around these types of cases. The Court has stressed the following, for example, in reference to an applicant:

> [O]ccupation of her caravan is an integral part of her ethnic identity as a Gypsy, reflecting the long tradition of that minority of following a travelling lifestyle. This is the case even though, under the pressure of development and diverse policies or by their own choice, many Gypsies no longer live a wholly nomadic existence and increasingly settle for long periods in one place in order to facilitate, for example, the education of their children. Measures affecting the applicant's stationing of her caravans therefore have an impact going beyond the right to respect for her home. They also affect her ability to maintain her identity as a Gypsy and to lead her private and family life in accordance with that tradition.[74]

What is more, states may be under the positive obligation to take active measures to respect and facilitate the development of these minority identities.[75] Finally, reference can be made to the right to a clean environment, which is also not contained in the Convention. Yet the Court is prepared to deal with cases revolving around noise pollution, air pollution, scent pollution and other forms of environmental damage under

---

[71] Article 15 UDHR.
[72] ECtHR, Slivenko v. Latvia, application no. 48321/99, 09 October 2003. ECtHR, Sisojeva a.o. v. Latvia, application no. 60654/00, 15 January 2007. ECtHR, Nasri v. France, application no. 19465/92, 13 July 1995.ECtHR, Aristimuno Mendizabal v. France, application no. 51431/99, 17 January 2006. ECtHR, Rodrigues Da Silva and Hoogkamer v. Netherlands, application no. 50435/99, 31 January 2006.
[73] P. de Hert, Human Rights and Data Protection. European Case-Law 1995–1997 [Mensenrechten en bescherming van persoonsgegevens. Overzicht en synthese van de Europese rechtspraak 1955–1997] (Jaarboek ICM, 1997 Antwerpen, Maklu, 1998.
[74] ECtHR, Chapman v. the United Kingdom, application no. 27238/95, 18 January 2001, §73.
[75] ECtHR, Aksu v. Turkey, application nos. 4149/04 and 41029/04, 27 July 2010, §49. ECtHR (Grand Chamber), Aksu v. Turkey, application nos. 4149/04 and 41029/04, 15 March 2012, §58 & 75.

the scope of the right to privacy of the Convention if such pollution affects the quality of life of the application, which the Court itself agrees is a very vague and broad term.[76]

2.3. ASSESSMENTS

With the shift from rights to duties and from protecting general interests to personal interests, a shift can also be witnessed with respect to how the Court determines the outcome of cases.[77] With the focus on duties and general interests, the ECtHR would mainly assess the quality and legitimacy of the policies and laws as such. Now, however, the focus is on the individual interest of the claimant, which is juxtaposed with the general interest, for example in relation to the protection of national security, public order and the economic well-being of the country. Balancing is currently one of the standard ways through which to determine the outcome of a case. The concept is so omnipresent, also in other jurisdictions, that some authors have stressed that we live in an 'age of balancing'.[78] Certainly, under the ECHR, weighing one right or interest against the other seems to be the standard approach for dealing with complaints:

> Establishing that the measure is necessary in a democratic society involves showing that the action taken is in response to a pressing social need, and that the interference with the rights protected is no greater than is necessary to address that pressing social need. The latter requirement is referred to as the test of proportionality. This test requires the Court to balance the severity of the restriction placed on the individual against the importance of the public interest.[79]

Likewise, when the rights of two individuals clash, for example the right to identity and reputation as protected under Article 8 ECHR, and the right to freedom of expression as guaranteed under Article 10 ECHR, the ECtHR balances the two rights against each other to determine the outcome of the matter.

It is important to stress, however, that the idea of balancing is not contained in the ECHR and was not in any way envisaged by the authors of the Convention. Rather, the Convention first and foremost provided minimum rules for the conduct of states; the focus was on duties (of care) for states, rather than individual and subjective rights. For

---

[76] ECtHR, Ledyayeva, Dobrokhotova, Zolotareva and Romashina v. Russia, application nos. 53157/99, 53247/99, 56850/00 and 53695/00, 26 October 2006, §90.
[77] This section is based in part on: B. van der Sloot, 'The Practical and Theoretical Problems with 'balancing': Delfi, Coty and the redundancy of the human rights framework', Maastricht Journal of European and Comparative Law, 2016-3. And on: B. van der Sloot, 'How to assess privacy violations in the age of Big Data? Analysing the three different tests developed by the ECtHR and adding for a fourth one', ICTL, 2015.
[78] T. A. Aleinikoff, 'Constitutional Law in the Age of Balancing', The Yale Law Journal, Vol. 96, No. 5, 1987.
[79] C. Ovey & R.C.A. White, 'European Convention on Human Rights', Oxford University Press, Oxford, 2002, p. 209.

example, the respect for life, except in respect of deaths resulting from lawful acts of war (Article 2 ECHR), the commandment that no one shall be subjected to torture or to inhuman or degrading treatment or punishment (Article 3 ECHR), the rule that no one shall be held in slavery or servitude (Article 4) and the prohibition on retrospective legislation (Article 7 ECHR), are principles which may never be violated by states, not even in the state of emergency (Article 15 ECHR). Besides the prohibition of retrospective legislation, the Convention lays down rules on fair trial (Article 6 ECHR), safeguards against unlawful or arbitrary detention or arrest (Article 5 ECHR) and the right to an effective remedy (Article 13 ECHR). These are all minimum conditions which states need to abide by; if they do not, for example by adopting retrospective legislation, it is not so much that individual rights have been interfered with, but that the state is held to be abusive of its powers.

Even with the four qualified rights – the right to privacy, the freedom of religion, the freedom of speech and the freedom of association – the prime focus of the Convention authors was on curtailing the conduct of states. First, regard should be had of Article 18 ECHR, specifying: 'The restrictions permitted under this Convention to the said rights and freedoms shall not be applied for any purpose other than those for which they have been prescribed.' This provision was aimed at the democratic legislator, who could only use its powers to adopt laws and policies to promote the general welfare of the population and the country. If it used its powers, for example, to suppress certain minority groups in society, it simply abused its powers. There is no case of balancing different interests, rather this doctrine functions as an intrinsic test. Democratic power should under no circumstances be used to promote exclusively the welfare of specific groups in society. This also holds true for the prohibition of discrimination contained in Article 14 ECHR, which provides:

> The enjoyment of the rights and freedoms set forth in this Convention shall be secured without discrimination on any ground such as sex, race, color, language, religion, political or other opinion, national or social origin, association with a national minority, property, birth or other status.

The same logic can be found in the limitation clauses of Articles 8–11 ECHR. The administrative power could only enter the private sphere, for example, if this was prescribed by law, if it was aimed at a general interest, such as national security or the protection of the rights and freedoms of citizens, and if it was necessary in a democratic society. It should be noted that this is a binary test: either an infringement is prescribed for by law or it is not, either it is aimed at one of the legitimate interests or it is not, either it is necessary in a democratic society or it is not. Take as an example the sanctity of one's home, as protected under Article 8 ECHR. If the police enters a person's house for a legitimate reason, for example if it has reason to believe that this person committed a murder and it wanted to search the premises for a murder weapon, this might qualify as necessary for the protection of the public order. If the police enters a person's home without a legitimate reason, for example because the person is a famous football player and the police-officers were curious to know the living conditions of that person, however, it is not. Note that no balancing of interests takes place, the test is simply whether an infringement is necessary or not. The same holds true for the question whether the infringement is prescribed by law – it is a binary test.

However, this approach has been moved to the background by the European Court of Human Rights. First, the ECtHR has reshifted the focus from prohibitions for states to abuse their power, to subjective rights by natural persons to protect their individual interests.[80] Second, it should be stressed that Article 18 ECHR, providing the first safeguard against the abuse of power by states has been of almost no relevance. In only 5 cases has the Court found a violation of Article 18 and even in these cases, it stressed that Article 18 cannot be invoked as a separate doctrine, but only in combination with an individual right as protected under the Convention. Thus, it is first necessary for a claimant to demonstrate that her individual right and personal interests have been harmed and only then is it possible for the Court to hold that a state has abused its powers. Holding states accountable for abuse of power as such is out of the question.[81] Likewise, Article 14 ECHR, under the interpretation of the Court, can only be invoked if an infringement with one of the subjective rights under the Convention has been established by the Court and if individual interests of natural persons are infringed. Finally, with regard to the four qualified rights, the common approach by the ECtHR is to balance different rights or interests against each other, for example the general interest in national security and the particular interest of a claimant to privacy.

The shift from a necessity test to a balancing test can be illustrated by analyzing a relatively simple case: *Delfi v. Estonia*.[82] In this case, an Estonian digital newspaper published a critical article about a company that provides ferry services and about L., its sole shareholder. The company would have planned to destroy ice roads for the benefit of its ferry services. In itself, the article was nuanced, balanced and the author has adhered to all journalistic principles. The site offered users the opportunity to respond to stories, and this particular article attracts some 200 comments. After some time, L. asked Delfi to remove twenty of those comments because he felt that they were defamatory, and to compensate him financially for the damage caused to his reputation. Delfi granted the former request, but denied the latter. The subsequent question was whether the site was legally responsible for comments posted by its users. In the national legal procedure, there was significant debate about which regime is applicable to Delfi. On the one hand, Delfi invoked the position of passive hosting provider under Article 14 of the

---

[80] B. van der Sloot, 'Privacy in the Post-NSA Era: Time for a Fundamental Revision?', JIPITEC, 2014–1.
[81] ECtHR, Ilgar Mammadov v. Azerbaijan, application no. 15172/13, 22 May 2014. ECtHR, Tymoshenko v. Ukraine, application no. 49872/11, 30 April 2013. ECtHR, Lutsenko v. Ukraine, application no. 6492/11, 03 July 2012. ECtHR, Cebotari v. Moldova, application no. 35615/06, 13 November 2007. ECtHR, Gusinskiy v. Russia, application no. 70276/01, 19 May 2004.
[82] See also: D. Voorhoof, 'Delfi AS v. Estonia: Grand Chamber confirms liability of online news portal for offensive comments posted by its readers', <https://strasbourgobservers.com/2015/06/18/delfi-as-v-estonia-grand-chamber-confirms-liability-of-online-news-portal-for-offensive-comments-posted-by-its-readers/>. L. Woods, 'The Delfi AS vs Estonia judgement explained', <http://blogs.lse.ac.uk/mediapolicyproject/2015/06/16/the-delfi-as-vs-estonia-judgement-explained/>.

e-Commerce Directive, which would exempt it from liability for actions taken by its users. On the other hand, it was also argued that Delfi could be seen as a journalistic online medium, which would mean it should be judged under the doctrine of the freedom of expression. Throughout the various stages of appeal, some courts applied the first regime and ruled in favor of Delfi, whereas others applied the second regime and held Delfi liable. At last instance, the Estonian Supreme Court chose the latter approach and awarded a small amount of damages to L. Subsequently, the ECtHR held, in first instance and on appeal before the Grand Chamber, that this judgment did not violate Delfi's freedom of expression as protected under Article 10 ECHR.

If the ECtHR had approached this case in the way intended by the authors of the Convention, it could have done the following. First, it could have analyzed whether the website could indeed invoke the right to freedom of expression under Article 10 ECHR. This is far from obvious, because Delfi itself argued that it was a passive internet intermediary, having no involvement with the comments – it only provided a platform for users to post comments on. The government highlighted this aspect before the Court:

> [The Government] pointed out that according to the applicant company it had been neither the author nor the discloser of the defamatory comments. The Government noted that if the Court shared that view, the application was incompatible *ratione materiae* with the provisions of the Convention, as the Convention did not protect the freedom of expression of a person who was neither the author nor the discloser.[83]

The question that could have been answered by the Court is: can a website that allows users to place comments invoke a right to freedom of expression with regard to the comments it has neither written nor disclosed, and if so, under which conditions? Second, if the first question is answered affirmatively, the Court could have assessed whether the limitation on Delfi's freedom of speech was prescribed for by law and necessary in a democratic society in relation to one of the goals enlisted in paragraph 2 of article 10 ECHR. In this case, the government relied on 'the protection of the reputation or rights of others' The Court could thus have assessed whether the comments authored by the users can actually be qualified as defamatory. Delfi's site contains thousands of user comments; the specific article in question attracted some 200. Of these 200, L. asked to remove 20. And of these 20 comments, at least half seem childish rather than illegal, such as, 'aha... [I] hardly believe that that happened by accident... assholes fck', 'rascal!!!' and 'I pee into [L.'s] ear and then I also shit onto his head.:)'.[84]

Subsequently, the Court could have assessed whether the limitation of Delfi's freedom of expression was prescribed by law and whether the law was accessible and foreseeable. Delfi argues that its conviction was not reasonably foreseeable. It refers to the fact that it is not unambiguously clear which legal regime applies to these types of cases; the e-Commerce framework or the freedom of expression. It also points out

---

[83] ECtHR, Delfi v. Estonia (first instance), application no. 64569/09, 10 October 2013, §48.
[84] ECtHR, Delfi v. Estonia (first instance), application no. 64569/09, 10 October 2013, §14.

that national courts did not agree on this point. Consequently, the ECtHR could have determined the extent to which Delfi could and should have known that it would be held liable under the freedom of expression for the comments written and posted by its users, instead of being judged under the e-Commerce framework. Finally, the Court could have assessed whether the restrictions on the freedom of expression, as provided for in the law, were indeed necessary in a democratic society. Note that what must be necessary in a democratic society are the restrictions *as such*. Paragraph 2 of Article 10 ECHR specifies:

> The exercise of these freedoms, since it carries with it duties and responsibilities, may be subject to such formalities, conditions, restrictions or penalties as are prescribed by law and are necessary in a democratic society (…) for the protection of the reputation or rights of others (…).

What the Court must determine is whether it is necessary in a democratic society to limit the freedom of expression of internet intermediaries and its users in general in order to prevent comments such as 'Rascal', 'assholes' and 'I pee in your ear and shit on your head'.

In conclusion, when the 'original test' is applied, as envisioned by the authors of the Convention, the focus is not on the balancing of the different interests at stake. However, in this case in particular but also more in general, the Court has increasingly emphasized the balancing act. It did not assess in detail whether internet intermediaries can invoke a right to freedom of expression with regard to the comments written and posted by their users.[85] Rather, it held that Delfi was required to pay a fine in relation to the user comments and that it was therefore unnecessary to answer this question in detail.[86] It did not assess whether and if so, which one of the comments could be seen as defamatory; rather, it stressed that it was clear that these comments were 'manifestly unlawful'.[87] It did not determine in any detail whether Delfi could and should have foreseen under which regime it would be judged.[88] It did not assess whether the restrictions on the freedom of speech were as such necessary in a democratic society. Rather, it balanced Delfi's right to freedom of expression with L.'s right to reputation as protected under Article 8 ECHR.[89]

---

[85] See the careful analysis on this point of: N. Cox, 'Delfi AS v Estonia: The Liability of Secondary Internet Publishers for Violation of Reputational Rights under the European Convention on Human Rights', The Modern Law Review, 77, 4, 2014. M. Susi, 'Delfi AS v. Estonia', The American Journal of International Law, Vol. 108, No. 2, 2014.

[86] ECtHR, Delfi v. Estonia (first instance), application no. 64569/09, 10 October 2013, §50.

[87] ECtHR, Delfi v. Estonia (Grand Chamber), application no. 64569/09, 16 June 2015, §117.

[88] If Delfi would have gone to the European Court of Justice, it might have been judged under the e-Commerce framework. Directive 2000/31/EC of the European Parliament and of the Council of 8 June 2000 on certain legal aspects of information society services, in particular electronic commerce, in the Internal Market ('Directive on electronic commerce'), Official Journal L 178, 17/07/2000 P. 0001 – 0016.

[89] The Court made this shift in the case from 2007. ECtHR, Pfeifer v. Austria, application no. 12556/03, 15 November 2007.

When examining whether there is a need for an interference with freedom of expression in a democratic society in the interests of the "protection of the reputation or rights of others", the Court may be required to ascertain whether the domestic authorities have struck a fair balance when protecting two values guaranteed by the Convention which may come into conflict with each other in certain cases, namely on the one hand freedom of expression protected by Article 10, and on the other hand the right to respect for private life enshrined in Article 8. The Court has found that, as a matter of principle, the rights guaranteed under Articles 8 and 10 deserve equal respect, and the outcome of an application should not, in principle, vary according to whether it has been lodged with the Court under Article 10 of the Convention by the publisher of an offending article or under Article 8 of the Convention by the person who has been the subject of that article.[90]

The peculiar thing is that the case revolves around a claim of Delfi against Estonia. Applying the original test, the core question would have been whether the Estonian government has illegitimately or unlawfully curtailed the fundamental right of Delfi. What the ECtHR does, however, is to bring into the equation L., who is not a party to this legal claim, and to focus instead on balancing the interests of two private parties. The actions of the Estonian state are only referred to on the side, when balancing the interests of Delfi and L. This is merely one example of a more general trend in which the ECtHR has shifted from applying a necessity test to a adopting a balancing test.[91] As will be shown in Subsection 2.3, a similar trend appears with respect to the right to data protection.

Necessity test	Balancing act
(1) The Court discusses whether Delfi can invoke a right to freedom of expression	(1) Delfi invokes the right to freedom of expression, as provided under Article 10 ECHR
(2) The Court assesses whether the fine Delfi had to pay is a limitation of its right	(2) L. invokes his right to reputation, as provided under Article 8 ECHR
(3) The Court determines whether this limitation is prescribed for by law and foreseeable	(3) The Court grants a wide scope to both provisions and gives no principled priority of one right over the other
(4) The Court checks whether the limitation serves a legitimate interest	(4) The Court balances the two rights against each other, setting out certain ad-hoc criteria
(5) The Court determines whether the limitation in law as such is necessary in a democratic society, for example, whether it serves a pressing social need	(5) The Court only discusses the particularities of the case, taking into account all relevant circumstances

---

[90] ECtHR, Delfi v. Estonia (Grand Chamber), application no. 64569/09, 16 June 2015, §138–139.
[91] Also critical of balancing is: C. J. Angelopoulos, 'European intermediary liability in copyright: A tort-based analysis', FdR: Instituut voor Informatierecht (IViR), 2016 <http://hdl.handle.net/11245/1.527223>.

2.4. ENFORCEMENT

The Convention in general, and its right to privacy in particular, have witnessed an enormous expansion in scope, an exponential increase in the number of cases and an increasing emphasis on juridical rules and enforcement measures. This follows in part from what has already been discussed. Section 2.2 showed that the material scope of Article 8 ECHR has grown. The 'living instrument' doctrine has meant that all provisions under the Convention have been interpreted broadly. The right to freedom of expression has been applied to the modern media environment, the right to education has also been interpreted in the light of Article 9 ECHR, and minority rights have been approached from the perspective of the freedom of religion as well as the right to expression and the right to education. Still, in contrast to the right to privacy, such 'new' freedoms are often directly associated with the core of those rights. For example, the Court has accepted that minorities are provided protection under a number of provisions under the Convention and its Protocols, such as the freedom from discrimination (14 ECHR), from which the right not to be discriminated against on the basis of a minority identity is derived; the right to education (Article 2(1)(e) Protocol), from which the right to special cultural or linguistic protection for the education of children is derived; the freedom of religion (9 ECHR), from which it follows that minorities and adherents of minority religions have a protected status; and the right to freedom of expression (Article 10 ECHR), in relation to which it has been accepted that minorities have a special claim to express their minority views.[92] In contrast to the right to maintain and develop one's minority identity and life style, which does not seem to be implicit in the respect for a person's private life or home, these are all matters that are either directly or indirectly linked to the core of those Convention rights.[93]

Consequently, the right to privacy has seen a vast expansion of its scope, not only because the Court has often relied on Article 8 when accepting new freedoms and third generation rights under the scope of the Convention, but also because it has been used to revert the exclusion of certain rights and freedoms from the ECHR and because it has encroached on a number of other rights specified in the Convention, such as the right to marry and found a family, the right to a fair trial, the right to reputation and honor, the right to property, the right to legalized stay and legal identity for immigrants, and the right to develop and express one's identity and personality.[94] There seems

---

[92] T. E. McGonagle, 'Minority rights, freedom of expression and of the media: dynamics and dilemmas', Intersentia, Cambridge, 2011. J. Castellino, 'Global minority rights', Burlington, Ashgate, 2011.
[93] The same might be argued in relation to the right to a name, which seems more directly connected to the right to marry and found a family under ECHR Art 12.
[94] Again, these are just a few or the examples; another example may be the right to a name, which is neither accepted under the UDHR and ECHR, but is accepted in subsequent human rights documents. It may already be derived from ICCPR Art 24. See further: ECtHR, Tekeli v. Turkey, application no. 29865/96, 16 November 2004. ECtHR, Guillot v. France, application no. 22500/93, 24 October 1996. ECmHR, Salonen v. Finland, application no. 27868/95, 2 July 1997. ECtHR, Bijleveld v. Netherlands,

no logical end to the expansion of the realm of Article 8 ECHR since the Court is faced with new questions and challenges on a daily basis. For example, consider the emerging principles tentatively described as 'fourth generation human rights'.[95] As suggested by different authors and commentators, these might include a right to general 'information management',[96] the 'rights of indigenous peoples',[97] the 'right to sustainable development of the future generation',[98] 'women's rights, the rights of future generations, rights of access to information, and the right to communicate'[99] and rights necessitated by 'phenomena like the great developments in the area of biotechnology (with very conflictive issues such as the cloning of and experimenting with stem cells for therapeutic or reproductive purposes) or the Internet (and the problem of its regulation)'.[100] If accepted, most if not all of these 'new' fourth generation human rights, suggested by different authors and commentators, would presumably be approached by the Court from the angle of Article 8 ECHR.

Secondly, Section 2.1 showed that natural persons now have direct access to the Court. Among the drafters of the Convention, the opponents of a right of individual complainants to have direct access to the Court, among the drafters of the Convention, feared for shoals of complaints being put forward by every person who believed that her interests were harmed. This seems indeed to have become a reality. The fact that individuals have direct access to the Courts, in combination with the increased material scope, the fact that Article 8 ECHR has also been applied to horizontal relationships (even though complaints can still only be brought against a state) and the fact that governments are often encouraged to take positive measures, has ensured that the amount of cases before the Court has exploded. The graphic below shows the number of cases per year. This graphic only shows the cases that were declared admissible, with 837 cases between 1959 and 1998 and a peak in 2009 of 1,625 a year. In other words, there were twice as many cases before the ECtHR in one year as in the first forty years of its existence. This graphic does not show the cases at first instance, the stage at which cases are either declared admissible or inadmissible. By far most cases are declared inadmissible, so the graphic only shows a minor component of the trend. Still, it should be acknowledged that the increase in cases also has other causes, such as that many more countries have acceded to the European Convention on Human Rights.[101]

---

application no. 42973/98, 27 April 2000. ECtHR, G.M.B. and K.M. v. Switzerland, application no. 36797/97, 27 September 2001. ECtHR, Tjerna v. Finland, application no. 18131/91, 25 November 1994.
[95] <www.s-j-c.net/main/english/images/humanrightsfinal.pdf>.
[96] <www.thejakartapost.com/news/2006/09/04/fourth-generation-human-rights.html>.
[97] M. Brinton Lykes, 'Human rights violations as structural violence', in: D. J. Christie, R. V. Wagner & D. A. Winter (eds), 'Peace, Conflict, and Violence: Peace Psychology for the 21st Century', Englewood Cliffs, New Jersey, Prentice-Hall, 2001.
[98] <www.csmcd.eu/downloads/Generations_of_Human_Rights.pdf>.
[99] R. P. Claude & B. H. Weston, 'Human Rights in the World Community: Issues And Action', University of Pennsylvania Press, 2006, p. 26.
[100] F. Falcón y Tella, 'Challenges for human rights', Martinus Nijhoff Publishers, Leiden, 2007, p. 66.
[101] See: <http://hudoc.echr.coe.int/>.

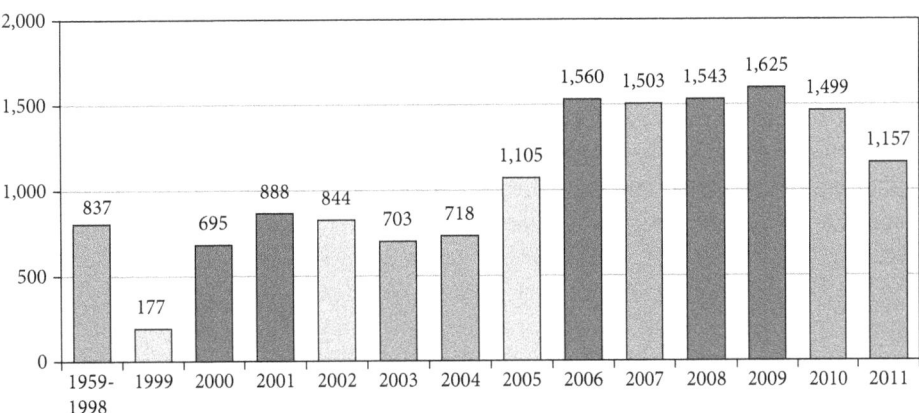

Third and finally, as has been explained in Section 2.1, when the Convention was drafted, two camps had opposing ideas. This concerned not only the question of whether individuals should have direct access to the Court, but also the question of whether a Court should be installed and if so, what kind of authority it should have. One group was hesitant to place a large emphasis on juridical solutions for human rights violations, as they feared, *inter alia*, that states that engaged in the mass violations of human rights, would not be persuaded by legal verdicts or sanctions. Consequently, emphasized non-juridical aspects of conflict resolution; they emphasized, for example, that, due to the moral authority of the European institutions, the publication of a report about a certain case might be enough to persuade the state to stop violating human rights, as it would fear damage to its national or international reputation. Besides, they hoped that mediation by the European Commission on Human Rights would lead to a friendly settlement by the parties. Under this model, the ECmHR was only authorized to assess the admissibility of cases. This group argued that there was no need to establish a European Court of Human Rights, as the work by the Commission would be sufficient. At most, the non-legalist group would have accepted a two-tiered model, with the possibility for states to pursue admissible applications before the International Court of Justice (ICJ).

Obviously, a compromise had to be reached between these two groups. What the legalist group won is that the European Court of Human Rights was established, so that the cases were not referred to the ICJ, but would be dealt with by ECtHR. Furthermore, the Court could establish a violation and impose sanctions or fines. For example, Article 50 of the original Convention specified:

> If the Court finds that a decision or a measure taken by a legal authority or any other authority of a High Contracting Party is completely or partially in conflict with the obligations arising from the present Convention, and if the internal law of the said Party allows only partial reparation to be made for the consequences of this decision or measure, the decision of the Court shall, if necessary, afford just satisfaction to the injured party.

On the other hand, however, it was merely optional for states to accept the authority of the Court and of the Commission.[102] Moreover, there was a large emphasis on non-legal aspects of conflict resolution in the Convention. Article 26, containing the rule on exhaustion of domestic remedies, ensured that the ECHR was only a last resort so that states could deal with the complaints themselves. And if an applicant did exhaust all domestic remedies, the ECtHR would not function as a fourth instance court, but as a court assessing whether the minimum principles for democratic states contained in the Convention had been respected. Furthermore, Article 28 provided that the Commission 'shall place itself at the disposal of the parties concerned with a view to securing a friendly settlement of the matter on the basis of respect for Human Rights as defined in this Convention' and Article 47 specified that the 'Court may only deal with a case after the Commission has acknowledged the failure of efforts for a friendly settlement and within the period of three months provided for in Article 32.' The approach was that juridical solutions should only be the *ultimum remedium*, to be applied if all other options had failed. Finally, Article 29 provided that the judges of the Court must be of 'high moral character', therewith emphasizing that the moral authority of the CoE's legal institutions might be of greater importance than the specific legal competences.[103]

Since the adoption of the original Convention however, this focus has changed, both through the conduct of the states, who have commonly accepted the jurisdiction of the Court, through the interpretation of the Convention by the Court and through the member states revising the original Convention on a number of points. For example, there are very few friendly settlements under the Court and the Court is willing to act (under certain circumstances) not only as court of fourth instance, which already is against the intention of the authors of the Convention, but increasingly also as a court of first instance, thereby circumventing the principle of exhaustion of domestic remedies and undermining the discretion of the member states (this will be explained in more detail in the next chapter). The number of cases has also seen an exponential growth. This means that the reputational influence of a decision by the Court has also lessened. Some countries, such as Russia and Turkey, are held to be in violation of the ECHR on such a regular basis that the moral influence of these decisions is almost nil. This is precisely as the non-legalist group among the drafters of the ECHR had feared: juridical solutions are powerless without a moral connotation. The reference to the 'high moral character' of judges has, however, been deleted from the Convention. In conclusion, the character of the European Convention on Human Rights has changed from a largely ethical document, with several juridical aspects, to a juridical instrument, with a few ethical components.

---

[102] See article 45–46 of the original Convention.
[103] This was later also included in the Convention with regard to the members of the Commission. Protocol No. 8 to the Convention for the Protection of Human Rights and Fundamental Freedoms.

3. DATA PROTECTION

The Charter of Fundamental Rights of the European Union from 2000 entered into force in 2009.[104] It contains provision for the right to data protection (Article 8) which is separated from the right to privacy (Article 7). A European Union wide General Data Protection Regulation has also been adopted recently. It would seem that the still young right to data protection has reached the point of maturity. The origins of the right to data protection lie partially in the data protection rules of northern European countries, which arose in several countries in the 1970s, and the Council of Europe's Resolutions on data processing[105] and partially in the USA and the realization of so called Fair Information Practices (FIPs), which were developed because the right to privacy was thought to be unfit for the 'modern' challenges of large automated data processing.[106] The increased use of large databases by (primarily) governmental organizations raised a number of problems for the modern 'individualized' concept of the right to privacy, which is aimed at protecting the private interests of citizens, *inter alia* by giving them a right to control over private and sensitive data.[107] First, data processing often does not handle private or sensitive data, but public and non-sensitive data such as car ownership, postal codes, number of children, etc.[108] A US governmental report from 1973 established that 'Dictionary definitions of privacy uniformly speak in terms of seclusion, secrecy, and withdrawal from public view. They all denote a quality that is not inherent in most record-keeping systems'.[109]

Secondly, and related to the first problem, many privacy doctrines at that time already emphasized the right of the data subject as having a unilateral role in deciding the nature and extent of her self-disclosure. None accommodated the observation that records of personal data usually reflect and mediate relationships in which both

---

[104] This section and section 3.1, 3.2 and 3.4 are based on: B. van der Sloot, 'Do data protection rules protect the individual and should they? An assessment of the proposed General Data Protection Regulation', International Data Privacy Law, 2014-3.

[105] U. Dammann, O. Mallmann & S. Simitis (eds), 'Data Protection Legislation: An International Documentation: Engl.–German: eine internationale Dokumentation = Die Gesetzgebung zum Datenschutz', Metzner, Frankfurt am Main, 1977. F. W. Hondius, 'Emerging Data Protection in Europe', North-Holland, Amsterdam, 1975. Organisation for Economic Co-operation and Development (OECD), Policy issues in data protection and privacy: concepts and perspectives: proceedings of the OECD seminar, 24–26 June 1974, 1976. H. Burkert, 'Freedom of Information and Data Protection', Gesellschaft für Mathematik und Datenverarbeitung, Bonn, 1983.

[106] See among others: Privacy Protection Study Commission, Personal Privacy in an Information Society (1977); Federal Trade Commission, Privacy Online: A Report to Congress (1998).

[107] See also: The Privacy Act of 1974 5 U.S.C. §552a. See further: H. Burkert, 'Freedom of Information and Data Protection', Gesellschaft für Mathematik und Datenverarbeitung, Bonn, 1983.

[108] See for the distinction between 'private' and 'personal' data: R. Wacks, 'Personal Information: Privacy and the Law', Clarendon Press, Oxford; Oxford University Press, New York, 1989. See for the distinction between 'private' and 'public' among others: S. Strömholm, 'Right of Privacy and Rights of the Personality', Norstedt, Stockholm, 1967.

[109] Secretary's Advisory Committee on Automated Personal Data Systems, Records, Computers and the Rights of Citizens (1973) <https://www.hsdl.org/?view&did=479784> accessed 24 June 2014.

individuals and institutions have an interest, and are usually made for purposes that are shared by institutions and individuals.[110] Because data processing often does not deal with private and sensitive data, the right to control by the data subject was felt undesirable, because governments need such general data to develop, among other things, adequate social and economic policies. It was also felt unreasonable because, in contrast to private and sensitive data, data subjects have no or substantially less direct and personal interest in controlling (partially) public and general information. Consequently, instead of granting a right to control, the focus of these principles was on the fairness and reasonableness of the data processing, for example by specifying that data should not be collected and processed when this was not necessary for or proportionate to the goal pursued and by laying down that the data should be correct and kept up to date, so as to guarantee that the profile of a person or a group of people was accurate.[111]

This first concern (that data processing often concerns non-sensitive or public data) has remained an identifying element of data protection instruments. The definition of personal data has been stretched even further to cope with the increased possibilities of identification.[112] The Council of Europe (CoE) adopted two Resolutions for data processing in 1973 and 1974, one for the public and one for the private sector, which defined 'personal information' simply as information relating to individuals (physical persons).[113] Here, the individual and subjective element in the definition of personal data is still prominent. Already by 1981, however, in the subsequent Convention for the Protection of Individuals with regard to Automatic Processing of Personal Data, adopted by the Council of Europe, 'personal data' were defined as any information relating to an identified or identifiable individual.[114] The explanatory report stressed that an 'identifiable person', an element which was new to this definition, meant a person who can be easily identified; it did not cover the identification of persons by means of very sophisticated methods.[115] Still, data which were not yet linked to an individual, but could be with relative ease, fell under the scope of the definition.

---

[110] Records, Computers and the Rights of Citizens.
[111] See further: A. F. Westin & M. A. Baker, 'Databanks in a Free Society: Computers, Record-keeping and Privacy', Quadrangle/The New York Times Book Co cop., New York, 1972.
[112] Likewise, the impossibility of owning and privatizing information may have had an influence: F. W. Hondius, 'Emerging Data Protection in Europe', 1975.
[113] Council of Europe, Committee of Ministers, Resolution (73) 22 On the Protection of the privacy of individuals vis-à-vis electronic data banks in the private sector. (Adopted by the Committee of Ministers on 26 September 1973 at the 224th meeting of the Ministers' Deputies). Council of Europe. Committee of Ministers, Resolution (74) 29 On the Protection of the privacy of individuals vis-à-vis electronic data banks in the public sector. (Adopted by the Committee of Ministers on 20 September 1974 at the 236th meeting of the Ministers' Deputies).
[114] Convention for the Protection of Individuals with regard to Automatic Processing of Personal Data, Strasbourg, 28 January 1981, article 2 sub a.
[115] <http://conventions.coe.int/Treaty/EN/Reports/HTML/108.htm>.

Chapter II. The Transformation of the Right to Privacy and the Right to Data Protection

In the Data Protection Directive of the European Union (EU) of 1995,[116] which has remained up to now the most important instrument for data protection in Europe, this concept was widened even further. The original proposal of the Commission contained the concept of 'depersonalisation', which signified modifying personal data in such a way that the information within it can no longer be associated with a specific individual or allow the identity of an individual to be determined without excessive effort in terms of staff, expenditure, and time.[117] The Directive would not be applicable to those data. However, the advisory report of the Economic and Social Committee suggested deleting the reference to 'excessive effort', 'for a processing task requiring an excessive effort today may require no effort at all next year'.[118] The European Parliament proposed to further limit this concept and in the final proposal it was deleted altogether,[119] although a special position has been reserved for personal data processed for statistical purposes.[120] At the same time, at the suggestion of the Parliament,[121] the definition of personal data was enlarged by specifying:

[A]n identifiable person is one who can be identified, directly or indirectly, in particular by reference to an identification number or to one or more factors specific to his physical, physiological, mental, economic, cultural or social identity.[122]

This not only introduces a very wide, non-exhaustive list of possible identifying factors, but also the possibility of 'indirect' identifiable data.[123] The Article 29 Data Protection Working Party ('the Working Party'), the advisory body installed by the Data Protection Directive, has clarified this as follows:

---

[116] Directive 95/46/EC of the European Parliament and of the Council of 24 October 1995 on the protection of individuals with regard to the processing of personal data and on the free movement of such data.

[117] Proposal for a Council Directive concerning the protection of individuals in relation to the processing of personal data COM(90) 314 final – SYN 287 (Submitted by the Commission on 27 July 1990) (90/C 277/03).

[118] Economic and Social Committee, opinion on: the proposal for a Council Directive concerning the protection of individuals in relation to the processing of personal data, – the proposal for a Council Directive concerning the protection of personal data and privacy in the context of public digital telecommunications networks, in particular the integrated services digital network (ISDN) and public digital mobile networks, and – the proposal for a Council Decision in the field of information security. 17 June 1991 Official Journal of the European Communities No C 159/38–48.

[119] No C94/176, Official Journal of the European Communities, 13 April 1992; Wednesday, 11 March 1992.

[120] Articles 6 and 11 Directive 95/46/EC.'

[121] No C94/176, Official Journal of the European Communities, 13 April 1992; Wednesday, 11 March 1992.

[122] Article 2 sub a Directive 95/46/EC.

[123] This was even broadened further: ECJ, Worten – Equipamentos para o Lar SA v Autoridade para as Condições de Trabalho (ACT), Case C-342/12, 30 May 2013.

Ancillary information, such as "the man wearing a black suit" may identify someone out of the passers-by standing at a traffic light. So, the question of whether the individual to whom the information relates is identified or not depends on the circumstances of the case.[124]

Finally, this trend of widening the scope may also be witnessed[125] in the General Data Protection Regulation, which will replace the Data Protection Directive over time, and in which personal data are defined in a slightly broader manner.[126] The reason for this, as is acknowledged by the Working Party and is increasingly emphasized by scholars, is that potentially all data could be personal data. Data which at one moment in time may contain no information about specific persons whatsoever, may in the future, through advanced techniques, be used to identify or single out a person.[127] Moreover, data that may not directly identify a person can increasingly be linked to them through means such as interconnecting and harvesting databases, and can be used to create profiles so that two or more non-identifying datasets may become identifying datasets if integrated.[128]

It is important to note once again that the focus on 'personal' data means that parties other than natural persons are in principle denied a right to invoke data protection rules. While the Convention of 1981 explicitly allowed Member States to specify in their national legislation 'that it will also apply this Convention to information relating to groups of persons, associations, foundations, companies, corporations and any other bodies consisting directly or indirectly of individuals, whether or not such bodies possess legal personality',[129] it is uncertain whether national authorities still have this power now that the General Data Protection Regulation is adopted. The Directive and the Regulation themselves are exclusively focused on natural persons.

---

[124] Article 29 Data Protection Working Party, Opinion 4/2007 on the concept of personal data, 01248/07/EN, WP 136, 20 June 2007, Brussels, p. 13.

[125] European Commission, Proposal for a Regulation of the European Parliament and of the Council on the protection of individuals with regard to the processing of personal data and on the free movement of such data (General Data Protection Regulation), (SEC(2012) 72 final), Brussels, 25 January 2012, COM(2012) 11 final, 2012/0011 (COD), article 4 (1).

[126] Article 4 sub (1) Regulation.

[127] D. Skillicorn, 'Knowledge Discovery for Counterterrorism and Law Enforcement', Boca Raton, CRC Press cop., 2009. D. T. Larose, 'Data Mining Methods and Models', Hoboken, Wiley cop., 2006. M. Hildebrandt & S. Gutwirth (eds), 'Profiling the European Citizen Cross-Disciplinary Perspectives', Dordrecht, Springer cop., 2008. C. Westphal, 'Data Mining for Intelligence, Fraud & Criminal Detection', Boca Raton, CRC Press cop., 2009. K. Guzik, 'Discrimination by Design: Data Mining in the United States's "War on Terrorism"', Surveillance & Society 7, 2009. P. Kuhn, 'Sex discrimination in labor markets: The role of statistical evidence', The American Economic Review 77, 1987. M. LaCour-Little, 'Discrimination in mortgage lending: A critical review of the literature', Journal of Real Estate Literature 7, 1999. G. D. Squires, 'Racial profiling, insurance style: Insurance redlining and the uneven development of metropolitan areas', Journal of Urban Affairs 25, 2003.

[128] See among others: M. R. Koot, 'Measuring and Predicting Anonymity', Amsterdam, Informatics Institute cop., 2012.

[129] Article 3.2(C) Convention 108, 1981.

In conclusion, the first of the two reasons underlying the creation of the FIPs and the early European data protection rules as separated from the right to privacy, was that personal data are often neither private nor sensitive. Currently, this is even more so and even non-identifiable information can be connected and harvested through the use of advanced techniques in order to create profiles. To cope with the fact that personal data are less and less linked to the individual subject, the definition of personal data has been broadened over time.[130] Like the right to privacy, the right to data protection has consequently seen an enormous expansion. It is agreed by most specialists and scholars that potentially all data can be(come) personal data and therefore that the data protection instruments could be applied to almost every form of data processing. Furthermore, in addition to this expansion in scope of the right to data protection, the exceptions to this right have also eroded.

For example, the Directive exempted the police, intelligence services and other bodies involved with national security from its scope of application.[131] Instead, it moved the rules for those institutions to a lower regulatory level, namely a Council Decision,[132] with less strict rules. Now, in the same way that the Directive has been elevated to the level of a Regulation, the Decision has been elevated to the level of a Directive, so that Member States have to implement the rules with respect to national security purposes in their national legislation as well.[133] Furthermore, while Article 9 of the Directive partially exempted the processing of personal data in relation to the exercise of the freedom of speech and while the ECJ had initially given quite a wide interpretation of this freedom in its *Satamedia* decision,[134] in its more recent *Google Spain* decision[135] it seems to adopt a narrow understanding of this exception and seems to suggest that in principle, data protection rules have priority over the freedom of expression. The Regulation provides a full and detailed provision on this point, in Article 85(1), but it is as of yet unsure how it should be interpreted. In any case, it is clear that there will be European oversight as the provision explicitly states: 'Each Member State shall notify to the Commission the provisions of its law which it has adopted pursuant to paragraph 2 and, without delay, any subsequent amendment law or amendment affecting them.'[136]

130　See also: ECJ, Tietosuojavaltuutettu v Satakunnan Markkinapörssi Oy, Satamedia Oy, Case C-73/07, 16 December 2008.
131　Article 3.1 Directive 1995.
132　Council Framework Decision 2008/977/JHA of 27 November 2008 on the protection of personal data processed in the framework of police and judicial cooperation in criminal matters.
133　Directive of the European Parliament and of the Council on the protection of individuals with regard to the processing of personal data by competent authorities for the purposes of prevention, investigation, detection or prosecution of criminal offences or the execution of criminal penalties, and the free movement of such data.
134　ECJ, Tietosuojavaltuutettu v. Satakunnan Markkinapörssi Oy & Satamedia Oy, Case C-73/07, 16 December 2008.
135　ECJ, Google Spain SL & Google Inc. v. Agencia Española de Protección de Datos (AEPD) & Mario Costeja González, Case C-131/12, 13 May 2014.
136　Article 85 §2 Regulation.

Finally, the Directive contains an exception for the processing of personal data by 'a natural person in the course of a purely personal or household activity'.[137] However, the ECJ has adopted a very narrow understanding of this clause. Although the term 'personal' in this clause refers to the activity and not the sphere in which the activity is conducted, the Court has taken the opposite view in its *Lindqvist*[138] and it *Rynes* decisions. In the latter, it held:

> To the extent that video surveillance such as that at issue in the main proceedings covers, even partially, a public space and is accordingly directed outwards from the private setting of the person processing the data in that manner, it cannot be regarded as an activity which is a purely 'personal or household' activity for the purposes of the second indent of Article 3(2) of Directive 95/46.[139]

This has also narrowed the scope of this exception and has ensured that the broadened scope of the concept of 'personal data' is curtailed only minimally by the various exceptions provided in the Directive.

The second principle, and the second reason for adopting data protection rules in addition to a right to privacy, which de-emphasized the concept of subjective rights and the individual's right to control over personal data in favor of general obligations of fairness and reasonableness for the data controller, is increasingly lost. More and more, the emphasis has been placed on (1) increasingly detailed and specific obligations for data controllers, (2) specific subjective rights of the data subject, (3) balancing the interests of the data subject with those of the data controller and (4) a high level of enforcement of duties and rights. The gradual development of these four points will be discussed in detail in the following four subsections. As an example of early data protection legislation, this chapter focuses on the FIPs and the CoE Resolutions, but the general conclusions reached about those rules are equally applicable to the early data protection rules in European countries such as Sweden, Germany (especially in the state of Hessen), France, and Austria, which are not discussed in detail.[140]

Similarly, this section will focus on the CoE's Convention from 1981, although similar rules might be found in the Guidelines Governing the Protection of Privacy and Transborder Flows of Personal Data from 1980 by the Organisation for Economic Co-operation and Development (OECD).[141] The table below provides an overview of the four main arguments made in this section, plus an overview of the development of the concept of 'personal data'. In the left column, the data protection instruments

---

[137] Article 3.2 Directive 1995.
[138] ECJ, Lindqvist, Case C-101/01, 6 November 2003.
[139] ECJ, František Rynes v. Úřad pro ochranu osobních údajů, Case C-212/13, 11 December 2014, para 33.
[140] Dammann et al., Data Protection Legislation; Hondius, Emerging Data Protection in Europe; OECD, Policy issues in data protection and privacy; Burkert, Freedom of Information and Data Protection.
[141] <www.oecd.org/internet/ieconomy/oecdguidelinesontheprotectionofprivacyandtransborderflowsofpersonaldata.htm>.

(discussed in this section) are listed in chronological order: the FIPs from 1972 to 1973, the two CoE Resolutions from 1973 and 1974, the CoE Convention from 1981, the EU Directive from 1995 and the General Data Protection Regulation from 2016. The second column shows the broadening of the concept of 'personal data' over time and with it, the expanded material scope of the data protection instruments. The last column shows an increased emphasis on the protection of the individual, her interests and her right to control personal data in the substantial provisions of those instruments. This part is divided into four subcolumns: the development from general duties of care to detailed and technology-specific obligations (Column 2a, corresponding to the section 'Obligations of the data processor'); the development from very marginal subjective rights to quite a strong emphasis on individual rights (Column 2b, corresponding to the section 'Rights of the data subject'); the development towards balancing the interests of the data subject against those of the data controller (Column 2c, corresponding to the section 'Assessments'); the development from a model with a focus on soft law (with code-of-conduct-like rules) to one which embeds strong rules on enforcement (Column 2d, corresponding to the section entitled 'Enforcement').

Finally, this section will only show the dominant approach in Europe, particularly in the European Union, to the right to data protection. It has to be stressed that there are exceptions to each of the four trends. It is impossible to discuss every nuance and detail and it is true that in its more recent jurisprudence, the Court of Justice has been forced to make exceptions to each of these points, especially in cases revolving around Big Data and mass surveillance. These cases and examples, and their significance, will be discussed in detail in the next chapter. That chapter discusses how the current data protection paradigm can be applied to Big Data and mass surveillance cases, which problems are involved and which solutions or alternatives have been proposed so far in order to overcome these problems.

	(1) Material scope of the regulations	(2) The substantive provisions of the regulations			
		(2a) Obligations	(2b) Rights	(2c) Assessments	(2d) Enforcement
FIPs	–	(1) Transparency (2) Principles of fairness	(1) Access to personal data (2) Marginal rights on rectification and erasure	–	Mainly a matter of good governance
Resolutions	Information relating to individuals (physical persons)	(1) Transparency (Pub. Sec) (2) Principles of fairness	(1) Access right	(1) Lawful, appropriate and relevant	Recommends governments to take all steps necessary
Convention	Information relating to an identified or identifiable individual	(1) – (2) Principles of fairness	(1) Access to and communication of personal data (2) Marginal rights on rectification and erasure	(1) Fairly and lawfully (2) Special rules sensitive data	(1) Parties shall establish sanctions and remedies (2) Cooperation states & DPAs & role CoM (3) Remedy of data subject if data controller denies request
Directive	Information relating to an identified or identifiable natural person; an identifiable person is one who can be identified, directly or indirectly, in particular by reference to an identification number or to one or more factors specific to his physical, physiological, mental, economic, cultural or social identity;	(1) Information to the data subject & Notification DPA (2) Principles of fairness (3) Grounds for legitimate data processing	(1) Access to and communication of personal data (2) Marginal rights on rectification and objection (3) Marginal right against automatic decision making	(1) Fairly and lawfully (2) Special rules sensitive data (3) Limitative grounds for processing personal data, e.g. balancing (4) Limitative grounds for processing sensitive data, balancing not included	(1) Parties shall establish sanctions and remedies (2) Cooperation states & DPAs + harmonisation through Directive and WP 29 (3) Marginal subjective right to remedy and compensation

Chapter II. The Transformation of the Right to Privacy and the Right to Data Protection

(1) Material scope of the regulations		(2) The substantive provisions of the regulations			
		(2a) Obligations	(2b) Rights	(2c) Assessments	(2d) Enforcement
Regulation	Any information relating to an identified or identifiable natural person ('data subject'); an identifiable natural person is one who can be identified, directly or indirectly, in particular by reference to an identifier such as a name, an identification number, location data, an online identifier or to one or more factors specific to the physical, physiological, genetic, mental, economic, cultural or social identity of that natural person	(1) Notification in case of data breach	(1) Access to personal data (scope broadened)	(1) Fairly and lawfully	(1) High sanctions
		(2) Principles of fairness	(2) Right to data portability	(2) Special rules sensitive data	(2) Total harmonisation trough Regulation; increased powers Commission and EDPB; better cooperation DPAs
		(3) Grounds for legitimate data processing – increased emphasis on consent	(3) Rights to rectification and objection	(3) Limitative grounds for processing personal data, e.g. balancing	(3) Several subjective rights to remedy and compensation
		(4) Accountability duty (multifaceted)	(4) Right to be forgotten	(4) Limitative grounds for processing sensitive data, balancing not included	
			(5) Right to object against profiling		

3.1. OBLIGATIONS OF THE DATA PROCESSOR

The Fair Information Practices were developed against the background of the rapid growth and proliferation of large databases. These databases were used to process large quantities of citizens' data, primarily, though not exclusively, by governmental agencies in relation to civil data such as marital status, car ownership, and number of children; statistical data, used for socioeconomic policies; and intelligence data used for security purposes. The principles primarily concerned the general fairness of these processes and specified two general obligations, which may be qualified as duties of care: to be transparent and to process data fairly and legitimately. First, agencies were encouraged to publish an annual public notice which contained, among other items: the name, nature and purpose of the data system, the categories and number of persons on whom data are maintained, the categories of data maintained, the organization's policies and practices regarding data storage, the duration of retention of the data, and details of the disposal thereof. This obligation of transparency was thus primarily linked to the principle of accountability; the public had an interest in knowing which data the government collected, for what reasons, and how they were processed. The annual notice was consequently directed at the public as a whole and not at specific individuals.

Secondly, the principles specified, *inter alia*, that personal data should not be further processed or transferred to third parties, that controllers should appoint a person in the organization responsible for the data processing, that reasonable precautions should be taken against data breaches, and that a complete and accurate record of every access to and usage of any data in the system should be maintained. Moreover, the principles detailed that the data should be stored with such accuracy, completeness, timeliness, and pertinence as is necessary to assure accuracy and fairness in any determination relating to an individual's qualifications, character, rights, opportunities, or benefits. Furthermore, they required data be eliminated from computer-accessible files when the data were no longer timely. These principles thus concerned very general obligations of fair processing, which may be linked to the principle of good governance. Note, moreover, that the requirement of keeping data correct and up to date may require gathering and processing more, not less data.[142]

Around the same time, the Council of Europe adopted two Resolutions, one for data processing in the public sector (1974) and one for the private sector (1973). They contained quite similar obligations for controllers. The Resolution for the public sector specified that the public should be informed regularly about the establishment, operation, and development of large databases (the principle of transparency and accountability),[143] and that the information stored should be obtained by lawful and

---

[142] B. van der Sloot, 'From Data Minimization to Data Minimummization', in: B. Custers, T. Calders, B. Schermer & T. Zarsky (eds), 'Discrimination and Privacy in the Information Society. Data Mining and Profiling in Large Databases', Heidelberg, Springer, 2012.
[143] Article 1 Resolution (1974).

fair means, be accurate and kept up to date, be appropriate and relevant, stored safely and processed confidentially, and that sensitive data should be processed with special care (the principle of fairness and good governance).[144] For the private sector, the obligation of transparency and accountability did not apply.[145]

The Convention of the CoE was directed at the members to the Council, who were encouraged to implement the rules with regard to the public and the private sector. The principles of fairness were transposed to the Convention, including the rules for data security, the additional protection of sensitive data and the quality of data. It prescribed that data should be obtained and processed fairly and lawfully, stored for specified and legitimate purposes and not used in a way incompatible with those purposes; that data should be adequate, relevant, and not excessive in relation to the purposes for which they are stored; and that data should be accurate, and, where necessary, kept up to date and preserved in a form which permits identification of the data subjects for no longer than is required for the purpose for which those data are stored.[146] Remarkably, however, as in the Resolution regarding the private sector (1973), the principle of transparency and the obligation to inform the public was omitted, which seems to reflect the consideration, contained in the explanatory report to the Convention, that 'most international data traffic occurs in the private sector'.[147]

The Commission's original proposal for the Data Protection Directive contained two separate regimes: one for the public sector and one for the private sector. However, on the suggestion of the Parliament, this distinction was deleted and the same principles were applied to both. Still, both the original proposal and the adopted version contain an important exemption for security-related data processing, such that a large part of governmental data processing falls outside its scope. Instead, these activities are regulated through a special Council Decision which contains less strict rules and obligations.[148] Thus the core framework for data protection is primarily aimed at the private sector, reflecting the trend of the so-called 'banalization of data processing'; that is, that governmental agencies, private companies and individuals alike can increasingly process large amounts of data with relative ease.[149]

Under the Directive, two important changes have been made. First, the transparency principle has been reintroduced, albeit in quite a quite different form. The Directive includes an obligation to notify the national Data Protection Authority (DPA) about the processing of personal data, although Member States are at liberty to adopt far-reaching exemptions. Moreover, the duty to inform the public of large scale data processing was

---

[144] Articles 2, 3, 4, 6 and 7 Resolution (1974).
[145] Articles 1, 2, 3, 4, 5, 7, 8 and 9 Resolution (1973).
[146] Articles 5, 6, and 7 Convention (1981).
[147] Article 3 Convention (1981).
[148] Council Framework Decision 2008/977/JHA of 27 November 2008 on the protection of personal data processed in the framework of police and judicial cooperation in criminal matters, OJ L 350, 30 Dec. 2008, p. 60.
[149] Council of Europe report: New technologies: a challenge to privacy protection? (1989). <www.coe.int/t/dghl/standardsetting/dataprotection/Reports/NewTechnologies_1989_en.pdf>.

transformed into a duty to notify the data subject herself. Thus, Article 10 specifies that the controller must provide a data subject from whom data relating to himself are collected with at least the identity of the controller, the purposes of the processing for which the data are intended and the recipients of the data.[150] Consequently, the transparency principle is transformed from a duty to notify the public, to a duty to notify the data subject herself.

Secondly, the obligations of fairness have been broadened. The principles transposed into the Directive include, among others, the principles of fair and lawful data processing, of safe and confidential processing, of data quality and of special care for sensitive data. What is new is that the Directive stipulates six grounds for legitimate data processing. The Commission in its original proposal suggested that processing in the private sector without the informed consent of the data subject could only be legitimate in specified and limited scenarios. On the suggestion of the Parliament, however, the informed consent of the data subject was made but one among several criteria.[151] Accordingly, personal data may only be processed (a) if the data subject has given her consent, (b) when this is necessary for the performance of a contract with the data subject, (c) for compliance with a legal obligation, (d) for the protection of the vital interests of the data subject, or (e) for the performance of a task carried out in the public interest,[152] or (f) when the interests of the controller to process the data outweigh those of the data subject.[153]

The European Court of Justice (ECJ), remarkably, has held that the principles of data quality and the obligation to obtain a legitimate ground for processing have direct effect, in that they may be relied on by an individual before the national courts to oust the application of rules of national law which are contrary to those provisions.[154] Although this does not make them a subjective right, the provisions may be invoked by the subject directly, even though they are formulated as obligations of the data processor and not as rights of the data subject. With the General Data Protection Regulation, a renewed emphasis on the element of consent and the control of the subject over her personal data (echoing the line proposed in the Commission's original proposal for the Directive) can

---

[150] Article 10 Directive 95/46/EC. See also: Article 11 Directive 95/46/EC.
[151] No C94/181, Official Journal of the European Communities, 13 April 1992; Wednesday, 11 March 1992.
[152] See further: ECJ, Heinz Huber v Bundesrepublik Deutschland, Case C-524/06, 16 December 2008.
[153] Article 7 Directive 95/46/EC.
[154] ECJ, Rechnungshof and Österreichischer Rundfunk, Wirtschaftskammer Steiermark, Marktgemeinde Kaltenleutgeben, Land Niederösterreich, Österreichische Nationalbank, Stadt Wiener Neustadt, Austrian Airlines, Österreichische Luftverkehrs-AG, and between Christa Neukomm, Joseph Lauermann, and Österreichischer Rundfunk, Joined Cases C-465/00, C-138/01, and C-139/01, 20 May 2003. See also: ECJ, Asociación Nacional de Establecimientos Financieros de Crédito (ASNEF), Federación de Comercio Electrónico y Marketing Directo (FECEMD) v Administración del Estado, intervening parties: Unión General de Trabajadores (UGT), Telefónica de España SAU, France Telecom España SA, Telefónica Móviles de España SAU, Vodafone España SA, Asociación de Usuarios de la Comunicación, Joined Cases C-468/10 and C-469/10, 24 November 2011.

be witnessed.¹⁵⁵ The definition of consent has been tightened,¹⁵⁶ it has been clarified that the controller shall bear the burden of proof for the data subject's consent¹⁵⁷ and a provision has been inserted which specifies that the processing of personal data of a child below the age of 13 years shall only be lawful if and to the extent that consent is given by the child's parent or custodian.¹⁵⁸

Secondly, although the general rules on fair and lawful processing, the conditions regarding sensitive data,¹⁵⁹ the grounds for legal processing, and the principles of data quality have largely been retained, they are supplemented with highly detailed and technology-specific rules, which are designed to regulate a particular existing technology. Not only does the controller have an obligation to verify whether personal data of children are being processed and whether consent has been given by the child's parents or custodian,¹⁶⁰ the controller also has a general 'accountability duty'.¹⁶¹ This duty is used as an umbrella concept which covers a myriad of obligations, such as keeping highly detailed and precise documentation on all processing operations, and conducting impact assessments to evaluate the risks involved in certain types of data processing.¹⁶² Based on such assessments, processors may be required to take further steps including additional technical measures,¹⁶³ or the appointment of a data protection officer, etc.¹⁶⁴

Perhaps most importantly, the principle of transparency has been lost almost completely.¹⁶⁵ The obligation to submit a general notification to the supervisory

---

155 F. Gilbert, 'EU Data Protection Overhaul: New Draft Regulation', The Computer & Internet Lawyer 2012-3, p. 3. P. De Hert & V. Papakonstantinou, 'The proposed data protection Regulation replacing Directive 95/46/EC: A sound system for the protection of individuals', Computer Law & Security Review 28, 2012. G. Hornung, 'A General Data Protection Regulation for Europe? Light and shade in the Commission's draft of 25 January 2012',1 Scipted 74, 2012.
156 Article 4 (11) Regulation. Compare Article 2 (h) Directive 95/46/EC.
157 Article 7 Regulation.
158 Article 8 Regulation.
159 See also: Case C-101/01 Bodil Lindqvist, ECJ, 6 November 2003.
160 Article 8 §2 Regulation.
161 Article 24 and further Regulation.
162 Article 35 and further Regulation. See already for risk assessments: R. Sizer & P. Newman, 'The Data Protection Act: a practical guide', Aldershot, Gower cop., 1984.
163 Article 32 Regulation.
164 Article 37 Regulation.
165 Which is remarkable because the evaluation of the directive showed that very little awareness existed about data processing and the data protection rules. Commission of the European Communities, First report on the implementation of the Data Protection Directive (95/46/EC), COM(2003) 265 final, Brussels, 15 May 2003. The reason the notification requirement being removed may lie partially in the costs associated with it. European Commission, Commission Staff Working Paper, 'Impact Assessment Accompanying the document Regulation of the European Parliament and of the Council on the protection of individuals with regard to the processing of personal data and on the free movement of such data (General Data Protection Regulation) and Directive of the European Parliament and of the Council on the protection of individuals with regard to the processing of personal data by competent authorities for the purposes of prevention, investigation, detection or prosecution of criminal offences or the execution of criminal penalties, and the free movement of such data' (COM(2012) 10 final) (COM(2012) 11 final)(SEC(2012) 73 final), Brussels, 25 Jan. 2012, SEC(2012) 72 final, p. 15.

authority has been replaced by the obligation for controllers and processors to maintain documentation of the processing operations under their responsibility.[166] Furthermore, the obligation to inform the data subject about data processing has been replaced by the obligation to provide transparent, easily accessible and understandable information with regard to the data processing.[167] Only when a data breach has occurred does the controller have an active obligation to inform the data protection authorities,[168] and the data subjects must be informed directly only when the breach is likely to have an adverse effect on their interests.[169]

3.2. RIGHTS OF THE DATA SUBJECT

Initially, the data protection rules essentially contained one subjective right, namely the right of the data subject to obtain information about the processing of her personal data. For example, the US Records, Computers and the Rights of Citizens Report of 1973 specified that the controller had a duty to inform an individual, upon her request, whether she is the subject of data processing, what use is made of her personal data, who has access to them, and for what reason. Some additional rights were also granted, such as that no personal data should be processed beyond the purpose of the data system, that the data subject may contest the accuracy, completeness, and pertinence of the personal data, and the right to request that the data be corrected or amended.

Even more narrowly, the CoE's Resolution on the public sector, provided merely that every individual 'should have the right to know the information stored about him',[170] and the Resolution on the private sector provided that as a general rule, 'the person concerned should have the right to know the information stored about him, the purpose for which it has been recorded, and particulars of each release of this information'.[171] The Convention from 1981 expanded the list of subjective rights and specified that any person shall be enabled to establish whether her personal data are processed and if so, which, for what purposes, and by whom. The data subject was also granted a right to communication to her of such data in an intelligible form and to request rectification or erasure of such data if these had been processed contrary to the obligations of fairness of the data controllers and to have a remedy if a request for confirmation or communication, rectification or erasure was not complied with.[172]

The Data Protection Directive expanded the data subject's rights somewhat by specifying three subjective rights. One was the right of access to personal data; that is, the right to request information about the processing of her personal data (which

---

[166] Article 30 Regulation.
[167] Article 12 Regulation.
[168] Article 33 Regulation.
[169] Article 34 Regulation.
[170] Article 5 Resolution (1974).
[171] Article 6 Resolution (1973).
[172] Article 8 Convention (1981).

data, who processes them, why, etc.)[173] and to receive the data undergoing processing in an intelligible form.[174] Secondly, the data subject has a right to rectification, erasure or blocking of personal data, the processing of which does not comply with the data protection rules[175] and a right to object to the processing of her personal data.[176] However, the right to rectification, erasure or blocking only applies to situations where the data are of an incomplete or inaccurate nature, and thus violate the data quality principle, and the right to object only where the processing is executed for direct marketing purposes or is based on grounds (e) and (f) for legitimate data processing. Moreover, data processors may reject such requests if overriding interests exist. Thirdly and finally, every person has a right to object to an automatic decision-making process. However, this rule only applies if a number of conditions are met: Firstly, the data processing must have legal effects concerning the data subject, or significantly affect the data subject in some other respect. Secondly, the decisions should be based solely on the automated processing of data and should be intended to evaluate certain personal aspects relating to her. Furthermore, the right to object to automatic decision making does not apply if such decisions are taken in the course of the entering into or performance of a contract or if it is authorized by a law which also lays down measures to safeguard the data subject's legitimate interests.[177]

With the General Data Protection Regulation, a radical shift seems at hand. The right to access personal information has been broadened by stressing, among other aspects, the right to be informed about the storage period.[178] A new right is introduced, which is partially based on the data subject's right to obtain the personal data being processed about him: the right to data portability. This right grants the individual the right to transfer data from one electronic processing system to another.[179] It includes the right to obtain those data from the controller in a structured and commonly used electronic format, for example facilitating the transfer from Facebook to another social network.[180] It is clear that the philosophy behind this rule is that personal data should be controlled by the data subject, perhaps even owned. The Commission has

---

[173] See also: ECJ, Heinz Huber v Bundesrepublik Deutschland, Case C-524/06, 16 December 2008.
[174] Article 12 Directive 95/46/EC.
[175] Article 12 Directive 95/46/EC.
[176] Article 14 Directive 95/46/EC.
[177] Article 15 Directive 95/46/EC.
[178] Article 13 and 14 Regulation. This is remarkable because it is questionable how effective this right really is: in the evaluation report of the Commission, it appeared that 'most of the data controllers responding to the questionnaire either did not have figures available or received fewer than 10 requests during the year 2001'. Commission of the European Communities, First report on the implementation of the Data Protection Directive (95/46/EC), COM(2003) 265 final, Brussels, 15 May 2003.
[179] S. Weiss, 'Privacy threat model for data portability in social network applications', International Journal of Information Management 29, 2009. U. Bojars, A. Passant, J. G. Breslin & S. Decker, 'Social network and data portability using semantic web technologies', < http://ceur-ws.org/Vol-333/saw1.pdf>.
[180] Compare to number portability: Article 30 Directive 2002/22/EC of the European Parliament and of the Council of 7 March 2002 on universal service and users' rights relating to electronic communications networks and services (Universal Service Directive).

accordingly stressed that 'retention by data subjects of an effective control over their own data' is an important precondition for ensuring that individuals enjoy a high level of data protection.[181] The right to control personal data is also in line with the thought that personal data are a modern form of currency on the internet, since they are often exchanged for free internet services.[182]

The Regulation goes even by stressing not only the subject's right to rectification,[183] but also introducing a right to be forgotten.[184] This right entitles the data subject to demand erasure of personal data relating to her and the abstention from further dissemination of such data, especially in relation to personal data which are made available by the data subject while she was a child.[185] The common fear that underlies this right is that children could post online pictures and videos of themselves and each other that may contain behavior or reveal aspects of their lives and may hinder them in their development. Without a right to erasure, such videos and pictures could haunt them for the rest of their lives. Accordingly, this right also entails an obligation for the controller that published the personal data to inform third parties to whom the data have been distributed of any data subjects' request to copy, replicate, or erase links to that personal data.[186] Although some exceptions remain, most importantly in relation to the freedom of speech, it seems that the underlying philosophy is that the data subject has a right to control her personal data.

Finally, the rights to object and resist automatic processing have been extended quite considerably. A data subject has the right to object to the processing of her personal information if not based on her consent, a contract, or a legal obligation.[187] Moreover, the burden of proof is shifted; while in the Directive the data subject had to convincingly demonstrate that the data processing should be stopped, the Regulation holds that the processing shall be stopped unless the controller brings compelling, legitimate grounds for the continued processing which override the interests or fundamental rights and freedoms of the data subject.[188] Moreover, the right to object to automatic decision

---

[181] European Commission, 'Communication from the Commission to the European Parliament, the Council, the Economic and Social Committee and the Committee of the Regions. A comprehensive approach on personal data protection in the European Union', Brussels, 4 Nov. 2010, COM(2010) 609 final, p. 7. Obviously, it also is an important means to stimulate competition, and avoid dominant position and lock-in effects.

[182] See also: M. Kuneva (then Commissioner for Consumer Protection), European Consumer Commissioner, Keynote Speech, p. 2, Roundtable on Online Data collection, targeting and profiling, Brussel, 31 Mar. 2009.

[183] Article 16 Regulation.

[184] See also the prior version: <www.statewatch.org/news/2011/dec/eu-com-draft-dp-reg-inter-service-consultation.pdf>.

[185] I. Szekely, 'The right to forget, the right to be forgotten: Personal Reflections on the fate of personal data in the informationsociety', in: S. Gutwirth, R. Leenes, P. De Hert & Y. Poullet (eds), 'European Data Protection: In Good Health?', Springer, Dordrecht, 2012. S. C. Bennett, 'The "Right to be Forgotten": Reconciling EU and US Perspectives', Berkeley Journal of International Law 30, 2012.

[186] Article 17 §2 Regulation.

[187] See further: F. Zuiderveen Borgesius, 'Improving privacy protection in the area of behavioural targeting', Alphen aan den Rijn, Kluwer Law International, 2015.

[188] Article 21 Regulation.

making has been transformed into a right to object to profiling in general.[189] Under the Regulation, every natural person shall have the right not to be subjected to a measure which produces legal effects or significantly affects her, and which is based solely on automated processing intended to evaluate certain personal aspects relating to this natural person or to analyze or predict in particular the natural person's performance at work, economic situation, location, health, personal preferences, reliability, or behavior.[190] This prohibition is lifted when the processing is based on her informed consent, is expressly authorized by a law which also lays down suitable safeguards or when this is done in relation to a contractual agreement with the data subject.[191] However, profiling is never legitimate when based solely on sensitive data, such as data regarding sexual orientation or health conditions.[192] Thus, although some limitations remain, this right has also been extended in scope and its level of protection has been raised.

3.3. ASSESSMENTS

The shift from a necessity test to a balancing test is less significant with regard to data protection than with respect to privacy (see Section 2.3).[193] Still, balancing has entered the realm of data protection and it has gained in prominence over the years – potentially, it may over time become as important as in privacy discussions. As has been stressed, the original data protection documents focused on obligations of data controllers. This corresponds to a focus on the general obligations for states under the

---

[189] Recommendation CM/Rec(2010)13 of the Committee of Ministers to member states on the protection of individuals with regard to automatic processing of personal data in the context of profiling (Adopted by the Committee of Ministers on 23 November 2010 at the 1099th meeting of the Ministers' Deputies).

[190] W. N. Renke, 'Who controls the past now controls the future: counter-terrorism, data mining and privacy' The Alberta Law Review 43, 2006. B. W. Schermer, 'The limits of privacy in automated profiling and data mining', Computer Law & Security Review 7, 2011. H. T. Tavani, 'Genomic research and data-mining technology: Implications for personal privacy and informed consent', Ethics and Information Technology 6, 2004.

[191] L. A. Bygrave, 'Minding the Machine: Article 15 of the EC Data Protection Directive and Automated Profiling', Computer Law & Security Report 17, 2001. M. Hildebrandt, 'Who is profiling who? invisible visibility', in: S. Gutwirth, Y. Poullet, P. de Hert, C. de Terwagne & S. Nouwt (eds), 'Reinventing Data Protection?', Dordrecht, Springer cop., 2009. M. Hildebrandt, 'The Dawn of a Critical Transparency Right for the Profiling Era', Digital Enlightenment Yearbook, 2012. C. Kuner, 'The European Commission's Proposed Data Protection Regulation: A Copernican Revolution in European Data Protection Law', Privacy & Security Law Report, 2012. Article 29 Data Protection Working Party, 'Opinion 01/2012 on the data protection reform proposals', 00530/12/EN, WP 191, 23 March 2012, Brussels, p. 19. See also: EDPS, 'Opinion of the European Data Protection Supervisor on the data protection reform package', Brussels, 7 March 2012.

[192] Recommendation CM/Rec(2010)13 of the Committee of Ministers to member states on the protection of individuals with regard to automatic processing of personal data in the context of profiling.

[193] This section is based in part on: B. van der Sloot, 'The Practical and Theoretical Problems with 'balancing': Delfi, Coty and the redundancy of the human rights framework', Maastricht Journal of European and Comparative Law, 2016-3.

necessity test of Article 8 ECHR. The principles of data minimization, for example, can easily be linked to this line of thought; collect data only when it is necessary, store it only as long as is necessary for achieving of a legitimate aim and delete personal data when it is no longer necessary to retain them, etc. Other data protection rules echoed the focus on necessity as well. Moreover, the first data protection instruments did not contain a balancing provision and did not even elaborate on the grounds for legitimate data processing.

The 1973 Resolution specified in Article 2 that the information should be appropriate and relevant with regard to the purpose for which it has been stored. In the same vein, the 1974 Resolution held in Article 2 that the stored information should be (a) obtained by lawful and fair means, (b) accurate and kept up to date, (c) appropriate and relevant to the purpose for which it has been stored. The 1981 Convention did not elaborate on this issue significantly. Article 5 specified:

> Personal data undergoing automatic processing shall be
> (a) obtained and processed fairly and lawfully;
> (b) stored for specified and legitimate purposes and not used in a way incompatible with those purposes;
> (c) adequate, relevant and not excessive in relation to the purposes for which they are stored;
> (d) accurate and, where necessary, kept up to date;
> (e) preserved in a form which permits identification of the data subjects for no longer than is required for the purpose for which those data are stored.

The explanatory report added: 'The way in which the legitimate purpose is specified may vary in accordance with national legislation.'[194] It was thus left up to the national authorities to specify under which circumstances the processing of personal data would be perceived as legitimate.

Article 6 of the The Convention continued with additional protection for sensitive data by specifying that certain data may not be processed automatically unless domestic law provides appropriate safeguards, namely: personal data concerning health or sexual life, personal data relating to criminal convictions and personal data revealing racial origin, political opinions or religious or other beliefs. The explanatory report held that while the risk of harm to persons generally depends not on the contents of the data but on the context in which they are used, there are exceptional cases where the processing of certain categories of data is as such likely to lead to encroachments on individual rights and interests. It should be noted that the list laid down in this article was not meant to be exhaustive; national authorities were granted the discretion to supplement the list with other types of sensitive data.[195]

In the Directive's drafting process, the balancing provision first entered the discourse at a time when a distinction was still being drawn between processing in the

---

[194] <http://conventions.coe.int/Treaty/EN/Reports/HTML/108.htm>.
[195] <http://conventions.coe.int/Treaty/EN/Reports/HTML/108.htm>.

public sector and processing in the private sector. In one of the first draft proposals of the Directive, the lawfulness of processing in the private sector was covered by Chapter III, containing Articles 8–11. Article 8 specified:

1. The Member States shall provide in their law that, without the consent of the data subject, the recording in a file and any other processing of personal data shall be lawful only if it is effected in accordance with this Directive and if:
   (a) the processing is carried out under a contract, or in the context of a quasi-contractual relationship of trust, with the data subject and is necessary for its discharge; or
   (b) the data come from sources generally accessible to the public and their processing is intended solely for correspondence purposes; or
   (c) the controller of the file is pursuing a legitimate interest, on condition that the interest of the data subject does not prevail.
2. The Member States shall provide in their law that it shall be for the controller of the file to ensure that no communication is incompatible with the purpose of the file or is contrary to public policy. In the event of on-line consultation, the same obligations shall be incumbent on the user.
3. Without prejudice to paragraph 1, the Member States may specify the conditions under which the processing of personal data is lawful.

By contrast, with regard to the public sector, the draft proposal specified that the creation of a file and any other processing of personal data shall be lawful insofar as they are necessary for the performance of the tasks of the public authority in control of the file.

Later in the drafting process, the Directive's distinction between the private and the public sector was dissolved. The grounds for legitimate data processing were merged in Article 7:

Member States shall provide that personal data may be processed only if:
(a) the data subject has unambiguously given her consent;
(b) or processing is necessary for the performance of a contract to which the data subject is party or in order to take steps at the request of the data subject prior to entering into a contract; or
(c) processing is necessary for compliance with a legal obligation to which the controller is subject; or
(d) processing is necessary in order to protect the vital interests of the data subject; or
(e) processing is necessary for the performance of a task carried out in the public interest or in the exercise of official authority vested in the controller or in a third party to whom the data are disclosed; or
(f) processing is necessary for the purposes of the legitimate interests pursued by the controller or by the third party or parties to whom the data are disclosed, except where such interests are overridden by the interests for fundamental rights and freedoms of the data subject which require protection under Article 1 (1).

Article 8 specified for sensitive data:

1. Member States shall prohibit the processing of personal data revealing racial or ethnic origin, political opinions, religious or philosophical beliefs, trade-union membership, and the processing of data concerning health or sex life.
2. Paragraph 1 shall not apply where:
   (a) the data subject has given his explicit consent to the processing of those data, except where the laws of the Member State provide that the prohibition referred to in paragraph 1 may not be lifted by the data subject's giving his consent; or
   (b) processing is necessary for the purposes of carrying out the obligations and specific rights of the controller in the field of employment law in so far as it is authorized by national law providing for adequate safeguards; or
   (c) processing is necessary to protect the vital interests of the data subject or of another person where the data subject is physically or legally incapable of giving his consent; or
   (d) processing is carried out in the course of its legitimate activities with appropriate guarantees by a foundation, association or any other non-profit-seeking body with a political, philosophical, religious or trade-union aim and on condition that the processing relates solely to the members of the body or to persons who have regular contact with it in connection with its purposes and that the data are not disclosed to a third party without the consent of the data subjects; or
   (e) the processing relates to data which are manifestly made public by the data subject or is necessary for the establishment, exercise or defence of legal claims(…).

It should be noted that there was an attempt to change the wording of Article 7(f) to include not only the legitimate interests of the controller or of a third party, but also the general interest. This proposal was rejected, however, and the wording remained unchanged. Recital 30 to the Directive clarifies:

Whereas, in order to be lawful, the processing of personal data must in addition be carried out with the consent of the data subject or be necessary for the conclusion or performance of a contract binding on the data subject, or as a legal requirement, or for the performance of a task carried out in the public interest or in the exercise of official authority, or in the legitimate interests of a natural or legal person, provided that the interests or the rights and freedoms of the data subject are not overriding; whereas, in particular, in order to maintain a balance between the interests involved while guaranteeing effective competition, Member States may determine the circumstances in which personal data may be used or disclosed to a third party in the context of the legitimate ordinary business activities of companies and other bodies; whereas Member States may similarly specify the conditions under which personal data may be disclosed to a third party for the purposes of marketing whether carried out commercially or by a charitable organization or by any other association or foundation, of a political nature for example, subject to the provisions allowing a data subject to object to the processing of data regarding him, at no cost and without having to state his reasons.

It is immediately apparent that a distinction was made between the processing of sensitive data and ordinary personal data. Although a number of the legitimation grounds from Article 7 reappear in Article 8, the balancing provision contained in Article 7 (f) does not. This ground was perceived as the weakest ground which therefore ought not to apply to more risky data processing activities. This difference has been retained in the final Directive. Moreover, the balancing provision was often perceived only as a matter of last resort, for when other grounds could not legitimize the processing of personal data. The fact that the balancing provision was concerned a weak legitimation ground is also apparent from Article 14, concerning the data subject's right to object, which specifies under (a): 'at least in the cases referred to in Article 7 (e) and (f), to object at any time on compelling legitimate grounds relating to his particular situation to the processing of data relating to him, save where otherwise provided by national legislation. Where there is a justified objection, the processing instigated by the controller may no longer involve those data.'

However, the relevance of the balancing provision has grown over the years. This is emphasized in one of the first recitals to the Regulation, specifying:

> The right to the protection of personal data is not an absolute right; it must be considered in relation to its function in society and be balanced against other fundamental rights, in accordance with the principle of proportionality.[196]

A number of points should be considered. First and foremost, since it concerns an act of balancing, the data processors have a large role in the initial assessment of the question whether the data processing is legitimate. They are the ones to determine whether their interests outweigh the interests of the data subject. Obviously, this allows data processors to tilt the balance in their favor; only afterwards, if the data subject does not agree with this manner of balancing, can she object and, eventually, go to court. By then, the practice may have existed for quite some time. Furthermore, courts are often hesitant to substitute their opinion on the balancing of the different interests for that of the data processor, because data processors are often better informed and equipped to execute the balancing test and because an overly restrictive court may create a chilling effect on data processing. Consequently, it is the balancing provision that is increasingly invoked by data processors, as it allows them to process personal data without the consent of the data subject, without a contract, without a societal interests being at stake, etc.

The Article 29 Working Party has also stressed the importance of this provision. It has emphasized that the provision entails something more than only 'weighing' the different interests involved and should not be conceived as an 'anything goes' provision. Still, it has acknowledged the special role of Subparagraph (f), which, in its view, must not only be seen as a last resort (for when all other legitimation grounds fall short). Rather, it argues that the balancing provision has an important added value and an independent field of application. Furthermore, it has stressed:

---

[196] Recital 4 Regulation.

[If] the interest pursued by the controller is not compelling, the interests and rights of the data subject are more likely to override the legitimate – but less significant – interests of the controller. At the same time, this does not mean that less compelling interests of the controller cannot sometimes override the interests and rights of the data subjects: this typically happens when the impact of the processing on the data subjects is also less significant.[197]

Consequently, even if the legitimate interests of the data controller are slim, the processing may be conceived as legitimate. The fundamental right to data protection contained in the European Charter of Fundamental Rights may be limited if significant interests of the data controller are served by a data processing activity.

As has been stressed in Section 3.2, perhaps the most important change in the conception of balancing has been initiated by the ECJ. The European Court of Justice has held that the principles of data quality and the obligation to obtain a legitimate ground for processing have direct effect, in that they may be relied on by an individual before the national courts to preclude the application of rules of national law which are contrary to those provisions.[198] In a case which revolved around Spain, which had implemented the Directive in its national legislation, but had limited the possibility of invoking the balancing provision, the ECJ held that the provision has direct effect and can be invoked not only by data subjects, but also by data controllers. This dovetails with the idea that the Directive has two aims, namely protecting the interests of data subjects, but also those of the data controllers. The ECJ held:

> Article 7(f) of Directive 95/46 must be interpreted as precluding national rules which, in the absence of the data subject's consent, and in order to allow such processing of that data subject's personal data as is necessary to pursue a legitimate interest of the data controller or of the third party or parties to whom those data are disclosed, require not only that the fundamental rights and freedoms of the data subject be respected, but also that those data should appear in public sources, thereby excluding, in a categorical and generalized way, any processing of data not appearing in such sources.[199]

Thus, data processors have a subjective right to legitimize their behavior by invoking the balancing provision.

---

[197] WP 29, 'Opinion 06/2014 on the notion of legitimate interests of the data controller under Article 7 of Directive 95/46/EC'.

[198] ECJ, Rechnungshof and Österreichischer Rundfunk, Wirtschaftskammer Steiermark, Marktgemeinde Kaltenleutgeben, Land Niederösterreich, Österreichische Nationalbank, Stadt Wiener Neustadt, Austrian Airlines, Österreichische Luftverkehrs-AG, and between Christa Neukomm, Joseph Lauermann, and Österreichischer Rundfunk, Joined Cases C-465/00, C-138/01, and C-139/01, 20 May 2003. See also: ECJ, Asociación Nacional de Establecimientos Financieros de Crédito (ASNEF), Federación de Comercio Electrónico y Marketing Directo (FECEMD) v Administración del Estado, intervening parties: Unión General de Trabajadores (UGT), Telefónica de España SAU, France Telecom España SA, Telefónica Móviles de España SAU, Vodafone España SA, Asociación de Usuarios de la Comunicación, Joined Cases C-468/10 and C-469/10, 24 November 2011.

[199] In Joined Cases C-468/10 and C-469/10, 49.

Furthermore, since the introduction of the right to data protection in the Charter of Fundamental Rights of the European Union, the ECJ, like the ECtHR, has increasingly adopted a balancing approach to fundamental rights cases. This is exemplified by its decision in *Coty v. Stadtsparkasse*. Like *Delfi v. Estonia*, this was a fairly straightforward case. Coty, a cosmetics company, held the trademark for a perfume brand. This perfume was sold illegally by B via website C to person D. However, Person D turned out to be Coty itself, which had been using pseudonyms to track down trademark violations. Coty contacted the website to determine the identity of B, who was also using a pseudonym. The website cooperated and disclosed B's identity; Coty then wrote to B to discuss the matter. B admitted to being the holder of the internet account, but denied having sold the perfume. So, finally, Coty turned to Stadtsparkasse, the bank that administered the account to which the money was deposited. It requested the bank to check whether B was the holder of this account. The bank, however, refused with reference to the legal principle of bank secrecy. In response, Coty sued Stadtsparkasse, succeeding at first instance but losing on appeal. Subsequently, the German Federal Supreme Court sent a preliminary question to the ECJ: 'Must Article 8(3)(e) of Directive 2004/48 be interpreted as precluding a national provision which, in a case such as that in the main proceedings, allows a banking institution to refuse, by invoking banking secrecy, to provide information pursuant to Article 8(1)(c) of that directive concerning the name and address of an account holder?' The Court of Justice responded in a fairly brief statement that Article 8(3)(e) of Directive 2004/48, which contains a provision regarding the protection of confidentiality of information sources and the processing of personal data, must be interpreted such that it precludes a national provision under which a banking institution may, in an unlimited and unconditional manner, invoke its banking secret in order to refuse to provide, pursuant to Article 8(1)(c) of the Directive, information concerning the name and address of an account holder.

How could the European Court of Justice have determined the outcome of this case without relying on a balancing test? First, it could have started with the observation that what is at stake here is the banking secret. The central question here is whether Stadtsparkasse can rely on the banking secret and, if so, to what extent. It is important to point out that, in many ways, the banking secret is comparable to the confidentiality between lawyer and client or between doctor and patient. Research shows that, if patients are not able to trust that the information they disclose to their doctor will be treated confidentially, they simply do not visit the doctor as often, and if they do, disclose less information than they would normally.[200] Essentially the same holds true for the confidentiality between lawyer and client. Therefore, many Western democracies have special rules for these types of relationships; there are privileges for doctors and lawyers and they have the duty to keep the information they receive from their clients or patients confidential. If they break this duty, they may be relieved from their profession or be subjected to disciplinary sanctions.

---

[200] A. L. Allen, 'Unpopular privacy: what must we hide?', Oxford University Press, New York, 2011.

It is important to emphasize that these kinds of principles do not protect the interests of individual patients or clients. Of course, patients and clients have an individual right to privacy, which they can invoke if it is violated. The additional value of the above privileges transcends these individual interests and protects the functioning of the profession as such. Professional secrecy is a necessary condition, a prerequisite for the functioning of the medical and legal sectors; without it they would not be able to function adequately. Only in exceptional cases can professional secrecy be curtailed, for example, if a client tells her lawyer in detail that and how she plans to commit a murder. The banking secrecy is cut from the same cloth. It protects the functioning of the banking sector as such. If citizens cannot trust that their financial situation will remain confidential, they will avoid banks or try to mask their assets, especially in cases of extreme wealth or poverty. Consequently, the banking secret protects a general interest and is a precondition for the functioning of the banking sector as such.[201]

The second issue the Court of Justice could have discussed is whether and if so under which circumstances the secrecy of banks can be curtailed and in particular whether the right to information by third parties such as Coty is one of such circumstances. Article 8 of the Directive 2004/48 holds:

1. Member States shall ensure that, in the context of proceedings concerning an infringement of an intellectual property right and in response to a justified and proportionate request of the claimant, the competent judicial authorities may order that information on the origin and distribution networks of the goods or services which infringe an intellectual property right be provided by the infringer and/or any other person who: (…) (c) was found to be providing on a commercial scale services used in infringing activities (…).
3. Paragraphs 1 and 2 shall apply without prejudice to other statutory provisions which: (…) (e) govern the protection of confidentiality of information sources or the processing of personal data.[202]

The ECJ could have investigated whether Coty could actually invoke the right to information. The question is whether Article 8(1)(c) applies, i.e. whether the bank 'was found to be providing on a commercial scale services used in infringing activities.' This is questionable because it is unclear whether the bank account is an intrinsic part of the infringing activities by B. For example, is the manufacturer of the computer that B used to create the account through which the deal was made also providing on a commercial scale products that are used to infringe on intellectual property? Finally, the ECJ could have assessed whether a limitation on the secrecy of banks would be necessary at all. It seems, for example, that Coty already knew who B was and that it had evidence to support that B was the holder of the account through which the trademark infringement

---

[201] S. Guex, 'The Origins of the Swiss Banking Secrecy Law and Its Repercussions for Swiss Federal Policy', Business History Review, 74, 2000.
[202] Directive 2004/48/EC of the European Parliament and of the Council on the enforcement of intellectual property rights, L 195/16.

was made. Coty could have gone to court on this basis and the burden would have on B to prove that although he was the holder of the internet account through which the trademark infringement was made, he was not actually the person who engaged in illegal activities.

The ECJ, however, took a different path. As with the ECtHR in *Delfi*, it avoided questions of broader significance. It did not assess the value of the banking secret, but pointed to the value of trademark protection; it did not assess whether the bank indeed provided services on a commercial scale for trademark infringements, holding instead that it is 'common ground that a banking institution, such as that at issue in the main proceedings, is capable of falling within the scope of Article 8(1)(c) of Directive 2004/48';[203] it did not assess whether the right to information of a trademark holder can justify curtailment of the banking secret; and it did not in assess whether such a limitation would generally be necessary. Rather, it engaged in a balancing activity. The peculiar thing is that, as with *Delfi*, the interests of a third party that was not an official party to the case were brought into the equation, namely the interests of B relating to his privacy and data protection. Consequently, instead of analyzing the general interest with respect to the banking secret and assessing to what extent a right to information might limit that interest, the Court balanced the specific interests of Coty against the specific interests of B. Interestingly, the banking secret is not even a part of this equation.

The ECJ stressed that '[a]rticle 8(1)(c) of Directive 2004/48 and Article 8(3)(e) thereof, read together, require that various rights be complied with. First, the right to information and, second, the right to protection of personal data must be complied with.'[204] That the Court interpreted the matter under the right to protection of personal data instead of the secrecy of banks is also evident in the following statement: 'It is also common ground that the communication, by such a banking institution, of the name and address of one of its customers constitutes processing of personal data, as defined in Article 2(a) and (b) of Directive 95/46.'[205] Subsequently, it elevated the right to information of Coty and the interests of B. to a fundamental rights discourse.

> The right to information which is intended to benefit the applicant in the context of proceedings concerning an infringement of his right to property thus seeks, in the field concerned, to apply and implement the fundamental right to an effective remedy guaranteed in Article 47 of the Charter, and thereby to ensure the effective exercise of the fundamental right to property, which includes the intellectual property right protected in Article 17(2) of the Charter. As noted by the Advocate General in point 31 of his Opinion, the first of those fundamental rights is a necessary instrument for the purpose of protecting the second.

---

[203] European Court of Justice, Coty Germany GmbH v. Stadtsparkasse Magdeburg, Case C-580/13, 16 Juli 2015, §26.
[204] European Court of Justice, Coty Germany GmbH v. Stadtsparkasse Magdeburg, Case C-580/13, 16 Juli 2015, §28.
[205] European Court of Justice, Coty Germany GmbH v. Stadtsparkasse Magdeburg, Case C-580/13, 16 Juli 2015, §26.

The right to protection of personal data, granted to the persons referred to in Article 8(1) of Directive 2004/48, is part of the fundamental right of every person to the protection of personal data concerning him, as guaranteed by Article 8 of the Charter and by Directive 95/46. As regards those rights, it is clear from recital 32 in the preamble to Directive 2004/48 that the directive respects the fundamental rights and observes the principles recognized by the Charter. In particular, that directive seeks to ensure full respect for intellectual property, in accordance with Article 17(2) of the Charter. At the same time, as is clear from Article 2(3)(a) of Directive 2004/48 and from recitals 2 and 15 in the preamble thereto, the protection of intellectual property is not to hamper, inter alia, the protection of personal data, so that Directive 2004/48 cannot, in particular, affect Directive 95/46. The present request for a preliminary ruling thus raises the question of the need to reconcile the requirements of the protection of different fundamental rights, namely the right to an effective remedy and the right to intellectual property, on the one hand, and the right to protection of personal data, on the other.[206]

Consequently, the ECJ transformed the case into a conflict of two private parties' fundamental rights, namely the right to intellectual property on the one hand, as protected by Article 17 paragraph 2 of the Charter of Fundamental Rights of the European Union, and the fundamental right to data protection on the other hand, as contained in Article 8 of the Charter. To determine the outcome of the case, according to the European Court of Justice, the rights of two private parties, namely Coty and B., each having a fundamental right under the Charter of the EU, neither one having priority over the other, must be weighed and balanced against each other.

Necessity test	Balancing act
(1) The Court discusses whether Stadtsparkasse could invoke the banking secrecy;	(1) Coty's claim is understood as referring to the right to intellectual property, as provided under 17.2 Charter
(2) The Court assesses whether giving the name of a client imposes a limitation on this principle.	(2) B.'s claim is understood to be referring to the right to intellectual property, as provided under 8 Charter
(3) The Court determines whether this limitation was prescribed by law, more in particular whether the bank provided on a commercial scale services used to infringe intellectual property	(3) The Court grants a wide scope to both provisions and gives no principled priority of one right over the other
(4) The Court checks whether this limitation served a legitimate aim.	(4) The Court balances the two rights against each other, setting out certain ad hoc criteria
(5) The Court determines whether the limitation was necessary in a democratic society, given that Coty already had evidence against B.	(5) The Court only discusses the particularities of the case, taking into account all relevant circumstances

---

[206] European Court of Justice, Coty Germany GmbH v. Stadtsparkasse Magdeburg, Case C-580/13, 16 July 2015, §29–33.

3.4. ENFORCEMENT

Initially, the data protection rules contained no or only marginal provisions on law enforcement. As has been stressed, the rules were primarily seen as principles of good governance for governments. Subsequently, the two Resolutions of the Council of Europe merely recommended member states of the CoE to adopt rules to protect the principles contained in the Resolutions. It was at their discretion to implement sanctions or rules regarding liability. Only in the Convention of 1981 was it explicitly provided that '[e]ach Party undertakes to establish appropriate sanctions and remedies for violations of provisions of domestic law giving effect to the basic principles for data protection set out in this chapter.'[207] The explanatory report to the Convention stressed that this could either be done through civil, administrative, or criminal sanctions.[208] Moreover, the Convention explicitly provided a number of rules regarding the application and enforcement of the rule on transborder data flows,[209] which was considered 'the most vague and elusive' of any of the data protection concerns.[210] It stimulated, *inter alia*, the cooperation between states and the national Data Protection Authorities to assist each other by providing full and detailed information of their laws and of data processing within their borders[211] and it specified that states and DPAs shall assist citizens living abroad, on the territory of another state.[212] Finally, the Convention installed a Consultative Committee,[213] which could advise the Committee of Ministers (CoM) on revising the Convention.[214]

The adoption of an EU-wide Directive was aimed at bringing uniformity in the national legislations of the different countries,[215] in order to provide an equal level of protection,[216] but also to facilitate the transfer of personal data in Europe.[217] This uniformity was further promoted by providing further and more detailed rules for cross-border data processing.[218] For example, personal data may only be transferred to third countries if they have an adequate level of data protection similar to that of the European Union.[219] As was alluded to before, the Working Party was installed,

---

[207] Article 10 Convention (1981).
[208] Article 11 Convention (1981).
[209] Article 12 Convention (1981).
[210] OECD, 'Policy issues in data protection and privacy', p. 197.
[211] Article 13 Convention (1981).
[212] Article 14 Convention (1981).
[213] Article 18 Convention (1981).
[214] Article 19 and 21 Convention (1981).
[215] See among others: Dammann et al., Data Protection Legislation; B. Niblett, 'Data Protection Act 1984', London, Oyez Longman, 1984.
[216] Article 1 Directive 95/46/EC.
[217] See for the tension between e-commerce and data protection among others: H. W. K. Kaspersen, 'Data Protection and e-commerce', in: A. R. Lodder & H. W. K., 'eDirectives: guide to European Union Law on E-Commerce', Kluwer Law International, The Hague, 2002.
[218] See further: R. Laperrière, 'Crossing the Borders of Privacy: Transborder Flows of Personal Data from Canada', Ottawa, Ontario, Communications and Public Affairs, Department of Justice Canada, 1991.
[219] Article 25 Directive 95/46/EC.

consisting of the representatives of all national DPAs, and with a broad mandate to give opinions on almost every aspect of the Directive – on how it should be interpreted, implemented, and amended, etc. The Directive also specifies that the Commission shall be assisted by a Committee composed of the representatives of the Member States when adopting measures pursuant to the Directive.[220]

Furthermore, the enforcement of the rules is promoted further by providing that each state should install an independent DPA,[221] which must be endowed with investigative powers, effective powers of intervention and the power to engage in legal proceedings.[222] The Directive further expands the role of these supervisory authorities by specifying that they shall hear claims lodged by any person and that they may carry out prior checks of data processing which is likely to present specific risks to the rights and freedoms of data subjects.[223] Finally, the Data Protection Directive lays down further and more specific rules by providing the right of every person to a judicial remedy for any breach of her rights, the right for data subjects to receive compensation from the controller for any damage suffered as a result of processing in violation of data protection rules, and the duty for Member States to lay down sanctions for the infringement of data protection rules.[224]

Under the Regulation, again, a quite radical shift is at hand.[225] The most important change is that a Regulation, in contrast to a Directive, has direct effect and need not be implemented in the national legal frameworks of the different countries.[226] Currently, countries have adopted a variety of different implementations and interpretations of the data protection rules in their national legislation, which means that a number of (American) companies choose the country with the least strict rules (e.g. Ireland) for their European headquarters.[227] The first evaluation of the Directive found:

> An overly lax attitude in some Member States – in addition to being in contravention of the Directive – risks weakening protection in the EU as a whole, because with the free movement guaranteed by the Directive, data flows are likely to switch to the 'least burdensome' point of export.[228]

---

[220] Article 31 Directive 95/46/EC.
[221] See also: ECJ, European Commission, v Federal Republic of Germany, Case C-518/07, 9 March 2010. ECJ, European Commission v Republic of Austria, Case C-614/10, 16 October 2012.
[222] See further: ECJ, Volker und Markus Schecke GbR and Hartmut Eifert (v Land Hessen, Joined Cases C-92/09 and C-93/09, 9 November 2010.
[223] Article 20 Directive 95/46/EC.
[224] Articles 22, 23, and 24 Directive 95/46/EC. See further: C. Kuner, 'European Data Protection Law: Corporate Compliance and Regulation', Oxford University Press, Oxford, 2007.
[225] Article 29 Data Protection Working, 'Opinion 8/2010 on applicable law', 0836–02/10/EN, WP 179, 16 December 2010, Brussels.
[226] Word has it though that the General Data Protection Regulation will be somewhere between the status of a Directive and of a Regulation, with much more wiggle room for countries to adopt their own approach than is normally the case with a regulation.
[227] 3.2. Subsidiarity and proportionality, European Commission Proposal (2012).
[228] Commission of the European Communities, First report on the implementation of the Data Protection Directive (95/46/EC), COM(2003) 265 final, Brussels, 15 May 2003.

Consequently, besides extended rules for cross-border data processing,[229] including rules to cope with new techniques such as cloud computing,[230] the Regulation grants DPAs more and wider powers[231] and introduces the concept of a lead supervisory authority. This entails that each supervisory authority exercise shall not only exercise its powers in the territory of its own Member State, but that, if a controller or processor is established in more than one member state, the supervisory authority of the main establishment of the controller or processor shall be competent for the supervision of their processing activities in all Member States. Thus, the Regulation not only encourages cooperation between DPAs; it also promotes uniformity of enforcement across the European Union regarding specific practices or towards specific companies.[232]

The Working Party will be replaced by a European Data Protection Board, which is granted wider powers,[233] and the Commission may adopt specific Regulations on a number of the provisions in the Regulation to provide further clarity and detail on the interpretation of the rights and obligations contained therein.[234] Both elements ensure that a further level of harmonization and effective protection of the data protection rules are achieved. Finally, the fines and sanctions connected to the violation of the provisions in the Regulation have gone up dramatically. For example, the supervisory authority can, in certain circumstances, impose a fine of up to € 20.000.000,- or, in case of an enterprise, up to four per cent of its annual worldwide turnover, which for companies such as Facebook and Google would be a dramatically high figure.[235] Interestingly, the enforcement of the rules is no longer seen as the primary concern and duty of the DPAs, but increasingly as a right of the data subject to seek redress and file a complaint or a law suit. Rights are introduced: to lodge a complaint with a supervisory authority,[236] to seek judicial remedy against a supervisory authority,[237] to seek judicial remedy against a controller or processor[238] and to seek compensation(the latter right was already partially contained in the Directive).[239] These are all subjective rights of the

---

[229] Articles 44–50 Regulation.
[230] European Commission, 'Communication from the Commission to the European Parliament, the Council, the Economic and Social Committee and the Committee of the Regions. A comprehensive approach on personal data protection in the European Union', Brussels, 4 Nov. 2010, COM(2010) 609 final, p. 5. See also: The Study on the economic benefits of privacy enhancing technologies, London Economics, July 2010, <http://ec.europa.eu/justice/policies/privacy/docs/studies/final_report_pets_16_07_10_en.pdf>, p. 14. Article 29 Data Protection Working, 'Opinion 05/2012 on Cloud Computing', 01037/12/EN, WP 196, Brussels, 1 July 2012.
[231] Articles 51–54 Regulation.
[232] See further: E. M. L. Moerel, 'Binding Corporate Rules Corporate Self-Regulation of Global Data Transfers', Oxford University Press, Oxford, 2012.
[233] Articles 68–76 Regulation.
[234] See also: Articles 92–93 Regulation.
[235] Article 83 Regulation.
[236] Article 77 Regulation.
[237] Article 78 Regulation.
[238] Article 79 Regulation.
[239] Article 77 European Commission Proposal (2012).

data subject which may be directly invoked by the individual, given that the Regulation has direct effect.

Thus, the provisions on the enforcement of the data protection instruments have been extended quite considerably. This fits with the general trend towards an increased focus on the individual and her interest as the core of data protection rules, since the tightened rules on enforcement have the explicit aim of safeguarding the interests of the data subject. For example, Recital 12 to the General Data Protection Regulation stresses:

> In order to ensure a consistent level of protection for natural persons throughout the Union and to prevent divergences hampering the free movement of personal data within the internal market, a Regulation is necessary to provide legal certainty and transparency for economic operators, including micro, small and medium-sized enterprises, and to provide natural persons in all Member States with the same level of legally enforceable rights and obligations and responsibilities for controllers and processors, to ensure consistent monitoring of the processing of personal data, and equivalent sanctions in all Member States as well as effective cooperation between the supervisory authorities of different Member States.[240]

Secondly, there is a sharp increase in the number of subjective rights on this specific point as well, namely to engage in legal proceedings, submit complaints and request (financial) compensation. Thirdly, the focus on the individual and her interests in terms of enforcement measures may also be witnessed from the structure of the Regulation's Article on administrative sanctions, which provides higher penalties for a violation of provisions which have the explicit aim of protecting individual interests than when other provisions engrained in the Regulation have been violated.[241] Finally, it should be recounted that as with the right to privacy, the material scope of data protection instruments has grown exponentially. This trend is invigorated by the fact that the exceptions for private use, freedom of expression and security-related data processing have all been or will be curtailed significantly. It should also be noted that the two Resolutions from 1973 and 1974 contained a total of 8 and 10 articles respectively. The Convention (1981) contained 27 provisions, the Directive 34 and the proposed Regulation 99. While the two Resolutions were one-pagers, the Regulation consists of 56 pages of rules (88 if the recitals are included).

A Regulation is also the most far-reaching instrument the EU can use to regulate a particular legal doctrine. The right to data protection is now regulated through an EU-wide Regulation, it is contained in the Charter of Fundamental rights, and the legal basis for regulating data protection in the EU is not merely the regulation of the internal market, as was the case with the Directive, but also the safeguarding of data protection as a fundamental right. Article 16 of the Treaty on the Functioning of the European Union reads as follows:

---

[240] Recital 12 Regulation.
[241] Article 83 Regulation.

1. Everyone has the right to the protection of personal data concerning them.
2. The European Parliament and the Council, acting in accordance with the ordinary legislative procedure, shall lay down the rules relating to the protection of individuals with regard to the processing of personal data by Union institutions, bodies, offices and agencies, and by the Member States when carrying out activities which fall within the scope of Union law, and the rules relating to the free movement of such data. Compliance with these rules shall be subject to the control of independent authorities. The rules adopted on the basis of this Article shall be without prejudice to the specific rules laid down in Article 39 of the Treaty on European Union.

4. CONCLUSION

This chapter has argued four points. First, both privacy and data protection were first primarily conceived as laying down duties of care and general obligations for states and data controllers. Gradually, however, they have come to be interpreted primarily as the subjective rights of natural persons. Second, this has had great significance for the type of interests that are protected by both doctrines. Although originally the focus was on protecting general and societal interests, related for example to the prevention of the abuse of power, currently, the core interests that are protected are personal and individual values such as human dignity, personal autonomy, and individual freedom. Third, this has influenced the way judges and courts assess and address privacy and data protection issues. The original paradigm embraced a binary necessity test. If a privacy infringement was necessary, it was deemed legitimate. If a privacy infringement was unnecessary, arbitrary or untimely, it was deemed illegitimate. Although this approach is still applied occasionally, it has been moved to the background and replaced by a balancing test. Under this approach, almost all interests are taken into account, both those of the individual and those of the state or data controller. In concrete cases, these interests are weighed and balanced against each other to determine the legitimacy of the privacy infringement. Finally, there has been an expansion in the scope of both doctrines in legal terms. This is partly due to the fact that the material scope of both the right to privacy and the right to data protection has been broadened considerably. Also, while the original instruments were conceived only partially as juridical doctrines and primarily as ethical guidelines and codes of conduct, the trend has been to focus more and more on juridical rules and the enforcement of those rules through legal means.

CHAPTER III
THE CHALLENGES FOR AND ALTERNATIVES TO THE CURRENT PRIVACY PARADIGM

1. INTRODUCTION

The previous chapter argued that both the right to privacy and the right to data protection are (1) increasingly seen as subjective rights of natural persons instead of duties (of care) for states and data controllers, (2) increasingly focused on individual instead of general interests, (3) increasingly balanced by courts against other interests instead of a necessity test being applied and (4) increasingly codified (in detail) and enforced through legal means. As has been suggested in the introduction, in the current technological environment with developments such as Big Data, however, the individualized and legalized approach to privacy is becoming increasingly problematic. This will be discussed in Section 2 of this chapter. Section 3 shows that the European Court of Human Rights is confronted with this tension, especially in large data processing cases but also other matters, and is subsequently faced with a principled choice when dealing with these cases. Either it sticks to the basic pillars of the current privacy paradigm, as discussed in detail in the previous chapter, and consequently is unable to address those cases adequately, or it chooses to develop a new approach to privacy in order to adequately tackle the problems involved with these types of cases. Interestingly, it chooses the latter approach. Section 4 will analyze some of the scholarly literature in which alternatives to the current privacy paradigm have been proposed.

2. THE CHALLENGES BIG DATA POSES TO THE CURRENT LEGAL PARADIGM

This section discusses the current legal framework and shows on which points Big Data practices and mass surveillance activities may challenge the fundaments of the legal framework.[242] It would go too far to discuss all points in detail. Instead, three

---

[242] This section is partly based on: WRR, 'Big Data in een vrije en veilige samenleving', WRR-rapport, Amsterdam University Press, Amsterdam 2016. See also: B. van der Sloot & D. Broeders & E.

conflicts will be shown. First, Big Data conflicts with the material provisions in the Data Protection Directive and the General Data Protection Regulation. Second, Big Data challenges law's focus on the individual. Third and finally, Big Data challenges regulation based exclusively on legal means. A few examples will be given to illustrate these three points, without aiming to be exhaustive.

2.1. BIG DATA AND DATA PROTECTION

The classic data protection principles seem to be challenged by Big Data processes. This is confirmed by a survey conducted among all DPAs in the European Union.[243] A few examples will be provided below, namely the purpose and purpose limitation principle, the data minimization principles, the confidentiality and security principles, the data quality principle and the transparency principle. Finally, a brief remark will be made with respect to discrimination and stigmatization.

- The current legal framework is based on the principles of purpose and purpose limitation. As explained in the previous chapter, the data protection instruments in Europe contain an exhaustive list of the legitimate grounds for processing ordinary personal data; they do the same with regard to the processing of sensitive personal data (e.g. about race, religion, sexual orientation, etc.). Furthermore, personal data must be processed fairly and lawfully and must be collected for specified, explicit and legitimate purposes and not further processed in a way that is incompatible with those purposes. The prohibition on further processing for different purposes is also known as the 'purpose limitation principle', from which it follows that 'secondary use' is in principle not permitted. The survey among DPAs shows that it is this principle (along with the data minimization principle) that is cited the most when it comes to the tension between Big Data and data protection. Big Data processes often have no fixed purpose – large amounts of data are simply collected and it may only become clear what the value or potential use of that data is after it has been collected. Moreover, in Big Data analysis, different kinds of databases with different types of data are often linked or merged. The original purpose for which the data were collected is then lost. For example, the Swedish DPA argues that the concept of Big Data 'is used for situations where large amounts of data are gathered in order to be made available for different purposes, not always precisely determined in advance.'
- The second principle that is often mentioned when it comes to Big Data is the principle of data minimization. This principle requires that as little data as possible

---

Schrijvers (eds.), 'Exploring the boundaries of Big Data', Amsterdam University Press, Amsterdam, 2016.

[243] Parts of this section has been published previously published: B. van der Sloot & S. van Schendel, 'International and comparative legal study on Big Data', WRR-rapport, working paper 20, <www.wrr.nl/publicaties/publicatie/article/international-and-comparative-legal-study-on-big-data/ >.

should be collected, and that the amount of data should in any event not be excessive in relation to the purposes for which it is collected. Additionally, personal data must be removed once the goal for which they were gathered has been achieved, and data should be rendered anonymous when possible. This principle obviously clashes with Big Data. The core idea behind Big Data is that as much data as possible is collected and that new purposes can always be found for data already gathered. Data can always be given a second life. This also challenges the requirement that data should be deleted or anonymized when it is no longer needed for achieving the purpose for which it was collected. Almost all DPAs mention this principle when it comes to the dangers of Big Data. The Dutch DPA summarizes the tension between Big Data and data minimization in very clear terms: 'Big Data is all about collecting as much information as possible.'

- Both the Data Protection Directive and the General Data Protection Regulation espouse the principle that data should be treated confidentially and should be stored in a secure manner. Many DPAs also mention this principle when discussing the dangers of Big Data; this holds especially for countries and DPAs that establish a link between Big Data and Open Data. The Slovenian DPA, argues, for example:

[P]rinciples of personal data accuracy and personal data being kept up to date may also be under pressure in Big Data processing. Data may be processed by several entities and merged from different sources without proper transparency and legal ground. Processing vast quantities of personal data also brings along higher data security concerns and calls for strict and effective technical and organizational data security measures.

- The current framework also requires that the data is accurate and kept up to date. This is aimed at ensuring that profiles created of or applied to an individual person, and any decisions taken on the basis of them, are appropriate and accurate. Often, however, Big Data applications do not revolve around individual profiles, but around group profiles; not around retrospective analyses, but around probability and predictive applications with a certain margin of error. Moreover, it is supposedly becoming less and less important for data processors to work with correct and accurate data about specific individuals, as long as a high percentage of the data on which the analysis is based provides a generally correct picture. 'Quantity over quality of data', so the saying goes, as more and more organizations become accustomed to working with 'dirty data'. In the public sector, too, it seems that working with contaminated data or unreliable sources is becoming more common. Examples include the use by government agencies of open sources on the Internet, such as Facebook, websites and discussion forums. The Dutch DPA, for example, describes the situation in the Netherlands as follows:

[There] has been a lot of media attention for Big Data use by the Tax administration scraping websites such as Marktplaats [an eBay-like website] to detect sales, mass collection of data about parking and driving in leased cars, including use of ANPR data, and profiling people to detect potentially fraudulent tax filings.

- An important principle of data protection instruments is transparency. This includes the right of the data subject to request information about whether data relating to her are processed, how and by whom. This principle is also at odds with the rise of Big Data, partly because data subjects often simply do not know that their data are being collected and are therefore not likely to invoke their right to information. This applies equally to the other side of the coin: the transparency obligation for data controllers. For them, it is often unclear to whom the information relates, where the information came from and how they could contact the data subjects, especially when the processes entail the linking of different databases and the re-use of information. The Slovenian DPA puts it as follows:

  Big Data has important information privacy implications. Information on personal data processing may not be known to the individual or poorly described for the individual, personal data may be used for purposes previously unknown to the individual. The individual may be profiled and decisions may be adopted in automated and non-transparent fashion having more or less severe consequences for the individual.

- Besides privacy and data protection principles, DPAs also place a good deal of emphasis on profiling and the risk of discrimination, stigmatization and inequality of power resulting from Big Data. These matters are covered in part by the provision on automatic decision making in the Directive and the provision on profiling in the Regulation, but in particular in the anti-discrimination laws of various countries. The best overview of these types of dangers is provided in the Working Paper 'Big Data and Privacy: Privacy principles under pressure in the age of Big Data analytics' by the International Working Group on Data Protection in Telecommunications. Four points are made in the working paper in this respect. First, there is a risk of power imbalance between those that gather the data (multinationals and states) and citizens. Second, there is a risk of determinism and discrimination, because algorithms are not neutral, but reflect choices about *inter alia* data, connections, inferences, interpretations, and thresholds for inclusion that advances a specific purpose. Big Data may, the Working Group makes clear, consolidate existing prejudices and stereotyping, as well as reinforce social exclusion and stratification. Third, there is the risk of chilling effects, which is the effect that people will restrict and limit their behavior if they know or think that they might be surveilled. Fourth and finally, the Working groups signals the chance of echo chambers, which may result from personalized advertising, search results and news items:

  The danger associated with so-called 'echo chambers' or 'filter bubbles' is that the population will only be exposed to content which confirms their own attitudes and values. The exchange of ideas and viewpoints may be curbed when individuals are more rarely exposed to viewpoints different from their own.[244]

---

[244] International Working Group on Data Protection in Telecommunications, 'Working Paper on Big Data and Privacy. Privacy principles under pressure in the age of Big Data analytics', 55th Meeting, Skopje, 5 – 6 May 2014.

2.2. FOCUS ON THE INDIVIDUAL

As shown in the previous chapter, the current privacy paradigm places much emphasis on the individual, her interests and rights. This focus is challenged by new technological developments such as Big Data and mass surveillance. A number of these points shall be discussed briefly below, namely the doctrine of *ratione personae,* the doctrine of *ratione materiae,* the concept of personal data and the balancing of rights and interests.

- The current legal framework is based on a number of principles which relate to the scope of legal doctrines, policies and laws. The principle of *ratione personae* entails that complaints about a violation of a doctrine, such as the right to privacy or the right to data protection, shall only be declared admissible if the complainant herself was harmed in the enjoyment of her right.[245] Especially with human rights, the premise is that juridical doctrines serve the protection of individuals and their interests, but in a sense this applies to the entire legal regime. In Big Data processes, the principle of *ratione personae* seems hard to maintain because these Big Data processes do not focus on specific individuals, but on large groups of people or potentially everyone. Briefly put, many Big Data processes and applications based thereon are general, large-scale projects that have an impact on big groups or on society as a whole, while the link to individuals and individual interests is increasingly vague and abstract. This imparity (particular vs. general) will become increasingly problematic.
- The principle of *ratione materiae* entails that complaints about the violation of a right shall be admissible only if the nature of the complaint falls under the scope of the relevant legal doctrine.[246] For example, to invoke the right to data protection, 'personal data' must be processed. Personal data are data that may identify someone directly or indirectly or that may identify a person in the future.[247] To invoke the right to privacy, there must be a breach of a person's private life, family life, home or correspondence. Even with more general doctrines, the material scope is often linked to the individual. As explained in the previous chapter, the ECtHR has suggested that Article 14 ECHR (prohibition of discrimination) and Article 18 ECHR (prohibition of abuse of power) can be invoked only if one of the individual rights, such as the right to privacy or the freedom of expression, is also at stake.[248] The material demarcation of rights and the link to the individual is also challenged in Big Data processes, not only because it is often difficult to prove personal interests and damage, but also because it is increasingly unclear whether a particular right is

---

[245] OECD Guidelines on the Protection of Privacy and Transborder Flows of Personal Data <www.oecd.org/sti/ieconomy/oecdguidelinesontheprotectionofprivacyandtransborderflowsofpersonaldata.htm>.
[246] OECD Guidelines on the Protection of Privacy and Transborder Flows of Personal Data <www.oecd.org/sti/ieconomy/oecdguidelinesontheprotectionofprivacyandtransborderflowsofpersonaldata.htm>.
[247] Data Protection Directive, Article.2 §1 (a).
[248] J. Vande Lanotte & Y. Haeck, 'Handboek EVRM. Dl.2 Artikelsgewijze commentaar, Vol. 2', Intersentia, Antwerpen, 2004.

at all involved with a certain practice. To give an example, the application of data protection instruments depends on whether personal data are processed. If the data that are processed cannot be traced back to a person, processing them will in principle fall outside their scope. However, increasingly, data is no longer stored and processed on the individual level; rather, the trend is to work with aggregated data and to generate general patterns and group profiles. These statistical correlations or group profiles cannot be qualified as personal data, but can be used to change the environment in which people live to a great extent. An individual as part of a group or as assigned to a particular category may not be identifiable directly herself, but can nonetheless be affected by the data processing. Of course, certain effects can be regulated, for example, if certain practices lead to discrimination or stigmatization. However, it will be increasingly difficult in the future to keep the concept of 'personal data' as the basis for regulation. For example, is the collection of nonpersonal data allowed if it can be used to significantly influence a person's life or can be reconnected to other data at a later stage so that it becomes a highly sensitive dataset?

– The current legal framework and the policy debate often assume a balance between interests. For example, a classic tension is often found between privacy and security. Traditionally, these interests are balanced against each other to see which weighs the heaviest either in general or in particular situations. There are some problems with balancing interests specifically related to Big Data processes. This has two causes. On the one hand it is increasingly difficult to specify individual interests (for example in relation to privacy), on the other hand the security interest is also becoming increasingly difficult to identify and determine.[249] Moreover, Big Data entails precisely that data are collected before a specific purpose is determined, so that the use and usefulness of data can only be assessed at a later stage. Because the interests on both sides are increasingly hypothetical and abstract, it becomes increasingly difficult to weigh and balance them in a sensible manner. Second, the dichotomy between "security = general interest" and "privacy = individual interest" is being eroded. Many of the security issues in fact revolve around human security, the question of whether individual citizens are safe and feel safe. Safety should therefore also be considered an individual interest. Conversely, privacy is also linked to general interests, as discussed earlier.

2.3. REGULATION THROUGH LEGAL MEANS

Finally, Big Data and mass surveillance challenge the legalized approach to privacy regulation. This is because law has traditionally focused primarily on subjective

---

[249] Privacy and Civil Liberties Oversight Board Report on the Surveillance Program Operated Pursuant to Sec7on 702 of the Foreign Intelligence Surveillance Act July 2, 2014. B. Schneier, 'Data and Goliath: The Hidden Battles to Collect Your Data and Control Your World', W. W. Norton & Company, 2015.

rights, and because it deals with specific categories and concepts, which are becoming increasingly blurry and vague in the age of Big Data. Some of those developments will be touched upon below, including a number of examples.

- The current legal system places much emphasis on subjective individual rights and does so to an increasing degree. In response to the survey mentioned earlier, DPAs frequently referred to the principle of informed consent. Individual rights traditionally also come with individual responsibility, namely to protect those rights and to invoke them if they are undermined. The question is whether this focus can be maintained in the age of Big Data. It is often difficult for individuals to demonstrate personal injury or an individual interest in a case; individuals are often unaware that their rights are being violated or even that their data has been gathered. In the Big Data era, data collection will presumably be so widespread that it is impossible for individuals to assess each data process to determine whether it includes their personal data, if so whether the processing is lawful, and if that is not the case, to go to court or file a complaint. This tension also appears from the survey. For example. the British DPA has stated the following:

[It] may be difficult to provide meaningful privacy information to data subjects, because of the complexity of the analytics and people's reluctance to read terms and conditions, and because it may not be possible to identify at the outset all the purposes for which the data will be used. It may be difficult to obtain valid consent, particularly in circumstances where data is being collected through being observed or gathered from connected devices, rather than being consciously provided by data subjects.

- More in general, the current system is primarily based on the legal regulation of rights and obligations. Big Data challenges this basis in several ways. Data processing is becoming increasingly transnational. This implies that more and more agreements must be made between jurisdictions and states. Making these agreements legally binding is often difficult due to the different traditions and legal systems. Rapidly changing technology means that specific legal provisions can easily be circumvented and that unforeseen problems and challenges arise. The legal reality is often overtaken by events and technical developments. The fact that many of the problems resulting from Big Data processes predominantly revolve around more general social and societal issues, as also highlighted by a number of DPAs, makes it difficult to address all the Big Data issues within specific legal doctrines, which are often aimed at protecting the interests of individuals, of legal subjects. That is why more and more national governments are looking for alternatives or additions to traditional black letter law when regulating Big Data – for example self-regulation, codes of conduct and ethical guidelines. For example, the British DPA has noted the following:

There is some evidence of a move towards self-regulation, in the sense that some companies are developing what can be described as an 'ethical' approach to Big Data, based on understanding the customer's perspective, being transparent about the processing and building trust.

- The legal framework often depends on static concepts and divisions. These are put under pressure by Big Data processes.
    - For example, the current legal regime is based on different levels of protection for different types of data. Article 8 of the ECHR protects private data (which do not necessarily have to be sensitive) and sensitive data (which do not have to be private) and provides limited protection only to personal data and metadata. The Data Protection Directive and the General Data Protection Regulation distinguish between ordinary personal data that may identify somebody, which are linked to the ordinary protection regime, and sensitive personal data that concern a person's race, sexual orientation, health statues, criminal record, and so on, which are linked to a stricter regime. In addition, the General Data Protection Regulation introduces a new regime for pseudonymous data,[250] and both instruments provide alternative rules for statistical data, which are aggregated and therefore not directly linked to specific individuals. In principle, completely anonymous data fall outside the scope of traditional privacy and data protection frameworks. In addition, the e-Privacy Directive makes a distinction between the protection of customer data, which may in principle be processed, and traffic and location data (or metadata), to which different rules apply.[251] However, it is increasingly questionable whether these distinctions are still tenable in the age of Big Data. Increasingly, these categories are merely temporary stages, because data can almost always be linked back to an individual or can be de-anonymized or re-identified. Overall, while the current legal system is focused on relatively static stages of data and links to these stages a specific protection regime, in practice, data processing is becoming a circular process: data are linked, aggregated and anonymized and then again de-anonymized enriched with other data in order to create sensitive profiles, etc. It is important to stress that it will often not be known in advance what role or status a specific datum will have, how it will be used and what it may reveal about an individual in the future. It is therefore questionable whether it is still tenable to apply a less stringent juridical regime to the collection of, for example, metadata or anonymized data than to the collection of sensitive data, if these data can be linked to other data with ease and may thus become sensitive data over time.
    - The law also depends on the division of responsibilities for upholding legal rights and obligations. This is also challenged by Big Data processes. Firstly, there is the increasingly transnational nature of data processing activities. The problem is that different countries have different levels of data protection. The danger is that private parties will settle in those countries where the regulatory pressure

---

[250] Article 4 (3) Regulation.
[251] E-Privacy Directive, Articles 6, 7 and 9.

is low. But public sector organizations might act in similar ways as well. For example, in the Netherlands there is a court case pending on the cooperation between the Dutch intelligence services and their counterparts abroad. Although the Netherlands limits the capacities of its intelligence services to collecting information about Dutch citizens, the US intelligence services, which are less constrained regarding the collection of data on Dutch nationals, might collect such data and then pass it on to the Dutch intelligence services. This might work the other way around, too. Consequently, intelligence services might effectively circumvent the rules that apply to them by cooperating with other international actors that are not bound by those rules. Secondly, there is increasing cooperation between the public and the private sectors, voluntary or otherwise. Again, the question is which responsibilities should be borne by which party. Often, it is not clear at first sight what role an organization has played in the value chain of the data processing activity. Also, very different regulatory frameworks often apply to public sector and private sector institutions, as also noted by a number of DPAs in their response to the survey. Thirdly and finally, there is also a trend towards sharing data and linking databases between governmental organizations. This implies that governmental agencies that have a limited legal capacity to gather and store data may still obtain a wealth of information from other governmental organizations that have a greater legal capacity to gather and store such data. For example, in the survey, the Dutch DPA refers to a lawsuit that revolves around the tax authorities' use of information gathered by the police. Again, the question is which party should bear responsibility for enforcing the legal regime and the restrictions it imposes. More generally, it should be noted that data flows are becoming more fluid and elusive, so that more and more organizations are involved and more and more parties share partial responsibility. This complicates the attribution of responsibilities. Just as the lifecycle of data is becoming increasingly circular, so the division of responsibilities is clearly shifting away from a rather static reality, in which one party controls, collects and processes data and should therefore enforce the relevant statutory rules and obligations, and towards a world in which different parties collect, share and link data; in which parties from the private and the public sectors cooperate; in which different governmental institutions share data and databases; and in which international data flows are becoming increasingly common.
- Constitutions usually have a special regime for the so-called state of exception or the state of emergency. This is the situation in which the existence of a country is at stake. The classic example is an act of aggression by another country, for example a hostile army invading another country. In such a state of emergency, the executive power of the invaded country has the right to curtail the rule of law and the human rights in whole or in part in order to ensure the survival of the country. The logic is that the defense of the country against invading armies would be almost impossible if the army and other services had to

respect, *inter alia*, everyone's right to property, privacy and freedom to the fullest extent. Traditionally, security and intelligence agencies fall under the same or a similar exceptionalist discourse, as they were installed to protect the stability of the country against foreign spies, insurrection and other aggressive intensions. Currently, the focus with respect to the state of emergency is almost exclusively on potential terrorist attacks. On the one hand, this entails a change in the nature of the relevant danger. However terrible a terrorist attack on, for example, a subway may be, it does not put the existence of a country at risk.[252] On the other hand, the nature of the aggressor has also changed significantly. In a war of aggression, it is relatively clear who the aggressor is, what she will attack and often when she will attack or at least when the danger of such an attack is over. With terrorism, the point is precisely that it is unknown who will carry out an attack (especially with lone wolves or small cells), what the target will be, and when the attack will take place. There is therefore a strong need to gather information on increasingly large groups of people and over an increasingly long period of time.[253] Another difference is that the danger no longer comes primarily from outside, but that potential aggressors may be among the population of a country. The question therefore arises how to deal with threats such as cyber wars and international terrorism in the future, as the classic dichotomy between war and peace, between the state of emergency and the rule of law is crumbling.[254] This is important because many of the Big Data and mass surveillance processes are initiated by intelligence agencies which partially fall under the exceptionalist discourse. In practice, there exists a hybrid between the two extremes of war and peace.[255] The threat of terrorism or a cyberwar has a distinctly different character than a war of aggression, but is also clearly distinguished from peacetime and traditional crime, like robbery or murder. On the one hand, it seems logical to place the exceptionalist legal framework for intelligence agencies under constitutional and democratic control. On the other hand, the question is whether it can still be asked of these services to operate only in cases where concrete and direct danger exists.

- A final example of how Big Data puts pressure on legal distinctions can be found in the notion of technology-neutral law. Many constitutions around the world contain a provision on the secrecy of correspondence, the protection of the home and of the physical body. Internet communications, privacy in the public sphere

---

[252] House of Lords, A (FC) and others (FC) (Appellants) v. Secretary of State for the Home Department, UKHL 56, 2004, §96.
[253] J. P. Loof, 'Mensenrechten en staatsveiligheid: verenigbare grootheden?: opschorting en beperking van mensenrechtenbescherming tijdens noodtoestanden en andere situaties die de staatsveiligheid bedreigen', Nijmegen, Wolf Legal Publisher, 2005.
[254] L. J. M. Boer, "Echoes of Times Past': On the Paradoxical Nature of Article 2(4)', *Journal of Conflict and Security Law*, 2014.
[255] B. van der Sloot, 'Is All Fair in Love and War? An Analysis of the Case Law on Article 15 ECHR', *Military Law and the Law of War Review*, 53/1, 2014.

and digital identities are protected to a lesser extent. The rights of citizens are not always defined in technology-neutral terms, nor are the powers of the police and the intelligence and security services. For instance, many police services face uncertainty regarding the extent of their investigative powers in the digital environment. How should the criterion of 'reasonable suspicion' as a condition for surveilling citizens, be interpreted on the internet; are police officers allowed to surveil public internet domains the same way as they are authorized to surveil public spaces in the physical realm; are they allowed to screen private social media pages and discussion fora, etc.? The distinction made between the various techniques and particularly between the online and offline world is becoming less and less clear. In fact, the online and offline environment are increasingly intertwined, especially with developments such as ambient technologies, smart robotics and the internet of things, where objects are equipped with a sensor and will be connected to the Internet and communicate with one another.[256]

3. HOW THE ECTHR IS GRADUALLY MOVING BEYOND THE INDIVIDUALIZED PRIVACY PARADIGM

Chapter II discussed the dominant privacy paradigm underpinning the European Court of Human Right's the interpretation of the right to privacy.[257] This approach is increasingly focused on individual interests and rights. However, ever since the late seventies, the Court has been struggling with its own approach. Some cases, especially those revolving around (bulk) data collection, seem to affect privacy without clearly violating individual rights and interests. At an early stage, the ECtHR already made exceptions to its own rules on *in abstracto* claims, on individual harm and on class actions. For a long time, it did so without explicitly acknowledging that it did so. In recent jurisprudence, namely the *Zhakarov* and *Szabó & Vissy* cases, the Court has finally made it clear that in exceptional cases, it will let go of its individualized approach to privacy in order to be able to address cases revolving around, in particular, mass surveillance by states.

This section will briefly explain the history of this development. It will discuss cases in which the Court was faced with the choice between sticking to its strict interpretation of the victim requirement and declaring the cases inadmissible, or derogating from this focus on individual harm and accepting jurisdiction to hear the case. The Court

---

[256] T.H.A. Wisman, 'Purpose and function creep by design: Transforming the face of surveillance through the Internet of Things', European Journal of Law and Technology, 2013 3-2. M. Hildebrandt, '*Smart Technologies and the End(s) of Law. Novel Entanglements of Law and Technology*', Cheltenham, Edward Elgar, 2015.

[257] This section is based on: B. van der Sloot, 'Is the Human Rights Framework Still Fit for the Big Data Era? A Discussion of the ECtHR's Case Law on Privacy Violations Arising from Surveillance Activities', IN: S. Gutwirth, R. Leenes & P. De Hert (eds.), 'Data Protection on the Move', Springer, Dordrecht, 2016.

typically chooses the latter option in three instances: (1) when there is a reasonable chance that the applicant has been harmed, (2) when it is likely that the applicant will be affected by the practice in the future and (3) when the mere existence of a law or policy as such leads to a violation of Article 8 ECHR. These three approaches will be briefly discussed in the following three paragraphs. Finally, the last subsection will discuss the recent *Zakharov* and *Szabó* cases, and explain what this implies for the protection of human rights in the age of Big Data.

3.1. REASONABLE LIKELIHOOD (HYPOTHETICAL HARM)

A discussion about the victim requirement under the European Convention on Human Rights, especially in relation to surveillance activities by the state, has to start with *Klass and others v. Germany*.[258] This case revolved around the applicants' claim that the contested German legislation permitted surveillance measures without obliging the authorities to notify the persons concerned after the event. They also complained about the lack of judicial remedies against the ordering and execution of such measures. According to them, this led to a situation of potentially unchecked and uncontrolled surveillance, as those affected by the measures were kept unaware and were consequently not able to challenge them in a legal procedure. In essence, the case revolved around hypothetical harm, as the applicants claimed that they could potentially have been the victims of surveillance activities employed by the German government, but could not be certain since the governmental services remained silent on this point. The claimants were judges and lawyers, professions which cannot function without respect for secrecy of deliberations and of contacts with clients. Moreover, by virtue of their profession, they are more likely to be affected by the measures than ordinary citizens, at least so the applicants claimed. The government, to the contrary, argued that the applicants could not substantiate their claim that they were victims of the contested surveillance activities and consequently, that they were bringing forth an *in abstracto* claim.

The Commission, deciding on the admissibility of the case, referred to Article 25 ECHR, the current Article 34 ECHR, which reads as follows:

> The Court may receive applications from any person, nongovernmental organisation or group of individuals claiming to be the victim of a violation by one of the High Contracting Parties of the rights set forth in the Convention or the Protocols thereto. The High Contracting Parties undertake not to hinder in any way the effective exercise of this right.

On this basis, the Commission argued:

> [O]nly the victim of an alleged violation may bring an application. The applicants, however, state that they may be or may have been subject to secret surveillance, for example, in course of legal representation of clients who were themselves subject to surveillance, and that

---

[258] ECtHR, Klass and others v. Germany, application no. 5029/71, 06 September 1978.

persons having been the subject of secret surveillance are not always subsequently informed of the measures taken against them. In view of this particularity of the case the applicants have to be considered as victims for purposes of Art. 25.[259]

Before the Court, which heard the case on its merits, the Delegates of the Commission argued that the government was setting too rigid a standard for the notion of 'victim'. They submitted that, in order to be able to claim to be the victim of an interference with the exercise of the right to privacy, 'it should suffice that a person is in a situation where there is a reasonable risk of his being subjected to secret surveillance.'[260] The Court took this reasoning a step further: 'an individual may, under certain conditions, claim to be the victim of a violation occasioned by the mere existence of secret measures or of legislation permitting secret measures, without having to allege that such measures were in fact applied to him.'[261] In this case, the Court thus accepted an *in abstracto* claim, instead of a hypothetical claim, as the 'mere existence' of a law may lead to an interference with Article 8 ECHR.[262] This contrasts with the test proposed by the Delegates, namely whether there is a 'reasonable likelihood' that the applicants were affected by the measures complained of. In the latter test, the requirement of personal harm remains, though it is not made dependent on actual and concrete proof, but on a reasonable suspicion; in the abstract test, the requirement of personal harm is abandoned, as the laws and policies are assessed as such.

Both approaches have played an important role in the Court's subsequent case law.[263] The abstract test was adopted in *Malone v. the UK*[264] and in *P.G. and J.H. v. the UK*,[265] among other cases. In *Mersch and others v. Luxembourg*, the Commission carefully distinguished between the two tests, applying them to two different types of complaints. The case was declared incompatible with the provisions of the Convention insofar as it regarded a violation of the Convention's provisions on account of measures taken under a legal instrument, as the claimants had not been subjected to surveillance measures. Likewise, the Commission stressed that legal persons, one of the applicants being a legal person, could not complain about such matters as they could not be

---

[259] ECmHR, Klass and others v. Germany, application no. 5029/71, 18 December 1974.
[260] ECtHR, Klass and others v. Germany, application no. 5029/71, 06 September 1978, §31.
[261] ECtHR, Klass and others v. Germany, application no. 5029/71, 06 September 1978, §34.
[262] There is also a discussion about the question whether surveillance in itself entails enough injury to bring a case under the scope of Article 8 ECHR. See among others: ECmHR, Herbecq and the Association Ligue Des Droits de L'Homme v. Belgium, application nos. 32200/96 and 32201/96, 14 January 1998. ECtHR, Perry v. the United Kingdom, application no. 63737/00, 17 July 2003. There is also discussion about in how far redress should go to render claims inapplicable. ECtHR, Rotaru v. Romania, application no. 28341/95, 04 May 2000.
[263] ECtHR, Case of Association "21 December 1989" and others v. Romania, application nos. 33810/07 and 18817/08, 24 May 2011. ECmHR, Spillmann v. Switzerland, application no. 11811/85, 08 March 1988.
[264] ECmHR, Malone v. the United Kingdom, application no. 8691/79, 13 July 1981. See further: ECtHR, Leander v. Sweden, application no. 9248/81, 26 March 1987. ECtHR, Huvig v. France, application no. 11105/84, 24 April 1990. ECtHR, Kruslin v. France, application no. 11801/85, 24 April 1990.
[265] ECtHR, P.G. and J.H. v. the United Kingdom, application no. 44787/98, 25 September 2001.

subjected to monitoring or surveillance ordered in the course of criminal proceedings because legal persons had no criminal responsibility. However, it continued to point out that another part of the claim concerned laws as such, namely the provisions allowing for surveillance not confined to persons who may be suspected of committing the criminal offences referred to therein. With regard to this abstract claim, the Commission accepted all applicants in their claim and declared the case admissible.[266]

Conversely, in *Hilton v. the UK*, the Commission argued as follows:

> '[T]he *Klass* case falls to be distinguished from the present case in that there existed a legislative framework in that case which governed the use of secret measures and that this legislation potentially affected all users of postal and telecommunications services. In the present case the category of persons likely to be affected by the measures in question is significantly narrower. On the other hand, the Commission considers that it should be possible in certain cases to raise a complaint such as is made by the applicant without the necessity of proving the existence of a file of personal information. To fall into the latter category the Commission is of the opinion that applicants must be able to show that there is, at least, a reasonable likelihood that the Security Service has compiled and continues to retain personal information about them.[267]

Subsection 3.3 will explore the use of the abstract test by the Court in more detail. What is important to note with regard to the reasonable likelihood test[268] is that two aspects can lead to the establishment of a reasonable likelihood.[269] First, the Court takes into account whether the applicant falls under a group or category that is specifically mentioned in the law on which the surveillance activities are based. In these types of cases, the Court is willing to accept that applicants who fall under these categories can demonstrate a reasonable likelihood that they had been affected by the matters complained of. Second, the Court takes into account specific actions by the applicants which make them more likely to be affected by surveillance measures. In *Matthews v. the UK*, for example, the Commission decided that the assumption of the applicants that they were wiretapped was not substantiated by their argument that they heard

---

[266] ECmHR, Mersch and others v. Luxembourg, application nos. 10439/83, 10440/83, 10441/83, 10452/83, 10512/83 and 10513/83, 10 May1985.
[267] ECmHR, Hilton v. the United Kingdom, application no. 12015/86, 06 July 1988.
[268] ECtHR, Stefanov v. Bulgaria, applicatioon no. 65755/01, 22 May 2008. ECmHR, Nimmo v. the United Kingdom, application no. 12327/86, 11 October 1988.
[269] ECtHR, Senator Lines GmbH v. Austria, Belgium, Denmark, Finland, France, Germany, Greece, Ireland, Italy, Luxembourg, the Netherlands, Portugal, Spain, Sweden and the United Kingdom, application no. 56672/00, 10 March 2004. ECtHR, Segi and others and Gestoras Pro-Amnistia and others v. 15 states of the European Union, application nos. 6422/02 and 9916/02, 23 May 2002. ECmHR, Tauira and 18 others v. France, application no. 28204/95, 04 December 1995. ECtHR, C. and D. and S. and others v. the United Kingdom, application nos. 34407/02 and 34593/02, 31 August 2004. ECtHR, C. v. the United Kingdom, application no. 14858/03, 14 December 2004. ECtHR, Berger-Krall and others v. Slovenia, application no. 14717/04, 12 June 2014. ECmHR, Esbester v. the United Kingdom, application no. 18601/91, 02 April 1993. ECmHR, Hewitt and Harman v. the United Kingdom, application no. 20317/92, 01 September 1993. ECmHR, Redgrave v. the United Kingdom, application no. 20271/92, 01 September 1993. ECmHR, T.D., D.E. and M.F. v. the United Kingdom, application nos. 18600/91, 18601/91 and 18602/91, 12 October 1992.

mysterious clicking noises during telephone calls. That being said, the Commission was prepared to accept this assumption on other grounds:

> [I]n view of the fact that the applicant was active in the campaign against Cruise (nuclear) missiles in the United Kingdom, the Commission will assume for the purposes of this decision that the applicant has established a reasonable possibility that her telephone conversations were intercepted pursuant to a warrant for the purposes of national security.[270]

3.2. CHILLING EFFECT (FUTURE HARM)

The chilling effect principle is mostly connected to the freedom of speech and the Court uses it to explain that certain actions by the government, although not directly limiting the freedom of speech of its citizens, may lead to self-restraint: a chilling effect in the lawful use of a right. The chilling effect is the effect which exists when people know that they are being watched or know that they might be watched. Afraid of the potential consequences, people will restrain their behavior and abstain from certain acts which they perceive as possibly inciting negative consequences.[271] However, the Court is also willing to accept this doctrine in certain cases relating to Article 8 ECHR, primarily when they regard surveillance measures, but also in relation to laws that discriminate or stigmatize certain groups in society. Here, the Court is willing to accept that although no harm has been done yet to an applicant, she may still be received in her (a priori) claim if it is likely that she will suffer from harm in the future, either because she is curtailed in her right to privacy by the government or because she will resort to self-restraint in the use of her right.

An example may be the case of *Michaud v. France*, in which the applicant, a lawyer, complained that because lawyers were under an obligation to report suspicious operations, he was required, subject to disciplinary action, to report people who came to her for advice. He considered this system to be incompatible with the principles of lawyer-client privilege and professional confidentiality. The government maintained, however, that the applicant could not claim to be a 'victim' as his rights had not actually been affected in practice, highlighting that he did not claim that the legislation in question had been applied to her detriment, but simply that he had been obliged to organize his practice accordingly and introduce special internal procedures. This would qualify as an *in abstracto* claim, according to the government. It continued to stress that if the Court accepted her status as a 'potential victim', this would open the door for class actions.

The Court pointed out that, indeed, in order to be able to lodge an application in pursuance of Article 34 of the Convention, a person must be able to claim to be a 'victim' of a violation of the rights enshrined in the Convention: to claim to be a victim

---

[270] ECmHR, Matthews v. the United Kingdom, application no. 28576/95, 16 October 1996. ECtHR, Halford v. the United Kingdom, application no. 20605/92, 25 June 1997, §48.
[271] J. Bentham, 'Panopticon; or The inspection-house', Dublin, 1791. M. Foucault, 'Discipline and punish: the birth of the prison', Vintage Books, New York, 1995.

of a violation, a person must be directly affected by the impugned measure. The Court continued by holding that the ECHR does not envisage an *actio popularis* for the interpretation of the rights set out therein, or permit individuals to complain about a provision of national law simply because they consider – without having been directly affected by that law – that it may contravene the Convention. Referring to *Marckx v. Belgium, Johnston and others v. Ireland, Norris v. Ireland* and *Burden v. the UK*, it stressed, however:

> [It is] open to a person to contend that a law violates his rights, in the absence of an individual measure of implementation, and therefore to claim to be a 'victim' within the meaning of Article 34 of the Convention, if he is required to either modify his conduct or risk being prosecuted, or if he is a member of a class of people who risk being directly affected by the legislation.[272]

The Court pointed out that if the applicant failed to report suspicious activities as required, he would expose herself by virtue of the law to disciplinary sanctions up to and including being struck off. The Court also accepted the applicant's suggestion that, as a lawyer specializing in financial and tax law, he was even more concerned by these obligations than many of his colleagues and exposed to the consequences of failure to comply. In fact, he faced a dilemma comparable, *mutatis mutandis*, to that which the Court already identified in *Dudgeon v. the UK* and *Norris*: either he applies the rules and relinquishes his idea of the principle of lawyer-client privilege, or he decides not to apply them and exposes herself to disciplinary sanctions and even being struck off. Therefore, the Court accepted that the applicant was directly affected by the impugned provisions and could therefore claim to be a 'victim' of the alleged violation of Article 8. In conclusion, the Court accepted the applicant's status as victim, not because he had actually suffered from any concrete harm, but because he was likely to be affected by it in the future, either because he would restrict or limit her behavior or because she would not and would face a legal sanction.

The references to the cases of *Marckx, Dudgeon* and *Norris*, amongst others, are particularly telling. It appears that the Court is also willing to relax its strict focus on individual harm in cases regarding potential discrimination and stigmatization of weaker groups in society. For example, it has accepted that where the national legislator had adopted a prohibition on abortion, a complainant could still be received even if she was not pregnant, had not been refused an abortion procedure, nor had been prosecuted for unlawful abortion.[273] Likewise, in *Marckx*, the inheritance laws complained of had not yet been applied to the applicants and presumably would not be applied for a certain period of time. Nonetheless, the Court argued that they had a legitimate interest in challenging a legal position, that of an unmarried mother and of children born out of wedlock, which affected them – according to the Court – personally.[274] *Dudgeon*

---

[272] ECtHR, Michaud v. France, application no. 12323/33, 06 December 2012, §51.
[273] ECmHR, Brüggemann and Scheuten v. Germany, application no. 6959/75, 19 May 1976.
[274] ECtHR, Marckx v. Belgium, application no. 6833/74, 13 June 1979, §27.

and *Norris* both involved claims by an applicant about the regulation of homosexual conduct. The Court held that the applicant could be received even without the law being applied to him and without there being any reason to believe that it might be:

> The very existence of this legislation continuously and directly affects his private life: either he respects the law and refrains from engaging – even in private with consenting male partners – in prohibited sexual acts to which he is disposed by reason of his homosexual tendencies, or he commits such acts and thereby becomes liable to criminal prosecution.[275]

This approach is becoming increasingly important in cases revolving around surveillance activities by the state, in which the Court is also willing to accept potential future harm and chilling effects. A good example may be the case of *Colon v. the Netherlands*, in which the applicant complained that the designation of a security risk area by the Burgomaster of Amsterdam violated his right to respect for privacy as it enabled a public prosecutor to conduct random searches of people over an extensive period in a large area without this mandate being subject to any judicial review. The government, to the contrary, argued that the designation of a security risk area or the issuing of a stop-and-search order had not in itself constituted an interference with the applicant's private life or liberty of movement. Since the event complained of, several preventive search operations had been conducted; in none of them had the applicant been subjected to further attempts to search him. According to the government, this was enough to show that the likelihood of an interference with the applicant's rights was so minimal that this deprived him of the status of victim.

The Court stressed again that, in principle, it did not accept *in abstracto* claims or an *actio popularis*:

> In principle, it is not sufficient for individual applicants to claim that the mere existence of the legislation violates their rights under the Convention; it is necessary that the law should have been applied to their detriment. Nevertheless, Article 34 entitles individuals to contend that legislation violates their rights by itself, in the absence of an individual measure of implementation, if they run the risk of being directly affected by it; that is, if they are required either to modify their conduct or risk being prosecuted, or if they are members of a class of people who risk being directly affected by the legislation.[276]

The Court went on to conclude that the applicant satisfied the victim requirement:

> The Court is not disposed to doubt that the applicant was engaged in lawful pursuits for which she might reasonably wish to visit the part of Amsterdam city centre designated as a security risk area. This made her liable to be subjected to search orders should these

---

[275] ECtHR, Dudgeon v. the United Kingdom, application no. 7525/76, 22 October 1981, §41. See further: ECtHR, S.A.S. v. France, application no. 43835/11, 01 July 2014. ECtHR, Mateescu v. Romania, application no. 1944/10, 14 January 2014. ECtHR, Vallianatos and others v. Greece, application nos. 29381/09 and 32684/09, 07 November 2013.

[276] ECtHR, Colon v. the Netherlands, application no. 49458/06, 15 May 2012, §60.

happen to coincide with her visits there. The events of 19 February 2004, followed by the criminal prosecution occasioned by the applicant's refusal to submit to a search, leave no room for doubt on this point. It follows that the applicant can claim to be a "victim" within the meaning of Article 34 of the Convention and the Government's alternative preliminary objection must be rejected also.[277]

As with the laws prohibiting homosexual conduct, the applicant was left a choice between two evils: either he avoided traveling to the capital city of the Netherlands or he risked being subjected to surveillance activities. This is enough for the Court to accept a victim status, which it has reaffirmed in later jurisprudence.[278] Currently pending before the Court is a case regarding mass surveillance activities by the British government and its intelligence services.[279] It will be interesting to see whether in future, the Court will take a similar approach to practices such as data retention practices[280] or mass wiretapping of telecommunications. By analogy to *Colon*, it could be argued that such are left only with the choice either to abstain from legitimately using the internet or other common (electronic) communication channels, or face the risk of being subjected to surveillance activities.

3.3. *IN ABSTRACTO* CLAIMS (NO INDIVIDUAL HARM)

Although in the cases discussed above involve a relaxation of the victim requirement, the Court still holds on to this principle. There are, however, cases, which have been briefly touched upon in Subsection 3.1, in which the Court allows *in abstracto* claims, regarding laws or policies as such without them having been applied to the claimant or otherwise having had a direct effect on her.[281] Sometimes, the Court, rather artificially, holds on to the victim requirement by holding that everyone living in a certain country is affected by a certain law. For example, in *Weber and Saravia v. Germany*, the applicants claimed that certain provisions of the Fight against Crime Act violated Article 8 ECHR. The Court reiterated that the mere existence of legislation which allows a system for the secret monitoring of communications entails a threat of surveillance for all those to whom the legislation may be applied:

> This threat necessarily strikes at freedom of communication between users of the telecommunications services and thereby amounts in itself to an interference with the

---

[277] Colon, §61.
[278] ECtHR, Ucar and others v. Turkey, application no. 4692/09, 24 June 2014.
[279] ECtHR, Big Brother Watch and others v. the United Kingdom, application no. 58170/13, 07 January 2014.
[280] ECJ, Digital Rights Ireland, C293/12 and C594/12, 8 April 2014.
[281] See further: ECmHR, M.S. and P.S. v. Switserland, application no. 10628/83, 14 October 1985. ECtHR, Tanase v. Moldova, application no. 7/08, 27 April 2010. ECtHR, Hadzhiev v. Bulgaria, application no. 22373/04, 23 October 2012. See further: ECtHR, Goranova-Karaeneva v. Bulgaria, application no. 12739/05, 08 March 2011.

exercise of the applicants' rights under Article 8, irrespective of any measures actually taken against them.[282]

In a similar fashion, the Court recalled in *Liberty and others v. the UK* its earlier case law:

> In previous cases to the effect that the mere existence of legislation which allows a system for the secret monitoring of communications entails a threat of surveillance for all those to whom the legislation may be applied. This threat necessarily strikes at freedom of communication between users of the telecommunications services and thereby amounts in itself to an interference with the exercise of the applicants' rights under Article 8, irrespective of any measures actually taken against them.[283]

The fact that everyone may claim to be a victim means that everyone may submit a claim before the Court, a situation which it had earlier hoped to prevent by introducing the prohibition on class actions.

Although in these cases, the Court still held on to the victim requirement, in most cases revolving around *in abstracto* claims, such as *Klass*, *Malone*, *P.G.* and *J.H.* and *Mersch*, the victim requirement is simply abandoned. This shift has had a large influence on the admissibility of cases and complainants more in general. While typical cases under Article 8 ECHR revolve around individual interests such as human dignity, individual autonomy and personal freedom, cases in which the Court accepts *in abstracto* claims revolve around societal interests, such as the abuse of power by the government. Abandoning the victim requirement means that other hurdles for invoking Article 8 ECHR are also minimized. This passage will briefly touch on three examples. First, the rejection of the Court of legal persons invoking the right to privacy; second, the obligation to exhaust all domestic remedies before submitting a claim under the system of supranational supervision; and third, the requirement that a case must be brought before the European Court of Human Rights within six months after the final decision has been made at the national level.

As has been discussed, in *Mersch and others v. Luxembourg*, the Court was willing to accept a legal person in its claim for the part of the case that regarded the mere existence of laws or policies as such. Besides *Mersch*, the Court has accepted the complaint of a legal person in *Liberty* and in *Association for European Integration and Human Rights and Ekimdzhiev v. Bulgaria*. The latter case regarded the authorities' wide discretion to gather and use information obtained through secret surveillance. The applicants suggested that, by failing to provide sufficient safeguards against abuse, by its very existence, the laws were in violation of Article 8 ECHR. The government disputed that the applicants could be considered victims (as they did not claim to be specifically harmed by the matter) and that legal persons should not be allowed to claim a right to privacy in general and in particular in this case because the legal person could not

---

[282] ECtHR, Weber and Saravia v. Germany, application no. 54934/00, 29 June 2006, §78.
[283] ECtHR, Liberty and others v. the United Kingdom, application no. 58243/00, 01 July 2008, §56–57.

have been harmed itself. The Court, however, pointed to the statutory objectives of the association and found to the contrary:

> The rights in issue in the present case are those of the applicant association, not of its members. There is therefore a sufficiently direct link between the association as such and the alleged breaches of the Convention. It follows that it can claim to be a victim within the meaning of Article 34 of the Convention.[284]

Essentially the same was held in *Iordachi and others v. Moldova*.[285] This means that legal persons who have statutes that incorporate references to the general protection of privacy and other human rights may have direct access to the court in the future when cases regard mass surveillance activities by the state.

As a second example, reference can be made to the requirement to exhaust all domestic remedies before submitting a claim before the ECtHR. This requirement is also relaxed with *in abstracto* claims. The admissibility criteria laid down in Article 35 ECHR specify that the Court may only deal with a matter after all domestic remedies have been exhausted, according to the general recognized rules of international law. This is connected to the principle that the Court dismisses cases in which the national authorities have acknowledged their mistake and have remedied their misconduct, either by providing compensation and/or by revoking the law or policy on which the abusive practices were based. If the national courts would be passed over by the claimant, national states would be denied this chance. However, the problem with *in abstracto* claims is that, especially when linked to mass surveillance by secret services, national oversight is often quite limited. More specifically, *in abstracto* claims can often not be brought forward by citizens or legal persons on the domestic level. Moreover, courts and tribunals often simply lack the power to annul laws or policies and can only assess specific individual cases. That is why the ECtHR is often willing to accept claimants which have not exhausted all domestic remedies if the claim regards the mere existence of laws or policies as such.

For example, the Court in *Kennedy v. the UK* concluded that the applicant had failed to raise his objections to the Regulation of Investigatory Powers Act 2000 (RIPA) before the Investigatory Powers Tribunal (IPT). However, it also stressed that where the government claims non-exhaustion it must satisfy the Court that the remedy proposed was an effective one, available in theory and in practice at the relevant time; that is to say, that it was accessible, was capable of providing redress in respect of the applicant's complaints and offered reasonable prospects of success. However, it found:

> '[I]f the applicant had made a general complaint to the IPT, and if that complaint been upheld, the tribunal did not have the power to annul any of the RIPA provisions or to find any interception arising under RIPA to be unlawful as a result of the incompatibility of the

---

[284] ECtHR, Association for European Integration and Human Rights and Ekimdzhiev v. Bulgaria, application no. 62540/00, 08 June 2007, §59.
[285] ECtHR, Iordachi and other v. Moldova, application no. 25198/02, 10 February 2009, §33-34.

provisions themselves with the Convention. (...) Accordingly, the Court considers that the applicant was not required to advance his complaint regarding the general compliance of the RIPA regime for internal communications with Article 8 §2 before the IPT in order to satisfy the requirement under Article 35 §1 that he exhaust domestic remedies.'[286]

The Court held essentially the same in *M. M. v. the UK*.[287] This means for *in abstracto* claims that the ECtHR is willing to rule as a court of first instance.

To offer a final example, the Convention specifies certain time-restrictive principles, which are also put under pressure with *in abstracto* claims, as these do not revolve around specific violations but the existence of laws or policies as such, and are thus not linked to a specific moment in time. The principle of *ratione temporis* signifies that the provisions of the Convention do not bind a national state in relation to any act or fact which took place or any situation which ceased to exist before the date of the entry into force of the Convention or the accession of a state to the ECHR. This means that, for example, if the right to privacy of an individual had been violated by a state before that state entered the Convention, this case will be declared inadmissible by the Court. Obviously, this principle does not apply to *in abstracto* claims, as the infringement continues to exist. The Convention, Article 35, also requires applicants to submit their application within a period of six months from the date on which the final decision on the national level was taken. This principle is also very difficult to maintain with regard to *in abstracto* claims, and the ECtHR has often adopted a flexible approach with this respect.

For example, in *Lenev v. Bulgaria*, the Court made a sharp distinction between the complaint regarding individual harm and the part of the application revolving around the mere existence of the law. Regarding the timeliness of the applicant's complaint, which occurred more than six months after he learned about the secret taping of his interrogation, the Court reasoned as follows:

> The fact that he did not have knowledge of the exact content of the recording is immaterial because the lack of such knowledge could not prevent him from formulating a complaint under Article 8 of the Convention in relation to the secret taping of his interrogation. Nor can the Court accept that the criminal proceedings against the applicant constituted an obstacle to his raising grievances in this respect. It follows that the complaints concerning the secret taping of the applicant's interrogation have been introduced out of time and must be rejected in accordance with Article 35 §§1 and 4 of the Convention. By contrast, the concomitant complaints concerning the mere existence in Bulgaria of laws and practices which have established a system for secret surveillance relate to a continuing situation – in as much as the applicant may at any time be placed under such surveillance without his being aware of it. It follows that his complaints in that respect cannot be regarded as having been raised out of time.'[288]

---

[286] ECtHR, Kennedy v. the United Kingdom, application no. 26839/05, 18 May 2010.
[287] ECtHR, M.M. v. the United Kingdom, application no. 24029/07, 13 November 2012.
[288] ECtHR, Lenev v. Bulgaria, application no. 41452/07, 04 December 2012.

Consequently, claims revolving around the mere existence of laws or policies are not bound by the time limits specified by the Convention. In conclusion, abandoning the victim requirement has the effect of dissolving many of the thresholds for invoking a right under the Convention.

3.4. CONVENTIONALITY

To summarize briefly, the following has been shown. The Court focuses on individual harm by natural persons when assessing the admissibility of cases under Article 8 ECHR, as discussed in the previous chapter. According to the Court, this provision guarantees protection only to individual interests such as human dignity, individual autonomy and personal freedom. Cases are declared inadmissible if they do not revolve around individual harm. Examples are: *in abstracto* claims, *a priori* claims, hypothetical complaints, class actions, claims about minimal harm, claims about harm which has been remedied, claims by legal persons and claims that do not regard strictly personal interests. However, it has also been explained that in certain types of cases, the Court is willing to relax its standards. It is sometimes willing to allow for hypothetical complaints if a reasonable likelihood exists that the applicant has been harmed; it is occasionally willing to accept *a priori* claims, when the applicant is forced to restrict its legitimate use of her right to privacy in order to avoid legal sanctions; and in exceptional cases, it is even willing to accept claims that revolve around the mere existence of laws and policies as such.

The reason why the Court is willing to relax its stance in cases revolving around (mass) surveillance activities specifically is clear. The citizen is mostly unaware of the fact that she is being followed or that her data are being gathered, why this is done, by whom, to what extent, etc. Likewise, especially with regard to laws allowing for mass surveillance and data retention, the fact is that the potential violations do not revolve around a specific person, but affect everyone living under that regime or at least very large numbers of people. Mostly, the issue is simply the presumed abuse of power by national authorities. This is a societal interest, related to the legitimacy and legality of the state.

The reason for discussing these matters in such detail is that these characteristics are shared to a large extent by privacy infringements following from Big Data initiatives in general. All notions connected to the victim requirement, such as the *de minimis* rule, the prohibition on hypothetical, future and abstract harm, the prohibition of class actions and of legal persons instituting a complaint, and the focus on individual interests, seem to be challenged by the developments known as Big Data. Some of the most salient privacy-related claims regarding mass surveillance and Big Data practices include claims about the potential chilling effect (e.g. users being afraid to use certain forms of communication), about hypothetical harm, and even abstract assessments of the policies and practices as such. Not the individual, but civil society groups and legal persons seem to be best equipped to file such complaints. Not individual interests are at stake in these types of processes, but general and societal interests. Thus, in order to retain the relevance of the rights to privacy and data protection in the modern technological era, the victim requirement and all its subrequirements should be relaxed.

And this is exactly what the ECtHR is willing to do in cases that revolve around surveillance activities. It does accept claims about future harm, potential chilling effects and about hypothetical harm; it does receive class actions, abstract claims and claims from legal persons; and it does take into account abstract and societal interests. Although the Court has done so for years without explicitly acknowledging the fact that, in exceptional cases, it is prepared to relax its individualized approach to privacy, it has finally made this unequivocally clear in in two recent cases, namely *Szabó & Vissy*[289] and especially *Zakharov*.[290] In *Zakharov*, the ECtHR argued as follows:

> [T]he Court accepts that an applicant can claim to be the victim of a violation occasioned by the mere existence of secret surveillance measures, or legislation permitting secret surveillance measures, if the following conditions are satisfied. Firstly, the Court will take into account the scope of the legislation permitting secret surveillance measures by examining whether the applicant can possibly be affected by it, either because he or she belongs to a group of persons targeted by the contested legislation or because the legislation directly affects all users of communication services by instituting a system where any person can have his or her communications intercepted. Secondly, the Court will take into account the availability of remedies at the national level and will adjust the degree of scrutiny depending on the effectiveness of such remedies. As the Court underlined in *Kennedy*, where the domestic system does not afford an effective remedy to the person who suspects that he or she was subjected to secret surveillance, widespread suspicion and concern among the general public that secret surveillance powers are being abused cannot be said to be unjustified. In such circumstances the menace of surveillance can be claimed in itself to restrict free communication through the postal and telecommunication services, thereby constituting for all users or potential users a direct interference with the right guaranteed by Article 8. There is therefore a greater need for scrutiny by the Court and an exception to the rule, which denies individuals the right to challenge a law *in abstracto*, is justified. In such cases the individual does not need to demonstrate the existence of any risk that secret surveillance measures were applied to her. By contrast, if the national system provides for effective remedies, a widespread suspicion of abuse is more difficult to justify. In such cases, the individual may claim to be a victim of a violation occasioned by the mere existence of secret measures or of legislation permitting secret measures only if he is able to show that, due to his personal situation, he is potentially at risk of being subjected to such measures.[291]

Although this development seems laudable in terms of concrete protection, the question is at what price this comes. What is left for the Court to assess in these types of cases, particularly with *in abstracto* claims, is the mere quality of laws and policies as such and the question is whether this narrow assessment is still properly addressed under a human rights framework. The normal assessment of the Court revolves around,

---

[289] ECtHR, Szabó and Vissy v. Hungary, application no. 37138/14, 12 January 2016.
[290] ECtHR, Roman Zakharov v. Russia, application no. 47143/06, 04 December 2015.
[291] Zakharov, §171.

roughly, three questions, as discussed in the previous chapter: (1) has there been an infringement of the right to privacy of the claimant, (2) is the infringement prescribed by law and (3) is the infringement necessary in a democratic society in terms of, *inter alia*, national security – that is, does the societal interest in this particular case outweigh the individual interest (balancing test). Obviously, the first question does not apply to *in abstracto* claims because there has been no infringement with the right of the claimant. The third question is also left untouched by the Court, because it is impossible, in the absence of an individual interest, to weigh the different interests involved. This means of course that another of the Court's principles, namely that it only decides on the particular case before it, is also overturned.

Even the second question – whether the infringement is prescribed by law – is not applicable as such since there is no infringement that is or is not prescribed by law. Although the Court regularly determines in cases, *inter alia*, whether the laws are accessible, whether sanctions are foreseeable and whether the infringement at stake is based on a legal provision, this does not apply to *in abstracto* claims. There is often a law permitting mass surveillance (that is exactly the problem) and these laws are accessible and the consequences are foreseeable (in the sense that everyone will be affected by it). Rather, it is the mere quality of the policy as such that is assessed; the content of the law, the use of power as such, may be deemed inappropriate. The question of abuse of power can of course be addressed by the Court, though not under Article 8 ECHR, but under Article 18 of the Convention, which specifies: 'The restrictions permitted under this Convention to the said rights and freedoms shall not be applied for any purpose other than those for which they have been prescribed.' But, as the Court has stressed, this provision can only be invoked if one of the other Convention rights are at stake. Reprehensible as the abuse of power may be, there are arguments for saying that it is only proper to address this question under a human rights framework if one of the human rights contained therein will be or has been violated by the abuse. The Court cannot assess the abuse of power as such (a doctrine which it also applies to, inter alia, Article 14 ECHR, the prohibition of discrimination).

However, what is assessed in cases in which *in abstracto* claims regarding surveillance activities have been accepted is precisely the use of power by the government as such, without a specific individual interest being at stake. This is a test of legality and legitimacy, which is well known to countries that have a constitutional court or body, such as France and Germany. These courts can assess the 'constitutionality' of national laws in abstract terms. Not surprisingly, the term 'conventionality' (or '*conventionalité*' in French) has been introduced in the cases discussed.[292] For example, in *Michaud*, the government argued that with a previous *in abstracto* decision, the

---

[292] See for the use of the word also: ECtHR, Py v. France, application no. 66289/01, 11 January 2005. ECtHR, Kart v. Turkey, application no. 8917/05, 08 July 2008. ECtHR, Duda v. France, application no. 37387/05, 17 March 2009. ECtHR, Kanagaratnam and others v. Belgium, application no. 15297/09, 13 December 2011. ECtHR, M.N. and F.Z. v. France and Greece, application nos. 59677/09 and 1453/10, 08 January 2013.

Court had 'issued the Community human rights protection system with a "certificate of conventionality", in terms of both its substantive and its procedural guarantees.'[293] Referring to the *Michaud* judgment, among other cases, in his partly concurring, partly dissenting opinion in *Vallianatos and others v. Greece*, justice Pinto De Albuquerque explained: 'The abstract review of "conventionality" is the review of the compatibility of a national law with the Convention independently of a specific case where this law has been applied.'[294]

He argued that the case of *Vallianatos and others*, which revolved around the fact that the civil unions introduced by a specific law were designed only for couples composed of different-sex adults, is particulary interesting in that the Grand Chamber performs an abstract review of the "conventionality" of a Greek law, while acting as a court of first instance:

> The Grand Chamber not only reviews the Convention compliance of a law which has not been applied to the applicants, but furthermore does it without the benefit of prior scrutiny of that same legislation by the national courts. In other words, the Grand Chamber invests itself with the power to examine *in abstracto* the Convention compliance of laws without any prior national judicial review.[295]

As explained earlier, when discussing *Lenev v. Bulgaria*, the Court is likewise willing to pass over the domestic legal system and act as court of first instance in cases revolving around mass surveillance. Subsequent to *Michaud* and *Vallianatos*, the term 'conventionality' has been used more often,[296] as well as the term 'Convention-compatibility', for example in the case of *Kennedy v. the UK* discussed earlier,[297] and most likely will only gain in dominance as the Court opens up the Convention for abstract reviews of laws and policies.

What is left in these types of cases is thus the abstract assessment of laws and policies as such, without a Convention right necessarily being at stake. Furthermore, the Court is willing to assess the 'conventionality' of these laws as court of first instance.[298]

---

[293] Michaud, §73. See also: ECtHR, Vassis and others v. France, application no. 62736/09, 27 June 2013.
[294] ECtHR, Vallianatos and others v. Greece, application nos. 29381/09 and 32684, 07 November 2013.
[295] Ibid.
[296] See among others: ECtHR, S.A.S. v. France, application no. 43835/11, 01 July 2014. ECtHR, Avotins v. Latvia, application no. 17502/07, 25 February 2014. ECtHR, Matelly v. France, application no. 10609/10, 02 October 2014. ECtHR, Delta Pekarny A.S. v. Czech Republic, application no. 97/11, 02 October 2014.
[297] See among others: ECtHR, Animal Defenders International v. the United Kingdom, application no. 48876/08, 22 April 2013. ECtHR, Emars v. Latvia, application no. 22412/08, 18 November 2014. ECtHR, Kennedy v. the United Kingdom, application no. 26839/05, 18 May 2010. ECtHR, Mikalauskas v. Malta, application no. 4458/10, 23 July 2013. ECtHR, Sorensen and Rusmussen v. Denmark, application nos. 52562/99 and 52620/99, 11 January 2006. ECtHR, Bosphorushava Yollari Turizm ve Ticaret Anonim Sirketi v. Ireland, application no. 45036/98, 30 June 2005. ECtHR, Lunch and Whelan v. Ireland, application nos. 70495/10 and 74565/10, 18 June 2013. ECtHR, Interdnestrcom v. Moldova, application no. 48814/06, 13 March 2012.
[298] Letting go of the personal and material scope of data protection rules could similarly lead to the application of certain principles *in abstracto*, such as the transparency principle, the requirement

As stressed before, in the Big Data era, what is needed is not more individual rights protecting individual interests, but general duties to protect general interests.[299] Accepting *in abstracto* claims and assessing the legality and legitimacy of laws and (Big Data) practices as such fits this purpose. But it seems to diverge in essence from the approach the ECtHR has taken to the right to privacy for a long time. Not individual interests of natural persons are the core of these types of cases, but general interests in relation to the legitimacy and legality of laws. When the Court does so, it seems to interpret the nature of the ECHR yet again. The first chapter of this book showed that it changed the Convention as a whole, and the right to privacy in particular, from a framework laying down duties of states not to abuse their power to a document protecting the specific interests of natural persons. Now, it is once more changing the nature of the Convention, namely from a human rights instrument which provides protection to the minimum principles of human life in last instance, to a document resembling a constitution, and its position from a supranational court overseeing severe human rights violations in last instance, to a first instance court for assessing the legality and legitimacy of laws and policies as such.

4. ALTERNATIVES FOR THE CURRENT PRIVACY PARADIGM IN THE SCHOLARLY LITERATURE

Section 2 showed that many of the aspects of the current legal paradigm are put under pressure by Big Data-related developments. Section 3 showed that in order to deal with these types of cases, the ECtHR is forced to move beyond the pillars of the individualized privacy paradigm. Section 4 will provide an overview of alternatives to the individualized privacy paradigm that have been proposed in scholarly literature. Subsection 4.1 will focus on theories that argue that privacy is constitutive for societal institutions, such as the healthcare sector, the legal system and journalism. Subsection 4.2 will discuss the aggregated, group and collective interests that relate to privacy protection. Subsection 4.3 will discuss theories that focus on potential and future harm, including the chilling effect. Subsection 4.4 will discuss theories that revolve around the (ethical) evaluation of agents, or potential privacy violators.[300]

---

of having a clear and defined purpose for the processing, the purpose limitation principle and the obligations to process data safely and confidentially and to keep the data correct and up to date. Again, although this abstract test might be in itself desirable, the question is whether it is appropriate to fit this under the regimes protecting personal data.

[299] See further: B. van der Sloot, "Do data protection rules protect the individual and should they? An assessment of the proposed General Data Protection Regulation", International Data Privacy Law 3, 2014.

[300] This section is based on: B. van der Sloot, 'The Individual in the Big Data Era: Moving towards an Agent-Based Privacy Paradigm', IN: B. van der Sloot & D. Broeders & E. Schrijvers (eds.), 'Exploring the boundaries of Big Data', Amsterdam University Press, Amsterdam, 2016.

4.1. CONSTITUTIVE INTERESTS

Many authors have struggled to find an exact definition and description of privacy. Most authors agree that the value and meaning of privacy differs between cultures, periods and persons. Still, the right to privacy is generally linked to underlying values such as human dignity,[301] individual autonomy[302] or personal freedom.[303] This means that in contrast to those values, the right to privacy is commonly viewed as an instrumental and not an intrinsic value. Solove, for example, holds that the problem with theories that ascribe to privacy an intrinsic value is that they tend to sidestep the difficult task of articulating why privacy is valued. 'The difficulty with intrinsic value is that it is often hard to describe it beyond being a mere taste. Vanilla ice cream has intrinsic value for many people, but reasons cannot readily be given to explain why. Individuals like vanilla ice cream, and that is about all that can be said. Privacy's value is often more complex than a mere taste, and it can be explained and articulated. Although it is possible that some forms of privacy may have intrinsic value, many forms of privacy are valuable primarily because of the ends they further'.[304] Privacy is thus generally described as an instrumental value, as a relative value (contrasting with absolute values such as the prohibition on torture) and a personal value. On this last point there is a contrast with, *inter alia*, the freedom of speech, which is generally said to be instrumental to individual expression and the possibility of personal development, but also to the search for truth through the market place of ideas and to the well-functioning of the press, which at its turn may be described as a precondition of a vital democracy.

Because of the points discussed earlier, scholars have increasingly argued that privacy is not only instrumental towards personal values, but also constitutive for general institutions. Constitutiveness, in contrast to instrumentality, signals a necessary relationship – privacy is described as a necessary precondition of societal institutions. One example is Spiros Simitis, who argued that privacy should be seen as a constitutive element of a democratic society.[305] Ruth Gavison, in similar vein, held: 'In the absence of consensus concerning many limitations of liberty, and in view of the limits on our capacity to encourage tolerance and acceptance and to overcome prejudice, privacy must be part of our commitment to individual freedom and to a society that is committed to the protection of such freedom. Privacy is also essential to democratic government because it fosters and encourages the moral autonomy of the citizen, a central requirement of a democracy'.[306] Of course, reference can also

---

[301] S. I. Benn, 'Privacy, Freedom, and Respect for Persons', in: F. Schoeman (red.), Philosophical Dimensions of Privacy: an Anthology, Cambridge: Cambridge University Press 1984, p. 223–244.
[302] B. Roessler, 'The value of privacy', Cambridge, Polity, 2005.
[303] J. S. Mill, "On Liberty' and Other Writings', Cambridge, Cambridge University Press, 1989.
[304] D. Solove, 'Understanding privacy', Cambridge, Harvard University Press, 2008, p. 84.
[305] S. Simitis, 'Reviewing Privacy in an Information Society', *University of Pennsylvania Law Review*, Vol. 135, No. 3, 1987.
[306] R. Gavison, 'Privacy and the Limits of Law', Yale Law Journal, 1980, 89, p. 455.

be made to Habermas, who argues that democracy and human rights are mutually constitutive.[307] For these types of theories, privacy is a necessary precondition for democracy, the rule of law or a free and equal society.

Similarly, a connection is often made between privacy and specific institutions. Many of the court cases revolving around mass surveillance by secret services, for example, are initiated not only by civil society organizations protecting the right to privacy in general, but also by professional organizations protecting the specific interests of lawyers and journalists. Those organizations point to the fact that both professions can only function properly when a degree of secrecy and confidentially is guaranteed. Without the possibility for secrecy between lawyer and client, the client might not feel free to speak about sensitive issues, which leaves the lawyers only partially informed and unable to defend the case of their client. This might undermine the right to a fair trial and ultimately the rule of law as such. Similarly, the argument is made that journalists cannot function without a form of secrecy of sources being guaranteed. Sources will not feel free to discuss sensitive matters with journalists or leak secret documents, which might ultimately undermine the position of the press as watchdog or fourth estate. The same might apply to the secrecy of ballot, an essential element of democratic elections.[308]

Finally, a similar argument has been made with regard to the confidentiality between patient and doctor. Anita Allen, for example, writes: 'First, confidentiality encourages seeking medical care. Individuals will be more inclined to seek medical attention if they believe they can do so on a confidential basis. It is reassuring to believe others will not be told without permission that one is unwell or declining, has abused illegal drugs, been unfaithful to one's partner, obtained an abortion, or enlarged one's breasts. [] Second, confidentiality contributes to full and frank disclosures. Individuals seeking care will be more open and honest if they believe the facts and impressions reported to health providers will remain confidential. It may be easier to speak freely about embarrassing symptoms if one believes the content of what one says will not be broadcast to the world at large'.[309] The fear is that surveillance in general and certain IT-projects in the health-care sector in particular might undermine the confidentially required for a well-functioning health care sector. Reference is sometimes made to underdeveloped countries, where the fear of others finding out about a certain disease or condition is often higher than the wish to be cured, but also to the United States, where patients may be skeptical about the influence of commercial parties and insurers.

---

[307] J. Habermas, 'Über den internen Zusammenhang zwischen Rechtsstaat und Demokratie', in: Preuß, Ulrich K. (Hrsg.), Zum Begriff der Verfassung. Die Ordnung des Politischen, Frankfurt am Main, 1994.
[308] A. Lever, 'Privacy and Democracy: What the Secret Ballot Reveals', Law, Culture and Humanities, 11(2), 2015.
[309] A. L. Allen, 'Unpopular privacy. What must we hide?', Oxford University Press, Oxford, 2011, p. 112.

4.2. GROUP AND COLLECTIVE INTERESTS

There are also theories that focus on the connection between individual harm and harm to others. The loss of privacy for one individual may have an impact on the privacy of others, but also on other important interests. It is stressed by some that a loss of privacy may undermine social relationships between individuals, which often consist of the very fact that certain information is disclosed between them and not to others. This is sometimes referred to as the social value of privacy.[310] But the loss of privacy for one individual may also have an impact on the privacy of others. This is commonly referred to as the network effect. A classic example is a photograph taken at a rather wild party. Although the central figure in the photograph may consent to the posting of their image on Facebook, it may also reveal others that attended the party. This is the case with much information – a person's living condition and the value of her home does not only disclose something about her, but also about her spouse and possibly their children. Perhaps the most poignant example is that of hereditary diseases. Data about this fact might reveal sensitive information not only about a specific person, but also about their direct relatives.

Alternative theories look not only to one specific individual, but to all individuals affected by a specific violation. These theories focus on aggregated harm and primarily aim against the common practice in the legal domain to focus on the specificities of a case, in combination with the fact that only individual victims can successfully file a complaint. What follows from this approach, according to some scholars, is a situation in which the effects of a certain law or policy are only measured and assessed with regard to its effects on the situation of the specific claimant. In reality, however, the law or policy has an effect on many people, sometimes millions. In contrast to the individual interest at stake, the countervailing general interest, for example national security, is often assessed at a general and societal level. The question is not how the monitoring of a specific individual (the claimant) has benefited the fight against terrorism, for example, but how the mass surveillance system as such aids this goal. Consequently, it might be worthwhile to assess the negative consequences of a particular law or policy in terms of privacy on a collective level as well.

These theories still focus on individual harm, though they broaden the scope of individuals being affected. More recent theories have proposed to transcend the focus on the individual when it comes to assessing privacy violations. Generally speaking, this might be done either by focusing on the privacy of a group or on the privacy of larger collectives and the value of privacy for society as a whole. With regard to group privacy,[311] two general lines of thinking exist. First, in accordance with the ideas of social privacy, it might be said that groups depend for their existence on a form of

---

[310] B. Roessler & D. Mokrosinska (eds.), 'Social Dimensions of Privacy: Interdisciplinary Perspectives', Cambridge University Press, Cambridge, 2015.
[311] L. Taylor, L. Floridi & B. Van der Sloot (eds.), 'Group Privacy: New Challenges of Data Technologies', Springer, Heidelberg, 2016.

privacy or secrecy. Consequently, if the right to privacy is undermined, this might have an effect on the group and its existence. Second, there is an increasing trend to use group profiles, not only with regard to crime fighting and the war against terrorism, but also when banks use risk profiles when deciding about loans, or health insurers when deciding whom to insure and against what price, etc. The fact is that decisions are increasingly made on the basis of these profiles, which might lead to discrimination and stigmatization as well as a loss of privacy. Because the problem is not so much that this or that specific individual is affected by being put in a certain category (whether rightly or wrongly), but the very fact that policies are based on stigmatizing or discriminating group profiles as such, the suggestion is that it might be worthwhile to look into the possibility of granting groups a right as such. Finally, as to the rights of future generations, not only a healthy living environment may be in their best interest. A good privacy environment may possibly be included in those interests too.

Others have argued that privacy should be regarded as a public good[312] or a societal interest,[313] rather than or in addition to an individual interest. For example, many of the current privacy violations are taking place at such a large scale and are affecting so many people that this might be qualified simply as abuse of power, undermining the trust of the citizen in the government and democratic institutions. Others have stressed, in reference to the Panopticon, that the fear following from mass surveillance hinders people in unfettered experimentation and in their development, which is not only detrimental to those specific individuals, but also to society as a whole.[314] When discussing privacy and the common good, Priscilla Regan distinguishes between three types of values. 'Privacy has value beyond its usefulness in helping the individual maintain his or her dignity or develop personal relationships. Most privacy scholars emphasize that the individual is better off if privacy exists; I argue that society is better off as well when privacy exists. I maintain that privacy serves not just individual interests but also common, public, and collective purposes. If privacy became less important to one individual in one particular contexts, or even to serval individuals in several contexts, it would still be important as a value because it serves other crucial functions beyond those that it performs for a particular individual. Even if the individual interests in privacy became less compelling, social interests in privacy might remain. (…) I suggest that three concepts provide bases for discussing a more explicitly social importance for privacy – privacy as a common value, privacy as a public value, and privacy as a collective value. The first two concepts are derived from normative theory, while the latter is derived from economic theory; the styles of analysis, therefore, are different, with the first two being conceptual and the third more technical'.[315]

---

[312] J. Fairfield & C. Engel, 'Privacy as public good', <http://papers.ssrn.com/sol3/papers.cfm?abstract_id=2418445>.
[313] B. van der Sloot, 'Privacy in the Post-NSA Era: Time for a Fundamental Revision?', JIPITEC, 2014-1.
[314] N. M. Richards, 'The dangers of surveillance', Harvard Law Review <http://harvardlawreview.org/2013/05/the-dangers-of-surveillance/>.
[315] P. M. Regan, 'Legislating privacy: technology, social values, and public policy', University of North Carolina Press, Chapel Hill, 1995, p. 211.

There is a common interest in privacy, Regan suggests, because individuals who have privacy not only become more valuable to themselves, but also become more valuable to society as a whole. Privacy as public value is the idea that privacy is not just valuable in itself, but is also instrumental towards other values, such as freedom of speech. Finally, the idea of privacy as a collective value is derived from the economists' concept of collective or public goods, which are those goods defined as indivisible or non-excludable; no one member of society can enjoy the benefit of a collective good without others also benefiting. Clean air and national defense, she suggests, are examples of public or collective goods. 'Currently a number of policies and policy proposals treat privacy as a "private good" and allow people to buy back or establish the level of privacy that they wish. For example, when you subscribe to a magazine, you can indicate that you do not want your name and information about you incorporated in a mailing list and sold for direct-mail purposes. Similarly, one policy proposal concerning Caller ID is that individuals be given the ability to "block" the display of their numbers. Such examples suggest that you can indeed "divide" privacy into components and allow people to establish their own privacy level. But three factors limit the effectiveness of this individual or market-based solution for privacy: the interests of third-party record holders; the nonvoluntary nature of many record-keeping relationships; and computer and telecommunication technologies'.[316]

4.3. POTENTIAL HARM

There is a third branch of privacy theories that focuses not on actual and concrete harm at the individual level, but on potential harm. This might be either hypothetical harm or potential future harm – these concepts have already been introduced in the previous section. Hypothetical harm can exist when a person might be affected by a given privacy violation, but cannot be certain. The classic example is the potential privacy violation following from the mass surveillance activities of secret services. As those services usually remain silent about their practices, the victim is often unaware of the fact that she might be affected by these practices. Normally, a person who cannot substantiate her claim that she has been harmed by a certain practice will not be able to successfully submit a complaint. However, as explained in the previous section, the European Court of Human Rights has stressed that it will make an exception in these types of cases because it will not accept a situation where mere fact that someone is kept unaware of her victimhood renders her powerless to challenge those practices and policies. It has stressed that if a person fits a category specifically mentioned in a law or policy or if a person engages in certain activities which gives her reason to believe that she might be subjected to surveillance activities, this might be enough to accept her status as victim.

Besides hypothetical harm, there is also increased attention for future harm. This again may be divided in two lines of thought: those focusing on potential future harm

---

[316] Regan, p. 228.

and those focusing on the harm following from self-restraint, also known as the chilling effect. The first category focuses on the possibility that certain harm might occur in the future. Although currently, for example, data, power or techniques may not be abused, they may in the future, especially if there are insufficient safeguards. *In ultima forma*, the Second World War hypothesis is applied, which posits a situation in which a Nazi-like regime takes power. If such a regime had access to all the data gathered and stored right now, including racial data, would it not be, so the argument goes, rather straightforward for it to execute its evil policies? The same argument may be applied to companies such as Facebook and Google, which might currently do no evil but could nevertheless do so in the future if their owners or board-members change.

Future harm is also receiving increased attention in the legal domain, for example in the General Data Protection Regulation. *Inter alia*, it contains rules on data protection impact assessments, which specify that where processing operations present specific risks to the rights and freedoms of data subjects by virtue of their nature, their scope or their purposes, the controller shall carry out an assessment of the impact of the envisaged processing operations on the protection of personal data.[317] Among other situations, this is the case when data controllers process privacy sensitive data. The idea of data protection impact assessments is borrowed from the domain of environmental law, where such assessments have already been introduced. Such impact assessments may focus on potential future harm on an individual level or on a societal level and on juridical, social or ethical consequences alike. There is a slight difference with regard to the type of harm that is at the heart of these types of assessments. While the Second World War argument stresses the fact that although there may be no reason now to believe that harm may take place or that power is abused, you never know for sure. By contrast, impact assessments focus on types of harm that are reasonably foreseeable, but ignore the unknown unknowns.

Second, future harm might lie in self-restricting behavior – when people know that they might be surveilled and possibly punished for their behavior or face other negative consequences. If people know that confidential information may fall in the hands of third parties, people may be discouraged from experimenting freely since they know that they might be confronted with their 'mistakes' in the future. Obviously, this fear also underlies the introduction of the hotly debated right to be forgotten. Proponents of this concept argue that children and adolescents may want to experiment freely with e.g. hairstyles, alcohol, or sex, without them being haunted for the rest of their lives by an unfortunate Facebook tag, Instagram photo or Youtube video. Not only would this limit their future social, societal and financial perspectives, the fear is that children may choose not to experiment altogether as they know that it is impossible to keep those experiments a secret. The latter is known in legal terms as the chilling effect, which is also increasingly accepted by the European Court of Human Rights when it considers data processing. A good example may be the case of *Colon v. the Netherlands*, as discussed previously.

---

[317] Article 35 Regulation.

4.4. AGENT-BASED THEORIES

There is a fourth and final branch of privacy theories that proposes to abandon the focus on harm altogether. Increasingly, scholars have suggested to move away from classic liberal theories focusing on (individual) harm, because this paradigm increasingly forces the notion of harm to be stretched so far as to appear far-fetched and unconvincing. A Second World War scenario is perhaps the most poignant target of such critiques, but the focus on hypothetical and future harm serves the point all the same. The problem with Big Data programs does not seem to be related directly to its impact on individuals and their interests, but rather to the fact as such that it enables companies, states or even individuals to obtain certain powers, have access to certain techniques, to possess certain types of data. The fourth branch of theories suggests not to focus on the 'patient', the individual being acted upon and potentially violated in her privacy, but on the 'agent', the one acting upon the individual and potentially violating her privacy. These types of theories are called agent-based theories. They focus on the behavior and the character of agents and evaluate them on the basis of either juridical or ethical principles. Theories that have been proposed focus, for example, on the existence of power, rather than its abuse (real or potential), on the possession of certain data, rather than the question of whether it can be linked to specific individuals, and on the access to certain techniques, instead of their actual use or application.

First, with regard to the abuse of power, it should be noted that there are certain doctrines in the legal realm that seek to prevent such abuse. For example, Article 18 ECHR specifies: 'The restrictions permitted under this Convention to the said rights and freedoms shall not be applied for any purpose other than those for which they have been prescribed.' This is a restriction on the abuse of power by states. Although the European Court of Human Rights has said that this doctrine can only be invoked by an individual claimant if she is curtailed in exercising in one or more of her individual rights, the Court accepts *in abstracto* claims in exceptional cases that revolve around the conduct of states as such, without any harm needing to be demonstrated. In a similar vein, it has been argued that not only the possession of power as such requires certain safeguards, but also the possession of certain types of data. In principle, legal instruments currently only provide protection to private, privacy-sensitive and personal data. The reason is that these types of data have a direct link to the individual and can be used to directly affect her. Sensitive data, regarding e.g. health and sexual or political preferences, are protected to a greater extent because they can be used in a way that has an even greater impact on the individual. However, in the current technological environment, the direct connection of data to the individual is becoming less evident. Increasingly, data have a circular life cycle, as has been explained in Section 2 of this chapter. They may begin as individual data, then be linked to other data so that they become sensitive data, then aggregated and anonymized in a group profile and finally, a specific individual may be linked again to the group profile. Consequently, the status of the data and the question of whether they can be linked at one specific moment to the individual is becoming less important. More important becomes the quality of the data as such, without it necessarily being linked to specific individuals. Thus it has been suggested that the sensitivity of the data or dataset itself should be the main determinant for data regulation. This has been discussed briefly in Section 2 of this Chapter and will be explored in further detail in Chapter V of this book.

Secondly, a similar argument has been made with regard to the technology. It has, for example, been argued that the capacity of a specific technology is most important, rather than how it is used in practice. Gray and Citron seem to hint at such an approach, when they argue that the core question should be

> whether an investigative technique or technology has the capacity to facilitate broad programs of indiscriminate surveillance that raise the specter of a surveillance state if deployment and use of that technology is left to the unfettered discretion of government. We think that the Fourth Amendment and the privacy issues at stake, as we have described them here, suggest taking a different tack. There are a number of ways that the Fourth Amendment status of a surveillance technique or technology could be determined. The most obvious would be for anyone who knows that he or she has been subject to surveillance by a novel technology, or dramatically improved existing technology, to file a civil suit seeking equitable relief or even damages. In such an action, a court would first need to determine whether the technology at issue should be subject to Fourth Amendment regulation. Among the important factors that a court would need to consider are: (1) the inherent scope of a technology's surveillance capabilities, be they narrow or broad; (2) the technology's scale and scalability; and (3) the costs associated with deploying and using the technology. If a court finds that a challenged technology is capable of broad and indiscriminate surveillance by its nature, or is sufficiently inexpensive and scalable so as to present no practical barrier against its broad and indiscriminate use, then granting law enforcement unfettered access to that technology would violate reasonable expectations of quantitative privacy.[318]

Following this line of thought, the main focus point for a regulatory approach could be access to the technique and the scope and reach of the technique or technical infrastructure.

Two theories have been put forward that try to give such privacy theories an ethical foundation, namely the republican theory and the virtue ethical theory. Both are agent-based theories that focus on the capacities or the character of the agent as such. Republicanism, in contrast to liberalism, views matters not as problematic if they affect a specific individual, but if an agent possesses power without there being sufficient checks and balances. Roberts, for example, notes that 'republicans are concerned about interference, but not interference per se. Concern is reserved for others' capacity to interfere in an agent's choices on an arbitrary basis. The individual who suffers such interference is at the mercy of the agent or agency that has power to interfere. But while such interference will always constitute domination – to a greater or lesser extent, depending on the nature of the interference – a person need not interfere with another's

---

[318] D. Gray & D. Citron, 'The Right to Quantitative Privacy', Minnesota Law Review, 2013, p. 101–102.

choices in order to exercise dominating control. If an agent or agency has the power to interfere arbitrarily in an individual's choices, freedom is diminished even if the power is never exercised'.[319] The core here is the idea that others should never have the capacity to interfere arbitrarily with another person's choices. This is wrong even without power being actually abused.[320]

Virtue theory also proposes to evaluate the ethical conduct of agents such as states, but it goes a step further. It not only stresses that states should not abuse their powers or have sufficient safeguards in place against abuse, it provides that states must use their powers in such a way that the lives of citizens are facilitated in their potential to grow on a personal, social or professional level. There is not only a negative obligation to abstain from harming individuals or a positive obligation to prevent harm, but also a positive obligation to help individuals to flourish to the optimal extent.[321] This will be explained in more detail in the next chapter.

5. ANALYSIS

As explained in the previous Chapter, the original privacy paradigm was only partially focused on the individual, her interests and the subjective rights of natural persons. The current privacy paradigm, however, is almost exclusively focused on protecting individual interests; it grants subjective rights to individuals and the outcome of cases is determined by balancing the individual with the societal interest at stake. This paradigm is wavering because Big Data processes do not revolve around individuals, but affect large groups and potentially society as a whole. It is increasingly difficult to link the effects of such processes back to individual interests, it is increasingly difficult for individuals to claim their subjective right in a world where data processing is so endemic, and the balancing of interests is difficult to maintain because both the individual and the societal interests at stake are increasingly difficult to capture.

Section 2 has argued that the core fundaments of the current legal paradigm are challenged by Big Data and mass surveillance activities. This holds true for the various substantive data protection provisions, the focus on the individual and the focus on legal regulation in the current privacy paradigm. Section 3 showed that the European Court of Human Rights, in exceptional cases mostly revolving around surveillance activities by states, is willing to relax its individualized approach to privacy. Finally, Section 4 discussed a number of scholars that have proposed alternatives to a privacy approach

---

[319] A. Roberts, 'A Republican Account of the Value of Privacy', European Journal of Political Theory, 2014, p. 6.

[320] See also: B. C. Newell, 'The Massive Metadata Machine: Liberty, Power, and Secret Mass Surveillance in the U.S. and Europe', /S: A Journal of law and policy, vol. 10:2, 2014. B. C. Newell, 'Technopolicing, Surveillance, and Citizen Oversight: A Neorepublican Theory of Liberty and Information Control', Government Information Quarterly, vol. 31 (3): 421–431, 2014.

[321] B. van der Sloot (2014C), 'Privacy as human flourishing: Could a shift towards virtue ethics strengthen privacy protection in the age of Big Data?', JIPITEC, 2014-3.

that is solely or primarily focused on individual interests and subjective rights. Each of these theories has appealing facets, but they also have specific downsides.

With theories focusing on the constitutionality of privacy towards societal institutions, the downsides are twofold. First, the value of privacy is primarily explained in relation to the value of societal institutions – the value of privacy itself is moved to the background. Second, these theories do not focus on privacy as such but rather on confidentiality. There is an obvious overlap between the two concepts, but privacy is far broader than merely a right to keep things secret. Theories focusing on group rights and societal interests have a number of practical problems in terms of granting rights: who should protect the interests at stake and invoke, for example, a group right to privacy? This is problematic because a group formed through group profiles is generally unstable; the group is mostly unaware of the very fact that it is a group, there is no hierarchy or leadership nor a legal representative of the group, and no way to determine what is in the interest of the group since interests may differ amongst its member. Theories focusing on hypothetical and potential future harm have the problem that they tend to become to hypothetical, unrealistic and far-fetched – particularly, the Second World War scenario faces this criticism. But also the chilling effect and future and hypothetical harm are in some sense forced attempts to stay within the liberal paradigm focusing on (individual) harm, while the strength of this approach is waning. Finally, with agent-based theories, the concept of privacy is moved to the background and is replaced by a focus on power and the safeguards against abuse and/or the obligation to use power in the best way. It thus runs the risk of no longer being a theory on privacy, but rather a theory on the rule of law.

Still, the latter type of theories may provide the most fruitful ground for future privacy regulation. Using agent-based theories, the focus is no longer on concrete individual interests, but on the general interest of being protected against the abuse of power and on the positive obligation of states to use their power in order to facilitate human flourishing. No balancing of interests takes place. Rather, an intrinsic assessment is applied to evaluate the behavior, power and actions of states, companies or even citizens, which requires checks and balances in place against abuse of power. An intrinsic assessment could address many of the current privacy and data protection issues, without having to link it to individual interests. Under an agent-based privacy paradigm, there is no need to attribute privacy claims to natural persons. Rather, it facilitates claims in the general interest (class actions) and *in abstracto* claims. This model has the further advantage that it lends itself to non-juridical forms of regulation, such as codes of conduct. This will be explained in further detail in the next chapter.

CHAPTER IV
DEVELOPING AN ALTERNATIVE PRIVACY PARADIGM THROUGH VIRTUE ETHICS

1. INTRODUCTION

Chapter II showed that both the privacy and the data protection paradigm have transformed of the years. These doctrines are (1) increasingly seen as subjective rights of natural persons instead of duties (of care) for states and data controllers, (2) increasingly focused on individual instead of general interests, (3) increasingly balanced by courts against other interests instead of a necessity test being applied and (4) increasingly codified (in detail) and enforced through legal means. Chapter III showed that these four characteristics are put under pressure by developments known as Big Data and mass surveillance. In particular, it argued that most of the material provisions in the Data Protection Directive and the General Data Protection Regulation are undermined and that the almost exclusive focus on the individual (rights, interests and balancing) and legal regulation are difficult to maintain.

Chapter III also showed that in jurisprudence, in the law and in the literature, there is an increasing awareness of these tensions. The European Court of Human Rights has been willing to let go of its individualized interpretation of privacy in exceptional cases, the General Data Protection Regulation has introduced the concept of Data Protection Impact Assessments in the realm of data protection, and in the literature scholars have suggested a focus on group privacy, relational privacy and collective interests. The chapter concluded by suggesting that it might be worthwhile to take a closer look at agent-based theories. Those theories focus on the agent of an action, instead of the patient of an action (the one being acted upon). One such theory is virtue ethics. This chapter will discuss what virtue ethics entails and how it could be implemented in the legal realm. The next chapter will suggest what such an approach to privacy regulation might look like and how it could be implemented in practice.

This chapter endeavors to do two things. First, Section 2 will discuss the notion of virtue ethics. Second, Section 2 will analyze some of the most prominent arguments against adopting a virtue ethical approach to (privacy) regulation. It will consist of 3 subsections. First, it will provide the general contours of virtue ethics. Second, it will discuss in some further detail what a virtue ethical approach to the legal regime in general might entail. It will do so by analyzing the work of Lon L. Fuller. Third and finally, it will briefly point out how such an approach might help to overcome the difficulties involved in applying the current privacy paradigm to Big Data and mass surveillance practices. Section 3 will analyze a number of arguments against adopting a virtue ethical approach to (privacy) regulation.

2. VIRTUE ETHICS AND LEGAL REGULATION

This section will discuss three matters. First, Subsection 2.1 will provide the general contours of virtue ethics. Second, Subsection 2.2 will discuss in some further detail what a virtue ethical approach to the legal regime in general might entail; it will do so by analyzing the work of Lon L. Fuller. Third and finally, Subsection 2.3 will briefly point out how such an approach might help to overcome the difficulties involved with applying the current privacy paradigm to Big Data and mass surveillance practices.

2.1. VIRTUE ETHICS

Three ethical theories are generally distinguished in scholarly literature, namely consequentialism, deontology and virtue ethics. The first has its roots in English utilitarian philosophers such as Bentham and Mill. The second takes as key reference Kantian thought and the idea of a categorical imperative. The third is both older and younger than the other two. It goes back to the work of Plato and especially Aristotle's *Ethica Nicomachea*, which significantly influenced, among others, stoicism, medieval Christian thought and even the early Enlightenment philosophy. However, roughly since the Enlightenment, virtue ethics lost its prominence and played only a minor role in philosophical discourse. It was only in the second half of the 20th century that virtue ethics was rediscovered and revived, most notably through the works of Anscombe[322] and MacIntyre.[323] These contributions inspired a number of books and articles defending virtue ethics as a viable alternative to deontology and consequentialism in the nineties and first decennium of the 21st century.

Consequentialism focuses on the consequences of actions, although a distinction is sometimes made between actual consequences, foreseen consequences and intended consequences. As such, consequentialism does not specify the ultimate good; however, most theories take as principle determinant the greatest happiness of the greatest number of people. In its most basic form, consequentialism holds that actions are good if the consequences are good, or if the benefits outweigh the costs. In contrast, actions are said to be bad if the consequences are bad, or if the costs outweigh the benefits. A distinction is often made between act consequentialism and rule consequentialism. According to the former, an act is good if and only if that act maximizes the good, while the latter holds that such an assessment must be made on the basis of a generalized rule

---

[322] E. Ascombe, 'Modern Moral Philosophy', *Philosophy*, 33, 1958.
[323] A. MacIntyre, 'After virtue: a study in moral theory', London, Duckworth, 1981.

of that act. For example, although theft might, in a particular situation, be morally good (i.e. the benefits outweigh the costs), it would have a mostly negative effect on human happiness if everyone, as a rule, would steal.

Deontology, deriving from duty (*deon*), prescribes what we ought to do, while *aretaic* (virtue) theories focus principally on how a good person should be, among others in terms of states of character. In contrast to consequentialism, deontology does not focus on the states of affairs choices and actions bring about, but on the question of whether those choices and actions accord to the duties of every person. Thus, the positive consequences of an act cannot lead (automatically) to the conclusion that it is morally good. Conversely, the negative consequences of an action cannot lead (automatically) to the conclusion that an agent should not perform it. Even if torturing a terrorist suspected of placing a time bomb could prevent thousands of fatal casualties, it would, in any case, be a wrongful act, as torturing a human being is wrong, period. Like consequentialism, deontology as such does not specify which actions are right and which actions are wrong, but mostly they derive from basic moral principles such as: do not lie, do not steal, do not kill, etc.

Virtue ethics places emphasis on the virtuous character of an agent, instead of the consequences of actions or the accordance of actions to pre-established moral norms. Still, it must be stressed that the outcome of applying the three different branches of ethics may actually be the same, even though their approaches might differ. A utilitarian, for example, could claim that being nice to your children is good because those children tend to flourish to a greater extent, which is to the benefit of society as a whole. A deontologist might simply stress that it is the duty of every parent to treat children with extra care. A virtue ethicists might say that virtuous parents should be nice to their children, because that is a benevolent thing to do, or perhaps even more precise, that parents should be nice to their children, because that is what a virtuous parent would do. Among the core concepts of virtue ethics are 'virtue', 'practical wisdom' (*phronesis*) and 'human flourishing' (*eudaimonia*).

A virtue is not merely a temporal or accidental habit or tendency to perform a certain act (or abstain from it). It is a more structural disposition – a character trait. Aristotle, for example, poses the question whether virtue is a passion, a faculty or a state of character. It is not a passion, such as anger, fear or joy, he argues, because 'we become angry or afraid without rational choice, while the virtues are rational choices or at any rate involve rational choice'.[324] Neither is it a faculty, he says, for 'we are neither called good or bad, nor are we praised or blamed, through being capable of experiencing things, without qualification. Again, while we have this capacity by nature, we do not become good or bad by nature (…).'[325] Thus, Aristotle concludes, it must be a state of character. It is important to note that although virtue ethics does not exclude moral judgments on the level of acts, these are not its principle focus. What makes a person good or bad is not based on the evaluation of one act, it is based on the character and

---

[324] Aristotle, 'Nicomachean Ethics', Cambridge University Press, Cambridge, 2000, 1106a.
[325] Aristotle, 'Nicomachean Ethics', Cambridge University Press, Cambridge, 2000, 1106a.

inclinations of a person to do good as a rule. More importantly however, the classic line of reasoning is not: 'If act Y is considered good and X performs that act, X is good'. Rather, it argues the other way around: 'If X is a good person and performs Y, then Y must be a good act'. Often, a hypothetical situation is invoked and the question is posed: 'what would a perfect human, shoemaker, doctor or lawyer do in such a case?' To effectuate such a thought experiment, Aristotle has for example introduced the *megalopsychos* or the 'god-among-man'.[326] Other virtue ethical theories have often worked with similar constructions, for example by discussing the lives and works of heroes. These theories describe the ideal – it is for mortals to strive towards that ideal.

As with the other two ethical theories, there is no exhaustive list of what *the* virtues are. Aristotle specifies, among others, courage, temperance, generosity and intellectual virtue. More in general, a difference can be made between philosophers that emphasize virtues that are directed at self-centered interests, such as power, health and strength. Machiavelli and Nietzsche are among the most well-known proponents of this branch of virtue ethics. There is also a branch, particularly defended by Christian philosophers, such as Thomas Aquinas, who emphasize the virtues of self-denial and self-sacrifice in the common interest. Hume mockingly called the latter 'monkish virtue':

> Celibacy, fasting, penance, mortification, self-denial, humility, silence, solitude, and the whole train of monkish virtues; for what reason are they everywhere rejected by men of sense, but because they serve to no manner of purpose; neither advance a man's fortune in the world, nor render him a more valuable member of society; neither qualify him for the entertainment of company, nor increase his power of self-enjoyment? We observe, on the contrary, that they cross all these desirable ends; stupify the understanding and harden the heart, obscure the fancy and sour the temper. We justly, therefore, transfer them to the opposite column, and place them in the catalogue of vices…[327]

Theories also differ as to the question whether virtues can conflict with each other, whether there is an objective test to determine the outcome of such potential conflicts and whether there is really one 'master virtue' among the different virtues, which must be taken as the guiding principle in such decision-making processes. Another open question is whether it is possible to be a fully virtuous person. Although most virtue ethicists (particularly the pre-modern philosophers) describe a 'heroic figure' who is fully in accordance with every virtue, mostly she is seen as a fictional character and it is held that only a divine being could be fully virtuous. As a final example, discussion exists about how to determine a particular virtue, such as, for example, courage. One of the common methods used is the Aristotelian mean – Aristotle holds that every virtue must be described as the mean between two vices. For example, courage is the mean between cowardice and recklessness. This is also known as the doctrine of the golden mean.

---

[326] Aristotle, 'The politics and The Constitution of Athens', Cambridge University Press, Cambridge, 2007, 3.1284a. H. J. Curzer, 'Aristotle's much maligned megalopsychos', Australasian Journal of Philosophy, 69:2, 1911, 131–151.

[327] D. Hume, 'An Enquiry Concerning the Principles of Morals', Clarendon Press, Oxford, 2010, §9, ¶3.

Another important aspect of virtue ethics is 'practical wisdom'. Virtue ethics hails (theoretical) wisdom as an important aspect of a virtuous life: not only knowing what things are, but also what, as a general principle, one should do or not do. However, such general principles only have limited value, according to virtue ethics. They need to be applied in concrete situations. For example, Thomas Aquinas, answered the question 'whether prudence takes cognizance of singulars' as follows:

> [T]o prudence belongs not only the consideration of the reason, but also the application to action, which is the end of the practical reason. But no man can conveniently apply one thing to another, unless he knows both the thing to be applied, and the thing to which it has to be applied. Now actions are in singular matters: and so it is necessary for the prudent man to know both the universal principles of reason, and the singulars about which actions are concerned.[328]

With this principle, virtue ethics diverges from classical deontology and consequentialism. Practical wisdom is largely dependent on experience; thus, even children may possess a virtuous disposition of some kind, but they lack any experience as to how to act in different situations and apply their virtuous dispositions in real life situations.

The practical wise know above all what makes their actions worthwhile and morally good: they have a true grasp of human flourishing, the key concept of virtue ethics. What this concept entails and how it should be determined who flourishes and to what extent, is, however, relatively vague and subject to extensive discussion. It is quite clear that it is not equal to personal happiness. Aristotle already distinguished between three types of live: the political life, the contemplative life and the life of pleasure. He denounces the life that most men and those of 'vulgar type' lead by seeking the good in pleasure and enjoyment.[329] Not only is the problem with a focus on personal happiness that it leads to a form of hedonism – more importantly, happiness is a subjective concept, which only the individual herself can determine. Mostly, however, human flourishing is said to have an objective quality as well, which can be determined not only by the subject itself.

But how to determine objectively which life is worth living? One part of virtue ethics embraces a form of naturalism, which, going against the Humean is-ought fallacy, derives an 'ought' from an 'is', from the nature of a being or a thing. For example, a duck that cannot fly and has a fear of water, we would normally call a bad or defective specimen of the species because we know that ducks normally tend to fly and swim. The same holds for a tree that does not grow and has no leaves or roots. We know from nature what it is for a tree to flourish and for a duck to prosper; similarly, according to the naturalistic presumption, we could distil from the nature of the human being how people ought to be. Many virtue ethicists apply a form of teleological thinking to 'lower

---

[328] T. Aquinas, 'The "Summa theologica" of St. Thomas Aquinas', Burns Oates and Washbourne, London, ca.1914–42, part II-II, Q 47 art. 3.
[329] Aristotle, 'Nicomachean Ethics', Cambridge University Press, Cambridge, 2000, 1095b.

life forms'. The end (*telos*) of a creature is that which it strives towards by nature; for example, the *telos* of a tree is to have a solid trunk, roots deep in the earth and many leaves to catch the sunlight.

The problems with such an assertion are multiple.[330] For one, there seems no clear and uniform answer to the question of how, as a fact, humans live, as the answer to this question differs over time, over culture and possibly, gender. What is natural and what is cultural in this respect is often hard to determine. Secondly, according to the doctrine of virtue ethics, there is a tripartite (or sometimes a dual) distinction in the different faculties possessed by humans. While plants are capable of living (eating, drinking, growing, reproduction, etc.) and animals are capable of living and having emotions (fear, joy, anger, etc.), humans have a capacity for living, emotions, and intellect. Thus, in order to flourish, humans must develop their intellect to the highest extent. But our intellectual capacity also allows us to reflect upon what it is for us to flourish, what goals we want to pursue, what makes life worth living for us. It follows that the interpretation of human flourishing becomes dependent upon each individual's personal reflections and thus remains highly subjective.

Connected to this issue is the question whether living a life in accordance with virtues is necessary and/or sufficient for human flourishing. For example, while Aristotle and Seneca agreed on the fact that the possession of a virtuous character is necessary for us to flourish, they disagree on the question as to whether possessing a virtuous character could ever be sufficient for a happy and rewarding life:

> Aristotle argues that human flourishing is ideally the flourishing of our whole natures – rational, emotional, social, and purely physical – so he concluded that a certain amount of luck in the material and social circumstances of life is also necessary for happiness. Seneca and other stoics disagreed, arguing that a conception of *human* flourishing should focus more narrowly on dispositions uniquely distinctive of human beings. While we may welcome gifts of fortune that permit the satisfaction of desires or impulses that we share with lower animals, such as the desire for physical pleasure, these are by no means necessary for human flourishing.[331]

One of the answers to this problem is that human flourishing has both an objective (universal) quality and a subjective (individual) quality:

> The happiness of a human being is not (…) a state of sensory pleasure, although such pleasures are also necessary for a successful human life, since man is not only a rational being but an animal with the biological capacity and need for sensory experiences as well. Instead the happiness or successful life of a person must involve considerations that depend upon his conceptual capacities. Man must be a success as a rational animal. He must live in such a way that he achieves goals that are rational for him individually but also as a human being. The former will vary depending on who he is. The latter are uniform and pertain to

---

[330] See more elaborate on this topic: M. C. Nussbaum, 'Human Functioning and Social Justice: In Defense of Aristotelian Essentialism', Political Theory, Vol. 20, No. 2, 1992.
[331] J. Welchman, 'The Practice of Virtue: Classic and Contemporary Readings in Virtue Ethics', Hackett Pub, Indianapolis, 2006, p. xx.

what he is; to his humanity – his goal as human being must be to do best what is his unique capacity: live rational.[332]

Another argument may be that, in Aristotelian fashion, man is qualified as a political animal, an animal that lives and thrives in social structures, in groups. Thus we could qualify a person that undermines the social cement of the group or that uses the group for purely selfish reasons as a morally wicked person, which may be compared to a free rider:

> And it will surely not be denied that there is something wrong with a free-riding wolf that feeds but does not take part in the hunt, as with a member of the species of dancing bees who finds a source of nectar but whose behavior does not let other bees know of its location. These free-riding individuals of a species whose members work together are just as *defective* as those who have defective hearing, sight, or powers of locomotion.[333]

Consequently, benevolence, altruism and charity would qualify as core virtues.

In the 18th century, partially as a reaction to this problem, a new 'sentimentalist' movement arose, with as main proponents Hutcheson and Hume.

> Instead of asking which characteristics any member of the human species ought to have to be a good example of humanity, they ask what dispositions do we in general find *preferable* based on our subjective experience of how different dispositions do, or do not, contribute to a happy and flourishing life.[334]

However, Hume and Hutcheson, differed as to what dispositions we generally find agreeable. For Hutcheson, the general sentiment we as humans have is a special feeling and approval for dispositions such as benevolence, which are directed at caring for others and their welfare.[335] Dispositions aimed at personal welfare are only of value if and to the extent that they are instrumental to altruistic virtues. Hume, by contrast, argues that we also value egocentric virtues valuable for their own sake, whether they promote their possessors' or others' welfare or not.[336]

To conclude, the sentimentalist view serves as the foundation for the theories of some modern virtue ethicists, such as Michael Slote, who tries to develop a neo-Aristotelian virtue ethics based on sentimentalism and bases his theory predominantly on the motives of the agent. It should be noted that both consequentialist and deontic theories exist that focus on the intention of the agent, i.e. whether the agent intended

---

[332] T. R. Machan, 'Human Rights and Human Liberties', Nelson-Hall, Chicago, 1975, p. 74–75.
[333] P. Foot, 'Natural goodness', Clarendon Press, Oxford, 2001, p. 16.
[334] J. Welchman, 'The Practice of Virtue: Classic and Contemporary Readings in Virtue Ethics', Hackett Pub, Indianapolis, 2006, p. xxi.
[335] F. Hutcheson, 'An inquiry into the original of our ideas of beauty and virtue: in two treatises. I. Concerning beauty, order, harmony, design. II. Concerning moral good and evil.', Glasgow, printed by Robert and Andrew Foulis, 1772.
[336] See further: D. Hume, 'A treatise on human nature: being an attempt to introduce the experimental method of reasoning into moral subjects, and Dialogues concerning natural religion', Longmans Green, London, 1878.

to procedure positive consequences or intended to accord her behavior to universal duties. Still, virtue ethics seems to provide a more obvious candidate, as focusing on the character of a person takes account of both the agent's actions and her intentions, the consequences and the motives. It has to be stressed that although virtue ethics focuses on the character of the person, the intentions and motives of a person are certainly not the only thing that is taken into account. Consequences and actions are just as important. If a person attempts, for example, to help her handicapped neighbor by mowing the lawn and, though genuine and thoughtful in her efforts, fails and ruins the lawn, a virtue ethical theory would not judge that agent culpable (in contrast to a basic consequentialist theory). However, if she does not learn from her mistakes and ruins the lawn a second time, she may be culpable, because 'in an important sense agent-based moralities *do* take consequences in account because they insist on or recommend an overall state of motivation that worries about and tries to produce good consequences.'[337]

Consequently, in such an interpretation of virtue ethics, the agent needs to improve herself if she is genuinely concerned with producing good results; it may even be so that a particular clumsy person or a person particularly bad at a certain task (e.g. mowing the lawn) needs to abstain from acting, even though her intentions are good. Likewise, a person should obtain sufficient information to be able to make a careful and reasoned judgment. If an agent acts without making a reasonable effort to gather relevant facts, she is not acting as a virtuous agent would act. This is obviously linked to the notion of practical wisdom. Finally, although most virtue theories refer primarily to individuals, they are also applicable to states, or in any case, to parliamentarians and those working at the executive branch. Slote, for example, refers to the introduction of the then recent 'Three Strikes, You're Out' policy in the USA and asks:

> But what about the motives of those who pass(ed) such legislation? Are they really trying to do the most good they can for society or the country or are they not, rather, pandering politically to the prejudices, fears and resentments of their own constituents (or subject to such irrational attitudes themselves)? It is not entirely implausible to suppose that those who are clamoring for or instituting such laws are motivated by desires and attitudes that are a far cry from anything like concern for the good of the country. Of course, legislators may, to relieve cognitive dissonance, convince themselves that such legislation is good for the country, but if this is self-deception and they really know better, then they are not really, or at the deepest level, concerned with that they tell themselves is their public-spirited objective.[338]

2.2. VIRTUE ETHICAL APPROACH TO THE LEGAL REALM

The best-known philosopher who has applied a virtue ethical thought to the legal regime is Lon L. Fuller. Although he never advertised himself as such, he was clearly inspired by virtue ethical and especially Aristotelian though. This is apparent from his

---

[337] M. Slote, 'Morals from Motives', Oxford University Press, New York, 2001, p. 34.
[338] M. Slote, 'Morals from Motives', Oxford University Press, New York, 2001, p. 104.

teleological approach to states, in addition to living creatures as virtue ethicists have commonly done. He also applied a form of professional ethics, which is rooted in virtue ethics, to the state and its employees. To provide a final example, Fuller believed that states not only have the obligation to abstain from curtailing the individual autonomy of its citizens, but also a positive obligation to promote their flourishing to the maximum. These are but a few examples from which it may become clear that Fuller endeavored to apply a virtue ethical way of thinking to the state and the legal order. Those and other examples will be further discussed below. This subsection will introduce some of his main ideas and theories. Obviously, this book does not attempt to adopt a 'Fullerian' approach to privacy regulation as such; there have been many critical reflections published about his work and some flaws in his thinking are irreparable. Still, his philosophy might provide useful building blocks for developing a novel approach to privacy regulation, which will be the focus of next chapter.

Fuller is most remembered for his debate with H.L.A. Hart about the possibility of separating law and morality. Although for decades the general sentiment was that Hart 'won' the debate, in recent years there has been renewed interest in the work of Fuller and attention for the arguments he made.[339] Though on many accounts, Fuller remains Hart's inferior in analytical clarity and philosophical rigor, the general outline of his legal philosophy and his skeptical view on legal positivism have gained many followers and have remained a great source of inspiration for modern legal philosophers.[340] It is not necessary to discuss in depth Hart's position as a legal positivist, as its general assumptions are well known. Hart, building on the utilitarian doctrine of Bentham and Austin, suggested that laws and morals are separable. It is important to note that Hart did not suggest that legal orders and morality, as a matter of fact, are detached or that they should be separated.[341] Hart's position could be best described as a separability thesis, which is the claim 'that there exists at least one conceivable rule of recognition (and therefore on possible legal system) that does not specify truth as a moral principle among the truth conditions for any proposition of law.'[342] The thesis that law and morals are separable, at least in theory, is mainly targeted at defenders of the natural law doctrine, who suppose that there is a pre-legal morality, either installed by nature

---

[339] W. J. Witteveen & W. Van der Burg, 'Rediscovering Fuller: Essays on Implicit law and institutional design', Amsterdam University Press, Amsterdam, 1999. P. Cane (ed.), 'The Hart-Fuller debate in the twenty-first century', Hart, Oxford, 2010. K. Rundle, 'Forms liberate: Reclaiming the jurisprudence of Lon L fuller', Hart Publishing, Oxford, 2012. R. S. Summers, 'Lon L. Fuller', Edward Arnold, London, 1984.

[340] See among others: D. Luban, 'The rule of law and human dignity: reexamining Fuller's canons', 2 Hague Journal of the Rule of Law 29, 2010. D. Dyzenhaus, 'The Morality of Legality', <www.law.berkeley.edu/files/The_Morality_of_Legality_DDyzenhaus.pdf>. J. Waldron, 'How Law Protects Dignity', <www.pem.cam.ac.uk/wp-content/uploads/2012/07/1A-Waldron-article.pdf>. S. J. Shapiro, 'Legality', Harvard University Press, Cambridge, 2011. J. Brunnée & S. J. Toope, 'Legitimacy and legality in international law: an interactional account', Cambridge University Press, Cambridge, 2010.

[341] H. L. A. Hart, 'Positivism and the Separation of Law and Morals', Harvard Law Review, Vol. 71, No. 4, 1958, p. 601.

[342] J. L. Coleman, 'Negative and Positive Positivism', the Journal of Legal Studies, Vol. 11, No. 1, 1982, p. 141.

or by God, to which the (positive) legal order must commit itself.[343] Law, under this doctrine, can only be called law if it accords to the pre-legal moral principles. Hart fervently opposed this view.

Fuller, against Hart, argued that there are minimum qualities which laws must abide by. However, these are not pre-legal moral norms, such as natural rights, but what he called standards of the 'inner morality' of law.[344] These were in fact elements of the state of law (*rechtsstaat*), such as the requirement that laws must be clear, general, non-contradictory and non-retroactive.[345] Fuller argued that legal orders must not be approached merely as factual objects, which might be studied as phenomena, such as Hart proposed. Rather, they should be viewed as purposive enterprises (teleological approach). Legal orders are made by men for a purpose, namely first to ensure order and second to achieve certain general, common goals. As an end in itself and as an instrument to reach these societal goals, legal orders must abide by the minimum standards of the rule of law, Fuller believed. Respect for the 'inner morality' of law, among others, ensures that citizens are able to take into account the norms the laws provide. If this 'inner morality' is violated, neither can the legal order bring order nor can the societal goals be adequately promoted.[346]

One of the matters at the center of the Hart-Fuller debate was the case of the grudge informer. This case builds on a famous example used by Gustav Radbruch,[347] which regarded a German woman who, during the Nazi period, had notified the local authorities about the anti-Nazi remarks her husband had made to her when returned home from the battlefront, who was then sentenced by a Nazi court.[348] After the war, the woman was charged with the illegal deprivation of her husband's liberty, while she argued that she had been obliged to act the way she did under Nazi laws. However, the post-war court rejected her claim and held that the statue on which she based the legitimacy of her actions 'was contrary to the sound conscience and sense of justice of all decent human beings.'[349]

Hart, to the contrary, believed that a law might be a law, even though it is a bad or immoral law. He did not so much oppose the punishment of the woman for her actions, but thought that it should not be a matter of judiciary discretion, resorting to personal moral sentiments, to decide on the quality of laws, and argued that such a conviction

---

[343] See also: L. Green, 'Positivism and the inseparability of law and morals', New York University Law Review, vol. 83, 1000, 2008.

[344] Hart's opposition to this suggestion, namely that these principle are not moral principles but principles of efficient legal orders, seems legitimate, but this is not essential for this chapter.

[345] L. L. Fuller, 'The Morality of Law', Yale University Press, London, 1969.

[346] See further: L. L. Fuller, 'Means and Ends'. In: L. L. Fuller, 'The Principles of Social Order', Duke University Press, Durham, 1981.

[347] G. Radbruch, 'Statutory Lawlessness and *Supra*-Statutory Law (1946)', Oxford Journal of Legal Studies, Vol. 26, No. 1, 2006.

[348] See on this topic amongst others: T. Mertens, 'Radbruch and Hart on the Grudge Informer: A Reconsideration',15 Ratio Juris 186, 186, 2002. D. Dyzenhaus, 'The grudge informer case revisited', New York University Law Review, vol. 83, 1000, 2008.

[349] H. L. A. Hart, 'Positivism and the Separation of Law and Morals', Harvard Law Review, Vol. 71, No. 4, 1958, p. 619.

should have been based on a law. Although a retroactive law to this course was clearly an evil, as retroactive punishment lacks basic legitimacy, it could be called the lesser of two evils.

> Odious as retrospective criminal legislation and punishment may be, to have pursued it openly in this case would at least have had the merits of candor. It would have made plain that in punishing the woman a choice had to be made between two evils, that of leaving her unpunished and that of sacrificing a very precious principle of morality endorsed by most legal systems.[350]

Fuller, although agreeing with Hart that the best solution might have been to enact a retroactive law, argued that in truth, it was dubious whether the Nazi laws on which the woman based the legitimacy of her actions, could properly be called laws and could be considered binding. He referred to the existence of secret laws, which were oftentimes not published and vague in formulation.[351] According to Fuller, the fact that the laws violated the principles that he had coined the 'inner morality' of the law, meant that they could not be called laws or only partially so.

Building on this suggestion, Fuller spelled out eight routes for failure for a fictional ruler, named Rex:

> The first and most obvious lies in a failure to achieve rules at all, so that every issue must be decided on an ad hoc basis. The other routes are: (2) a failure to publicize, or at least to make available to the affected party, the rules he is expected to observe; (3) the abuse of retroactive legislation, which not only cannot itself guide action, but undercuts the integrity of rules prospective in effect, since it puts them under the threat of retrospective change; (4) a failure to make rules understandable; (5) the enactment of contradictory rules or (6) rules that require conduct beyond the powers of the affected party; (7) introducing such frequent changes in the rules that the subject cannot orient his action by them; and, finally, (8) a failure of congruence between the rules as announced and their actual administration.[352]

From these routes for failure, eight positive principles might be derived which form part of what Fuller saw as law's 'inner morality'. Abiding by these principles is a duty for the legislator and the ruler, not a right of the citizen.

Fuller relates this to the principle of reciprocity, namely between citizen and state. Citizens are generally held to obey and respect the rules and, at least most of the time

---

[350] H. L. A. Hart, 'Positivism and the Separation of Law and Morals', Harvard Law Review, Vol. 71, No. 4, 1958, p. 619.

[351] Fuller also thought the law in the case of the grudge informer had been incorrectly applied on the private domain by the nazi-court. 'This question becomes acute when we note that the act applies only to public acts or utterances, whereas the husband's remarks were in the privacy of his own home. Now it appears that the Nazi courts (and it should be noted we are dealing with a special military court) quite generally disregarded this limitation and extended the act to all utterances, private or public." Is Professor Hart prepared to say that the legal meaning of this statute is to be determined in the light of this apparently uniform principle of judicial interpretation?' L. L. Fuller, 'Positivism and Fidelity to Law: A Reply to Professor Hart', 71 Harvard Law Review 630, 1958, p. 654.

[352] L. L. Fuller, 'The Morality of Law', Yale University Press, London, 1969, p. 39.

and with regard to most of the rules, follow them. States, in turn, must respect the basic dignity and autonomy of the citizens. The eight routes for failure and the rules following therefrom may all be seen as guarantees for respecting the autonomous citizen. If citizens do not know the rules, are unable to adept their behavior to them or do not understand the rules, they cannot follow them. If they are then prosecuted or punished for violating the rules, the state is not only showing disrespect for the citizen and her dignity, but is also ignoring the basic human capacity to choose and to be responsible and accountable for her actions.

> Every departure from the principles of the law's inner morality is an affront to man's dignity as a responsible agent. To judge his actions by unpublished or retrospective laws, or to order him to do an act that is impossible, is to convey to him your indifference to his powers of self-determination. Conversely, when the view is accepted that man is incapable of responsible action, legal morality loses its reason for being.[353]

Fuller suggests that if the state structurally ignores these eight principles and the related principle of *mens rea*, it is not showing proper respect for its citizens and is thus not fulfilling its side of the reciprocal relationship; in turn, the citizens are not, or only to a limited extent, held to obey the laws.[354]

It is good to note at this point that Fuller distinguished between two kinds of morality, namely the morality of duty and that of aspiration. He explained the morality of aspiration as the striving for the Good Life and for excellence, in whatever form it might be thought best described. This morality is aimed at the ideal, the maximum achievable. The morality of duty, in contrast, starts at the bottom, at the minimum rules which need to be respected and without which ordered societies cannot exist. In terms of language, he compared it to the difference between the rules of aesthetics and that of grammar; in economic terms, it relates to the difference between the rules of marginal utility, regarding the most efficient use of scarce resources, and the rules of the economy of exchange, facilitating the exchange of goods as such.

> In default of some highest moral or economic good, we resort ultimately, both in the morality of aspiration and in marginal utility economics, to the notion of balance – not too much, not too little. (…) It is a characteristic of normal human beings that they pursue a plurality of ends; an obsessive concern for some single end can in fact be taken as a symptom of mental disease.[355]

The morality of aspiration should be conceived as an ideal which can never be attained to the fullest. Likewise, there are always a multitude of different aspirations working at the same time; the attempt should be here to find the right balance between those different ideals, as the pursuit of one may block or hinder the pursuit of the others.

---

[353] L. L. Fuller, 'The Morality of Law', Yale University Press, London, 1969, p. 162–163.
[354] L. L. Fuller, 'The Morality of Law', Yale University Press, London, 1969, p. 39.
[355] L. L. Fuller, 'The Morality of Law', Yale University Press, London, 1969, p. 18.

The morality of duty, to which the minimum standards of legal orders are related, is not something which aims at high standards, but ensures the preconditions of legal orders, or in economic terms, rules of exchange. Both the morality of duty and the rules of exchange are characterized by the relationship of reciprocity; to provide for social, legal or economic interactions, there must be minimal procedural standards to facilitate the interaction and both interacting partners must show a minimum of basic respect for each other. Fuller believes that the morality of duty and the minimum standards it provides can be derived in large part from that simple saying, the golden rule: Do not do to others what you do not want others to do to you.

Although the respect of the rulers and lawgivers for the basic dignity and autonomy of the citizens is part of the morality of duty, the eight principles of legality are in themselves best characterized as matters of aspiration. Only in a utopia can all eight elements be respected to a maximum; as the example provided by Radbruch shows, some situations may necessitate deviation from those principles and moreover, in a number of cases the different principles may conflict with each other. As it is, according to Fuller, with the morality of aspiration in general, a balance should be found between the different aspirations. He refers anecdotally to the efforts of Communist Poland to make the laws so clear that they would be intelligible even to the workers and the peasants. It appeared, however, that this clarity could only be achieved at the cost of legal consistency and the overall coherence of the system. Similarly, although legal orders and laws must be relatively stable over time, rules cannot and should not be written in stone.

Laws and legal orders should thus strive or aspire to abide by all the principles of legality. What is 'internal' about these principles is that Fuller believes that they are intrinsically connected to the essence of laws. We may, to use an example, compare legal orders to a chair, which is also man made, and the art of law making to the craft of carpentry.[356] A legal order must respect the 'inner morality' of laws, as just provided, in order to be called a legal order proper, like a chair must have legs and a seating to be called a chair. If a chair has one uneven leg, we might call it dysfunctional, if it lacks one leg altogether we might call it defect or broken and if it has no legs whatsoever, we might call it a cushion instead of a chair. So too, it is for a legal order. It exists in gradations; if it respects all principles of the 'inner morality' of law to an absolute extent, it is a utopia. If, however, it respects none of those elements, it cannot be called a legal order.

Finally, it should be noted that the principles of 'inner morality' are in themselves neutral to the societal goals which legal orders aim at.[357] Thus, in principle, a Nazi-like regime could aim at morally corrupted goals and at the same time respect the principles of legality. Still, Fuller believed that there is a close affinity between legality and justice and he believed that in fact, morally corrupted regimes are inclined to ignore the rules of legality.[358] Even the most corrupted regimes, in his opinion, are afraid to explicitly and openly acknowledge the horrors they (want to) commit. Often, the worst atrocities

---

[356] L. L. Fuller, 'The Morality of Law', Yale University Press, London, 1969, p. 96.
[357] L. L. Fuller, 'The Morality of Law', Yale University Press, London, 1969, p. 152.
[358] L. L. Fuller, 'Positivism and Fidelity to Law: A Reply to Professor Hart', 71 Harvard Law Review 630, 1958, p. 631.

are based on *ad hoc* decisions, without any explicit legal basis and without those decisions being communicated openly to the public.[359]

It is thus clear that respecting the principles of 'inner morality' of the law is the duty of the state and is not formulated as a right of the individual. There is a duty for a minimum level of respect, on the one hand, and an obligation to aspire to a maximum level of respect, on the other hand. It is important to consider what values are at stake with respecting the principles of legality. These principles should be respected, according to Fuller, for two reasons, which relate to the two functions of legal orders; namely, as a goal in itself, to provide order; and as an instrument to reach societal goals. IT also relates to to the distinction between the morality of duty and the morality of aspiration. As an end in itself, legal orders must respect the basic principles of legality to ensure and facilitate the principle of reciprocity and basic legitimacy of the state. As an instrument, legal orders must respect them as a matter of efficiency and effectiveness. Without abiding by the 'inner morality' of laws, legal orders will not be effective, Fuller believed.

To start with the later point, Fuller, at a number of occasions, provided the example of an extreme brute, though rational, tyrant who is only concerned with his own interest. Even to achieve only his own private interests, Fuller suggested, the tyrant will understand that he needs to abide by the principles of legality. First, Fuller argued, this tyrant will understand that he has to limit his own freedom to a certain extent. He cannot do whatever he feels like, at any time, if he wants to be successful in steering and influencing the population according to his desires. He will comprehend that there must be some consistency in his behavior and the demands he poses on the people for them to understand his demands and take them into account when planning certain actions. Thus, the tyrant will acknowledge that he cannot decide on *ad hoc* basis, but must limit his freedom to ensure a basic sense of consistency and clarity.

'With this consideration in mind, our intelligent tyrant now proceeds to plan how to employ his subjects as tools for the realization of his purposes. A little reflection will remind him that he cannot effectively use another human being as a tool without according to him some power of choice, some opportunity to use his own discretion. When I hire the neighbor's boy to mow my lawn I do not begin by imposing on him a long and abstruse definition of what I mean by "lawn"; I assume he will have the good sense not to push the mower into my tulip bed just because he sees a few blades of grass growing up among the tulips. Simply from the standpoint of engineering efficiency in achieving a goal, some discretion and choice must, then, be accorded the human agent. This conclusion is reinforced when we recall that a favored and often successful mode of revolt is to carry out instructions with a wooden literalness; many a domineering parent has had his inclinations toward tyranny curbed by the retort, "But I did just what you told me to do!"'[360]

---

[359] Also, Fuller believed 'that coherence and goodness have more affinity than coherence and evil.' L. L. Fuller, 'Positivism and Fidelity to Law: A Reply to Professor Hart', 71 Harvard Law Review 630, 1957, p. 636.

[360] L. L. Fuller, 'Freedom as a Problem of Allocating Choice', Proceedings of the American Philosophical Society, Vol. 112, No. 2, 1968, p. 105–106.

The tyrant, Fuller continued, then discovers that citizens will obey him more effectively if they are happy and satisfied with the role they play in his system. But to be happy and satisfied, as a minimum, citizens need to feel that they are not merely means to the tyrant's ends; they must be approached as though they were ends in themselves. Finally, Fuller suggested, the tyrant will understand that the citizens need not only to develop capacities and skills that directly relate to their immediate assigned tasks, they must be able to fully explore their capacities and fully flourish as a human being in order to be happy and satisfied. This will also maximize, in the long run, their 'usefulness' for the tyrant. In conclusion, the rational tyrant will come to respect the principles of the rule of law even out of self-interest. What is more, he understands that he must aspire for his citizens to flourish as humans to the highest and fullest extent. If this extremely selfish tyrant will come understand to understand these lessons, so will every (rational) legislator and ruler.[361]

Not only is the respect for human beings an essential necessity to achieve effectively and efficiently the societal goals of legal orders, it is also a minimum quality of basic legitimacy. This is the second fundamental value at stake with respect to the principles of the 'inner morality' of the law. Human interaction and reciprocity are the basis on which all legal forms, according to Fuller, are built. Human interaction, as a minimum, requires respect for individual autonomy and human dignity. In this respect, it is important to stress that much if not most of Fuller's work is concerned with the non-legal elements in legal orders and the limits of legal orders, which always go back to human interaction.

Reciprocity is not only the key factor in the relationship between citizen and ruler, as explained earlier, Fuller also suggested that it is a key factor for the position of the judge. Fuller argued that a judge must always take into account the expectations of the lawgiver regarding the purpose and the application of the rules, and those of the citizens regarding what the rules mean and how they might be applied to them. Fuller stressed that the judiciary often takes:

> into account what effect a given interpretation would have on the interactional expectancies that have developed tacitly in the world beyond courts and statutes. If these expectancies are innocent and beneficial, a judge familiar with them will incline, often unconsciously, toward an interpretation of legislative intent that will not needlessly disturb them. Second, in the field of statutory law a practical realization of legislative intent through judicial action cannot be obtained without some stabilization of expectations between the legislature and the courts charged with interpreting and applying its enactments. If the courts of a given state have habitually adopted a severely restrictive and letter-bound attitude in interpreting statues, the legislature will take this practice into account in its craftsmanship. But if the courts make a sudden and unexpected shift toward a more expansive and liberal interpretation, the

---

[361] This example is repeated by Fuller with regard to the gunman situation in: L. L. Fuller, 'Irrigation and Tyranny', Stanford Law Review, Vol. 17, No. 6, 1965, p. 1027. Obviously, this example only works when two assumptions are made the tyrant or the gunman is rational and he sees laws or rules as instruments to further his interests.

legislature will obviously not attain its objective or, perhaps, will attain objectives it had no intention of achieving.[362]

Moreover, Fuller thought that all law was based on customary law (sometimes called implicit law), which is in its turn based on human interaction (customs).[363] It is here in particular that Fuller emphasized his proposed openness of the legal system:

> Customary law can be viewed as being implicit law in a double sense. In the first place, the rules of customary law are not first brought into being and then projected upon the conduct they are intended to regulate. They find their implicit expression in the conduct itself. In the second place, the *purpose* of such rules never comes to explicit expression.[364]

Customs are pre-legal; the patterns they create in human conduct bring forth implicit rules, rights and obligations, which are based on the supposition and reasonable expectation that under similar conditions, similar conduct will be adopted. Customs are based in this sense on reciprocity and interrelational expectancies.[365]

Fuller believed that positive law is built on these customs and pre-legal norms; for example, a rule prohibiting vehicles in the park presupposes some general understanding of what a park and a vehicle are, why the rule was adopted and in which contexts it should be applied.[366]

> In reality, a modern system of written statutory law depends for its successful functioning on what may be called a form of customary law, in the sense of a system of stabilized interactional expectancies. Statutes are put into textual form by legislatures; their meaning and application to specific situations of fact are authoritatively determined by the judiciary. When a legislator drafts a statute, he takes into account, tacitly or explicitly, the established attitudes that courts have displayed toward the task of interpreting legislative enactments.[367]

Contract law, to Fuller, is a hybrid between customary law and made law, containing both implicit and statutory rules. 'Customary law may, indeed, be described as the inarticulate older brother of contract.'[368] Contract law, like customary law, is based on the rational capacity of individuals and their reciprocal interaction. This is what Fuller called the interactional foundations of contract law.[369] Contract law's basic function is

---

[362] L. L. Fuller, 'Some presuppositions shaping the concept of "Socialization"', p. 39–40. In: J. L. Tapp & F. J. Levinne, 'Law, justice and the individual in society: psychological and legal issues', New York, Holt, Rinehart and Winston, 1977.
[363] Vice versa, customary law always contains, at least in embryonic form, elements statutory law or legal procedures.
[364] L. L. Fuller, 'Anatomy of the law', Penguin Books, Harmondsworth, 1971, p. 44.
[365] L. L. Fuller, 'Human interaction and the Law', 14 American Journal of Jurisprudence. 1 1969.
[366] L. L. Fuller, 'Anatomy of the law', Penguin Books, Harmondsworth, 1971, p. 60.
[367] L. L. Fuller, 'Law as an Instrument of Social Control and Law as a Facilitation of Human Interaction', 1975 Birmingham Young University Law Review 89 1975, p. 95.
[368] L. L. Fuller, 'Means and Ends', p. 176. In: L. L. Fuller, 'The Principles of Social Order', Duke University Press, Durham, 1981.
[369] L. L. Fuller, 'Human interaction and the Law', 14 American Journal of Jurisprudence 1 1969, p. 224.

to facilitate the interaction between citizens and to support their autonomy; contract law, in contrast to for example criminal law, does not so much restrict human choices and actions, but provides legal and procedural forms.[370] Different from customary law though, contract law lays down procedural rules through which the parties can interact and some minimum limits on what parties can agree upon.

However, Fuller went further and suggested that criminal law, international law and basic administrative law could all be best understood as based on reciprocity and human interaction. First, international law does not contain (or only partially so) positive law nor is there a supernational authority to enforce those rules; consequently, Fuller argued, international law is mostly a matter of interstate relationships and agreements. These agreements and the attitude of different nations are based on their reciprocal relationship. Second, Fuller believed that human interaction is also the key element of administrative law. Traffic rules, for example, are meant to guide and facilitate human interaction, rather than at corrective behavior.

Finally, even criminal law is best explained in terms of reciprocity, according to Fuller, as it is installed to ensure freedom, not curtail it, and to facilitate and encourage inter-human relationships. The prohibition on murder, for example, not only prohibits the type of action which denies someone a basic sense of dignity and respect, it also breaks the vicious circle of eye-for-an-eye, in which interhuman relations are annulled rather than promoted.[371] To Fuller, criminal law should not be seen as an instrument of social control but as a way to facilitate human interaction. To the argument that the origins of criminal law might lie in the attempt to put a stop to the *lex talionis*, he submitted two more arguments in support of the claim that criminal law is also based on human interaction.

Fuller started with the example in which A threatens B with his fist and appears to be reaching for something in his pocket and B at once draws a revolver, kills A and pleads that his act was done in self-defense. A judge is faced with the difficulty in determining as to just what happened and in judging the reasonableness of the actions in the circumstances confronting him. 'As in other interactional situations, we are here concerned with interpreting the meanings reciprocally conveyed by the behavior of men in interaction with one another.'[372] Secondly, Fuller continued:

[A] rule against murder, effectively enforced, serves to enlarge the scope of the individual's interactions with others. In many of our cities are areas that strangers cannot enter without some risk to their physical safety. Here a failure of legal control results in a restriction on interaction, an interaction that in the long run might promote reciprocal understanding and, with it, a reduction in the risks that now aggravate distrust.[373]

---

[370] L. L. Fuller, 'Source Consideration and Form', Columbia Law Review, Vol. 41, No. 5 (May, 1941), p. 806.
[371] L. L. Fuller, 'Human interaction and the Law', 14 American Journal of Jurisprudence 1 1969, p. 231–232.
[372] L. L. Fuller, 'Law as an Instrument of Social Control and Law as a Facilitation of Human Interaction', 1975 Birmingham Young University Law Review 89, 1975, p. 90.
[373] L. L. Fuller, 'Law as an Instrument of Social Control and Law as a Facilitation of Human Interaction', 1975 Birmingham Young University Law Review 89 1975, p. 90.

In conclusion, according to Fuller, reciprocity plays a dual role in legal systems. First, it ensures the basic effectiveness in realizing social goals and aspirations. As the example of the brute tyrant already indicated, facilitating reciprocity and human interaction is or should be the goal of legal orders in terms of aspiration. Second, as the basis for all rules and the legal order as such, reciprocity forms an intrinsic limit. This then, is the second value at stake with respecting the intrinsic limits of the law. Violating the principles of reciprocity is more than merely undesirable; it undermines the very foundations of legal orders. If the legal order violates these principles, it undermines its own foundation and lacks basic legitimacy.

To understand on the basis of what criteria and how, according to Fuller, governmental policies may be evaluated, the term eunomics (potentially inspired by the virtue ethical term *eudaimonia*, the good life) should be introduced. Eunomics again plays a dual role, relating to the morality of duty and the morality of aspiration, the guarantee of order and the aim for societal goals and the basic legitimacy and the effectiveness of legal systems. This has to do with finding the right balance between means and ends and negative and positive freedom. The term was first coined by Fuller in a review article on Edwin W. Patterson's 'Jurisprudence, Men and Ideas of the Law'.[374] Fuller comes back at his favorite subject, his attack on legal positivism and his defense, at least in some sort, of natural or implicit law. Fuller proposed two important additions to Patterson's treatment of the natural law philosophy.

First, with a reference to Plato and Aristotle, he challenges the is-ought/fact-value distinction on the basis of, what he called, the 'Direction-giving Quality of purposive facts'. Purposes, Fuller argues, can properly be regarded as facts, namely as facts that set a target or direction. If we want to interpret a text, for example, we have to know what the writer wanted to convey and it should best be read by someone who is aware of this purpose. If a mechanic with poor English were to write an instruction on how to build a machine, Fuller illustrates, and two persons were to read his instructions, an English professor English and another mechanic, Fuller argues that the latter would not get lost in the 'literal or factual' interpretation of the text, but try to find its essence and would thus understand the instructions better than the English professor. Facts and literal meaning, in conclusion, cannot be separated from value and purpose.

> As for the application of the dichotomy of *is* and *ought* to the law, it is fairly clear that with legal precepts, as with the instructions for assembling a machine, what a direction *is* can be understood only by seeing toward what end result it is aimed. The essential meaning of a legal rule lies in a purpose, or more commonly, in a congeries of purposes. Within the framework of this purpose, or set of related purposes, the sharp dichotomy between fact and evaluation cannot be maintained; the "fact" involved is not a static datum but something that reaches toward an objective and that can be understood only in terms of that reaching.[375]

---

[374] L. L. Fuller, 'American Legal Philosophy at Mid-Century: A Review of Edwin W. Patterson's Jurisprudence, Men and Ideas of the Law', 6 J. Journal of Legal Education 457, 1953–1954.

[375] L. L. Fuller, 'American Legal Philosophy at Mid-Century: A Review of Edwin W. Patterson's Jurisprudence, Men and Ideas of the Law', 6 J. Journal of Legal Education 457 1953–1954, p. 470–471.

Secondly, Fuller introduces the term eunomics to discuss the 'natural laws of social order', which he describes as 'a neglected branch of jurisprudence'. Fuller here refers to welfare economics, political science and business administration which, according to him, all assume (1) that men can choose to adopt one form of social order or another and (2) that the achievement of particular ends may require the choice of particular forms of order, the available forms being limited in number. 'All of these studies are directed towards discovering and utilizing what may be called the "laws" of social order. These "laws" are in turn "natural" in the sense that they represent compulsions necessarily contained in certain ways of organizing men's relations with one another.'[376] For example, he suggests that it is commonly agreed that if the goal is to maximize the satisfaction of diverse wants while there is a situation of scarce resources, then the instrument of choice is something similar to a market mechanism. A certain goal thus leads to a certain type of social order and, in turn, a certain type of social order determines the boundaries between and forms in which human interaction is casted.

Fuller then turns to legal science and distinguishes between the drafting and implementation of constitutions and laws, on the one hand, and the study of the implemented rules, on the other. He suggests that the latter has been almost the exclusive focus of legal scholars. Eunomics, the new jurisprudential branch Fuller tries to introduce, is to the contrary defined as the science, theory or study of good order and workable arrangements. It involves no commitment to ultimate ends, although it may be that there are ends which seem in the abstract desirable, but for the attainment of which no social form can be devised that will not involve an obviously disproportionate cost. 'But the primary concern of eunomics is with the means aspect of the means-end relation, and its contribution to the clarification of ends will lie in its analysis of the available means for achieving particular ends.'[377]

Fuller, never tired of analogies, compares it to devising a not yet existing game. Suppose, he suggests, that one would propose to first decide on what kind of enjoyment the projected game should serve and only afterwards decide on the rules of the game itself, the means to accomplish this end.

> The pleasures derived from any form of play are always complex, and the enjoyment yielded by any particular game is the unique product of its own peculiar nature. If we are to invent a game, we shall have to start with ends vaguely perceived and held in suspension while we explore the problem of devising a workable system of play.[378]

The point is that means and ends can never be fully separated. Setting the goals has an impact on the choice of instruments and likewise, the choice of instruments has an impact on which goals might be pursued.

---

[376] L. L. Fuller, 'American Legal Philosophy at Mid-Century: A Review of Edwin W. Patterson's Jurisprudence, Men and Ideas of the Law', 6 J. Journal of Legal Education 457 1953–1954, p. 475–476.
[377] L. L. Fuller, 'American Legal Philosophy at Mid-Century: A Review of Edwin W. Patterson's Jurisprudence, Men and Ideas of the Law', 6 J. Journal of Legal Education 457 1953–1954, p. 477–478.
[378] L. L. Fuller, 'American Legal Philosophy at Mid-Century: A Review of Edwin W. Patterson's Jurisprudence, Men and Ideas of the Law', 6 J. Journal of Legal Education 457 1953–1954, p. p. 479.

This rudimentary idea proposed in a book review was never fully explored by Fuller.[379] At the time of his death, he had the plan to write a book on eunomics, but only the first chapter, entitled 'Means and Ends', was finished.[380] In this piece, Fuller suggests, *inter alia*, that means, such as institutions, procedures and rules, are not only necessary evils to achieve the social ends, but are also valuable in and of themselves. It is important that the evaluation of the good arrangement of society and the legal order is thus not measured on the basis of its capacity to reach certain societal goals, but is primarily linked to an intrinsic assessment of the quality of the institutions and the laws themselves.

Fuller suggested that the touchstone of good governance, or eunomics, is human freedom:

> The only permissible form of legislation is the sort that lets individuals plan their own lives. Simply put, legislative enactments are baselines for self-directed conduct by citizens, providing the minimal restraints necessary for continuing interaction. Legislation properly conceived permits citizens to order their own affairs, to pursue their own good in their own way (in the words of John Stuart Mill).[381]

However, freedom is always experienced in relation to others. Fuller stressed that freedom as a form of social ordering, and order, as essential to freedom, are interrelated.[382]

> Society is, of course, impossible without some limits on individual freedom, that is, without some form of constraint. If freedom means the absence of constraint, the problem then becomes that of avoiding constraints at particular points and for particular reasons – or, reversing the emphasis, of assigning sound reasons for imposing constraint at particular points. The respective functions of freedom and constraints are, therefore, two aspects of the same question. The pattern of freedom is the reversed image of the pattern of constraint. The two form the structure of society as a whole.[383]

Freedom can thus not be unbound, which is further emphasized by the fact that our options are not unlimited. Here, Fuller compared law to language, which are both necessary to facilitate reciprocity and human relations, but also structure our options. Fuller argued that although language is often unsuitable to precisely say what we mean

---

[379] See also the related: L. L. Fuller, 'Human Purpose and Natural Law', The Journal of Philosophy, Vol. 53, No. 22, 1956.

[380] See also: See further: L. L. Fuller, 'Two principles of human association'. In: L. L. Fuller, 'The Principles of Social Order', Duke University Press, Durham, 1981.

[381] Editor's note, L. L. Fuller, 'The implicit Laws of Lawmaker', p. 158. In: L. L. Fuller, 'The Principles of Social Order', Duke University Press, Durham, 1981. See also: L. L. Fuller, 'Irrigation and Tyranny', Stanford Law Review, Vol. 17, No. 6 (Jul., 1965).

[382] This may be summarized by the words 'forms liberate', which is one of the final fragments found in Fullers documents after his death.

[383] L. L. Fuller, 'Means and Ends', p. 59. In: L. L. Fuller, 'The Principles of Social Order', Duke University Press, Durham, 1981.

(he provides the example of the difficulty of choosing between how we should address someone we just met, feeling that it should be somewhere between the formal and the informal tense), these limits in choice are necessary if we want to communicate at all. 'Language imposes on us a sometimes unwelcome allocation of choice; if it did not, we would be unable to talk.'[384] Fuller believed that there should always be a balance between positive and negative freedom. Both were equally important, he argued, and moreover, he stressed that the one cannot do without the other. As an example, he described the freedom to vote:

> [The freedom] to cast one's ballot loses its point where the voter is not also free from restraints that prevent him from voting as he decides he should. The ridiculous 'elections' held under the Nazi regime are an extreme case in point. A 'freedom from' certain kinds of interference must, then, be presupposed in every 'freedom to.'[385]

2.3. BUILDING BLOCKS FOR AN ALTERNATIVE PRIVACY PARADIGM

The previous two subsections can provide building blocks for the development of a new approach to privacy that can overcome the four tensions between the current privacy paradigm and the developments known as Big Data and mass surveillance can be overcome. The following chapter will look at this aspect in further detail, but this subsection will already provide some of the more general ways in which virtue ethics can help to overcome the four tensions.

(1) As has been stressed, privacy was originally conceptualized as a responsibility of the state not to abuse its powers, for example, by entering the home of a person without any clear or legitimate reason. Gradually, however, it has been rephrased into a subjective right of the natural person to protect its interests. This has worked well for decades, because most privacy infringements where aimed at specific individuals or small numbers of people. Now, however, in the age of Big Data, data collection is often aimed at large groups with an undefined number of members. The effects of such data processes are often difficult to specify on an individual level. That is why last chapter suggested that it might be worthwhile to go beyond the model of individual rights. Virtue ethics, in a way, combines the 'original' with the 'current' approach to privacy regulation. It lays down obligations (to be virtuous), while those obligations do not correlate with any specific rights of others. For Fuller, the state has certain obligations to respect the minimum conditions of the legal order. If it does not, it runs the risk of no longer being a proper legal order. Likewise, the legal order is, according to Fuller, a purposive enterprise. It is by nature directed towards a certain end (*telos*), namely to

---

[384] L. L. Fuller, 'Freedom as a Problem of Allocating Choice', Proceedings of the American Philosophical Society, Vol. 112, No. 2, 1968, p. 102.
[385] L. L. Fuller, 'Freedom: A Suggested Analysis', Harvard Law Review, Vol. 68, No. 8, 1955.

promote order and human flourishing. Again, this is not something that citizens have a subjective right to; it is an obligation of the state in itself. How such a disconnection of rights and duties could be applied to privacy regulation will be discussed in further detail in the next chapter.

(2) As has been stressed, privacy was originally primarily linked to protecting general or societal interests, for example related to the prevention of the abuse of power. Gradually, however, in the wake of privacy becoming an individual right, the main focus was directed at individual interests. As has been stressed in the previous chapter, however, in the age of Big Data, privacy infringements are often problematic because they undermine general and societal interests, instead of individual and particular interests. Virtue ethics proposes to move beyond the mere concept of individual interests. As has been stressed, flourishing as a human being means striving towards being the most perfect self, not towards individual pleasure or happiness. The state should strive towards the most perfect legal order, in which general and societal interests are warranted, such as the basic legitimacy and legality of laws. It is important to point out again that Fuller focused on the idea of eunomics. For Fuller, the legal order is not only an instrument in reaching certain ends (aspirations), such as societal interests; the quality of the instrument itself is essential, as means and ends are to a large extent interdependent. Upholding the quality of the legal order is thus not only important in order to promote general interests, such as human flourishing, but it is an end in itself. How such an addition to individual interests could be applied to privacy regulation will be discussed in further detail in the next chapter.

(3) As has been discussed, the original privacy paradigm focused primarily on the intrinsic qualities of governmental actions. Potential privacy violations were assessed on the basis of whether they were prescribed by law, served a legitimate interest and were necessary in a democratic society. Gradually, however, a different approach was adopted by courts, namely one in which the societal goal promoted through a certain law, measure or action was weighed and balanced against the private interest of a natural person harmed by that law, measure or action. The previous chapter argued that this approach is often difficult to apply to Big Data processes, both because the individual interest at stake is often difficult to substantiate and because the societal interests are increasingly abstract, not in the last place because data are often gathered without a specific and predetermined goal. As discussed above, neither virtue ethics nor Fuller reject the idea of balancing altogether, but there are two important limits. First, Fuller differentiates between the 'morality of duty' and the 'morality of aspiration'. The morality of duty regard minimum requirements; they must be respected at all times. Balancing is not a part of this part of morality.

With aspirations, however, balancing does take place. If a person strives to be, for example, both the perfect father and the perfect employee, some middle ground has to be found in terms of time management. It is important to stress that finding a middle ground is exactly what virtue ethics proposes. A virtuous agent, in general, would not spend all her time to be with her child, and fully neglect her work, nor the other way around. Thus, it is generally not the case that one interest outweighs or outbalances the other interests. Rather, an equilibrium must be found. Moreover, although virtue ethics is not blind to the consequences of actions, its main focus is on the character of the agent. Consequently, the potential benefits of a certain law or measure are not balanced and weighed against the potential negative effects, as consequentialist theories would propose. How such an alternative approach to determining the outcome of cases can be applied to privacy infringements will be discussed in further detail in the next chapter.

(4) Finally, as explained previously in this book, the original privacy paradigm was only partly focused on juridical doctrines and legal sanctions for violating those doctrines. Rather, early privacy and data protection instruments could be seen as codes of conduct and ethical guidelines, containing many open norms and depending mostly on reputational enforcement mechanisms. It was shown, however, that gradually, more and more focus has been placed on legal instruments with very broad and detailed legal provisions and severe sanctions for violation. The previous chapter showed that many of the current data processing efforts challenge this focus, *inter alia* because the fixed categories which laws are by necessity based upon are often ill-suited to address Big Data initiatives, and because of the transborder nature of many data processes. Virtue ethics and Fuller place much emphasis on open norms, as they regard human behavior and customs as the basis of the legal order. This does not mean that virtue ethics do not or cannot come up with concrete and hard rules, but it does mean that this branch of ethics is more prone towards providing open norms that could be used for soft law and code-of-conduct-like instruments, much like the 'original' privacy paradigm. How such an alternative approach can be used for regulating privacy will be discussed in further detail in the next chapter.

3. COUNTERARGUMENTS AGAINST ADOPTING A VIRTUE ETHICAL APPROACH TO PRIVACY

Before explaining in detail what a virtue ethical approach could mean for privacy regulation in practice, which shall be the main goal of the next chapter, this section will discuss in further detail which elements of virtue ethics and Fuller's interpretation of the legal regime will be adopted. This will be done by discussing several counterarguments against adopting a virtue ethical approach to (privacy) regulation. The three most dominant critiques will be discussed, while others remain largely untouched, such as the critique that virtue ethics embraces a form of perfectionism (for the state in the case of Fuller), which undermines the neutrality of the state and, potentially, democratic rule. The three points of critique that will be discussed are, first, that law supposes a correlation between rights and duties, while virtue ethics does not (Section 3.1); second, that law separates is from ought, while virtue ethics does not (Section 3.2) and; finally, that law provides action guidance, while virtue ethics does not (Section 3.3).

3.1. THE CORRELATION OF RIGHTS AND DUTIES

Immanuel Kant is commonly seen as the founding father of the human rights framework; similarly, deontology is often regarded as the theoretical foundation of the modern legal regime as such. Kant is well-known for his belief that in the legal realm, as opposed to the moral realm, rights and duties correlate. Kant sees the fundamental distinction between the legal realm and the moral realm, or what is called the doctrine of right and the doctrine of virtue (virtue in fact refers to *ethica,* while right refers to *ius*), in the fact that legal obligations may be coercively enforced from outside the agent, while ethical duties should not be externally enforced, as those are dependent on the agent's inner life.[386]

In consequence, Kant thought virtues to be an important part of a moral theory, but he thought they could not be codified in law because they have no corresponding right on the other side. This is still an often-heard critique. Virtue ethics lays down many obligations for virtuous agents (do what is honest, brave, temperate, etc.) without a clear correlative right of another. It is a duty to oneself or sometimes to others or mankind as such, without a corresponding legal claim. However, law and the legal regime, so it is said, are based on the correlativity of rights and duties.[387] This thesis has been made especially famous by Hohfeld.[388] In its strong variant, there is a double correlativity: a right of A implies a duty of B and a duty of B implies a right of A.

Remarkably, the examples given to illustrate such a supposed double correlativity are almost without exception taken from private/civil law, which regulates the relationships between private parties. For example, if A borrows B's bicycle for 10 euros a month, B has a right to get 10 euro a month from A and A has a duty to pay 10 euro to B; A has a right to use B's bicycle and B has a duty to lend A her bicycle for a month. The thesis of double correlativity indeed works well to explain private law, in particular contract law, but it is difficult to uphold when applied to criminal, administrative and constitutional law. For example, the obligation of A to stop for a red traffic light has no direct correlative right of another person. Perhaps, it could be argued that A has a duty towards all other participants in the traffic, but this is already a weaker correlativity

---

[386] I. Kant, 'The Metaphysics of Morals', Cambridge University Press, Cambridge, 1996.
[387] See on this topic among others: J. Feinberg, 'The Rights of Animals and Future Generations', in W. Blackstone (ed.), 'Philosophy and Environmental Crisis', University of Georgia Press, Athens, 1974. J. Feinberg, 'Duties, Rights, and Claims', American Philosophical Quarterly, Vol. 3, No. 2, 1966. J. Feinberg, 'Review', The Journal of Philosophy, Vol. 70, No. 9, 1973. W. N. Eskridge, ' Relationship between Obligations and Rights of Citizens', 69 Fordham Law Review 1721, 2001. S. S. Silbey, 'The Availability of Law Redux: The Correlation of Rights and Duties', Law & Society Review, Volume 48, Number 2, 2014. A. Corbin, 'Rights and Duties', Faculty Scholarship Series. Paper 2932, 1924. T. S. N. Sastry, 'Introduction to human rights and duties', <www.unipune.ac.in/pdf_files/Final%20 Book_03042012.pdf>. P. Biasetti, 'Rights, Duties, and Moral Conflicts', Ethics & Politics, XVI, 2014-2. H. K. Michael, 'The Role of Natural law in Early American Constitutionalism: did the founders contemplate judicial enforcement of 'unwritten' individual rights?', 69 North Carolina Law Review 421 1990-1991. E. Curran, 'Hobbes's Theory of Rights – A Modern Interest Theory', The Journal of Ethics, 6 (1), 2002.
[388] W. N. Hohfeld, 'Fundamental Legal conceptions', Yale University Press, New Haven, 1966.

than in contract law. Moreover, it seems that this argument is false as A is also under such a duty when there are no people on the road. Potentially, it could be argued that this duty is directed toward the hypothetical traffic participant, but this seems again much less convincing then the examples take from private law. The hypothetical participant has no correlative claim-right.

A similar problem is often faced when trying to apply the double correlativity thesis to constitutional law, as can be derived, inter alia, from H.L.A. Hart's discussion of natural rights. He pointed out first that there seem to exist rights of persons that do not correlate with duties of others. Suppose, he argued, that two persons went into the dessert and found a ten dollar bill which did not seem to belong to anyone. Both of them would have a right to pick it up, while there is no corresponding duty (of course both have many rights and duties to one another, but not in relation to picking up the 10 dollar). He then continued to distinguish between what he called special rights and general rights. Special rights are those that a person has against one or several clearly distinguishable others, while general rights are those one has against everyone. He also discussed the meaning of the sentence 'I have a right' and argues:

> It is I think the case that this form of words is used in two main types of situations: (A) when the claimant has some special justification for interference with another's freedom which other persons do not have ("I have a right to be paid what you promised for my services"); (B) when the claimant is concerned to resist or object to some interference by another person as having no justification ("I have a right to say what I think"). (A) *Special rights.* When rights arise out of special transactions between individuals or out of some special relationship in which they stand to each other, both the persons who have the right and those who have the corresponding obligation are limited to the parties to the special transaction or relationship. I call such rights special rights to distinguish them from those moral rights which are thought of as rights against (i.e., as imposing obligations upon) everyone, such as those that are asserted when some unjustified interference is made or threatened as in (B) above.'[389]

There are two things that might be interesting in this respect. First, Hart refers to general rights as 'moral rights'. Second, while special rights are (again) mostly exemplified by discussions about private law, general rights seem to equate with constitutional rights:

> (B) *General rights.* In contrast with special rights, which constitute a justification peculiar to the holder of the right for interfering with another's freedom, are general rights, which are asserted defensively, when some unjustified interference is anticipated or threatened, in order to point out that the interference is unjustified. 'I have the right to say what I think.' 'I have the right to worship as I please.'[390]

Hart stresses that special rights and general rights are similar in that, to have them is to have a moral justification for determining how another shall act, namely that that

---

[389] H. L. A. Hart, 'Are There Any Natural Rights?', The Philosophical Review, Vol. 64, No. 2, 1955, p. 183.
[390] H. L. A. Hart, 'Are There Any Natural Rights?', The Philosophical Review, Vol. 64, No. 2, 1955, p. 187.

person shall not interfere. Also, the moral justification does not arise from the character of the particular action to the performance of which the claimant has a right; what justifies the claim is simply that this is a particular exemplification of the equal right to be free. However, there are also some important differences. Most importantly:

> '[General rights] have as correlatives obligations not to interfere to which everyone else is subject and not merely the parties to some special relationship or transaction, though of course they will often be asserted when some particular persons threaten to interfere as a moral objection to that interference. To assert a general right is to claim in relation to some particular action the equal right of all men to be free in the absence of any of those special conditions which constitute a special right to limit another's freedom; to assert a special right is to assert in relation to some particular action a right constituted by such special conditions to limit another's freedom.'[391]

Consequently, it seems that in any case, there is a big difference between private (contract) law and public (criminal, administrative, constitutional) law. While for contract law, the correlation between rights and duties seems quite natural, this seems so to a lesser extent for other branches of law. And even for private law, it seems difficult to explain all doctrines in terms of rights and duties, which can be exemplified by Kant's oft-discussed description of marriage as a contractual agreement to use on another's reproduction organs.[392] Framing such 'moral' agreements in law in terms of hard legal rights and correlative duties seems rather uncomfortable to the modern reader. But more importantly, the duty of A to stop for a red traffic light seems not directed at B or several Bs. That this also holds for more extreme examples, such as murder, can be shown by pointing out that A is under the duty not to kill B, even if B permits A to kill him. In contrast with a right, for example, to lend a bicycle, A cannot normally defeat her right to life in this way.[393] Likewise, the correlation between a constitutional right seems not with the duty of another to respect it, but rather with the state not to (ab)use its power in certain ways.

The latter point is made in length by several authors, among others by David Lyons in his article 'The correlativity of rights and duties'.[394] He takes as example the freedom of speech. Does the right of A to say something correlate to the duty of B to listen to what A has to say? Obviously not. Rather, it could entail a duty for B not to actively disturb A in his freedom of expression. Suppose that A is atop a soap box speaking to a crowd against the state's military involvement in the Iraq war. 'His act is perfectly lawful, but he is assaulted by some private citizens, driven from the box and silenced.

---

[391] H. L. A. Hart, 'Are There Any Natural Rights?', The Philosophical Review, Vol. 64, No. 2, 1955, p. 188.
[392] I. Kant, 'The Metaphysics of Morals', Cambridge University Press, Cambridge, 1996, 6:280–6:281. Also, his discussion on 'public right' seems to be of quite different nature than his discussion of 'private right'.
[393] Assisted suicide or euthanasia may be the exception, though it is only decriminalized in very few countries around the world.
[394] D. Lyons, 'The Correlativity of Rights and Duties', Noûs, Vol. 4, No. 1, 1970. Critical to Lyons: J. Donnelly, 'How are rights and duties correlative?', Journal of Value Inquiry 16 (4), 1982.

Their behavior is unlawful and constitutes unwarranted and prohibited interference with the exercise of his legal rights. In saying this we may refer to his general right of free speech or to a specific right to stand there addressing the crowd. In either case the right might be construed as a right to do something. How is that to be understood?'[395] The problem, of course, is that the described behavior is illegitimate as such. Whether someone is using their freedom of speech or not, it is never allowed for other individuals to assault a person. Rather, having a right to freedom of expression means, Lyons suggests, that congress and other governmental agencies with legislative power to enact laws are limited and curtailed in their freedom to make certain laws.

It is important, Lyons stresses, that A's material right to say certain things or not does not correlate with parliament's duty not to enact certain laws.

> To see this, imagine the First Amendment repealed: then Congress would acquire the "power" to enact legally binding laws restricting speech now unrestrictable. But Congress could have this power without exercising it, and thus it could happen that speech was no more restricted than it is right now and that one's speaking and remaining silent were equally lawful and protected against interference even though we could no longer truly say that we have Constitutional rights of free speech.[396]

Consequently, there is no correlative 'duty' of parliament with A's right; A's right is in fact a legislative disability, namely that parliament is not empowered to enact certain laws.[397]

As a result, most commentators agree that there are both rights that have no correlative duty and duties that have no correlative right. 'The non-correlative duty is owed to the state alone, and the rationale for imposing that duty is either disconnected from any right or is broader ranging than ensuring the protection of an individual right. An example of a non-correlative duty disconnected from any right is contained in article 29(2) of the African Charter, which states that an individual must 'serve his national community by placing his physical and intellectual abilities at its service.'[398]

---

[395] D. Lyons, 'The Correlativity of Rights and Duties', Noûs, Vol. 4, No. 1, 1970, p. 49.
[396] D. Lyons, 'The Correlativity of Rights and Duties', Noûs, Vol. 4, No. 1, 1970, p. 51.
[397] In conclusion, it seems that the correlativity between rights and duties seems not the most obvious candidate to describe rights and obligations in public law. Though some philosophers have stressed that the right of the state to punish criminals, for example, correlates with the duty of citizens to obey the law, this is a very general and weak correlation and does not regard the material provisions in criminal law, but only the meta-ethics of criminal law.
[398] L. Lazarus, B. Goold, R. Desai & Q. Rasheed, 'The relationship between rights and responsibilities', University of Oxford, Ministry of Justice Research Series 18/09, December 2009. <https://www.matrixlaw.co.uk/uploads/other/21_08_2013_04_20_27_The%20relationship%20between%20rights%20and%20responsibities%20Ministry%20of%20Justice%20Research%20Series%20December%202009.pdf>. Article 29 of the African Charter on Human and Peoples' Rights reads: 'The individual shall also have the duty: (1) To preserve the harmonious development of the family and to work for the cohesion and respect of the family; to respect his parents at all times, to maintain them in case of need. (2) To serve his national community by placing his physical and intellectual abilities at its service; (3) Not to compromise the security of the State whose national or resident he is; (4) To preserve and strengthen social and national solidarity, particularly when the latter is strengthened; (5) To preserve and strengthen the national independence and the territorial integrity of his country and to contribute to his defence in accordance with the law; (6) To work to the best of his abilities and competence, and to

Similarly, Joel Feinberg has discussed a variety of rights and duties without an obvious counterpart. He has referred, among others, to 'manifesto rights',[399] of which an example may be article 24 of the Universal Declaration of Human Rights which holds: 'Everyone has the right to rest and leisure, including reasonable limitation of working hours and periodic holidays with pay.'[400]

Consequently, the critique is that law supposes correlativity between rights and duties, while virtue ethics also accepts duties without correlative rights. This critique is false, because the legal realm contains quite some doctrines that do not reflect the supposed correlativity. It can thus be concluded that the supposed correlativity cannot be brought as an argument again applying a virtue ethical approach to legal regulation. What is more, there are already concepts in law that seem to reflect a virtue ethical way of thinking. An example might be the duty of care. The classic reference here is to the obligation to act as a *bon père de famille*. In most jurisdictions, parents are under the legal obligation to take good care of their children and act as 'a good parent' or 'good father' would do. Similarly, doctors are under a legal obligation to act as 'a good doctor', that is, to act just like a hypothetical virtuous doctor would act. The education of medical students is also mostly focused on this aspect. Duties of care are quite similar to v-rules or virtue-rules, which will be explained in more detail below. A virtue ethical rule could be 'do as the most virtuous person would do'; the duty of care in relation to caring for children, for example, currently already embedded in many Civil Codes around the world, could be framed as 'do as a virtuous father/parent would do'.

Second, one could also refer to professional ethics, which is often inspired by a virtue ethical way of thinking. For example, in the legal regime, there are obligations for private parties to prevent damage to others, even if there exists no contractual or other legal relationship. For example, internet intermediaries have a duty of care to prevent damage to third parties, *inter alia* if users violate the intellectual property of third parties, damage their reputation or violate their right to privacy or data protection.[401] They should do what is reasonable to prevent such damage and act as a 'diligent economic operator' would.[402] In a similar vein, criminal law often takes as a standard the reasonable foreseeability test, i.e. that which the reasonable man would foresee.[403]

---

pay taxes imposed by law in the interest of the society; (7) To preserve and strengthen positive African cultural values in his relations with other members of the society, in the spirit of tolerance, dialogue and consultation and, in general, to contribute to the promotion of the moral well being of society; (8) To contribute to the best of his abilities, at all times and at all levels, to the promotion and achievement of African unity.' <www.achpr.org/instruments/achpr/>.

[399] J. Feinberg, 'The nature and value of rights', Journal of Value Inquiry, 1970.
[400] Universal Declaration on Human Rights <www.un.org/en/universal-declaration-human-rights/>.
[401] N. A. N. M. van Eijk, 'Moving Towards Balance: A study into duties of care on the Internet', <www.ivir.nl/publicaties/download/679>.
[402] European Court of Justice, L'Oréal SA, Lancôme parfums et beauté & Cie SNC, Laboratoire Garnier & Cie, L'Oréal (UK) Ltd v. eBay International AG, eBay Europe SARL, eBay (UK) Ltd, Stephen Potts, Tracy Ratchford, Marie Ormsby, James Clarke, Joanna Clarke, Glen Fox, Rukhsana Bi, Case C-324/09, 12 July 2011, §124.
[403] There are, however, also exceptions to this principle, for example the egg-scull doctrine: if person A hits person B on the head, in a way which would normally not have killed another, but it does, due to

As in contract law, the doctrine of the reasonable man is sometimes substituted in professional environments from which an extra duty of care may arise. A restaurant owner may have an extra duty to inquire whether costumers have certain allergies and to double check whether the information provided about the ingredients on the packaging is actually correct; the owner of a boxing school may be required to provide her students with extra protection against possible head injury; etc. Consequently, certain positions may entail extra obligations.

Third and finally, it should be taken into account that, as discussed in Chapter II of this book, both privacy and data protection law were originally focused on the character of the state and the data controller. Both doctrines specified primarily how a good state or good data controller would behave. It should be noted that virtue ethics does not spell out hard rules on what a person should or should not do, but rather what a person ought to strive for, in order to be, for example, a good father or a good data controller. A good example may be the obligation for data controllers to take technical measures to protect the personal data of data subjects. The General Data Protection Regulation specifies that the data controller must implement appropriate technical and organizational measures to ensure a level of security appropriate to the risk, taking into account the state of the art, the costs of implementation and the nature, scope, context and purposes of processing as well as the risk of varying likelihood and severity for the rights and freedoms of natural persons.[404] This is a rather open norm, the core of which is that data controllers should behave as a good or virtuous data controller would, namely by doing everything reasonably possible to secure the data in their possession.

Consequently, it seems that law does contain rules that are inspired by or consistent with a virtue ethical approach to regulation. Like v-rule, duties of care specify, for example, 'act as the most virtuous doctor would act' or 'do as the most virtuous parent would do'. Furthermore, these types of rules are applicable to legal persons. Most professional ethics and many legal doctrines revolving around diligent economic operators and professional and responsible behavior embody a virtue ethical approach. Finally, it was stressed that the original privacy and data protection paradigm, and even some of the doctrines engrained in the current privacy and data protection paradigm, can be related to a virtue ethical way of thinking. This is not to argue that the regulators and lawmakers were thinking of Aristotle when they designed these rules, but it is to say that there is no immediate problem adopting a virtue ethical approach to privacy regulation.

3.2. IS-OUGHT FALLACY

One of the classic moral principles is that 'is' and 'ought' should be separated. This thesis was made famous by David Hume in *A treatise of Human Nature*, in which he argued

---

the victim's unusually soft scull, this is mostly said to be part of the risk-acceptation/assumed risk of the aggressor and lead to culpability.
[404] Article 32 General Data Protection Regulation.

that an 'ought' may never be derived from an 'is'.[405] The is-ought fallacy has remained one of the fundamental pillars of ethics. One cannot derive moral obligations from facts. One should provide reasons for accepting an 'ought', there must be convincing moral arguments for doing so. The fact that the sun rises in the east, wolves eat rabbits and humans have the capacity for sexual reproduction does not imply an 'ought'. It would be absurd to say that it follows from these factual observations that the sun *should* rise in the east, that wolfs *should* eat rabbits and that humans *should* sexually reproduce or that humans *should* have the capacity to do so. 'Is' and 'ought' can coincide, but it is not *because* something 'is' that something 'ought' to be. Yet, this is exactly what some virtue ethical scholars do. They do derive 'oughts' from 'isses' and they do make moral claims about specimens who do not follow the normal or natural path of their species. This is because virtue ethics places much emphasis on the natural ends (*telos*) of creatures. 'The *telos* is not the point at which the process of growth happens to finish, it is that point which the whole process was *for*'.[406]

Virtue ethics looks at animate creatures and observes their nature. One could study trees and find that most trees have roots, branches and leaves. Similarly, we can see that wolves eat rabbits and other little creatures, can sexually reproduce and have a fur. Virtue ethics could hold that if one comes across a mature wolf that grows no fur, has undeveloped sexual reproduction organs and eats grass, one might (under usual circumstances) call it a defective wolf or a bad specimen of the category wolf. Similarly, if a tree has no roots, leaves or branches, one would normally call this a degenerate tree. In extreme cases, one might not even be able to call it a tree or a wolf at all, because it does not fit its definition. Because virtue ethics looks to aspirations and ends, it will stress that a tree does not have roots for the looks of it or as a superfluous show piece,; it has roots in order to absorb water, which it needs for survival and for producing leaves, seeds and nuts. A peacock has its plumage to attract females or to show its superiority over other males, a wolf has fur to keep it warm, etc. Virtue ethics generally holds that species have the aspiration to survive and that certain elements aid them in this aspiration. That is why virtue ethics would not derive a moral claim from every 'is'; many aspects of ducks, wolfs and trees are not essential to these aims. If a duck has green instead of yellow legs, this would normally not be called a defective duck. However, as has been stressed, the application of these types of arguments to human beings is not uncontroversial. This is because humans can reflect on their behavior and can decide that an 'is' should not be an 'ought'. An obvious example may be the fact that throughout history, mankind has eaten meat; still, given the fact that we can by now get the nutrition we need without killing animals, it might be argued that we need to change how we behave.

Consequently, along with Fuller, most contemporary virtue ethicists reject this thesis when it comes to humans, as does as this book. Still, the separation of 'is' from

---

[405] D. Hume, 'A treatise of human nature', San Bernardino, 2014, p. 254.
[406] Aristotle, 'The Politics and the Constitution of Athens', Cambridge University Press, Cambridge, 2007, introduction xxiii.

'ought' is important because their separability is also an important part of the Hart-Fuller debate, as stressed earlier. Hart, introduced the topic of his article 'Positivism and the Separation of Law and Morals' by stating the following:

> [J]urisprudence trembles so uncertainly on the margin of many subjects that there will al-ways be need for someone, in Bentham's phrase, "to pluck the mask of Mystery" from its face. This is true, to a pre-eminent degree, of the subject of this article. Contemporary voices tell us we must recognize something obscured by the legal "positivists" whose day is now over: that there is a "point of intersection between law and morals," or that what is and what ought to be are somehow indissolubly fused or inseparable, though the positivists denied it.[407]

Hart did defend the legal philosophy known as legal positivism. Legal positivism can be seen as a response to classic natural law theories. It is not necessary to give a full overview of the discussion, but insofar as relevant here, legal positivism defends two theses. First, the origins of law cannot be found in (human) nature or in God, but in an act of a sovereign or parliament. Austin's command theory classically proposed that all positive law is man-made and that laws can simply be defined as the commands of the sovereign. He also described the position of the sovereign in *de facto* terms, namely as the person (or body) whose rules are followed in general by the bulk of the population most of the time and who himself does not habitually obey others. Rules, Austin continued, are general commands applying to a class (people have a freedom of speech) and not to individuals (Sarah has freedom of speech). Finally, it is important to point out that for Austin and for most legal positivist, positive law does not include laws of honor, international law, customary law and constitutional law. For example, Austin argued:

> The admirers of customary law love to trick out their idol with mysterious and imposing attributes. But to those who can see the difference between positive law and morality, there is nothing of mystery about it. Considered as rules of positive morality, customary laws arise from the consent of the governed, and not from the position or establishment of political superiors. But, considered as moral rules turned into positive laws, customary laws are established by the state: established by the state directly, when the customs are promulgated in its statutes; established by the state circuitously, when the customs are adopted by its tribunals.[408]

The second point legal positivists make is that law and morals can be separated and that laws are laws, even if they are unjust. Hart, for example, made reference to the case of the grudge informer discussed earlier. The post-war court held that the statue on which she based the legitimacy of her actions 'was contrary to the sound conscience and sense

---

[407] H. L. A. Hart, 'Positivism and the Separation of Law and Morals', Harvard Law Review, Vol. 71, No. 4, 1958, p. 594.
[408] J. Austin, 'The Providence of Jurisprudence determined. Being the first part of a series of lectures on jurisprudence, or, the philosophy of positive law. Lecture I.'. <www.heinonline.org/HOL/Page?handle=hein.beal/profjdete0001&id=1>.

of justice of all decent human beings.'[409] The Court thus relied on supralegal morality to judge the legitimacy of laws. Hart, and many legal positivists, however, hold that the law is a law, even if it is immoral, even if it does not promote the common good, even if it is unclear, etc. Lon L. Fuller, in the Hart-Fuller debate, disagreed on both points, not by taking a natural law perspective, but by adopting a novel approach which is very much inspired by virtue ethics.

What is important here is to note that virtue ethics has difficulty accepting both arguments made by legal positivism. First, it does regard customs and human behavior as the basis of law. This is perhaps due to a historical coincidence, because in the Ancient Greece of Plato and Aristotle, the word for law (*nomoi*) also signified customs. Laws, customs and culture can all be considered legitimate translations of *nomos*. It has been pointed out, for example, that by Herodotus' time:

> '[N]omos could mean a law formally enacted at a known date and recorded in writings; it could refer to aspects of human behavior observed to vary from one culture to another, in opposition to *physis*; and it had also been used by the Presocratics to denote regularities in the working of the cosmos – what we might call 'laws of nature.'[410]

Later, in the Socratic writings and from then onwards, *nomoi* (customary, human laws) were contrasted with the *physis* (natural laws). While the former were man-made and relative, the latter were natural and absolute. Most early virtue ethicists strongly emphasized the added value of customary law and customs. For example, Aristotle emphasized:

> [I]t is evident that in seeking for justice men seek for the mean, for the law is the mean. Again, customary laws have more weight, and relate to more important matters, than written laws, and a man may be a safer ruler than the written law, but no safer than the customary law.[411]

Consequently, it is true that virtue ethics does not wholeheartedly embrace the separability thesis proposed by legal positivism. First of all, it senses that the separation between customary law and written law is not particularly clear and in any case, that customary law is the basis of written law rather than the other way around.[412] This should be linked to the doctrine of *phronesis* or practical wisdom. As has been stressed, a child may be 'good' and may follow moral principles, but it lacks practical wisdom; it does not know how to interpret and apply moral principles in practice or in difficult situations. Such a practical wisdom can only be gained from experience, on which customs are based. Aristotle, for example, explains this by referring to a doctor. It is not

---

[409] H. L. A. Hart, 'Positivism and the Separation of Law and Morals', Harvard Law Review, Vol. 71, No. 4, 1958, p. 619.

[410] S. Humphreys, 'Law, custom and culture in Herodotus', <http://kainani.hpu.edu/sschwartz/HIST4911_Lectures/Humphreys1987.pdf>.

[411] Aristotle, Politics, 1287b. See also 1269A and 1286A.

[412] Later on, written laws were referred to as *thesmoi* and not as *nomoi*. L. Foxhall & A. D. E. Lewis, 'Greek law in its political setting: justifications not justice', Oxford University Press, Oxford, 1996.

optimal if a doctor only acts on its own insights, but it is also not optimal if he merely follows and applies written rules or protocols. Rather, if in doubt he should call upon a more experienced doctor, who has gained practical wisdom and knows what to do in these types of situations.[413]

Second, virtue ethics does not subscribe to the idea that everything the ruler or the sovereign commands should be called law. Both Plato and Aristotle discussed whether 'the best men' or 'the best laws' should rule the *polis*. Plato, in his republic, seemed to suggest that the ideal city would be ruled by a philosopher-king. Such a person would not be bound by the laws of the *polis*. However, later on, Plato developed a new political philosophy, which contrasted sharply with his prior work. The last work he wrote was entitled *Nomoi* (the Laws) and described a society regulated in detail through law:

> Not only is the person of the philosopher-ruler split in two (into the philosopher-lawgiver and the virtuous Young tyrant), but *neither of these persons simply rules*. The tyrant is a *means* to the establishment of the Legal code devised by the philosopher-legislator.[414] (emphasis added)

Mostly the same applied for Aristotle:

> There may indeed be cases which the law seems unable to determine, but such cases a man could not determine either. But the law trains officers for this express purpose, and appoints them to determine matters which are left undecided by it, to the best of their judgment. Further, it permits them to make any amendment of the existing laws which experience suggests. Therefore he who bids the law rule may be deemed to bid God and Reason alone rule, but he who bids man rule adds an element of the best; for desire is a wild beast, and passion perverts the minds of rulers, even when they are the best of men. The law is reason unaffected by desire.[415]

Consequently, Aristotle holds that it is in fact the ruler or the sovereign who should be bound by the rule of law, the only exception being when the hypothetical god-among-men would actually come into existence.[416]

In light of the above, virtue ethics views things as having a natural end (*telos*), which might also, be applied to states and legal orders, as discussed previously when introducing the work of Lon L. Fuller. In general, the state and the law, in virtue ethical thinking, have as aim 'justice' and 'human flourishing'.[417] If laws are devoid of justice, it is doubtful whether under a virtue ethical paradigm they would be called laws at all.

---

[413] Aristotle, 1287a-1287b.
[414] V. Bradley Lewis: 'Politeia kai Nomoi: On the Coherence of Plato's Political Philosophy', Polity Vol. 31, No. 2, 1998, p. 342.
[415] Aristotle, 1287a.
[416] C. A. Bates, 'Law and the Rule of Law and Its Place Relative to Politeia in Aristotle's Politics', in: L. Huppers-Cluysenaer & N.M.M.S. Coelho (eds), 'Aristotle and the philosophy of law: theory, Parctice and Justice', Springer, Dordrecht, 2013.
[417] See also: Aquinas, 1 95 art.3 pt. I-II.

If a state does not provide citizens with the bare necessities of life and if it does not help citizens to strive for maximum flourishing, it is questionable whether it would be called a state. It is important to stress that for both Plato and Aristotle, the state is regarded as having a *telos* itself, namely on the one hand providing the minimum necessities of life for its citizens (minimum requirements) and on the other hand helping and encouraging them to become perfect virtuous beings (aspirations). Legal orders are thus in themselves purposive enterprises, is and ought are to a certain extent intertwined.

So, to conclude, it is true that virtue ethics defies the separation between 'is' and 'ought' in both the moral and in the legal realm, but this cannot lead to the conclusion that virtue ethics cannot serve as the basis for (legal) regulation. Virtue ethics in no way opposes written law, but it does hold that written law is often a codification of human behaviour and subjected and dependent on customs. It is important to stress that it is perfectly possible to base a juridical system to a large extent on customs and unwritten rules, as is evidenced by the legal systems of common law countries. Also, it is important that in civil law jurisdictions, written laws are often interpreted on the basis of customs and there are open juridical doctrines in civil law jurisdictions which are interpreted on the basis of customs.

For example, the tort law in the Netherlands places a large emphasis on unwritten law and common accepted principles of morality:

1. A person who commits a tortious act (unlawful act) against another person that can be attributed to him, must repair the damage that this other person has suffered as a result thereof.
2. As a tortious act is regarded a violation of someone else's right (entitlement) and an act or omission in violation of a duty imposed by law or of what according to unwritten law has to be regarded as proper social conduct, insofar as there was no justification for this behavior.
3. A tortious act can be attributed to the tortfeasor [the person committing the tortious act] if it results from his fault or from a cause for which he is accountable by virtue of law or generally accepted principles (common opinion).[418]

In conclusion, although the argument that virtue ethics does not perfectly separate 'is' and 'ought' is correct, it does not mean that virtue ethics cannot be used for (privacy) regulation or that virtue ethical principles cannot be embedded in law.

3.3. ACTION GUIDANCE

Another critique against virtue ethics is that it is unable to produce hard and stable rules. In contrast to deontology and utilitarianism, so it is argued, virtue ethics cannot give clear action guidance to agents. The critique from utilitarians and deontologists is that law should try to come up with a code providing universal rules. For example,

---

[418] Article 6:162 Civil Code. Definition of a 'tortious act'.

it is said that while in utilitarianism and deontology, it is clear what an agent should do, virtue ethics can only provide that a person must do what is virtuous or what the most virtuous person would do, but is in itself empty. This critique, however, is false, as Rosalind Hursthouse argues. She explains that all three ethical theories actually work according to the same scheme. Each has a moral premise and each takes a second step, in which this moral principle is provided with substance. The moral premise for utilitarianism could be framed as: 'an action is right if it promotes the best consequences'. The moral premise for deontology could be framed as: 'an action is right if it is in accordance with a correct moral rule or principle'. And the moral premise for virtue ethics could be: 'an action is right if it is what a virtuous agent would characteristically (i.e. acting in character) do in the circumstances'. Neither of these three premises gives actual guidance, it only provides how a particular branch of ethics would approach the question of right and wrong.[419]

It is only with the second step that material rules can be produced. Utilitarians must decide on what they view as the best consequences, deontologists must decide on what they view as moral rules or principles and virtue ethicists must decide on what they regard as virtuous or what they think a virtuous agent would do. About each of these decisions, there is considerable discussion among scholars. Although most utilitarians hold that the guiding principle should be 'achieving the maximum happiness for the maximum number of people', a utilitarian goal could as well be 'getting as many sheep in Scotland as possible'. The point of utilitarianism is that actions are judged on their utility, on the consequences they produce. In principle, this branch of ethics is neutral to the end goal that is picked. Likewise, although most deontologists agree on a basic set of moral principle, such as 'do not lie', 'do not steal' and 'do not kill', there is considerable discussion about defining the broader set of duties. Likewise, although most virtue ethicists agree on a basic set of virtues, such as 'do what is honest', 'do what is just' and 'do what is brave', there is a debate about the scope and definition of the virtues. So, it can be concluded that the basic premise of the three branches of ethics are all empty and that virtue ethics is not exceptional in that respect.

A similar attack directed at virtue ethics is that the only moral principle it provides is 'do what a virtuous agent would do', and that it cannot produce any substantial insight on what a virtuous agent would do concretely in certain circumstances. Clearly, virtue ethicists have pointed out, this critique is based on a misunderstanding. 'Blinkered by slogans that described virtue ethics as "concerned with Being rather than Doing", as addressing "What sort of person should I be?" but not "What should I do?" as being "agent-centred rather than act-centred", its critics maintained that it was unable to provide action guidance and hence, rather than being a normative rival to utilitarian and deontological ethics, could claim to be no more than a valuable supplement to them. The rather odd idea was that all virtue ethics could offer was "Identify a moral exemplar and do what he would do" as though the raped fifteen year old trying to decide whether or not to have an abortion was supposed to ask herself "Would Socrates have

---

[419] R. Hursthouse, 'On virtue ethics', Oxford University Press, Oxford, 1999, p. 25–30.

had an abortion if he were in my circumstances?"[420] This would be absurd to virtue ethics; there are many virtue ethicists who have engaged in specific debates on difficult topics such as abortion and euthanasia.

But, it is objected, deciding on what virtues are and what a virtuous person would do, is highly subjective. Consequently, virtue ethics cannot produce stable and objective rules. However, as has been stressed, deciding on the question what the moral principles in deontology or the goal for utilitarianism should be is just as subjective. Moreover, virtue ethicists believe that in common circumstances, what is right and wrong for an agent to do can be derived from common knowledge and understanding. But, a further critical argument goes, a non-virtuous being cannot understand or estimate what a virtuous being would do. While deontology is clear on what the guiding principles are, for example, 'do not lie', virtue ethics asks an agent to imagine what a most virtuous agent would do. The question is, can, for example, a criminal imagine what it would be like to be a fully virtuous being? Mostly, the answer is yes, maybe with an exception of pathological liars, thieves, etc., if a set of virtues such as honesty, charitableness, truthfulness and bravery are provided.

> So, given such an enumeration of the virtues, I may well have a perfectly good idea of what the virtuous person would do in my circumstances, despite my own imperfection. Would she lie in her teeth to acquire an unmerited advantage? No, for that would be both dishonest and unjust. Would she help the wounded stranger by the roadside even though he had no right to her help, or pass by on the other side? The former, for that is charitable and the latter callous. Might she keep a death-bed promise even though living people would benefit from its being broken? Yes, for she is true to her word. And so on.[421]

Still, it is argued, virtue ethics cannot produce any rules, such as 'do not steal', 'do not lie' and 'do not kill'. However, virtue ethicists would argue that virtue ethics can provide so-called 'v-rules'.[422] These are rules that stress 'do what is honest', 'do what is charitable', 'do what is brave', or negatively formulated, 'do not do what is dishonest', 'do not do what is uncharitable' and 'do not do what is un-brave'. However, it is often said that these rules are less absolute than the rules provided by deontology. This may be the case, although even in the moral realm it can be questioned whether modern deontologists would actually feel that one should never kill a person, or that, for example, killing out of self-defense is not immoral. In any case, as the attack discussed here is particularly on its codifiability, it is important to stress that the legal realm knows (almost) no absolute rules, perhaps with the exception of the prohibition of torture in the European Convention on Human Rights.[423] In the legal domain, it is legitimate to kill someone in self-defense, or potentially as an act of war, and certain

---

[420] R. Hursthouse, 'Virtue Ethics', in: E. N. Zalta (ed.), 'The Stanford Encyclopedia of Philosophy', 2013 Edition.
[421] R. Hursthouse, 'On virtue ethics', Oxford University Press, Oxford, 1999, p. 36.
[422] R. Hursthouse, 'On virtue ethics', Oxford University Press, Oxford, 1999, p. 37.
[423] Article 3 ECHR.

states still have the death penalty as an ultimate form of punishment. Every other legal principle is similarly non-absolute. So, although it is true that virtue ethics does not produce absolute rules, this does not in any way mean that it is uncodifiable. The fact that virtue ethics turns more to open norms and soft rules could actually be an advantage, as discussed in Chapter III of this book.

4. CONCLUSION

This chapter provided a brief introduction into virtue ethics and discussed the work of one legal philosopher, namely Lon L. Fuller, to see how a virtue ethical approach could be adopted in the legal regime. It sketched some initial ideas about how such an approach might complement the current privacy paradigm; the next chapter will develop this in further detail. In addition, this chapter has discussed and rebutted a number of arguments against adopting a virtue ethical approach to (privacy) regulation. These regarded the correlativity between rights and duties, the separability of is and ought and the codifiability of virtue rules. It was shown that law can adopt a virtue ethical approach to (privacy) regulation and that there are already doctrines engrained in the legal domain that lend themselves for such an approach. How such an approach might be applied to privacy regulation will be discussed in the next chapter.

CHAPTER V
EMBEDDING A VIRTUE-BASED APPROACH IN PRIVACY REGULATION

1. INTRODUCTION

Chapter II has discussed both the current and the original privacy and data protection paradigm. In broad strokes, it signaled a shift on four points, by contrasting the 'original' with the 'current' approach – both were presented in idealized form. First, there has been a shift away from protecting privacy through duties of care and doctrines based on the abuse of power, and towards granting subjective rights to natural persons. Second, there has been a shift away from the protection of general and societal interests and towards an, almost exclusive, focus on the protection of personal interests of natural persons. Third, there has been a shift away from a more fundamental, rule-of-law-based perspective when determining the outcome of privacy cases and towards adopting the method of balancing as a standard approach. Fourth and finally, there has been a shift away from an approach which combined legal and ethical forms of regulation, and towards a paradigm which almost exclusively focuses on legal regulation and black letter law.

Chapter III showed how the current privacy paradigm conflicts with new technological developments, such as, for example, Big Data processes. First, it showed that claiming individual rights is increasingly difficult for natural persons in the age of Big Data. Second, it stressed that these types of processes increasingly go beyond individual interests, and instead tend to affect general and societal interests. Third, it pointed out that the method of balancing is often difficult to apply in cases concerning Big Data processes. Fourth, it argued that solely relying on black letter law does not allow for an adequate regulation of Big Data processes. Chapter III also showed that alternatives to the current privacy paradigm have been developed, both in the literature and in case law. Although some of these alternatives are insightful and provide useful building blocks, they do not lay down a fully developed and theoretically grounded alternative privacy paradigm that overcomes the difficulties faced by the current privacy paradigm.

Chapter IV argued that such a foundation may be found by turning to virtue ethics, especially through its reinterpretation by Lon L. Fuller. This chapter demonstrated that a virtue-based approach may provide alternatives to each of the four points mentioned. Virtue ethics does not focus on the rights of the patient, the data subject, but on the obligation on the agent to be virtuous, in this case the state. Virtue ethics does not focus on particular individual interests of specific natural persons; it focuses on the duty of the agent to perfect herself. The core obligation of the state is to promote the human flourishing of its citizens. This means that by virtue of its very existence, the state is or should be directed at aspiring human autonomy and freedom for its subjects. As a prerequisite, the legal order should abide by certain minimum conditions to ensure effectiveness and efficiency as an instrument in promoting human freedom. These minimum conditions are part of the duty of morality. Since they are minimum standards, no balancing takes place; they must be respected at all times. With respect to aspirations, it should be taken into account that different goals might conflict. Here, an equilibrium must be found, a middle ground between the different aspirations. Finally, it should be taken into account that the legal order and the state are limited not only because they are directed at human freedom, but also because they are based on human behavior. Both virtue ethics and Lon L. Fuller place a large emphasis on customs, customary law and open norms in legal systems.

This chapter will analyze how such an approach could be applied to privacy regulation. Obviously, this is an argumentative rather than a descriptive task. And the argument is limited, as it is impossible to rewrite the entire corpus of privacy and data protection legislation in such a way that it incorporates virtue ethical elements, or in such a way that an entirely new legal regime is constructed that complements the current one. Rather, a few examples will be provided of how such an approach might complement what is currently in place and how those rules might be able to address problems that current rules are unable to address. The commonality between the examples provided is that they lay down obligations for the state, which one might call v-rules, and that these obligations are not linked to the individual rights or interests of natural persons.

The examples will be divided in two categories. First, minimum requirements, which are obligations that states must always take into account. They can be seen as prerequisites for a legitimate state and a democratic legal order. They correspond to what Fuller has called the 'morality of duty'. Second, aspirations, i.e. obligations for states to strive towards their *telos* or end, which is promoting human flourishing and freedom. These aspirations are formulated as open norms and can conflict with each other. While minimum requirements could be called obligations aimed at results, aspirations could be seen as obligations aimed at best efforts.

The minimum requirements are deeply rooted in considerations regarding the rule of law. There are certain minimum requirements that laws and democratic states must always respect. These rules and conditions focus predominantly on curtailing governmental power and laying down checks and balances to prevent abuse of power. The principles of the rule of law apply independent of any subjective, individual right; they are the preconditions for the legal order, the foundations on which the state is built. The aspirations are based on the fact that virtue ethics embraces the idea of a teleological regulatory framework, or as Fuller put it: the state is not a neutral object, it is designed for a certain purpose. Such a focus provides a theoretical framework for building non-rights-based policies, such as those directed at duties of care, codes of conduct and best practices.

Section 2 of this chapter will specify which minimum requirements related to the principles of the rule of law can be applied to privacy regulation. It will use the building blocks discussed in Chapter II and III in order to craft a fully developed theoretical and normative foundation for this additional privacy approach. Section 3 will demonstrate how a focus on goals and aspiration could be applied in practice with respect to privacy regulation. It will use the building blocks developed in Chapter IV, and relate them back to some elements of the 'original' privacy paradigm, as discussed in Chapter II. Finally, Section 4 will briefly analyze the previous points and discuss how these rules can be enforced through legal and other means.

2. MINIMUM REQUIREMENTS

This section will provide three examples of potential minimum requirements under a virtue ethical approach to privacy regulation. Such obligations are directed at the state and do not correlate with subjective rights of natural persons. The obligations have the goal of protecting the legitimacy and legality of the legal order; they are linked to the rule of law and provide safeguards for the abuse of power. The examples will suggest how such an approach might be of added value when compared to the current regulatory privacy and data protection framework.

The first example, as described in Subsection 2.1, goes as follows. First, the current legal paradigm distinguishes between quite a number of different types and categories of data, each with a particular level of protection. In general, the closer a datum is linked to the individual, the higher the level of protection. Second, this model is under pressure for two reasons in particular: One reason is that data re being processed in an increasingly hybrid fashion; their type and status may change in a split second. Sticking to fixed and static categories of data will prove increasingly difficult in this constellation. The other reason is that the use of ordinary, nonpersonal, aggregated and metadata can have a significant impact on individuals, even if they are not identified or identifiable on an individual level. Third, and consequently, it may prove fruitful to regulate 'data'. A virtue ethical model of privacy regulation could provide the basis for such an approach, as it is not linked to the protection of individual interests, but to the virtuous behavior of the agent. Although a number of individual rights contained in the current privacy and data protection instruments cannot be upheld with regard to processing nonpersonal data, other principles could be applied as minimum requirements when states process 'data'.

The second example, provided in Subsection 2.2, can be described as follows. First, it suggested that under the dominant European privacy paradigm, as described in Chapter II, it is difficult to invoke rule of law principles for natural or legal persons that have not been directly and personally affected by the matter complained of. Second, as shown in Chapter III, in Big Data and mass surveillance cases, rule of law principles are often undermined without specific individuals being harmed. Third, as discussed in Chapter III, the European Court of Human Rights has in recent jurisprudence stressed that in specific circumstances it is willing to abandon its strict focus on individual harm and will assess rule of law principles *in abstracto*. Fourth, it is nevertheless unclear how this exception could be reconciled on a theoretical level with the dominant paradigm, which focuses on individual rights and individual interests. Fifth, a virtue ethical approach could provide a theoretical framework by explaining why it is important to uphold rule of law principles even without individuals being directly affected.

The third and final example, which was provided in Subsection 2.3, picks up on an idea mentioned in the introduction to this book. First, the current regulatory framework is mostly focused on gathering and using data, not on the phases in between, in which the data are analyzed, aggregated and turned into categories, patterns and group profiles. Second, the reason for this focus, related to the argument discussed in Subsection 2.1, is that the gathering of data and the application of data profiles in practice may have an impact on individuals, whereas the analysis of data as such rarely does. Third, the phase in which the analysis is conducted is increasingly important and the choices made in that stage do in fact have a large impact on society as a whole and on individuals in particular, albeit in indirect ways. Fourth, certain minimum requirements for analyzing data could be enshrined in law when adopting a virtue ethical approach to privacy regulation.

2.1. REGULATING 'DATA'

Currently, there are many different types of data and categories of data distinguished in the legal paradigm, each having their own regime and level of protection. For example, in the General Data Protection Regulation, a distinction is made between non-personal data, statistical data, personal data and sensitive data. Nonpersonal and anonymized data, in principle, fall outside the scope of the data protection principles,[424] which only apply to cases in which data related to identifiable natural persons are processed.[425] The Regulation defines personal data as any information relating to an identified or identifiable natural person and explains that 'an identifiable natural person is one who can be identified, directly or indirectly, in particular by reference to an identifier such as a name, an identification number, location data, an online identifier or to one or more factors specific to the physical, physiological, genetic, mental, economic, cultural or social identity of that natural person'.[426] The many data protection principles, such as the data minimization requirement, the purpose and purpose limitation principle,

---

[424] Recital 26 Regulation.
[425] Article 1 Regulation.
[426] Article 4 (1) Regulation.

the transparency principle and the duty to provide for adequate technical and organizational standards, apply only to the processing of personal data. Nonpersonal data are mostly left unregulated.

There is a special regime under the Regulation for 'sensitive data'. Sensitive data are data that have a special status because they have a particularly close link to the individual or reveal particularly sensitive information about that person. The Regulation specifies that the processing of personal data revealing racial or ethnic origin, political opinions, religious or philosophical beliefs, or trade union membership, and the processing of genetic data, biometric data for the purpose of uniquely identifying a natural person, data concerning health or data concerning a natural person's sex life or sexual orientation, shall in principle be prohibited.[427] The Regulation does specify a number of exceptions to that rule, but it is clear that the data qualified as sensitive enjoy a higher level of protection. This is also clear from the fact that the grounds on which the processing of sensitive data can be legitimized are stricter in comparison to the grounds that can be used for legitimizing the processing of non-sensitive personal data.

Then there is the category of statistical data. These are data that may have been personal data or even sensitive personal data, but have been aggregated to serve as the building blocks for group profiles and statistical patterns. For example, a group profile may be that of the people living in neighborhood Y, 70% of the males drive a red car. It is unlikely that such a profile itself will be qualified as a personal datum, because it does not relate to one or a number of specific individuals. Consequently, many of the data protection principles will not apply, even although the profile was based on personal data. The Regulation contains a specific provision on the processing of personal data, holding that many of the classic data protection principles should be respected in these circumstances.[428] However, it is unclear whether this will also be the case with respect to the processing of non-personal or aggregated data for statistical purposes. Given the explicit delineation in the scope of the Regulation, it must be presumed that this is not the case.

Finally, the Regulation introduces even more categories and types of data:
- There are special rules for pseudonymized data, pseudonymization meaning the processing of personal data in such a manner that the personal data can no longer be attributed to a specific data subject without the use of additional information, provided that such additional information is kept separately and is subject to technical and organizational measures to ensure that the personal data are not attributed to an identified or identifiable natural person.[429]
- There are rules new on 'genetic data', which are personal data relating to the inherited or acquired genetic characteristics of a natural person which give unique information about the physiology or the health of that natural person and which

---

[427] Article 9 Regulation.
[428] Article 89 Regulation.
[429] Article 4 sub 5 Regulation.

result, in particular, from an analysis of a biological sample from the natural person in question.[430]
- There are rules on 'biometric data', meaning personal data resulting from specific technical processing relating to the physical, physiological or behavioral characteristics of a natural person, which allow or confirm the unique identification of that natural person, such as facial images or dactyloscopic data.[431]
- And there are so called 'data concerning health', meaning personal data related to the physical or mental health of a natural person, including the provision of health care services, which reveal information about his or her health status.[432]

Each of these data have a special regime and level of protection, because they have a special relation to the individual.

A similar structure may be found in the e-Privacy Directive.[433] This Directive contains specific rules on the processing of personal data in the electronic environment, for example with respect to directories of subscribers.[434] It applies to the processing of personal data in connection with the provisioning of publicly available electronic communications services in public communications networks.[435] It also is intended to harmonize the provisions of the Member States required to ensure an equivalent level of protection of fundamental rights and freedoms, and in particular the right to privacy, with respect to the processing of personal data in the electronic communication sector and to ensure the free movement of such data and of electronic communication equipment and services.[436]

However, there are also a number of rules that apply to other types of data, such as location data and traffic data – sometimes referred to as metadata:
- Traffic data are defined by the e-Privacy Directive as any data processed for the purpose of the conveyance of a communication on an electronic communications network or for the billing thereof. Location data, within the meaning of the Directive are any data indicating the geographic position of the terminal equipment of a user of a publicly available electronic communications service.[437] The Directive specifies, *inter alia*, that traffic data relating to subscribers and users processed and stored by the provider of a public communications network must be erased or made anonymous when it is no longer needed for the purpose of the transmission of a communication.[438]

---

[430] Article 4 sub 13 Regulation.
[431] Article 4 sub 14 Regulation.
[432] Article 4 sub 15 Regulation.
[433] Directive 2002/58/EC of the European Parliament and of the Council of 12 July 2002 concerning the processing of personal data and the protection of privacy in the electronic communications sector (Directive on privacy and electronic communications).
[434] Article 12 e-Privacy Directive.
[435] Article 3 e-Privacy Directive.
[436] Article 1.1 e-Privacy Directive.
[437] Article 2 e-Privacy Directive.
[438] Article 6 e-Privacy Directive.

- Regarding location data other than traffic data, the e-Privacy Directive specifies, *inter alia*, that data relating to users or subscribers of public communications networks, may only be processed when they are made anonymous, or with the consent of the users or subscribers to the extent and for the duration necessary for the provision of a value added service. The service provider must, prior to obtaining their consent, inform the users or subscribers, of the type of location data other than traffic data which will be processed, of the purposes and duration of the processing and whether the data will be transmitted to a third party for the purpose of providing the value added service.[439]
- The e-Privacy Directive also contains rules protecting the secrecy of communication and the integrity of communication devices. For example, it is stressed that the provider of a publicly available electronic communications service must take appropriate technical and organizational measures to safeguard the security of its services, if necessary in conjunction with the provider of the public communications network with respect to network security.[440] To conclude, the Directive stresses that Member States must also ensure that the use of electronic communications networks to store information in the terminal equipment of a subscriber or user, or to access to the information stored therein, is only allowed on condition that the subscriber or user concerned is provided with clear and comprehensive information.[441]

To give a final example, as discussed at length in Chapters II and III, under the right to privacy laid down in Article 8 of European Convention on Human Rights, different types of data and communications are also distinguished by the European Court of Human Rights. Most of them have already been explained in Chapter II and III. In general, it has been shown that the ECtHR in principle rejects cases that revolve around the processing of ordinary data in what could be considered day-to-day processing activities. It also provides less protection to metadata than to the content of communications and provides a higher level of protection for certain categories of data, for example those related to health, sexual preferences and criminal records. Consequently, under this regime too, distinctions are made as regards types and categories of data and the level of protection afforded.

However, as discussed in Chapter III, it is questionable whether these distinctions are still tenable in the age of Big Data. Ordinary data and metadata are increasingly collected and the information that can be distilled from them can provide a very detailed picture of a person's life. Also, these data, particularly if linked and connected to other information, can be used to determine the content of communication.

> Possible inferences from metadata can invade a user's privacy in the same way as sensitive personal information obtained from posted content. This includes identifying information

---

[439] Article 9 e-Privacy Directive.
[440] Article 4 e-Privacy Directive.
[441] Article 5 e-Privacy Directive.

(directly or indirectly), general descriptive data (interests, political attitudes, health condition, etc.) as well as more SNS-specific information such as social relationship data (number of friends, nature of relations, etc.), or behavioral data (activity, location, etc.).[442]

It is generally also agreed upon that ordinary 'data' can increasingly be used to influence the behavior and lives of natural persons, even without knowing their precise identity. In this sense, the distinction between ordinary data and metadata on the one hand and personal and sensitive data on the other hand seems to be crumbling.

In addition, insensitive personal data are increasingly linked to other insensitive data and general statistical profiles, for example through merging databases, so that sensitive and very significant profiles may be created. The general profile "in district X, 80% of people have disease Y" (which is not a personal datum) may be linked to an insensitive datum "person Z lives in district X", in order to create a very sensitive profile. This fact also challenges the distinction between personal data and sensitive personal data, engrained in the current regulatory approach to privacy and data protection regulation. The same applies to aggregate data and anonymous data. Increasingly, these categories are merely temporary stages, because data can almost always be linked back to an individual or can be de-anonymized or re-identified.[443]

Overall, while the current legal system is focused on relatively static stages of data and links to these a specific protection regime, in practice, data processing is becoming a circular process: data are linked, aggregated and anonymized and then again de-anonymized enriched with other data, in order to create sensitive profiles, etc. It is important to point out that it will often prove impossible to assess beforehand what status or role a specific datum will play, how it will be used and what it may tell about an individual in the future. It is therefore questionable whether it is still tenable to apply a less stringent juridical regime to the collection of, for example, metadata or anonymized data than to the collection of sensitive data, if these data can be linked to other data with ease and, as a result, may become sensitive data all the same.

Both trends (the fact that nonsensitive data can be used for means that have a high impact on the individual and the fact that it becomes increasingly difficult to apply static categories of data to an increasingly circular and volatile data life-cycle) beg the question: why not regulate plain 'data'? This would apply in particular to digital data. Doing so might also have a practical advantage, because both data subjects and data controllers are increasingly unaware of whether certain data bases and data processing activities include personal data or sensitive personal data, and if so, to whom the data can be linked. Determining these facts with care might demand significant

---

[442] B. Greschbach, 'The Devil is in the Metadata – New Privacy Challenges in Decentralised Online Social Networks', <www.nada.kth.se/~gkreitz/metadata/sesocMetaPrivacy.pdf>.
[443] P. Ohm, 'Broken promises of privacy: responding to the surprising failure of anonymisation', UCLA Law Rev., 2010-57. M. R. Koot, 'Measuring and predicting anonymity', Amsterdam, Informatics Institute, Amsterdam, Universiteit van Amsterdam, 2012. L. Sweeney, 'k-anonymity: A model for protecting privacy', International Journal of Uncertainty, Fuzziness and Knowledge-based Systems, 10-5, 2002.

organizational efforts and costs, if at all successful, which could be avoided if legal regulation simply turned to 'data' instead of creating numerous different categories and types of data.

It is also important to point out that stretching the concept of personal data in data protection regimes is not a novelty; as shown in Chapter II, the concept 'personal data' has been broadened and widened time and again. One of the reasons was that companies and governments became capable of having an effect on people and their lives with data that was ever less directly connected to the individual. In order to ensure that the data protection rules would still apply to these data uses, the definition of 'personal data' was broadened in every subsequent data protection instrument. In this sense, because it is now possible to influence people's lives on the basis of non-personal data, applying the data protection principles to 'data' as such seems only the next logical step.

A final practical advantage would be that there are currently many discussions over what should be considered personal data and what not, such as IP addresses, cookies, group profiles and human tissue samples. In a recent opinion addressing the question whether IP addresses are personal data, the advocate general of the Court of Justice stressed:

> Conformément à l'article 2, sous a), de la directive 95/46/CE du Parlement européen et du Conseil, du 24 octobre 1995, relative à la protection des personnes physiques à l'égard du traitement des données à caractère personnel et à la libre circulation de ces données, une adresse IP dynamique par laquelle un utilisateur a accédé au site Internet d'un fournisseur de médias électroniques constitue pour celui-ci une donnée à caractère personnel, dans la mesure où un fournisseur d'accès au réseau possède des informations supplémentaires qui, combinées à l'adresse IP dynamique, permettraient d'identifier l'utilisateur.[444]

Even if the ECJ would follow this advice, there will be many other difficult dilemmas regarding the scope of personal data, which may take years before they will be resolved and, in the meantime, may be used by companies and governmental institutions to collect and process large quantities of data, as they may claim the data do not qualify as 'personal data'. Regulating 'data' would avoid these and similar discussions.

The question is whether the data protection principles contained in the various data protection instruments could be applied to 'data' instead of 'personal data'. Under a virtue ethical approach to privacy, many of them arguably could, because the core question is how states should behave; how they should process data and under which conditions. Obviously, this does not count for the rules and principles under the current framework that are directly linked to the individual, her rights and her interests. These are the principles that lay down the rights of individual data subjects, for example the right of a data subject to access her data, the right to correct them, to right to object to

---

[444] Opinion of Advocate General Campos Sanchez-Bordona, Patrick Breyer v. Bundesrepublik Deutschland, Case C-582/14, 12 May 2016.

the processing of her data, the right to be forgotten and the right to data portability.[445] The underlying reason for granting individuals a right to access and control personal data is because the data relate to them specifically – these are 'their' data. When the focus of data protection instruments turns to plain 'data', this underlying rationale no longer applies. Consequently, if data protection instruments would indeed take 'data' as their core concept and if one would want to preserve the subjective access and control rights, a separate rule should be introduced stressing that these rights only apply to cases in which personal data are processed.

It seems that the other principles in the current data protection instruments could also be applied to 'data' in general, and it could be argued that they should if the underlying rationale for these rules is the prevention of abuse of power and laying down checks and balances. As stressed in Chapter II, the origins of the data protection instruments were grounded in providing duties for data controllers. The underlying reason was that processing personal data granted the data controller power over the data subjects. The data controller could influence the behavior of individuals or base decisions and policies on the data processes, and in doing so, positively or negatively affect the interests of these individuals. That is why a number of duties of care were laid down in order to ensure checks and balances that could mitigate potential risks. As stressed above, in the current technological reality, the same argument can be applied to the processing of 'data'. Through the use of statistical correlations, algorithmic patterns and group profiles, people's lives can be affected significantly. It is no longer essential whether the data that are processed are personal or aggregated, ordinary or sensitive, private or public; all data can be used in ways that have a large impact on individuals and society as a whole. Consequently, it seems logical apply the duties of care to the processors of 'data' in general.

To provide an example, the current data protection principles specify that personal data must be stored safely and confidentially. Data controllers should take all reasonable technical measures to prevent data leaks and to minimize harm when data leaks occur. Data controllers should also ensure that access is limited to those persons within their organization that actually need it. Given the fact that nonpersonal, nonsensitive and anonymized data can often be linked back to individuals and be de-anonymized, and can be used to affect people even without knowing their identity, it seems that there is no guarantee that these types of data will not be abused in a way that negatively affects individuals or society as a whole when they fall into the wrong hands. That is why is seems pivotal to apply the requirement of safe and confidential data processing to 'data' in general.

A similar reasoning could be applied to the requirement of a legitimate aim and the requirements of necessity and proportionality. The current data protection principles specify that data controllers may only gather, store and process personal data when the processing serves one of various (enumerated) legitimate purposes. Data controllers may only gather data insofar as they are necessary for achieving that legitimate goal and if gathering those data is proportionate to the aim pursued. It seems that, especially

---

[445] Chapter III of the Regulation.

in relation to governmental institutions, the requirement that the state may only use its power (in this case for gathering and processing data) if that serves a legitimate aim and is necessary in a democratic society, seems to be a minimum condition for every legitimate state. Random exercises of power without any clear or concrete purpose conflict with the basic principles of the rule of law. There seems to be no reason why a state or governmental institution should be allowed to use its power (to process data) without there being a clear need, without there being a legitimate aim, and without the use of power being proportionate.

Current data protection instruments also include the principle of data quality, which prescribes that; the data should be correct and that they must be kept up to date. The underlying reason for such rules is that incorrect or outdated personal data may lead to incorrect decisions and to negative or unfair results for individuals. The same logic seems to apply to the processing of nonpersonal data. Suppose, for example, that the profile '70% of the people living in neighborhood Y have disease Z' is based on outdated information, and suppose that the relevant data were gathered 20 years ago. It would be wrong for either the government or an insurance company to use this database to develop a general policy. Again, it seems expedient to apply this principle not merely to 'personal data', but to 'data' in general.

To provide a final example, the current data protection instruments also include the principle of transparency. Although the current General Data Protection Regulation links this transparency principle exclusively to the individual and her individual interest, this was not the case originally, as explained in detail in Chapter II. In earlier documents, a distinction was made between, on the one hand, the right of the individual to request access to her personal data and to receive information about the specific data processing activities, and on the other hand the general transparency obligation of the data controller. While the data controller incurred a correlative duty with respect to the rights of the data subject, namely to grant access to the personal data and/or to provide further information about the processing activities, it is important to stress that the transparency duty did not correlate with any individual right. It was a duty as such of the data controller to provide clarity about her activities. For example, the first article of the Resolution of the Council of Europe from 1974 on the processing of personal data in the public sector specified: 'As a general rule the public should be kept regularly informed about the establishment, operation and development of electronic data banks in the public sector.'[446] Note that this duty is directed at the public in general. The underlying reason for this principle can be found in the need for transparency of governmental power, among other reasons to ensure control over the exercise of that power. In light of the previous discussion on the processing of nonpersonal data, it might be pertinent to apply such a transparency rule to 'data' in general.

In conclusion, it has been demonstrated that the current regulatory framework is based on a number of different categories and types of data and that each of them

---

[446] Resolution (74) 29 on the protection of the privacy of individuals vis-à-vis electronic data banks in the public sector.

receives a different level of protection. It has been shown that in Big Data processes, the underlying reason for these differentiations no longer holds, because nonpersonal, aggregate and metadata can be used to impact individuals just as well as personal and sensitive personal data, and because the nature of data is increasingly circular and volatile. That is why it seems expedient to regulate 'data'. A good starting point for finding principles for the regulation of 'data' might be the rules provided by the General Data Protection Regulation. Some of these rules are only applicable to 'personal data', namely the rules granting individuals subjective rights, but the basic principles of fair and adequate data processing seem to be applicable to the processing of 'data' in general – and especially to data kept in digital formats. There may also be other principles that could be applied to data processing in general, when the core rationale is no longer protecting the rights and interests of individuals, but laying down safeguards against the abuse of power by states. These will need to be developed further; one particular set of rules that might be applied to the analysis of data will be discussed in Subsection 2.3.

2.2. APPLYING THE RULE OF LAW TEST IN ABSTRACTO

Chapter II showed that the original privacy paradigm under the European Convention of Human Rights, as contained in Article 8 ECHR, was primarily focused on providing protection to general and societal interests, and only marginally relied on individual, subjective rights to protect personal interests. It was also shown that over time, this focus has shifted quite a bit. The Convention has been revised on a number of points and the European Court of Human Rights in particular has radically reinterpreted the meaning and function of the Convention. It has focused almost exclusively on granting subjective rights to natural persons and on the protection of personal interests of individuals. This has meant that in principle, only natural persons can submit a complaint if they have suffered from the law or practice complained of personally and directly. Conversely, claims from individuals, groups or legal persons who have not suffered individually and directly have generally been declared inadmissible. An example of such an application is a so-called *in abstracto* claim, in which a claimant asks the Court to assess the quality of a law or policy as such.

Chapter III showed that in Big Data and mass surveillance cases, it is increasingly difficult to prove or substantiate individual harm. It raised questions such as: how did the data gathering by the NSA affect an ordinary American or European citizen? Similarly, it referred to cities such as London in which there are apparently more CCTV camera's than people. Again, it is very difficult to prove how this affects an individual personally. The problem, it seems, with these types of processes is not that one specific individual is filmed or surveilled, but rather that everyone is or might be – indiscriminately and without a pre-established reason. Rather than affecting individual and personal interests, such practices have an impact on general and societal interests. In particular, they put pressure on the classic principles of the rule of law, which limit governmental power and mitigate risks related to its abuse.

Chapter III also showed that since the *Klass* judgement, the ECtHR has struggled with its own approach centered on individual rights and individual interests, especially in cases revolving around large data gathering and surveillance practices. Ever since that judgment in 1978, the Court has been willing to occasionally allow *in abstracto* claims through the backdoor, without explicitly acknowledging that it did so. Rather, it used terms that obscured its relaxed position on individual rights and individual interests, e.g. by emphasizing that certain practices affected everyone residing in a certain country. This has changed in the more recent case of *Szabó & Vissy v. Hungary* and especially in *Zakharov v. Russia*. With these decisions, the European Court of Human Rights has finally accepted unequivocally that in exceptional cases, it will allow *in abstracto* claims and that it will assess as such the basic principles of the rule of law, relating *inter alia* to the basic legality and legitimacy of the laws and practices underlying the mass surveillance practices. These are minimum standards that the state needs to abide by, even when no individual rights have been infringed or individual interests have been harmed.

To reiterate, in *Zakharov* the ECtHR specified the following:

[T]he Court accepts that an applicant can claim to be the victim of a violation occasioned by the mere existence of secret surveillance measures, or legislation permitting secret surveillance measures, if the following conditions are satisfied. Firstly, the Court will take into account the scope of the legislation permitting secret surveillance measures by examining whether the applicant can possibly be affected by it, either because he or she belongs to a group of persons targeted by the contested legislation or because the legislation directly affects all users of communication services by instituting a system where any person can have his or her communications intercepted. Secondly, the Court will take into account the availability of remedies at the national level and will adjust the degree of scrutiny depending on the effectiveness of such remedies. As the Court underlined in *Kennedy*, where the domestic system does not afford an effective remedy to the person who suspects that he or she was subjected to secret surveillance, widespread suspicion and concern among the general public that secret surveillance powers are being abused cannot be said to be unjustified. In such circumstances the menace of surveillance can be claimed in itself to restrict free communication through the postal and telecommunication services, thereby constituting for all users or potential users a direct interference with the right guaranteed by Article 8. There is therefore a greater need for scrutiny by the Court and an exception to the rule, which denies individuals the right to challenge a law *in abstracto*, is justified. In such cases the individual does not need to demonstrate the existence of any risk that secret surveillance measures were applied to him. By contrast, if the national system provides for effective remedies, a widespread suspicion of abuse is more difficult to justify. In such cases, the individual may claim to be a victim of a violation occasioned by the mere existence of secret measures or of legislation permitting secret measures only if he is able to show that, due to his personal situation, he is potentially at risk of being subjected to such measures.[447]

---

[447] Zakharov, §171.

In this case, the Court assessed in general terms whether a law allowing for mass surveillance practices abided by the minimum principles of the rule of law. *Inter alia*, it assessed the accessibility of the domestic law and the scope and duration of the secret surveillance measures. It also assessed the procedures for authorization, supervision and notification of these measures, and for storing, accessing, examining, using, communicating and destroying the intercepted data, as well as the available remedies. The ECtHR concluded that Russian legal provisions governing interceptions of communications did not provide for adequate and effective guarantees against the risk of arbitrariness and abuse, which it considered inherent in any system of secret surveillance, especially in a system where the secret services and the police have direct access, by technical means, to all mobile telephone communications.

In particular, the Court stressed that the circumstances in which public authorities are empowered to resort to secret surveillance measures were not defined with sufficient clarity; the provisions on discontinuation of secret surveillance measures did not provide adequate guarantees against arbitrary interference; the domestic law permitted automatic storage of clearly irrelevant data and was not sufficiently clear as to the circumstances in which the intercepted material would be stored and destroyed after the end of a trial; the authorization procedures were not capable of ensuring that secret surveillance measures would be ordered only when 'necessary in a democratic society'; the supervision of interceptions did not comply with the requirements of independence, powers and competence which are sufficient to ensure effective and continuous control, public scrutiny and effectiveness in practice; and the effectiveness of the remedies was undermined by the lack of notification at any point of interceptions, or adequate access to documents relating to interceptions.

In conclusion, the European Court of Human Rights held as follows:

> It is significant that the shortcomings in the legal framework as identified above appear to have an impact on the actual operation of the system of secret surveillance which exists in Russia. The Court is not convinced by the Government's assertion that all interceptions in Russia are performed lawfully on the basis of a proper judicial authorisation. The examples submitted by the applicant in the domestic proceedings and in the proceedings before the Court indicate the existence of arbitrary and abusive surveillance practices, which appear to be due to the inadequate safeguards provided by law. In view of the shortcomings identified above, the Court finds that Russian law does not meet the "quality of law" requirement and is incapable of keeping the "interference" to what is "necessary in a democratic society". There has accordingly been a violation of Article 8 of the Convention.[448]

Chapter III ended by lauding this turn by the ECtHR; in fact, one of the main arguments of this book is that courts should apply a rule of law test independently of the question of whether a specific individual has been harmed. The principles of the rule of law are the minimum conditions for legal orders; these principles should always be respected

---

[448] Zakharov, §302.

because they are the foundation of the state. If the principles of the rule of law are disrespected, the state will undermine its own legitimacy and legality. The European Court of Human Rights now seems to fully acknowledge this fact. However, as Chapter III concluded, it remains unclear how this approach relates to or can be reconciled with the Court's dominant approach, which is focused strongly on subjective rights and individual interests. If it is true, as seems to be the premise of the Court, that human rights protect humans and their interests, it remains unclear how this can be reconciled with an approach in which *in abstracto* claims are declared admissible. In cases such as *Zakharov*, not human rights are undermined, but the principles of the rule of law.

Obviously, on a practical level, it is laudable that the European Court of Human Rights has signaled that its dominant approach does not provide an adequate level of protection in cases concerning Big Data and mass surveillance practices. It is also laudable that it tries to find new ways to afford protection to principles that it considers important. However, since an abstract test of legality and legitimacy of laws is so diametrically opposed to its focus on subjective rights and individual interests, such a novel approach seems to require a theoretical and ethical foundation. This helps to understand and explain what the ECtHR actually does when it accepts *in abstracto* claims, and it can grant legitimacy to such an approach.

Chapter IV provided such an ethical foundation by turning to virtue ethics. Virtue ethics, as has been explained, is a third branch of ethics, next to consequentialism and deontology. It does not rely on the maximization of the general wellfare nor does it build on a set of categorical duties. Rather, it assesses the virtuousness of agents. An agent has an ethical duty to act in the most virtuous manner; such a duty applies irrespective of any correlative rights of other persons or institutions. The state is approached as a man-made artifact and compared to other objects. A chair is designed by man with a certain goal; typically a chair is designed to sit on. We might call a chair optimal if it allows us to relax, or, depending on the context in which it is used, to work behind our desk. The virtuous furniture maker should always aim to design a chair that is the most perfect given the circumstances. There are also a number of minimum conditions. A chair that has no legs, no back and no surface to sit on, might no longer be called a proper chair. A similar logic may be applied to other man-made objects, such as the legal order – though this argument is of course more abstract since the legal order was not designed at one moment, by one person, with one specific purpose.

Still, Chapter IV proposed to apply the same reasoning to the state. Lon L. Fuller stressed that, like a chair, the legal order is man-made; it is designed with a certain purpose and goal. Its goal is to protect and promote human autonomy and freedom. Choosing a legal order as the way to regulate the state is nontrivial, because laws, as opposed to e.g. monarchical orders and dictates, are designed to give the citizen guidance. The essential difference between laws and orders by dictators is precisely that the latter are often unstable, directed at specific persons or situations and are often unintelligible to the ordinary citizen. Laws are relatively stable, general and transparent, such that citizens know the rules applicable to them and can take those rules into account when making decisions. The very essence of the legal order is thus that it is based on human autonomy. The legal order is based on the idea that humans can access the law, can understand the law and can modify their conduct accordingly. If laws lose these essential characters or when the executive order is left unrestrained and thus has the capacity to issue ad hoc and unintelligible decrees, the very essence of the legal regime is undermined. Arguably, this is precisely what is central to cases such as *Zakharov*.

Just like a chair without legs or seat would normally not be called a chair, there are certain minimum conditions for legal orders to be called a legal order. This is the case when the legal order in general no longer functions as a vehicle for ordering human life in such a way that human autonomy is respected. This is the case, for example, with retroactive, unclear, unstable and intransparent legislation. It is precisely these types of principles that are put under pressure in cases concerning mass surveillance. In the case of *Zakharov*, for example, the problem at issue was the broad and unrestricted attribution of power to organizations within the state, without a minimum level of transparency and checks and balances being in place. As described in Chapter IV, respecting these minimum principles of the rule of law is a duty of the state without a correlative subjective right of citizens. This is precisely what happens in *in abstracto* claims; states are held to obligations that need to be respected even if no concrete subjective rights have been violated. Consequently, while a rights-based approach to privacy regulation cannot explain or provide a theoretical basis for such *in abstracto* claims, virtue ethics can.

2.3. REGULATING THE ANALYSIS PHASE

The introduction to this book signaled the fact that the current regulatory regime is mostly focused on the phase in which data are gathered and stored. Just to recall a number of relevant data principles: data may only be gathered as far as they are necessary and proportionate to the goal pursued; the goal must be legitimate and clear; data may subsequently not be processed for other purposes; and data must be stored confidentially and safely. Data usage is also regulated to a certain extent, in particular when the use has a direct effect on the individual, for example through direct or indirect discriminatory practices. The reason that these two phases (the collection and the usage of data) are prominent in the current regulatory framework is that in these phases, a link can be made between the data processing activities and the individual.

The phase in between, however, where data are aggregated, analyzed and turned into valuable knowledge, is mostly left unregulated. In this phase, databases are merged, data are selected for aggregation, algorithms are deployed, factors and their relative weight are determined, statistical correlations are found and interpreted, and group profiles, patterns and general policies are developed. The reason that this phase is mostly left unregulated is, as already pointed out in Subsection 2.1, that the data are often not directly connected to specific individuals. To find general patterns and statistical correlations, increasingly large datasets are harvested and combined on an aggregated level. The data analyzed may no longer have a direct link to any particular individual, which also holds true for the patterns and profiles produced. A statistical correlation could be, for example, that 70% of the people who attend classical music concerts also like expensive red wine. Such a profile in itself is not a personal datum, nor does it, in itself, have any impact on individuals; it is only when it is applied in practice, for example by showing advertisements of red wine to particular individuals, that the current regulatory regime might come into play.

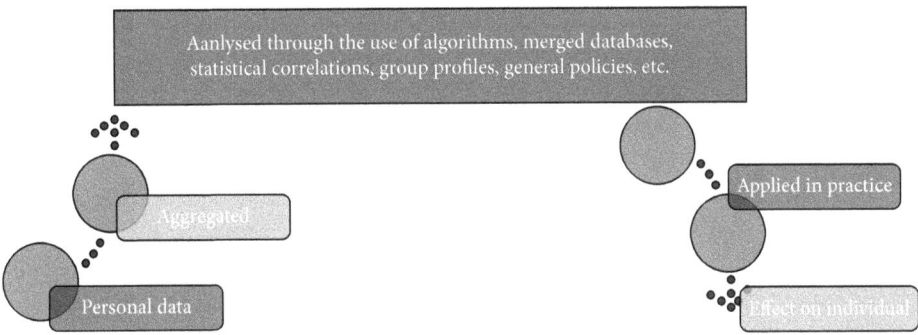

Although the phase in which the data are analyzed has no direct effect on specific individuals, it may still be important to regulate it for a number of reasons. Three of those will be discussed briefly. The first ground for regulation is that the quality of the data analysis process has enormous relevance for the eventual outcome and the further application of the results in practice. It is therefore essential to adopt rules to ensure the quality of the phase in between of the collection and usage of data. The second point is that the same might be said about the choices that are made in designing the analytics process, for example which data are taken into account, how they are analyzed and how the various factors are weighed. Third and finally, the general patterns and statistical correlations found should always be assessed on their quality and societal acceptability, for example in relation to precluding false or potentially discriminatory results.[449]

First is the quality of the process. Subsection 2.1 already pointed to the rule of data quality, engrained in many data protection instruments, which entails that data must be reliable and kept up to date. For example, Article 5, Paragraph 1, Subparagraph d of the General Data Protection Regulation specifies that personal data must be 'accurate and, where necessary, kept up to date; every reasonable step must be taken to ensure that personal data that are inaccurate, having regard to the purposes for which they are processed, are erased or rectified without delay'.[450] As stressed in Subsection 2.1, it is important to apply this principle to the processing of 'data' in general, because data analysis currently relies mainly on aggregated data that do not qualify as 'personal data'.

---

[449] See more in detail: WRR, 'Big Data in een vrije en veilige samenleving', WRR-rapport, Amsterdam University Press, Amsterdam 2016.
[450] Article 5, Section 1, sub d of the General Data Protection Regulation.

The same applies to the quality of the categorization of data and the merging of different databases. Although there is much talk about analyzing so-called unstructured data, often these data are often nevertheless labeled and categorized. Designing and selecting those data in a logical and transparent manner, in a way that allows for reliable, scientific data analysis, is pivotal. The same applies to the merging of databases. Often, databases are integrated though they are essentially incomparable due to inherent differences in the types of data, and in the methods applied for their collection, selection and organisation. Even if two databases contain similar categories, for example the category 'young white males', the criteria for including a person in this group may differ between these databases. In one database, people might be qualified as 'young' if they are younger than 35, whereas the other database may use 30 as its criterion and only contain data on people who have reached the age of 18. The same goes for the category of 'white' and 'male'. The results found with respect to the group 'young white males' by merging and harvesting the two databases may thus turn out to be corrupt.

As a final example of the importance of the quality of the data analysis process, reference can be made to algorithm design and research methods. Obviously, the algorithm used to analyze the data must itself be adequately designed to yield reliable and valuable results. However, few legal standards currently guarantee the minimum reliability of such tools, or of research methods in general. One of the terms now often used is 'data-driven' research, which is defined by some as 'letting the data do the work'. The essential thought is that it would be possible to do data analysis without a proper research plan or question, because algorithms and data analysis will produce valuable results by themselves. One proponent of this belief is Anderson, who developed a similar argument in his article 'The End of Theory: The Data Deluge Makes the Scientific Method Obsolete'.[451] Although this is a provocative claim, the general consensus is that it is untrue. To provide anecdotal evidence, some Dutch municipalities are now merging several databases in their position to scan for 'irregularities', without having specified what type of 'irregularity' they are looking at, on the basis of which factors it will be determined what an irregularity is, and which purpose such analysis would serve. Data analysts at those municipalities have indicated that such a broad research question and defunct research method will result in finding everything and thus nothing. Consequentially, inadequate research methods will lead to corrupt or invaluable results.

In essence, it is simply untrue that data-driven research will lead to valuable results all by itself. Although such research is often presented as objective and neutral, it is not. Even this type of research depends on a number of human choices – important ones. This leads to the second point made in this subsection, namely that there must be more clarity about the decision-making process in the phase in which data are analyzed. Currently, this stage of the data processing activities is often referred to as the 'black box', a metaphor developed by Frank Pasquale, among other scholars, in his book *The*

---

[451] C. Anderson, 'The end of theory: The data deluge makes the scientific method obsolete', Wired Magazine 16.07, 2008 <www.uvm.edu/~cmplxsys/wordpress/wp-content/uploads/reading-group/pdfs/2008/anderson2008.pdf>.

Black Box Society: the Secret Algorithms that Control Money and Information. He holds that this metaphor is useful for understanding the current status quo:

> The term 'black box' is a useful metaphor for doing so, given its own dual meaning. It can refer to a recording device, like the data-monitoring systems in planes, trains, and cars. Or it can mean a system whose workings are mysterious; we can observe its inputs and outputs, but we cannot tell how one becomes the other. We face these two meanings daily: tracked ever more closely by firms and governments, we have no clear idea of just how far much of this information can travel, how it is used, or its consequences.[452]

It is important to know more about this black box because choices are made in the analysis-phase that influence the final outcomes and results. These decisions often contain a certain bias in that they prioritize one approach over the other. For example, when data are gathered or selected from an already existing database, it should be assessed where the data were gathered and by what means. A classic example is that databases from the police contain an important bias, for example towards race. It may be so that in a certain neighborhoods, more criminal activities take place. Given this fact, it is logical that the police would surveil more in such areas. Such areas may have an overrepresentation of citizens with a migrant background. As a consequence, the database created by the police is primarily the result of the surveillance activities in certain neighborhoods, while others neighborhoods are surveilled to a lesser extent and are thus only marginally represented in the data. From a data-analytics perspective, this is in itself not an insuperable problem, but the bias in the database towards certain neighborhoods, and people living therein, should be acknowledged. Thus, when analyzing the data, information must be included on where the data were gathered and what the average background of the inhabitants of those neighborhoods is, in order to be able to correct the bias. However, current databases often lack such metadata.

The foregoing example is based on location, on where the data were gathered. But the same counts for the collection method, i.e. by whom the data were gathered and how. As is known in academia, the choices with respect to all these factors are determinative for finding reliable and valuable outcomes. Yet it seems that the standard of research methodology is underdeveloped in the governmental sector. Consequently, although data-based research may be perceived as factual, neutral and objective, in fact its results are often corrupt, outdated and unreliable. Because governmental agencies are relying more on data analytics by the day, it might be valuable when employees working with the data would be trained for those tasks. Also, the government should structurally monitor and store data on how databases are created, in what way data are collected, in which ways databases are merged or linked, which data are selected for a certain research project, which algorithm was deployed, how this algorithm was designed, which factors were taken into account and which weight were attributed to

---

[452] F. Pasquale, 'The Black Box Society: the secret Algorithms that Control Money and Information', Harvard University Press, Cambridge, 2015, p. 3.

them, etc. This allows third parties to assess the reliability of the data analysis process and potentially, to reproduce the research when necessary. It must be pointed out that such a requirement may be too burdensome for companies that may use biased databases or unreliable analytics to produce profiles for personalized advertising. For the government, however, a higher standard applies.

Consequently, there should be rules guaranteeing the quality of the data, the database and the research methods deployed, and there should be transparency about the various choices that are made in the data analysis process. Even if these principles are taken into account, it is important to assess the outcomes of the data analysis process – the patterns, statistical correlations and (group) profiles – for a number of reasons. The first is that profiles are always both under- and over-inclusive. Not all people in a certain profile will like the chocolate cookie they are advertised and there are people not included in the profile that do in fact appreciate chocolate cookies; similarly, not all people included in the profile of a potential terrorist are actually terrorists and there are people not included in the profile who are potential terrorists. Although this under- and over-inclusion is a natural element of predictive group profiling, more standards should be adopted with regard to which margin of error is allowed for certain practices. The two factors that should be taken into account are on the one hand, the impact of being profiled on the group of individuals, and on the other hand, the interests served by profiling.

The two examples provided above are two extremes. Advertising chocolate cookies to the wrong group of people has a relatively low impact on those people and the interest served by the profiling activity is, broadly speaking, unimportant. Being profiled as a potential terrorist, however, may have a severe impact and even lead to death when used for drone strikes. Furthermore, profiling for this purpose serves a significant interest, namely national security. For many other applications, the equation is different. It would be valuable if governmental organizations were to specify per profile what percentage of false positives and what percentage of false negatives they find acceptable. This allows for an assessment by a third party of whether those objectives are met in reality. If, for example, there are structurally too many false positives and/or false negatives, this may be a reason to start redesigning the data profile.

It should also be determined whether, and if so to what extent, unconnected elements and factors can be used to create profiles and determine policies. Potentially, a statistical correlation might be found between driving a red car and being a potential terrorist, or between people having felt pads under their chair legs and those who repay their loans on time. Although there may be a statistically reliable correlation, such correlations might still be applied hesitantly by governmental authorities, because the decompartmentalization of society and different aspects of citizens' lives might be perceived as unfair, because there is no causal relationship. This might in time undermine the perceived legitimacy of those policies and the trust of citizens in the government.

Similarly, it is important to stress, as has been stressed by many, that statistical correlations are not always reliable since they do not necessarily indicate causal relationships. An example often referred to is the fact that in airplanes crash landing at sea, more people die while wearing a life jacket than without wearing one. Obviously, the conclusion is not that wearing a life jacket is dangerous, but that most passengers involved in a crash landing at sea tend to wear their life jacket. Another example is the book plan project of the State of Illinois. Research had shown a strong correlation between the number of books at home and the performance of children at school. The State, so the story goes, almost decided to acquire and distribute additional books, but after second analysis it was shown that there was no *causal* relationship between the number of books at home and the school results. Rather, the environment in which children grew up had a positive effect on their learning curves; parents that stimulated children's learning activities owned a higher number of books on average than parents that did not. Merely distributing additional books would not address the underlying problem.

This ties in with a more general point which builds on what has been signaled above, namely that there is a tendency to regard the outcomes of data analytics as neutral and objective. As has been argued, this is not the case. Perhaps more importantly, these outcomes are often general and context-blind, while the specific situation in which a profile is applied is often of great importance. There is a prohibition on automatic decision making processes in the General Data Protection Regulation, but, as is generally the case, this rule only applies when the decision making process has a direct effect on the individual interests of a specific person. 'The data subject shall have the right not to be subject to a decision based solely on automated processing, including profiling, which produces legal effects concerning him or her or similarly significantly affects him or her.'[453] Given all that has been said in this Subsection and Subsection 2.1, it might be valuable to apply a similar rule to the use of profiles and statistical correlations in general. It is a valuable asset in general to take into account the specific context when a natural person applies a general profile.

Finally, there has always been fear for discriminatory processing activities. Using profiles based on racial information, on sexual or religious preferences and on health care data is generally considered dangerous. That is why many countries, for example the Netherlands, used to have a codified prohibition on collecting and storing certain types of data about their population, such as race. Now, however, such rules have mostly disappeared and gathering such data is a common practice around the globe. The difficulty is that condemning such practices is problematic, because gathering such data may also be used to enhance the position of certain groups. If it is known that there is a higher crime rate among people of Moroccan descent, the government might invest more in terms of education and coaching for this group. If it is known that there is a high number of violent incidents against the LGBT community, the police might want to invest more in protecting certain nightlife areas.

The difficulty is that indirect sensitive data can also be used to discriminate against groups. The most well-known example being the so-called *redlining* practice, in which American banks did not outright discriminate against Afro-American citizens, but did

---

[453] Article 22 General Data Protection Regulation.

take into account postal codes. It so happened that postal code areas in which there was a high percentage of Afro-Americans living were treated in an unfavorable manner when compared to the areas in which people with a different background lived. As stressed previously, this might be a reason to process more data when in designing a profile or policy; for example, if policies are based on postal code areas, a data controller could be under a duty to assess whether the population living in certain areas has a specific ethnic background.[454]

In conclusion, it has been argued that it might be worthwhile to regulate the phase in between of the collection and use of data, namely the stage in which the data are analyzed, harvested, aggregated, mined, in which profiles are made and statistical correlations are found. Three points have been made. First, that the quality of the data and the research methods should be guaranteed. Second, that the choices made in the analysis phase should be transparent and auditable. Third, that the outcomes of the data analysis process, the correlations, patterns and profiles, should be assessed on the basis of reliability, usefulness and unforeseen negative consequences. One of the reasons why the current regulatory approach is incapable of providing such rules, it was argued, is because it is primarily focused on providing protection to individual interests, while the analysis phase in itself has no impact on such interests. Complementing the current rights-based approach with a virtue ethical understanding of privacy regulation, under which the data processor is under a general obligation to ensure good and qualitatively correct data analysis processes, has additional benefits as well.

A first advantage is that a rights-based approach only allows individuals to invoke their rights when their interests are harmed. A virtue-based approach would make it possible to intervene much earlier, namely when the policies and profiles are designed. A second advantage is that a rights-based approach, in many cases, seems to miss the point. If a health insurer designs a profile that refuses coverage to people with a handicap, the problem is not that this or that specific person is denied insurance because she has a handicap. The problem is the design of the health insurers' policy as such. A third advantage is related, namely that rights-based models tend to focus on providing relief to individuals whose interests are harmed or rights are violated – for example, providing relief to the handicapped person that was denied health insurance. The policy, however, may remain intact if a governmental organization or company decides that it is willing to occasionally pay damages to victims. A virtue ethical approach to privacy regulation has the advantage of being able to tackle the underlying problem.

A fourth advantage is that it is often difficult to specify the concrete and direct harm that has been done, which is problematic under a rights-based regulatory model. Suppose the police would decide to analyze all governmental databases for suspicious patterns and focus its activities only on people of Moroccan descent. It would then take action, e.g. by wire-tapping the communications or surveilling the behavior of

---

[454] B. van der Sloot, 'From Data Minimization to Data Minimummization', in: B. Custers, T. Calders, B. Schermer & T. Zarsky (eds.), 'Discrimination and Privacy in the Information Society. Data Mining and Profiling in Large Databases', Springer, Heidelberg, 2012.

individuals, only against those people against which there is a concrete suspicion. It will be difficult for suspects to submit a complaint about this procedure because the police has concrete grounds to believe that they are involved with criminal behavior. Furthermore, it will be difficult for the group of 'innocent Moroccans' to submit a complaint, both because they are mostly unaware of the fact that their data have been analyzed and because there are no concrete negative effects on their interests. A virtue ethical approach has the advantage that it allows for a legal and ethical evaluation of the research methods used by the police as such.

A final advantage may be that the rights-based model is unfit for addressing problematic forms of positive discrimination. If the police should decide to concentrate its surveillance activities to 6 of the 10 districts in a certain city, lightly monitoring 3 districts, and mostly leaving 1 district unsurveilled because this is a wealthy area with mostly well-educated, white inhabitants. A rights-based model could potentially address the negative discrimination of certain groups or inhabitants, but it cannot address the fact that the police structurally decides not to gather information and create databases about suspicious behavior in white and wealthy neighborhoods. Obviously, however, these forms of positive discrimination are equally important and signal a form of structural and social injustice. A virtue ethical approach can evaluate such policies and intervene at an early stage.

3. ASPIRATIONS

The previous section explained the added value of a virtue ethical approach to privacy regulation in terms of legal obligations. In short, its added benefit is that it does not hinge on subjective rights and correlative duties to respect those rights, but rather embraces duties that agents should respect independent of whether they protect a particular individual interest. These duties are related to the principles of the rule of law, which should always be respected by states and governmental organizations. This section analyzes the other side of the coin, namely the aspirations and goals of the state and its governmental agencies. Again, these are not related to specific rights and interests of subjects. Rather, the state has a general obligation to strive towards policies and laws that promote human freedom to the largest extent possible. These aspirations are best-effort obligations and can only be embedded in the legal regime in open terms; also, the different aspirations can conflict with each other. That is why an equilibrium, a golden mean, must be found between the different aspirations. Three points will be made in particular in this section.

First, it is often suggested that in the current political and juridical environment, national security interests often outweigh the interests related to privacy, according to some even almost completely overriding the latter interests. Obviously, it does not lie within the scope of this project to verify or falsify this claim, even if it were possible to do so. Rather, what will be suggested is that if this claim in true, in whole or in part, virtue ethics might be used to reflect on the fact why this might be problematic. In general, it can be said that in order to be truly free as a human being, one needs both privacy and safety. These are equally important interests which must be respected to the maximum extent possible. If choices have to be made, either on a legal, policy or practical level, an equilibrium must be found. The state should strive for neither total security nor total privacy, if promoting the one means structurally sacrificing the other. Virtue ethics, especially in the interpretation of Lon L. Fuller, places natural limitations to the state's aspirations and the means it deploys to achieve them. This argument and the various examples of potential limitations on policies, goals and aspirations will be discussed in Subsection 3.1.

Second, as has been stressed in the previous chapter, the legal order and the state should aim at the promotion of human freedom and autonomy. This means, *inter alia*, that the state should adopt policy that aims at promoting privacy related interests. These are positive obligations that a state might have, not to refrain from abusing its powers, but to actively use its powers in a good, or better, perfect manner. The state, under a virtue ethical model, should strive to perfect itself, not only by respecting minimum requirements, but also by using its power in a way that it optimally promotes human freedom. Just as with the minimum requirements discussed in Section 2 of this chapter, it is not for this book to specify exhaustively or determinatively what this might mean in practice. Rather, as with Section 2, three examples will be provided to give an idea about in what direction a virtue ethical approach to the use of governmental power might hint. These are combatting social stratification, promoting diversity and promoting individual autonomy. This argument, and the three examples, will be discussed in further detail in Subsection 3.2.

Third, the question is discussed how such positive obligations might be embedded in a legal discourse. With minimum requirements, there are already quite a few examples and legal instruments to build on. With the aspiration, this might be more difficult, *inter alia* because they are often formulated as an open norm or a best-effort obligation, and embedded in code-of-conduct-like instruments. The question is if and how such open norms can be embedded in the current legal and regulatory framework. This will be discussed in Subsection 3.3. This subsection will for the most part recapitulate what has been shown in Chapters II, III and IV of this book and tie those arguments together.

3.1. THE LIMITS OF ASPIRATIONS OVERRIDING PRIVACY INTERESTS

From a virtue ethical perspective to privacy regulation, it is important that agents search for the mean with respect to their actions. This means that there are natural limits to setting aspirations and goals for states as well. The exact limits of such goal setting are by necessity difficult to pinpoint precisely, but a few examples from virtue ethics in general and the work of Lon L. Fuller in particular will be provided to illustrate this argument. A first example may be that an agent must strive for an equilibrium between its goals or aspirations and the procedural or legal safeguards. Fuller, for example, distinguished between two types of association, or forms of living: on the one hand, the association that is based on a shared commitment, and on the other hand, the association that is based on the legal principle. An association that is primarily focused on a shared commitment is focused on an *end* or a *goal* that it wants to achieve; an association that is focused on the legal principle is focused primarily on the *means* or *instruments* of getting there. A book club is typically more aligned to the first form of association, although even such clubs have certain procedural rules (even though they may be unwritten), such as on who decides what the next book will be that the members of the club will read. Consequently, Fuller stressed that existing organizations will always contain both elements.

The goal is something that is shared by most of the members of the organization, or that dominates its operations. The legal principle ensures that each individual has some level of protection against the group and the shared commitment. The danger of too much focus on the shared commitment is obviously that it tends to override individual interests and might undermine procedural fairness. The danger of too great a focus on legal principles is that of 'creeping legalism'. Kenneth Winston, discussing Fuller's texts, describes it as follows:

> [The trend of creeping legalism] shows itself in three ways: (1) a greater reliance on rules to define members' duties and entitlements, (2) a concordant shift in accountability based on tangible harms or benefits which flow from specific acts rather than on more judgmental assessments of character and motive, and (3) the articulation of strict procedural requirements for distributing benefits and burdens.[455]

Consequently, an equilibrium should be found between legal principles and shared commitments.

A second and related principle is that there should be a balance between striving for common interests and individual interests. Because the legal order is aimed at promoting individual autonomy and freedom, there should always be an equilibrium in democratic states between the common and the individual interest and, perhaps more importantly, the common interests may never structurally override the individual interests of the citizens. 'In order to grasp the force of Fuller's argument, one has to understand that the "internal morality" is an enumeration of the moral duties that attach to the role of legislator, and underlying the definition of that role is a special conception of the legislator's task. In Fuller's view, the only permissible form of legislation is the sort that lets individuals plan their own lives. Simply put, legislative enactments are baselines for self-directed conduct by citizens, providing the minimal restraints necessary for continuing interaction. Legislation properly conceived permits citizens to order their own affairs, to pursue their own good in their own way (in the words of John Stuart Mill). In this respect legislation differs fundamentally from what

---

[455] Editor's note, L. L. Fuller, 'The implicit Laws of Lawmaker', in: L. L. Fuller, 'The Principles of Social Order', Duke University Press, Durham, 1981, p. 67.

Fuller calls managerial direction, which provides detailed regulations for accomplishing objectives set by a political superior. To the contrary, legislation involves complete deference to citizen's powers of self-determination and so can be said to promote their autonomy. Thus, Rex's failure to make "laws" is a special affront to the dignity of citizens as autonomous agents'.[456] Consequently, the state should find an equilibrium between common and individual interests.

A third essential principle that black letter law, according to virtue ethics, is mostly based on implicit or customary law, that is, on human behavior and individual autonomy. These principles should, according to Fuller, be used to interpret laws and legal actions and serve as the natural limits of the legal order. 'The prevailing tendency to regard all social order as imposed from above has led to a general neglect of the phenomenon of customary law in modern legal scholarship. (…) The fact is that the operation of a system of state-made law is itself permeated with internal customary practices that enable it to function effectively by facilitating a collaboration among its constituent elements.'[457] That is also why Fuller placed so much emphasis on the role of the judiciary, as opposed to the lawmaker. The judicial branch, in his opinion, bridges the gap between customs and black letter law and vice versa. Consequently, the state should find an equilibrium between written and customary, black letter and open norms.

The fourth limit that Fuller describes relates to the practical limits of laws. One of the principles of the rule of law, Fuller described, is that laws should not require the impossible of citizens. One of the conclusions that follow from this principle is that there are natural limits to the width and scope of laws and regulatory policies. In principle, Fuller stressed, these should be primarily aimed at the public and the public domain and not at the private and the private domain. There are two reasons for this. On the one hand, it will often prove difficult to enforce laws and policies in the private domain. Although the law should of course not be silent and leave this domain unregulated, it should not strive to fully regulate it either. 'The result is that though an aloof justice is bound at times to be harsh, an intimate justice, seeking to explore and grasp the boundaries of a private world, cannot in the nature of things be evenhanded. The law knows no magic that will enable it to transcend this antinomy.'[458]

On the other hand, there is certain behavior that the state can simply not banish. An example, which was still very prominent at the time of Fuller's writing, was that of states prohibiting homosexual conduct, even in the private sphere. Fuller rejected this endeavor outright:

> The conception underlying John Stuart Mill's Essay is essentially a negative one: liberty consists in leaving a man alone, in not imposing restraints on him. It is no accident, I believe, that modern discussions drawing on the thought of Mill relate chiefly to the wisdom of legal

---

[456] Editor's note, L. L. Fuller, 'The implicit Laws of Lawmaker', in: L. L. Fuller, 'The Principles of Social Order', Duke University Press, Durham, 1981, p. 158.
[457] L. L. Fuller, 'The Role of contract', In: L. L. Fuller, 'The Principles of Social Order', Duke University Press, Durham, 1981, p. 177.
[458] L. L. Fuller, 'The Morality of Law', p. 72.

restraints on sexual activity. In this arena of human concern, the negative conception of liberty is quite at home. It is not necessary to make arrangements for the sexual freedom of a man; nature has seen to that. The problem is how far to go in placing social restraints on that freedom.[459]

Consequently, the state should find an equilibrium between subjecting the private domain and private conduct in full to the norms of general justice and leaving part of it beyond its reach.

A fifth and final principle is that states should adopt an equilibrium between certain aspirations. Fuller, for example, referred to the principles of the rule of law and stressed that states should not only ensure a minimum level of respect for those principles, but that they should also endeavor to promote those principles to the maximum extent possible. For example, states should not only strive to make laws reasonably legible for the common man, but also easily legible for people with very few knowledge of laws and a poor understanding of the language. However, Fuller stressed, achieving one aspiration might conflict with achieving another aspiration. He provides an example:

> During a visit to Poland in May of 1961 I had a conversation with a former Minister of Justice that is relevant here. She told how in the early days of the communist regime an earnest and sustained effort was made to draft the laws so clearly that they would be intelligible to the worker and peasant. It was soon discovered, however, that this kind of clarity could be attained only at the cost of those systematic elements in a legal system that shape its rules into a coherent whole and render them capable of consistent application by the courts. It was discovered, in other words, that making the laws readily understandable to the citizen carried a hidden cost in that it rendered their application by the courts more capricious and less predictable. Some retreat to a more balanced view therefore become unavoidable.[460]

Consequently, the state should find an equilibrium between its different aspirations.

The limits that are suggested above are of obvious relevance to the current regulatory approach to privacy and data protection. It is often said, for example, that there is too much emphasis on one policy goal, namely national security and public order. Other policy goals are often subordinate to this goal. Moreover, it is said that this common interest (national security) often overrules the personal interests of private individuals. Also, the private domain is entered more and more by the state, and the reach of the legal domain has grown quite significantly over time. The fear that such an application of the legal order on the private domain is often not effective, which was discussed above, is also voiced with regard to mass surveillance activities. Moreover, although human autonomy and freedom are the basis of the law and the legal order as such, it is often put under pressure by far-reaching surveillance and profiling activities. Finally, secret services often operate in an extra-legal domain, in which the promotion of shared goals is not or only marginally limited by procedural and legal requirements.

---

459 L. L. Fuller, 'Freedom as Allocating choice', p. 103.
460 L. L. Fuller, 'The Morality of law', p. 45.

These are but a few examples of how a virtue ethical approach to privacy regulation may be used to impose limits on aspirations and policy goals that override potential privacy interests. The next section will give a few examples of how such an approach might produce positive obligations for states in relation to data processing activities.

3.2. ASPIRATIONS DIRECTED AT PROMOTING HUMAN FREEDOM

If it is accepted that the legal order is aimed at promoting human autonomy and freedom, the state has a positive obligation to promote this goals. What this means in practice is difficult to specify in general, and depends on the circumstances of the case. Still, three tentative examples will be provided to illustrate the policy goals states may embrace, for example in a code–of–conduct-like document. These examples are merely intended to illustrate the type of reasoning and the type of obligations that could be derived from a virtue ethical approach to privacy regulation. The examples are neither exhaustive nor fully developed. It will be mainly up to states themselves and the democratic process to decide on the actual rules and obligations. The examples provided below relate to combatting social stratification, promoting diversity and promoting individual autonomy. What promoting those positive aspirations might mean in practice for virtuous states will be suggested below.

First, an aspiration could be not only to design algorithms, patterns and data-based profiles that do not discriminate, but also to combat social injustice. There is much discussion about the role of computer programs and algorithms that produce biased and even discriminatory results. If this is due to the design of the computer program or the algorithm, obviously, this may and should be tackled. But if the bias is due to the fact that the algorithm is programmed to copy or learn from human behavior, the problem is less easy to tackle. An example is the computer trained to learn from human discussion forums on the internet in order to join the discussions as if it were a human. It had to be taken down because it turned into a racist commentator, not, so the story goes, due to the design of the computer bot, but because real humans on discussion fora often say dubious things. An even more obvious example might be the fact that search engines learn from search queries in order to provide useful suggestions and results. However, the word 'Jew' is apparently often searched in combination with negative qualifications. This begs the question, should companies and states actively counter existing biases or racism that exist in society?

Omer Tene and Jules Polenetsky have raised this question in a paper still in draft, which will be cited here nevertheless because it is one of the best on this topic. They are hesitant about such a positive obligation for a number of reasons:

> Implementing editorial discretion and social engineering raises a broad array of ethical dilemmas. Are all companies well placed to identify societal consensus and norms or should they be trailblazers adopting progressive agendas? An approach requiring companies to

"tame the Golem," bringing algorithmic decisions to heel by instilling them with liberal values, is based on rickety grounds. First, it could incentivize companies to sweep socially fraught issues under the carpet, sanitizing decisions to present users with a *Shallow Hal* view of the world. If Google suppressed hateful search results for the word "Jew", the underlying social problems would not be solved but rather concealed from public view. Second, it places business entities, which are undemocratic bureaucracies with little transparency, due process and accountability, in an unenviable position as final arbiters of ethical dilemmas and social norms. Corporations are legal constructs intended to maximize profit and shareholder value. Many do not have ethics review processes, chief privacy officers or other mechanisms for arbitrating social values and norms. A case in point is the European Court of Justice's decision establishing a "right to be forgotten," which effectively charged Google with balancing delicate values, norms and fundamental rights including freedom of speech, freedom of information and the right to privacy, and doing so in a variety of cultural and legal environments all over the world. Although privacy advocates claimed victory, critics argued that at the end of the day, the decision endowed the company with tremendous discretion with little legal guidance. Third, when viewed by users from other countries and cultures in Asia, Africa and beyond, resolution of these issues under Silicon Valley ethics could be viewed as American-centric socio-technological colonialism, presuming to impose Western liberal values on societies that have broadly divergent views about gender and family, religion and politics. Even within the U.S., advocates of proactive corporate editorializing should bear in mind that this approach could cut both ways. For example, in the recent debate over North Carolina's legislation prescribing transgenders' access to public bathrooms, companies such as Target and Bank of America led the charge for more liberal laws. But in other cases, companies have promoted a conservative agenda out of sync with those arguing for additional involvement.[461]

From the perspective of privacy as virtue, another line of reasoning may be put forward, at least in the case of the state using computer programs and algorithms to make decisions. As discussed in Subsection 2.3 of this chapter, there may be biases and differences in terms of socioeconomic background and crime rate with respect to different neighborhoods, groups with different ethnic backgrounds and between other social strata. Subsection 2.3 suggested that the state has an obligation to be aware of potential biases and existing differences and an obligation not to reinforce such differences. However, a positive approach to data use may go further. If it is accepted that the legal order is or should be directed at promoting human autonomy and freedom, it might be suggested that the state should aim at correcting existing biases and differences and should impose, in this sense, 'liberal values', such as human autonomy and equality, and implement them in algorithms and computer decision making programs.

A second example may be provided by discussing some of the ideas about filter bubbles.[462] A common fear is that once a person is profiled in a certain group, for

---

[461] O. Tene & J. Polenetsky, 'Taming The Golem: Challenges of Ethical Algorithmic Decision Making', working paper <https://fpf.org/wp-content/uploads/2016/05/Golem_May153–1.docx>, p.12-13.

[462] E. Pariser, 'The filter bubble: what the Internet is hiding from you', Viking, London, 2011.

example 'conservative, male, sports lover', he will only or primarily get news items, search results and personalized advertising that fits that profile. That might have an enormous impact on his life, because there would be a high chance of him staying in or being substantially influenced by that profile. Thus, room for serendipity and personal development is minimized and the fear is that society will become more and more one-dimensional over time. This undermines the individual autonomy and capacity human flourishing of citizens in a society in general. The question is in how far the government can and should enter this domain, promoting or requiring of private parties to offer more diverse media content to users or allowing more choice. It has to be stressed that traditionally, promoting media diversity by the state has always been an explicit goal in policy making. For example, public radio and television channels often have the goal to promote social, cultural and regional diversity. Even in the digital media environment, certain provisions have been adopted that promote diversity, for example Electronic Programme Guides that by law need to prioritize programs by public broadcasters, because public broadcasters have an obligation to promote diversity.[463] Still, there has been relatively few active governmental policies in this field.

Natali Helberger, for example, stresses that it is surprising 'that at least in Europe the possible contribution of choice intermediaries to the realization of media diversity (and here particularly the exposure to diverse media content) is still a topic that has hardly been discussed seriously in media law and policy. This can be partly explained by the uncertainty of policymakers about the permissibility of interference in an area that is as politically and legally sensitive as is individual information consumption. This uncertainty, moreover, has stood in the way of a more fundamental debate about the possible contribution of choice intermediaries to the realization of media diversity policies. To have such a debate would require tackling a number of difficult and yet open questions. First, what are "diverse choices" and for what reasons would it be a concern for media law and policy that people choose diversely? This question is closely related to another open question. Namely, how can we conceptualize exposure diversity as a possible policy goal? What is the possible role of choice intermediaries in promoting exposure diversity, and what is the role of the government, if any?'[464]

Helberger indeed suggests a number of ways to promote diversity, choice freedom and serendipity by implementing certain principles in the technical infrastructure and design of platforms and choice intermediaries, such as search engines and Electronic Programme Guides. One of the questions remains how far a state should go in embracing such far reaching policy goals. It seems difficult to distill such a policy goal from a rights-based perspective, because the impact of personalized news content, search results and advertising is difficult to measure, because individuals are often unaware of the fact that they are offered personalized content and because if they are aware of this fact, they generally accept or even welcome content that is tailored to their profile. Embracing a virtue ethical approach to privacy regulation might provide

---

[463] B. van der Sloot, 'Walking a thin line: the regulation of EPGs', JIPITEC, 3 2012 (2).
[464] N. Helberger, 'Diversity by Design', Journal of Information Policy 1, 2011, p. 443.

a theoretical basis for and legitimation of such choices. If it is accepted that the state and the legal order are in their very essence directed at promoting human autonomy and freedom and that the legal order is based on human autonomy and freedom, promoting human autonomy and freedom of its citizens by the state is not only its raison d'être, it is also a condition for the legal order to stay vital.

A final example may be provided by discussing the work of Rosamunde van Brakel.[465] She discusses the use of Big Data practices for predictive policing and other security-related purposes by the government. Van Brakel has studied the use of Big Data in relation to predictive policing. She signals both potentially disempowering and empowering effects that the use of Big Data may have on citizens. With regard to the disempowering effects, she suggests that it is possible that in the future, it will no longer be a human who makes the assessments and decisions, but a computer, or rather the technology, which mayhave serious consequences for questions of accountability. Moreover, these types of algorithms and computer programs are often not transparent, which may have a disempowering effect on the position of citizens. The use of algorithms may also lead to algorithmic discrimination if the algorithms or the data on which they are based are biased. Furthermore, there is also the danger of both false positives and false negatives, which may lead to stigmatization and may have serious consequences for citizens' well-being and life chances. The cumulative surveillance effect signals that predictive policing and Big Data may have a cumulative disadvantage effect, and groups such as Amish, Roma, and Luddites may be socially excluded. Van Brakel concludes by suggesting that Big Data may also have an empowering effect on citizens, but that Big Data is rarely applied in such a way at present. Still, Big Data could potentially be used to provide more and more detailed information to citizens, about crime rates, for example, so they are better able to protect themselves against crime, or to use profiling to provide more protection to the weak.

In this context, Van Brakel writes:

> To give a concrete illustration in the context of crime prevention, there are two ways in which you can think of using predictive Big Data policing for preventing people from committing crime in the future. The first response is the pre-emptive repressive response: to develop software that will analyze Big Data to predict what people are at risk of committing crime so the police can intervene before the crime is committed by them. An example here is the beware software. The second response is the positive criminology response: similar to the abovementioned Cedar Grove initiative, a consortium of police, social workers, neighbourhood workers, schools, civil society organizations, and city planners could work together and use Big Data applications to identify what areas in a city need more attention (areas where, for example, an increasing number of young people are more at risk of

---

[465] R. van Brakel, 'Pre-emptive Big Data Surveillance and its (Dis)Empowering Consequences: the Case of Predictive Policing', in: B. van der Sloot & D. Broeders & E. Schrijvers (eds.), 'Exploring the boundaries of Big Data', Amsterdam University Press, Amsterdam 2016. This description follows partially from: B. van der Sloot, D. Broeders & E. Schrijvers, 'Introduction: Exploring the Boundaries of Big Data', IN: B. van der Sloot & D. Broeders & E. Schrijvers (eds.), 'Exploring the boundaries of Big Data', Amsterdam University Press, Amsterdam 2016.

radicalizing) and identify what specific problems in that area need to be addressed. Data could include school quality measures, percentage of neighbourhood green, crime rates, mean income, percentage of unemployment, etc. If you have areas that are run down, lacking green spaces, with a concentration of people who are disadvantaged or unemployed with no future prospects, crime figures will be higher than in other areas. A caring intervention here might be to improve schooling and urban space, to invest in community policing, to invest in parenting and family support programmes, public health, building up trust with the community, empowering victims of crime, etcetera (for knowledge and evidence-based crime prevention policy). It is a more positive long-term strategy to change the conditions in society so as to prevent people from embarking on crime. A repressive intervention will only take place if it is really necessary, but budgets are divided equally over both controlling and caring measures.[466]

Again, embracing a virtue ethical approach to privacy regulation might provide a normative basis for such an approach. The state does not only have a negative obligation not to violate the rights of its citizens, but also an active duty to promote the human freedom and autonomy of its citizens, without them having any explicit correlative right to it. This might mean, as Van Brakel has suggested, that data processing by the police and other security-related agencies must not only be aimed at control, surveillance and punishment, but also at helping people that might be pushed towards criminality due to, for example, their socioeconomic background. This might help them in their personal development and be an important tool in preventing criminal behavior. Also, it might help to ensure that people support such data use by the government. In a similar vein, an oft-mentioned example is that data processing by Tax Authorities should not only be aimed at detecting fraud and errors in tax forms, but also to actively inform people if they forget to ask for certain deductions or tax benefits that they have a right to.

In conclusion, the legal order and the state should aim at the promotion of human freedom and autonomy to the maximum extent. What this means precisely in privacy and data protection contexts cannot be determined here, both because this is dependent on the context and the particulars of the case and because goal setting is something that is primarily up to the democratic process and the state itself, although obviously, viewing the legal order in a teleological manner sets limits to the democratic process. Still, three examples have been provided of how a positive approach to data use might play a role in privacy regulation when it is accepted that the state is or should be aimed at promoting human autonomy and freedom in a general. These examples were: combatting social stratification, promoting diversity, and promoting individual autonomy. These examples are not meant to be exhaustive or determinative in any way, but merely serve to illustrate what a positive duty to data processing might mean for a state in a virtue ethical approach to privacy regulation.

---

[466] R. van Brakel, 'Pre-emptive Big Data Surveillance and its (Dis)Empowering Consequences: the Case of Predictive Policing', in: B. van der Sloot & D. Broeders & E. Schrijvers (eds.), 'Exploring the boundaries of Big Data', Amsterdam University Press, Amsterdam 2016, p. 130.

3.3. HOW TO EMBED ASPIRATIONS IN A JURIDICAL FRAMEWORK

The question is how such rules could be implemented in a juridical framework. It seems that their nature is quite different from the standard rules and doctrines engrained in privacy and data protection law. To argue that, and in what ways, such open norms and duties of care could be used to complement the current regulatory framework, four steps will be taken in this Subsection. First, it will briefly be recapitulated how and on which points the current privacy and data protection have been transformed over time. It will be clear that these trends are diametrically opposed to accepting open norms. Second, the arguments provided in Chapter III, regarding the need for soft law standards and open norms will be recapitulated. Third, it will be pointed out that there are already open norms and duties of care engrained in the current legal frameworks. Consequently, it is not impossible to rely on such standards in the legal realm. Fourth and finally, two arguments against relying on open norms, that have been discussed in Chapter IV, will be recalled, as will the counter-arguments presented in that chapter.

As shown in Chapter II, the privacy and data protection paradigm has been transformed quite significantly. Over time, it has increasingly emphasized individual rights. Although originally, there were only one or two subjective rights contained in data protection instruments, namely the right to access personal data and, sometimes, the right to rectify or delete outdated information, this list has grown substantially. Under the General Data Protection Regulation, the individual has a right to resist profiling, a right to be forgotten, a right to data portability, a right to access personal data, a right to remedy, and many more rights. A typical example of this trend may be transparency principle. Originally, this was a duty of care imposed on the data controller as such, as recalled in the previous section. The first article of the Resolution of the Council of Europe from 1974 on the processing of personal data in the public sector specified: 'As a general rule the public should be kept regularly informed about the establishment, operation and development of electronic data banks in the public sector.'

Under the General Data Protection Regulation, even this general duty of care is linked to the data subject and her interests directly. Article 12 provides:

> The controller shall take appropriate measures to provide any information referred to in Articles 13 and 14 and any communication under Articles 15 to 22 and 34 relating to processing to the data subject in a concise, transparent, intelligible and easily accessible form, using clear and plain language, in particular for any information addressed specifically to a child. The information shall be provided in writing, or by other means, including, where appropriate, by electronic means. When requested by the data subject, the information may be provided orally, provided that the identity of the data subject is proven by other means.

There is also an increased focus on black letter law and more elaborate juridical rules. Rights-based doctrines have the regulatory advantage of transferring the primary responsibility for the protection of rights and interests to the natural person, as the holder of a subjective right. If her interests are violated, she should complain to the organization or person who allegedly violates her rights and interfere with her interests and if that is to no avail, a legal procedure is open to her. Black letter law too seems to have several assets that regulators look upon as favorable. Data protection in particular is often called the procedural branch of privacy regulation, which provides for a set of rules in a quasi-neutral, -technical and -objective fashion. The newly adopted General Data Protection Regulation certainly continues this trend and imposes many specific rules on data controllers and describes in an almost cookbook-like fashion how they should act and what measures they should adopt when processing personal data. While the original data protection instruments were literally one-pagers, embedding open norms like 'be transparent', 'do not collect more data than necessary' and 'store data safely and confidentially', the General Data Protection Regulation consist of no less than eighty-eight pages, containing many very detailed rules, principles, exceptions and exceptions to the exceptions.

The document has the character of market regulation, rather than a fundamental rights framework. Instead of containing a dozen rules as was originally the case, or the thirty-four articles of the Directive, the Regulation contains ninety-nine provisions and one hundred and seventy-three recitals. These norms have not only changed in type, but that they are also looked upon differently. While the original data protection frameworks contained rules that were regarded as guidelines rather than absolute standards, the General Data Protection Regulation not only harmonizes the rules within the European Union, it also lays down very high sanctions for data controllers that do not abide by the data protection principle. Data controllers such as Google, Microsoft and Apple, may be levied with a fine, if they do not live up to European standards on data protection, of as much as € 20 million or 4% of the company's worldwide revenue.[467]

A final trend that has been signaled is that quite ordinary principles are increasingly transferred to higher regulatory levels. In data protection, there has been a move from adopting code-of-conduct-like documents, to a Directive, and finally to a EU-wide Regulation, which has direct effect. The right to data protection has also been included as a separate doctrine in the Charter of Fundamental Rights of the European Union, independent of the right to privacy. To give a final example, within the Council of Europe, the European Convention on Human Rights in general and the right to privacy under Article 8 ECHR in particular, has expanded their scope grown significantly over time. Many relatively inconsequential personal interests are now protected under the right to privacy and consequently, treated as a human right.

Given these trends, it seems clear that embracing more open and ethics-based norms in privacy and data protection instruments would go against the grain. Yet, there are many arguments that seem to point in that direction. Chapter III concluded that it is increasingly questionable whether and to what extent black letter law and rights-based models of regulation are still tenable in the Big Data era. This is because data processes are becoming ever more transnational, technologies change rapidly so that legal provisions become outdated quickly and the many general and societal interests at

---

[467] Article 83 Regulation.

stake are difficult to regulate in concrete juridical provisions. Future regulation, Chapter III suggested, may need to focus to a greater extent on other types of regulation, such as on soft law, codes of conducts, best practices and duties of care, to allow for more flexibility while maintaining and protecting the underlying core values of the legal regime. Finally, it stressed that it may be necessary to rely on more open norms because these can adapt more easily to the constant technological changes.

Open norms are also easier to use in transnational contexts, because it is easier to agree upon a core rule or basic ethical principle than it is to agree on specific legal provisions. More in general, it has been suggested that Big Data processes have an effect on a more general and societal level, which rights-based models cannot adequately address but a virtue-based regulatory model can. Open norms may also have the additional benefit that they are not directed at one particular player, but rather at data controllers in general. One of the problems faced under the current regulatory regime is that it is often unclear where the responsibilities lie, because data are shared between many different organizations, and subsequently combined, harvested and used. In this reality, it is often unclear who, for example, is under the obligation to ensure that the data being processed are correct and kept up to data. A virtue-based model will have an advantage in this respect, because open norms and duties of care do not rely on specific legal positions of 'data controller', 'data processor', 'third party', or any other status.

Furthermore, it has the advantage that black letter law and rights based models tend to produce very specific, detailed regulatory frameworks. This potential disadvantage of black letter law was already signaled clearly by Lon L. Fuller, as discussed in Chapter 3 and Sub-section 3.1 of this Chapter. A virtue-based model to privacy and data protection regulation might have an advantage on this point, because it focuses in part on aspirations and goals, on general policies and societal interests. Among others, Wibren van der Burg has pointed to this possible advantage when discussing the work of Lon L. Fuller. To this end, he used the medical context as source of inspiration:

> One of the leading legal ideals in Western culture is the ideal of respect for the autonomous person. This is a very broad ideal, which can give rise to many more specific norms. A more concrete way to formulate a part of the ideal is to say that we should protect and enhance autonomous decision-making with respect to medical treatment. A deontological interpretation of this ideal might lead to a principle holding that the patient's informed consent should be obtained before performing any treatment. A teleological interpretation of the ideal might lead to policies that foster conditions for autonomous decision-making such as easy access to information and counseling services. Both could give rise to concrete rules. A principle-based rule would be that a doctor must always obtain the informed consent from her patient, unless the patient is unconscious or there is some other kind of emergency. A policy-based rule would be that every hospital must have leaflets available containing information about common diseases and treatments, in every language that is frequently spoken in the hospital's area.[468]

---

[468] W. van der Burg, 'The morality of aspiration', in: W. J. Witteveen & W. Van der Burg, 'Rediscovering Fuller. Essays on Implicit law and Institutional Design', Amsterdam University Press, Amsterdam, 1999, p. 180.

Both policies can obviously complement each other, but Van der Burg also warns for too much focus on patient rights and hard rules. 'The recognition of patients' rights is clearly a matter of principle. To a certain extent, we can formulate them as rules, as strict rights, but beyond a certain point, we may go too far, which may be counterproductive. Many health-care professionals claim that legislation aimed at protecting patients' rights has indeed gone too far. In the Netherlands, even patients organizations now admit that strict regulations stating that only if psychiatric patients constitute a real danger to themselves or to others it legally permitted to give them involuntary treatment, frustrate the good care for some categories of schizophrenic patients. Legal recognition of patients' rights with the purpose of protecting patients might lead to more defensive and bureaucratic medicine, and would thus, in the end, go against patients' interests.'[469] Van der Burg thus contrasts 'the strict rules of the morality of duty and the general principles and policies of the morality of aspiration,' and points out that it might be worthwhile to rely to a greater extent on self-regulation and open norms. It is not difficult to see the similarities between healthcare and privacy regulation on this point.

Consequently, it seems that a greater emphasis on aspirations and open norms might be beneficial, given the current regulatory approach. It should be pointed out that it seems possible to incorporate such norms in the legal regime, because there are already a number of doctrines and rules engrained in law that rely on such rules. Chapter IV pointed out that the general structure of so called v-rules (virtue-rules) is: 'do what is most virtuous' or 'do not what is unvirtuous'. It also suggested that there are a number of doctrines engrained in law that seem to reflect that structure. Perhaps the most prominent is the notion of the duty of care, already engrained in a number of juridical doctrines. Such a rule specifies, for example, 'act like the most virtuous/best parent would act' or 'act like the most virtuous/perfect doctor would act'.

Also, more in general, there seems to be a renewed interest in open norms and soft law in Europe and beyond. The European Union has, for example, embraced the idea of soft law with respect to environmental challenges, which is praised by many scholars: 'Soft law instruments are often the most effective means for governments to change behavior in a policy environment where uncertainties are high and their authority is limited. In these cases, the alternative to soft law may be no law at all.'[470] Other authors, looking at the financial sector, have precisely called for combining the two regulatory approaches (soft law and black letter law) and for cementing the open norms in legal instruments:

> We argue that dominant perspectives' view of the role of soft law in global finance is misguided, as soft law in global finance cannot be understood in isolation from domestic law. We advocate viewing the role of soft law through the prism of multilevel governance and argue that European integration in particular promotes soft law diffusion. Across multiple issues in global finance, the European Union (EU) acts as a legalization mechanism that

---

[469] Ibid, p. 184.
[470] M. Dreyfus & A. Patt, 'The European Commission White Paper on adaptation: appraising its strategic success as an instrument of soft law', Mitig Adapt Strateg Glob Change (2012) 17, p. 850.

transforms soft law from informal transnational best practice into embedded rules backed by domestic law.[471]

The European Union and other international organizations have turned to open norms and ethical principles in their legislative approach when that is regarded opportune.[472] This trend is also reflected in the private sector, in which hard commitments are increasingly combined and supplemented with general aspirations and best practices.[473] A company endorsing the concept of Corporate Social Responsibility will, for example, not only look at profits, margins and revenue, but will also commit itself to reducing environmental pollution, promoting the conditions of the workers they rely on in third world countries and support projects in those countries that promote education, healthcare infrastructure and women's rights. These aspirations are not duties that correlate with subjective rights of others; rather, they are the goals that an organization commits itself to. Reference can also be made to the European Court of Human Rights' use of the concept of 'positive obligations' and to the fact that the original privacy and data protection frameworks primarily relied on duties of care.

4. ANALYSIS

This chapter has discussed a number of rules that may be produced by a virtue ethical approach to privacy regulation. These can be used to complement the current rights-based approach. In essence, it's goal is to sandwich doctrines that focus on subjective rights and individual interests between, on the one hand, minimum requirements that are related to the rule of law, and, on the other hand, goals and aspirations. The first are preconditions for the state and the exercise of governmental power, which must be respected even if no individual interests or subjective rights are at stake. The second are goals that will mostly focus on general and societal interests, even though policies that promote human freedom and diversity have an obvious impact on the citizens living in a country. The previous sections and it subsections discussed which rules might be produced by a virtue ethical approach to privacy regulation, but left largely undiscussed how such rules could be applied and enforced in practice. Providing such a discussion is what this final section shall endeavor to do.

---

[471] A. Newman & D. Bach, 'Soft law and the diffusion of global financial regulation', Journal of European Public Policy, 2014. p. 430–431.

[472] C. Bailliet', 'Non-state actors, soft law, and protective regimes: from the margins', Cambridge, Cambridge University Press, 2012. O. Stefan, 'Soft law in court: competition law, state aid and the Court of Justice of the European Union', Kluwer Law International, Alphen aan den Rijn, 2013.

[473] OECD, 'Corporate Social Responsibility Partners for Progress', OECD Publishing, Paris, 2001. C. S. Frederiksen, S. O. Idowy, A. Y. Mermod & M.E.J. Nielsen, 'Corporate Social Responsibility and Governance Theory and Practice', Springer, Cham, 2015. E. Werna, R. Keivani & D. F. Murphy, 'Corporate social responsibility and urban development: lessons from the South', Palgrave Macmillan, Basingstoke, 2009.

First, it has been suggested that it would be worthwhile to regulate not just personal data or sensitive personal data, but 'data' in general. Most general rules contained in the current data protection instruments could be applied to data in general; examples that have been given are the transparency requirement, the purpose and purpose limitation principle, the requirement to keep data correct and up to date and the obligation to store data safely and confidentially. It has been suggested that the same does not apply to the subjective rights engrained in data protection instruments. Conversely, the rules that can be applied to 'data' in general cannot be enforced through subjective rights, precisely because there is not direct link between the individual and the data. There is, however, no problem in granting Data Protection Authorities the power to enforce these rules; they are equipped to do so and have both the knowledge and expertise needed. Given what has been said in Subsection 2.1, it seems both logical and desirable for DPAs to extend their audits and enforcement activities to data processing in general.

Second, it has been suggested that it would be valuable to assess laws and policies on the basis of whether they respect the basic principles of the rule of law. These minimum principles must be taken into account even if an infringement does not result in direct individual harm or a violation of subjective rights. It was suggested that although the main focus in the current privacy paradigm is on individual rights and personal interests, in recent times the European Court of Human Rights has accepted so-called *in abstracto* claims that focus on assessing the legality and legitimacy of the laws as such. It was also stressed that although such claims are currently declared admissible (though only in exceptional circumstances), they seem incompatible with a rights-based approach to privacy regulation. It was suggested that addressing such claims by a human rights court seems out of place, because the very essence of *in abstracto* claims is precisely that no human rights have been violated. Finally, it has been suggested that a virtue ethical approach to privacy regulation provides a better understanding of and theoretical foundation for such claims. Rather than a human rights court, it would seem logical if constitutional courts would accept and assess class actions and *in abstracto* claims.

Third, it has been suggested that it would be valuable if the analysis phase were to be regulated. The current regulatory regime focuses primarily on the phase in which data are gathered, and to some extent on the phase in which the data are used. The phase in between, however, is mostly left unregulated. One of the reasons is that, although a link can be made to particular individuals when gathering and using the data, this is mostly impossible with respect to modern data analytics. It would nevertheless be expedient if the regulatory framework would incorporate rules on the analysis of the data, such as to guarantee the quality of the data analysis process, making the many decisions that are furnished during this phase transparent and auditable and allowing for an assessment of the outcomes of the process sas to their reliability and social desirability. It was suggested that a virtue-based approach to privacy and data protection regulation could produce such rules. Obviously, not all companies and governmental authorities can be fully transparent; there are legitimate reasons for some level of opacity, such as that the algorithm, the selection, weighing and categorization of data can be an important business secret for many companies, giving them a competitive advantage over other businesses. For governmental authorities, especially in the field of law enforcement, such reasons may be found in the fact that full transparency might allow criminals to adjust their behavior and calculate the risks of being caught and punished for illegal conduct.

However, it must be stressed that this logic does not apply to all governmental organizations and businesses. For example, when the government gathers and analyzes data for developing general socioeconomic policies, full transparency might be promoted. For other organizations, such as those involved with law enforcement, a form of multilevel transparency could be promoted. Under such a model, DPAs or similar agencies would have access to the black box, and would be able to audit the quality of the data, the decisions made and the outcomes of the analysis process. These organizations could then report to their superiors, for example the parliament. Such a report would not contain any details on, for example, the exact design of algorithms, but the authority could present the results of the audits on an annual basis.[474]

One of the aspects of such audits may be an assessment of whether the governmental organization has achieved the goals it wanted to achieve through the data processing activities. One the one hand, this might regard an evaluation of the percentage of false positives and negatives indicated as acceptable. One the other hand, this might imply an evaluation of the goals which the data processing activities were intended to further. For example, when an intelligence agency starts a mass surveillance project for the fight against terrorism, it would be for the intelligence agency to specify beforehand which specific goals it wants to achieve through the use of the data processing activities. It would be for that agency to prove that the data processing activities actually achieved those goals and to demonstrate that the same results would not have been reached if the time and money would have been invested in other means. When a governmental agency cannot prove such effectiveness, or when the original reasons for starting the data processing activities no longer hold, such activities would need to be stopped or fundamentally redesigned.

Another option might be to require that governmental organizations install a data commission. The task of such a commission would be to assess the quality and the presumed effectiveness of the plans of the organization to gather, analyze and use large quantities of data. Such a commission might exist of lawyers, ethicists, informatics experts, specialists in scientifically reliable data analytics, and experts in other fields that might be of relevance. In the medical realm, an ethical commission or board usually assesses the necessity, design and potential use of a research plan that uses or relies on personal healthcare data and tissue samples. Such a model could be taken as a best practice and implemented with respect to data analysis processes within the public sector in general. Such a commission would need to be consulted before a data processing initiative is deployed; it would have the power to authorize or forbid such plans.

---

[474] See more in detail: WRR, 'Big Data in een vrije en veilige samenleving', WRR-rapport, Amsterdam University Press, Amsterdam 2016.

Fourth, it has been suggested that, from a virtue ethical approach, there are a number of natural limits on the aspiration of governmental organizations. Democratic states cannot focus blindly on aspiration, but must also take into account procedural justice; they must be concerned with promoting human autonomy; they must take into account the practical limits of laws and policies; they must find a balance between different aspirations; and they must find a balance between different means of promoting those aspirations. The problem is obviously that these are mostly extra-legal limits. Yet it is not impossible to embed those limits in a regulatory regime; rather, it seems that there are already a number of building block in the current legal realm that could be used to cement such limits. With respect to finding a balance between law and policy, procedural justice and shared aspirations, it seems that this is precisely one of the aims of the European Convention on Human Rights, holding *inter alia* that whenever a policy has an effect on a human rights, it should be 'prescribed by law'. The principle of proportionality requires states to strike a balance between different aspiration and the ECtHR has stressed a number of times that governments can only go so far in regulating the private sphere, for example in relation to sexual conduct. By example, reference can also be made to a Dutch case in which a judge annulled a law which prohibited fishing on Sunday, because the law was formulated too broadly. It also prohibited fishing in one's private pond; this, the judge stressed, went beyond the legitimate reach of the legal order.[475]

Fifth and finally, this chapter has suggested that agents processing large amounts of data can also adopt certain positive aspirations. Which aspirations an organization embraces should be left largely to its own discretion. With respect to democratic states, choosing and setting goals and aspirations is the *raison d'être* of the democratic process *par excellence*. Still, if it is accepted that the essence of the legal order is that it is aimed at promoting human autonomy and freedom, a few examples of natural aspirations might be provided, namely combatting social injustice, promoting diversity and strengthening human autonomy. Obviously, other examples might also apply. An organization that commits itself to certain aspirations might also choose to install a disciplinary court which could have the power to assess whether and in how far the professional ethics within an organization is maintained at a sufficiently high level.

It should also be recalled that, as discussed in Chapter II of this book, the European Convention on Human Rights originally did focus only marginally on juridical means of enforcement. Rather, it relied to a large extent on a form of reputational enforcement. The belief was that if a Commission would determine that a state might be in violation of the Convention's provisions, a state would curtail or change its behavior out of fear for damage to its national and international reputation. Although this model has been underused, it might be valuable to rely on such forms of enforcement to a greater extent in the future. If organizations publicly commit themselves to certain aspirations, but do little to promote them, pressure through social media and outrage on Twitter might force such organizations to adapt their policies.

---

[475] Hoge Raad, Wilnisse Visser, NJ 1922, 473, 13 February 1922.

To conclude, there are also juridical ways to enforce self-ascribed goals and aspirations. In certain cases, it might be possible to submit an *actio polularis* claim before a court of law. An example may be a recent decision in the Netherlands, commonly known as the *Urgenda*-case.[476] The Dutch government has committed itself to certain environmental goals in a document that did not contain any subjective rights. Still, the applicants in this case claimed that it was clear that the government had not done enough to achieve those goals. More importantly, it was clear that if the government did not change its policy, the objectives, which were agreed upon under a certain time frame, would not be met. The court agreed with the applicants and imposed on the Dutch government the obligation to develop a policy that enabled it to meet the goals it had committed itself to.

---

[476] Rechtbank Den Haag, C/09/456689 / HA ZA 13-1396, 24 June 2015. ECLI:NL:RBDHA:2015:7145.

CHAPTER VI
CONCLUSION

1. MAIN ARGUMENT

The core question of this book is whether a rights-based approach to privacy regulation still suffices to address the challenges triggered by new data processing techniques such as Big Data and mass surveillance. A rights-based approach generally grants subjective rights to individuals to protect their personal interests. However, large-scale data processing techniques often transcend the individual and her interests; they may affect broader and more general values. To provide an example, it is very difficult to specify whether and if so, to what extent the large-scale data gathering activities of the NSA have negatively affected the personal interests of an ordinary U.S. or E.U. citizen, which holds true even for broader values such as human dignity, individual autonomy and personal freedom. Similarly, although specific individuals may be filmed by the thousands of CCTV camera's surveilling some European cities, the problem is not so much that these camera's film specific individuals; the problem is that everyone or almost everyone living in these cities is filmed almost constantly and everywhere. Consequently, rather than affecting specific personal interests, such data processing initiatives seem to revolve around general and societal interests.

On a practical level, the problem is that people are often simply unaware that their personal data are gathered by either fellow citizens (e.g., through the use of smart phones), by companies (e.g., through tracking cookies) or by governments (e.g., through covert surveillance). Obviously, people who are unaware of their data being gathered will not invoke their right to privacy in court. But even if people were aware of these data collections, given the fact that data gathering and processing is currently so widespread and omnipresent and will become even more so in the future, it will quite likely be impossible for them to keep track of every data processing initiative involving (or potentially involving) their data, to assess whether the data controller abides by the legal standards applicable, and if not, to file a legal complaint. Consequently, it is increasingly the question whether individuals are able to effectively exercise their rights.

It is important to stress, however, that a rights-based approach to privacy regulation will need to be preserved to address issues in which individual interests are at stake. For example, when the government enters the private home of an individual or when a data controller collects sensitive personal data about a specific subject, it makes sense to grant that individual a subjective right to protect her personal interests. The effects of such matters are limited to one person or a small group of persons, they generally know that they have been affected by the privacy infringement and such infringements are usually temporal and incidental. In these circumstances, individuals are generally capable of invoking their rights in order to protect their personal interests. The question is, however, whether a broader conception of privacy regulation can be introduced, which aims not only at protecting the subjective rights of private individuals, but also the interests at stake that cannot be (directly) linked to a specific individual. This book has developed such an approach by turning to virtue ethics.

Virtue ethics is seen as a third approach in ethics, next to consequentialism and deontology. Virtue ethics argues that an action is good if a virtuous person would perform that action, while consequentialism holds that an action is good if it promotes the maximum amount of happiness for the maximum number of people, and deontology argues that an action is good if it accords to the categorical imperative. Human rights and even the legal framework as such are commonly held to be based on a deontological framework, even though the current human rights framework is often critiqued for being overly consequentialist. This book proposes to base privacy protection not only on the question of respect for the (human) rights of citizens, but also on the broader question of whether the actions of an agent are the actions a virtuous agent would perform.

Leaving the rights-based focus intact, the virtue ethical approach to privacy regulation can be used to tackle the broader implications of Big Data and mass surveillance initiatives. A virtuous agent not only respects the rights and interests of others; a virtuous agent has a broader duty to act in the most careful, just and temperate way possible. The type of agent that is central to this book is the state, although the conclusions reached are potentially also applicable to other agents, such as large data companies like Apple, Facebook and Google. This book has developed two sets of virtues that states must take into account when gathering, analyzing and using data, even if no individual interests or subjective rights are at stake: on the one hand a set of 'minimum requirements' and on the other hand a set of 'maximum requirements' or aspirations. The minimum requirements are procedural conditions, related to the rule of law, which must always be respected, the maximum goals or aspirations, which can never be reached in full.

Virtue ethics produces these two sets of requirements by using the idea of *telos* (purpose or goal). Things, objects and beings have a natural goal towards which they strive, so virtue ethics holds. A tree strives to flourish to the maximum extent and needs roots, branches and leaves to do so. This also applies to man-made instruments. A hammer or a chair, for example, is a non-neutral object – a hammer is designed for hitting other objects such as nails; a chair is designed to sit on. The intrinsic purpose of these tools follows from their design, their embedded aspiration. The best hammer is the hammer that is optimally capable of hitting other objects such as nails and the best chair is the one in which it is best to sit. Two things must be kept in mind. First, that the optimal hammer or chair will never exist – it is a utopian idea. Second, that what is conceived as the best hammer or chair may differ from person to person and from time to time. One person may want to sit comfortably in a chair, another person may want a chair which is good for working in, etc.

Still, it is important that there is a correlation between means and ends. If one chooses a certain goal, for example 'sitting', there are a number of means suited to this goal (chairs, beer crates, cushions, etc.), but most objects, such as plants, umbrellas and lamps, are intrinsically unfit for this purpose. Likewise, a cotton swab is unsuited for hitting other objects. The other way around, instruments are only suitable for certain goals and not for others; a hammer, for example, may be used for hitting other objects and, perhaps, for opening a bottle of beer, but it is unsuitable for the goal of playing rugby or baking bread. This leads to the point that from the aspirations, not only may the maximum goals be derived, but also a set of minimum conditions. A hammer that is made out of cotton instead of wood and steel is a bad hammer, or not a hammer at all; a chair that has no legs, no back and no seat is a deficient chair, or no chair at all.

The same type of logic is often used in professional ethics. A doctor should not only strive to be a decent doctor; she has a professional duty to be the best doctor. A parent should not only strive to be a decent parent; she has a social duty to strive to be the best parent – and so forth. Again, two types of duties or requirements may follow from this. First, a doctor that does not cure any patient and even expedites their sudden death is generally seen as a bad doctor not worthy of her profession; a parent that hits or sexually molests her children, leaves them underfed or does not care for their hygiene is generally seen as such a bad parent that she should be relieved from her parental authority. Second, the doctor has a duty to strive to be the best doctor and the parent has a duty to strive to be the best parent. These are aspirations, the exact definition and scope of which may be a matter of debate. Still, we have a general idea of what a good doctor is and what good parents are. A good doctor, for example, is not only someone who cures the diseases suffered by her patients, but also provides optimal information to her patients, is empathetic towards them and their family, etc.

It is important to stress that although minimum requirements ('do not assault or molest your children', 'do not expedite the death of your patients', etc.) make up the larger part of the law, aspirations are not absent from the legal realm. For example, most legal regimes around the world embed both a duty of care for doctors and for parents, specifying 'act as a good doctor would act' or 'do as a good parent would do'. These are open norms, which are interpreted according to the prevailing societal norms. It is mostly left to courts of law or disciplinary councils to decide whether in concrete cases, parents, doctors and others acting under a duty of care have done enough to be the best possible parent, doctor or otherwise. Moreover, most professional standards and codes of conduct are based on aspirations and goals, rather than on minimum requirements. To provide a final example, some human rights courts have stressed that states are not only under the negative obligation not to abuse their power by violating human rights, but also under a positive obligation to promote human freedom and autonomy, create a healthy living environment and to promote minority identities and life styles. They have a duty to use their power to strive for 'the good' and to use their power in the best way.

This book suggests that the idea of professional ethics may also be applied to the state and the legal order as such. It is argued that these are non-neutral institutions. Why live in a legal order rather than a tyranny? Because legal orders tend to have stable and accessible rules that enable humans to take them into account when making certain choices. Tyrannies, in general, are more prone to ask the impossible of people and to punish them retroactively, because punishment is dependent on the will of the tyrant only. The nature of a legal order is thus that it is aimed at preserving human autonomy and individual freedom to the greatest extent possible. This is the essence, the intrinsic quality, of a legal order. Thus, its aspiration or *telos,* its natural direction is aimed at promoting human autonomy and freedom to the maximum extent. In addition, as Fuller specified, there are minimum requirements; if the state or legal order flagrantly ignores or disrespects human autonomy, for example by structurally adopting retroactive laws, by not making them public, by relying on unstable and *ad hoc* decisions, it can no longer be called a state or a legal order proper. Rather, it would constitute a form of tyranny. In addition to these minimum requirements, the state and its legal order are, or should be, striving towards promoting human autonomy and freedom to the optimal extent.

The introduction of minimum and maximum requirements to privacy regulation could address the problems faced by the current paradigm. The main problem is that there is currently a tension between, on the one hand, a technical reality (Big Data and other large data processing operations) which affects general and societal interests, and on the other hand a legal realm that is focused on the individual, her rights and her interests. A virtue ethical approach to (privacy) regulation is, by contrast, not uniquely focused on individual interests. For example, the virtue ethical approach to privacy regulation does not depend on the question of whether personal data are processed or whether the private life of an individual is at stake. This is because virtue ethics looks at the virtuousness of the agent's behavior as such, without individual interests and rights of others necessarily being at stake. As has been stressed, it goes further than merely respecting the rights or interests of others. Thus, a virtue ethical approach to privacy regulation can specify rules for the gathering, analysis and use of 'data' as such. This solves two tensions under the current regulatory framework that become increasingly evident. First, the fact that data processes are increasingly based on nonpersonal data, such as metadata, statistical data and aggregated data. The processing of such data is difficult to assess under the current regulatory framework, because these data often do not directly or indirectly identify a person. Second, as stressed, the effects of such processes often transcend the individual and her interests. This is problematic because courts often only accept cases by applicants who can demonstrate that they have been or will be affected by the acts or laws complained of. Regulating the processing of data as such might provide a solution for both of these two problems. The gathering, analysis and use of 'data' by states might be regulated as such, irrespective of whether they are linked to specific individuals, and legal complaints could be assessed without it being necessary that the claimants can demonstrate that they have been harmed significantly by the practices complained of.

A virtue ethical approach applies minimum requirements to data processing techniques. Data processing should accord to some, though not all, of the principles currently linked to the processing of 'personal data', such as purpose limitation, data security and data quality. It proposes, second, that the laws and data processing programs they facilitate must always abide by the minimum requirements of legality, legitimacy, transparency and accountability. It proposes, third, as a minimum requirement, that a number of additional duties should be applied in the phase between gathering and using data, when data are combined, harvested through the use of algorithms, analyzed and aggregated in group or statistical profiles. These include the duty that data controllers must ensure that the datasets are not biased, that the data that are combined actually entail the same types of data, that the algorithms used are not biased and that metadata are kept on the data analysis process. These are merely three examples of minimum requirements that a virtue ethical approach to privacy regulation might produce. Others may be derived from such an approach as well. A virtue ethical approach to privacy regulation also proposes maximum goals. The exact content of these aspirations cannot be written in stone. Still, some examples of policies promoting human autonomy and freedom have been provided in the realm of privacy and data protection, namely promoting diversity, autonomy and combatting social stigmas. Moreover, it has been stressed that there are natural limits to these and other aspirations, meaning that an equilibrium has to be found by the state.

Finally, it is important to stress that both these minimum and maximum requirements have already been sporadically suggested, both in the literature and in the jurisprudence of the European Court of Human Rights. For example, starting with the *Klass* judgement and culminating in the *Zakharov*, the Court has gradually accepted that focusing solely on individual rights and individual interests does not do justice to the complexity of cases addressing large scale data processing techniques. It has stressed that in exceptional cases, it is willing to accept *in abstracto* claims and assess the legitimacy and legality of laws and policies as such, without requiring that the laws and policies have had a direct impact on the rights and interests of specific individuals. On the other hand, the ECtHR also uses the concept of positive obligations. Essentially, these are obligations for states to use their power in the optimal way for the promotion of human happiness and the well-being of the country. Similarly, some scholars have suggested that courts and lawmakers should focus on general and societal interests in addition to individual privacy interests.

On a practical level, a virtue ethical approach to privacy regulation might facilitate this move and bring the alternatives suggested to a higher and more consistent level. On a theoretical level, the problem is that the suggestions that have been made so far remain mostly without ethical/theoretical foundation – they are mainly practical solutions to concrete problems. Virtue ethics could provide a solid basis. More importantly, it seems that the alternatives in the case law and literature seem to diverge from and even conflict with the dominant approach to human rights in general and privacy regulation in particular. It is mostly unclear how the alternative approaches relate to the fundamental premises of the current human rights framework, namely that human rights are designed to protect humans by granting them subjective rights to protect their individual interests. For example, when the ECtHR assesses the legitimacy and legality of laws as such, without any harm having been done, it is acting as a constitutional court rather than a human rights court. Similarly, some commentators have critiqued the notion of positive obligations for states, because in effect it allows judges to decide which aspirations and goals states should ascribe to, while this should be left to the democratic legislator. Consequently, more thought is needed on how an alternative approach to (privacy) regulation could be reconciled with the current privacy paradigm.

2. OUTLINE OF THIS BOOK

The first chapter of this book identified two approaches to the regulation of privacy and data protection. The original approach was only marginally based on the protection of the individual and her interests and focused primarily on laying down obligations for states and data controllers. Gradually, the focus of privacy and data protection has shifted towards granting subjective rights to natural persons and protecting their personal interests. It has to be stressed that although many legal provisions and cases were discussed in this chapter, they were presented in an idealized way. The original paradigm did not disregard individual rights and interests absolutely, nor does the current paradigm focus exclusively on personal interests and subjective rights. Still, showing this gradual transformation from an approach which focused primarily on societal interests and general duties, to an approach in which the individual is central, serves two purposes. First, it shows that it is not true that by definition, privacy regulation must focus on private interests and subjective rights. Second, contrasting the current with the original approach to privacy and data protection regulation offers the reader a better understanding of some of the core characteristics of the current legal paradigm.

The second chapter discussed the development of privacy and data protection rules over time. It primarily discussed the instruments developed on a European level, though the American Fair Information Practices, the OECD's guidelines for the protection of personal data and some national European laws and case law were also referred to occasionally. For privacy regulation, the main objects of study were the Council of Europe's European Convention on Human Rights and the jurisprudence of the European Court of Human Rights. For data protection regulation, the main focuses were the European Union's Data Protection Directive and the upcoming General Data Protection Regulation. It has to be stressed that the Directive is to a large extent inspired by the Council of Europe's Convention for the Protection of Individuals with regard to Automatic Processing of Personal Data and that the ECtHR often refers to the EU's Charter of Fundamental Rights when delivering its decision. The instruments of both organizations are increasingly intertwined and interrelated and can (and perhaps need to) be studied in connection to each other. Furthermore, it is important to stress that although privacy and data protection are discussed separately, it is by no means the intention of this book to enter into the discussion whether privacy and data protection are two strictly separated rights or in fact two sides of the same coin.

The second chapter was divided in an introduction (Section 1), a description of the development of privacy regulation (Section 2) and data protection regulation (Section 3) over time and a conclusion (Section 4). Section 2 started by showing in general how privacy has transformed from a classic negative right into a personality right, and then made four specific points. Though the right to complain was originally not or only marginally granted to individuals, it is now solely or almost exclusively granted to natural persons (Section 2.1); though the ECHR as a whole and the right to privacy in particular were originally primarily concerned with the protection of societal and general interests, Article 8 ECHR is now predominantly concerned with the protection of the private and individual interests (Section 2.2); although originally, laws and policies by the states were judged primarily on their intrinsic qualities, such as their effectiveness, legitimacy and legality, the preferred methodology of the ECtHR to determine the outcome of cases is currently the balancing of interests (Section 2.3); although originally, the protection of privacy was only partially done through juridical means, currently, legal regulation is the dominant approach (Section 2.4). Section 3 started off by showing that the term 'personal data' has broadened over time, which means that like the right to privacy, the material scope of the data protection instruments has widened significantly. Subsequently, four arguments were made. Over time, the duties of data controllers have become more and more elaborate and less and less like general duties of care (Section 3.1); there has been an increased focus on the interests and rights of individuals, *inter alia*, to control their data and to submit complaints about a violation of the data protection rules (Section 3.2); like with the right to privacy, though to a lesser extent, there has been an increased focus on balancing the rights and interests of the different parties involved (Section 3.3); the instruments have changed from code-of-conduct-like documents to almost market-regulation-like, full-fledged juridical regimes with high fines and penalties in case of a violation (Section 3.4).

While Chapter II showed how privacy and data protection regulation became increasingly individualized and legalized, Chapter III analyzed the problems of the current privacy paradigm when applied to Big Data and mass surveillance. These problems were explained and analyzed on the four points featuring in chapter II, namely the focus on individual rights, on individual interests, on the balancing of interests to determine the outcome of a case and on legal forms of regulation. Also, a number of the material provisions in the European Data Protection instruments were discussed. The goal of this chapter was not to provide an exhaustive list of the questions raised by modern data processing initiatives, but to show that Big Data and mass surveillance challenge some of the fundaments of the current regulatory framework as such and of the privacy and data protection paradigm in particular. The core argument made here is that Big Data and mass surveillance often transcend the rights of individuals and instead affect general and societal interests. Obviously, this tension has been signaled by others already, both in jurisprudence and in the literature. That is why alternatives to the focus on subjective rights and personal interests developed by others, were discussed in detail in this chapter.

With respect to jurisprudential alternatives, the case law of the European Court of Human Rights with respect to the application of Article 8 ECHR, especially in (mass) surveillance cases, served as an example. Although in *Klass and others v. Germany* from 1978, the ECtHR already made an exception to its rejection of *in abstracto* claims, and has been willing to do so in a handful of cases since then, it was only in the *Zakharov* case from 2015 that it explicitly acknowledged that, in exceptional cases revolving around mass surveillance activities by the state, it is willing to abandon its victim requirement and assess laws and policies on their intrinsic qualities, such as on effectiveness, legitimacy and legality, without any individual interests or personal rights needing to be affected. This jurisprudential precedence serves as a building block for developing an alternative to the rights-based approach to privacy regulation.

Such building blocks have also been found in the literature, where many authors have tried to develop alternatives to an exclusive focus on individual rights and interests. It has to be stressed that although the legal regulation of and case law on privacy discussed in this book are almost exclusively European, the literature is predominantly American. This is unproblematic because these theories are not used to reflect on or interpret the European laws or cases as such, but to find alternatives to the focus on individual rights and interests in privacy regulation, which is as dominant in the U.S.A. as it is in Europe, perhaps even more so. Again, the goal of this discussion was not to provide a full and exhaustive list of theories and proposals, but to give a brief overview of some of the most appealing suggestions made so far. It was suggested that one branch of these theories, namely the agent-based theories, might be used to further develop a virtue ethical approach to privacy regulation.

Chapter III started with an introduction (Section 1) and then discussed the problems of the current regulatory framework in general and the privacy and data protection rules in particular when applied to Big Data and mass surveillance processes (Section 2). To illustrate this argument, the tensions were shown on three aspects, namely the material data protection principles (Section 2.1), the focus on individual rights and interests (Section 2.2) and the focus on legal regulation (Section 2.3). Subsequently, the cases in which the ECtHR has struggled with the focus on subjective rights and individual interests were discussed (Section 3). It appeared that, in exceptional cases, the court has in fact been willing to relax the victim requirement when there is a reasonable likelihood that a person is harmed by a specific law or policy (Section 3.1), when it is likely that harm will result from specific laws or policies (Section 3.2) and in exceptional circumstances, it is even willing to assess cases *in abstracto* (Section 3.3). Finally, the *Zakharov* case was briefly discussed and it was argued that in *in abstracto* cases, the ECtHR acts as a quasi-constitutional court (Section 3.4). Subsequently, Section 4 discussed some of the most prominent theories proposed in scholarly literature that try to develop alternatives to the approach based on individual rights and interests, namely theories that focus on the constitutive value of privacy (Section 4.1), group and collective interests (Section 4.2), potential harm (Section 4.3) and agent-based theories (Section 4.4). Finally, the analysis suggests that the focus on *in abstracto* claims and the agent based theories developed in the literature could be used as building block for developing an alternative approach to privacy regulation (Section 5).

Chapter IV developed the fundaments of a virtue ethical approach to privacy regulation. It did so by explaining the core characteristics of virtue ethics, such as human flourishing, virtue and practical wisdom. The work of Lon L. Fuller was discussed. He believes states and legal orders are in fact teleological (purposive) institutions, aimed at promoting justice and human autonomy and freedom. These goals provide the 'inner morality' of states, from which both minimum and maximum requirements may be derived. It was also briefly pointed out that such an approach might provide alternatives to the four aspects of the current privacy paradigm as discussed. First, virtue ethics does not believe that duties necessarily correlate with the rights of others; the state may have certain duties that transcend the mere respect for the (human) rights of its citizens. Second, the duties of states may transcend the protection or promotion of mere individual interests; virtue ethics focuses on more general and societal interests, on the society as such and the environment people live in. Third, virtue ethics does not merely focus on external moral concepts or on a clash of different interests; it focuses on the 'inner morality' of law and the character of the state. Fourth and finally, virtue ethics lays down minimum requirements for states and suggests positive obligations through the use of data.

Chapter 3 started with an introduction (Section 1) and discussed the notion of virtue ethics (Section 2). First, Subsection 2.1 provided the general contours of virtue ethics. Second, Subsection 2.2 discussed in further detail what a virtue ethical approach to the legal regime in general might entail; it did so by analyzing the work of Lon L. Fuller. Third and finally, Subsection 2.3 briefly pointed out how such an approach might help to overcome the difficulties involved with applying the current privacy paradigm to Big Data and mass surveillance practices. Section 3 analyzed some of the most prominent arguments against adopting a virtue ethical approach to (privacy) regulation. The counter-arguments that have been discussed are: virtue duties do not correlate with rights of subjects, while law supposes a correlation between rights and duties (Subsection 3.1); the legal regime separates is from ought and thus an 'inner morality' of law must be rejected (Subsection 3.2); law must provide action guidance, while virtue ethics is unable to do so (Subsection 3.3).

Chapter V picked up where chapter IV left off. It started with an introduction (Section 1) and subsequently developed the minimum and the maximum requirements for virtuous states with respect to data processing. First, regarding the minimum requirements (Section 2), three examples were provided. It was argued that regulation should apply to 'data' independent of whether they are personal, private or sensitive or not (Section 2.1). Second, it was suggested that there are a number of intrinsic qualities of laws and policies that could be assessed irrespective of whether personal interests have been harmed (Section 2.2) Third, several minimum conditions for analyzing data were developed (Section 2.2). Then, the maximum requirements were developed with respect to data processing (Section 3). It was argued that an equilibrium must be found between the different means and ends of the state (Section 3.1); that states, when using data processing techniques, should strive towards promoting the flourishing of its citizens (Section 3.2); and that there are good reasons for adopting more open, ethics-inspired doctrines in privacy regulation (Section 3.3). The chapter concluded with a brief analysis of the possibility of embedding minimum and maximum requirements in the current legal paradigm (Section 4).

3. CONCLUSIONS

(1) LETTING GO OF THE FOCUS ON INDIVIDUAL RIGHTS

a. Allow in abstracto claims

The current legal regime primarily focuses on *in concreto* judgements. It requires that the applicants must be harmed individually by the law or policy complained of. Courts then assess matters on a case by case basis, that is, on the particular circumstances of the case. However, it is often difficult to substantiate individual harm in Big Data processes. Moreover, it is increasingly difficult for individuals to uphold their individual rights in a world where data processing is so omnipresent. That is why it may be valuable to accept *in abstracto* claims. In such cases, laws or policies are assessed on their own merits, without it being necessary that they have been applied in practice of that they have or will have potential negative effects on the interests of the individual when applied in practice. Rather, the laws and policies are assessed in abstract terms, for example by assessing their intrinsic qualities.

b. Allow class actions (actio popularis)

The current privacy regime grants rights specifically to individuals, that is, natural persons. This also holds true for the right to data protection, because 'personal data' are commonly defined as data that identify a 'natural person'. The difficulty with this approach is twofold. First, people are often simply unaware that their personal data are gathered. Secondly, there is often an inequality of arms. Big Data processes are often initiated by large multinationals such as Google, Apple and Facebook or by states' intelligence services, police or tax authorities. Individual citizens are mostly ill-equipped and underfinanced to engage in long and difficult legal proceedings regarding highly complex, sophisticated technologies. That is why it may be valuable to allow for class actions (*actio popularis*). In such claims, civil society organizations and groups are allowed to submit complaints about a privacy violation. Allowing these types of claims in European case law might mean that over time, specialized organizations may be created that have as primary goal engaging in these types of class actions.

(2) LETTING GO OF THE FOCUS ON INDIVIDUAL INTERESTS

a. Focus on societal interests

The current privacy paradigm is primarily, though not exclusively, focused on protecting personal interests. This is increasingly problematic in the age of Big Data, because large scale data processing practices often transcend the individual and her interests. That is why it might be valuable to also take into account general and societal interests when assessing cases regarding large data processing initiatives. Such societal interests may be linked, *inter alia*, to the prevention of abuse of power by states, but also to the question of whether the state is using its power optimally, for example, by creating a (technological) environment that allows for diversity, for human flourishing and for citizen empowerment.

b. Regulate data

The current legal regime differentiates between, *inter alia*, private and public data, content and metadata, anonymous and personal data, statistical and sensitive personal data, etc. Their protection depends on the question of whether the data can be linked to the individual, can be used to identify a person or has an impact on a natural person. There are generally two problems with this approach. First, as was stressed previously, the link to a specific individual and her interests is increasingly insufficient to address all the relevant aspects of data gathering, processing and usage. Second, distinguishing between different types and categories of data, and linking to them a specific regime of protection and of powers for data controllers, is outdated because data are increasingly going through a circular life cycle. That is why it may be valuable to introduce additional regulation of the processing of data as such, independently of whether these data can be qualified as personal, private or sensitive data. Similarly, rules could be developed for the analysis of data by computerized means.

(3) LETTING GO OF THE FOCUS ON BALANCING INTERESTS

a. Focus on intrinsic qualities of laws and policies

The current regulatory regime is primarily concerned with determining the outcome of cases and assessing the quality of laws and policies on the basis of their potential positive and negative effects. A privacy violation is primarily seen as a negative effect that may result from data processing activities, while efficiency, security or transparency are the positive effects that may result from them; while the negative effects are primarily focused on the individual level, the positive effects are mostly formulated on a societal level. The negative and positive consequences are weighed and balanced against each other. However, because both individual and societal interests in Big Data processes are increasingly abstract and vague, balancing those interests becomes increasingly difficult. That is why it may be worthwhile to focus on the minimum requirements of the law. These rule-of-law-based principles, guaranteeing the basic legitimacy and legality of laws and policies, should be respected even when no individual rights or interests are at stake. As these are minimum requirements, they should be respected at all times; no balancing exercise takes place.

b. *Focus on the aspirations of laws and policies*

The current legal (privacy) paradigm is primarily focused on laying down duties and minimum requirements. Because technological developments are so rapid and because the interests at stake are often abstract and societal in nature, it might be worthwhile to focus more on the aspirations of laws and policies. Seeing the legal order as a purposive enterprise allows for such an approach, as the legal order is created and designed in such a way that human freedom is respected. The natural end of a legal order is promoting human freedom to the maximum extent possible. Such aspirations could be, *inter alia*, promoting a society with maximum diversity, autonomy and freedom.

(4) LETTING GO OF THE FOCUS ON BLACK LETTER LAW

a. *Focus on ethical rules*

The current paradigm places its bets mainly on the legal regulation of rights and obligations – black letter law. Yet it is increasingly questionable whether and to what extent this form of regulation still suffices in the Big Data era. That has to do with a number of issues. First, data processing is increasingly transnational. This implies that more and more agreements need to be made between different states and organizations in different jurisdictions. Hard legal rules are often difficult to agree upon due to the difference in traditions and legal systems. Furthermore, rapidly changing technology has the effect that specific legal provisions can easily be circumvented and that unforeseen problems and challenges may arise. And, as discussed, many of the problems arising from Big Data practices are social and societal. It is questionable whether those concerns should be dealt in full within the juridical discourse. It could be promising to regulate Big Data processes additionally through forms of soft law and ethical standards, such as duties of care and codes of conduct. The underlying normative principles and values to be guaranteed in Big Data processes remain relatively stable.

One could also look to other sectors for inspiration, for example the idea of installing ethical oversight committees, such as is a common practice in the medical sector. An interdisciplinary group of experts, consisting for instance of lawyers, ethicists, engineers and practitioners, could assess specific plans, policies and experiments.

b.   *Adopt a more hybrid approach*

The current regulatory regime is based on numerous categorizations, labels and distinctions. For example, distinctions can be made between the offline and online, between the analog and digital environment, between the protection of privacy in the private and in the public domain, between different nations and jurisdictions, between times of war and times of peace, between the powers and capacities of organizations in the private sector and in the public sector, and between different organizations in the public sector (for example in relation to which data they may gather, how they might use them and for what purposes; the intelligence agencies have broader powers to process data than the police, and the police has broader powers than the social services). In the Big Data era, however, the world is becoming increasingly fluid. Although the rights of citizens are currently linked mainly to physical objects such as the body and the home, and certain forms of communication such as the secrecy of correspondence, the Big Data era requires that one's digital identity, internet communications and privacy in the public domain be protected equally. Likewise, in Big Data processes, data streams increasingly circulate between the private and the public sector and between different governmental agencies. Future regulation will need to standardize the rules applicable to those different sectors.

BIBLIOGRAPHY

1. COUNCIL OF EUROPE

1.1. TEXTS AND DOCUMENTS

Council of Europe, Original European Convention on Human Rights <www.echr.coe.int/library/annexes/CEDH1950ENG.pdf>

Council of Europe, Current European Convention on Human Rights < www.echr.coe.int/Documents/Convention_ENG.pdf>

Council of Europe, Committee of Ministers, Resolution (73) 22 On the Protection of the privacy of individuals vis-à-vis electronic data banks in the private sector. (Adopted by the Committee of Ministers on 26 September 1973 at the 224th meeting of the Ministers' Deputies).

Council of Europe, Committee of Ministers, Resolution (74) 29 On the Protection of the privacy of individuals vis-à-vis electronic data banks in the public sector. (Adopted by the Committee of Ministers on 20 September 1974 at the 236th meeting of the Ministers' Deputies).

Council of Europe, Convention for the Protection of Individuals with regard to Automatic Processing of Personal Data Strasbourg, 28 January 1981.

<http://conventions.coe.int/Treaty/EN/Reports/HTML/108.htm>.

Council of Europe, Protocol No. 8 to the Convention for the Protection of Human Rights and Fundamental Freedoms, Vienna, 1985.

Council of Europe, Protocol No. 9 to the Convention for the Protection of Human Rights and Fundamental Freedoms Rome, 6 November 1990. This Protocol has been repealed as from the date of entry into force of Protocol No. 11 (ETS No. 155) on 1 November 1998.

Council of Europe, Protocol No. 11 to the Convention for the Protection of Human Rights and Fundamental Freedoms, restructuring the control machinery established thereby. Strasbourg, 11 June 1994. Since its entry into force on 1 November 1998, this Protocol forms an integral part of the Convention (ETS No. 5).

1.2. CASE LAW OF THE ECMHR AND THE ECTHR

ECtHR, Case "Relating to certain aspects of the Laws on the Use of Languages in Education in Belgium" v. Belgium, application nos. 1474/62, 1677/62, 1691/62, 1769/63, 1994/63 and 2126/64, 23 July 1968.

ECmHR, Klass and others v. Germany, application no. 5029/71, 18 December 1974.

ECmHR, X. v. Germany, application no. 7407/76, 13 May 1976.

ECmHR, X. v. Iceland, application no. 6825/74, 18 May 1976.

ECmHR, Brüggemann and Scheuten v. Germany, application no. 6959/75, 19 May 1976.
ECtHR, Kjeldsen, Busk Madsen and Pedersen v. Denmark, application nos. 5095/71, 5920/72 and 5926/72, 7 December 1976.
ECtHR, Klass and others v. Germany, application no. 5029/71, 06 September 1978.
ECtHR, Marckx v. Belgium, application no. 6833/74, 13 June 1979.
ECmHR, X. v. Germany, application no. 8741/79, 10 March 1981.
ECmHR, Malone v. the United Kingdom, application no. 8691/79, 13 July 1981.
ECtHR, Dudgeon v. the United Kingdom, application no. 7525/76, 22 October 1981.
ECmHR, G. and E. v. Norway, application no. 9278/81, 3 October 1983.
ECtHR, Malone v. the United Kingdom, application no. 8691/79, 2 August 1984.
ECmHR, Mersch and others v. Luxembourg, application nos. 10439/83, 10440/83, 10441/83, 10452/83, 10512/83 and 10513/83, 10 May 1985.
ECmHR, M.S. and P.S. v. Switserland, application no. 10628/83, 14 October 1985.
ECtHR, Leander v. Sweden, application no. 9248/81, 26 March 1987.
ECtHR, W. v. UK, application no. 9749/82, 8 July 1987.
ECtHR, B. v. the United Kingdom, application no. 9840/82, 8 July 1987.
ECtHR, R. v. the United Kingdom, application no. 10496/83, 8 July 1987.
ECmHR, Spillmann v. Switzerland, application no. 11811/85, 08 March 1988.
ECmHR, Hilton v. the United Kingdom, application no. 12015/86, 06 July 1988.
ECtHR, Lawlor v. the United Kingdom, application no. 12763/87, 14 July 1988.
ECmHR, Nimmo v. the United Kingdom, application no. 12327/86, 11 October 1988.
ECtHR, Huvig v. France, application no. 11105/84, 24 April 1990.
ECtHR, Kruslin v. France, application no. 11801/85, 24 April 1990.
ECmHR, Spire v. France, application no. 13728/88, 17 May 1990.
ECtHR, Moustaquim v. Belgium, application no. 12313/86, 18 February 1991.
ECtHR, Campbell v. the United Kingdom, application no. 13590/88, 25 March 1992.
ECmHR, T.D., D.E. and M.F. v. the United Kingdom, application nos. 18600/91, 18601/91 and 18602/91, 12 October 1992.
ECtHR, Drozdowski v. Poland, application no. 20841/02, 06 December 1992.
ECtHR, Niemitz v. Germany, application no. 13710/88, 16 December 1992.
ECmHR, Esbester v. the United Kingdom, application no. 18601/91, 02 April 1993.
ECmHR, Hewitt and Harman v. the United Kingdom, application no. 20317/92, 01 September 1993.
ECmHR, Redgrave v. the United Kingdom, application no. 20271/92, 01 September 1993.
ECmHR, K.B. v. Netherlands, application no. 18806/91, 01 September 1993.
ECtHR, Tjerna v. Finland, application no. 18131/91, 25 November 1994.
ECmHR, Church of Scientology of Paris v. France, application no. 19509/92, 09 January 1995.
ECtHR, Nasri v. France, application no. 19465/92, 13 July 1995.
ECmHR, Tauira and 18 others v. France, application no. 28204/95, 04 December 1995.
ECtHR, C. v. Belgium, application no. 21794/93, 07 August 1996.
ECmHR, Matthews v. the United Kingdom, application no. 28576/95, 16 October 1996.
ECmHR, Glass v. UK, application no. 28485/95, 16 October 1996.
ECtHR, Guillot v. France, application no. 22500/93, 24 October 1996.
ECtHR, Halford v. the United Kingdom, application no. 20605/92, 25 June 1997.
ECmHR, Salonen v. Finland, application no. 27868/95, 2 July 1997.

ECmHR, Herbecq and the Association Ligue Des Droits de L'Homme v. Belgium, application nos. 32200/96 and 32201/96, 14 January 1998.
ECtHR, Marzari v. Italy, application no. 36448/97, 4 May 1999.
ECtHR, Asselbourg and 78 others and Greenpeace Association-Luxembourg v. Luxembourg, application no. 29121/95, 29 June 1999.
ECtHR, Bijleveld v. Netherlands, application no. 42973/98, 27 April 2000.
ECtHR, Rotaru v. Romania, application no. 28341/95, 04 May 2000.
ECtHR, Chapman v. the United Kingdom, application no. 27238/95, 18 January 2001.
ECtHR, Cyprus v. Turkey, application no. 25781/94, 10 May 2001.
ECtHR, Erdem v. Germany, application no. 38321/97, 05 July 2001.
ECtHR, Boultif v. Switzerland, application no. 54273/00, 02 August 2001.
ECtHR, P.G. and J.H. v. the United Kingdom, application no. 44787/98, 25 September 2001.
ECtHR, G.M.B. and K.M. v. Switzerland, application no. 36797/97, 27 September 2001.
ECtHR, Pretty v. the United Kingdom, application no. 2346/02, 29 April 2002.
ECtHR, Segi and others and Gestoras Pro-Amnistia and others v. 15 states of the European Union, application nos. 6422/02 and 9916/02, 23 May 2002.
ECtHR, Christine Goodwin v. the United Kingdom, application no. 28957/95, 11 July 2002.
ECtHR, I. v. the United Kingdom, appliclation no. 25680/94, 11 July 2002.
ECtHR, Nazarenko v. Ukraine, application no. 39483/98, 29 April 2003.
ECtHR, Lich v. Ukraine, application no. 41707/98, 29 April 2003.
ECtHR, Perry v. the United Kingdom, application no. 63737/00, 17 July 2003.
ECtHR, Slivenko v. Latvia, application no. 48321/99, 09 October 2003.
ECtHR, Senator Lines GmbH v. Austria, Belgium, Denmark, Finland, France, Germany, Greece, Ireland, Italy, Luxembourg, the Netherlands, Portugal, Spain, Sweden and the United Kingdom, application no. 56672/00, 10 March 2004.
ECtHR, Gusinskiy v. Russia, application no. 70276/01, 19 May 2004.
ECtHR, C. and D. and S. and others v. the United Kingdom, application nos. 34407/02 and 34593/02, 31 August 2004.
ECtHR, Tekeli v. Turkey, application no. 29865/96, 16 November 2004.
ECtHR, C. v. the United Kingdom, application no. 14858/03, 14 December 2004.
ECtHR, Py v. France, application no. 66289/01, 11 January 2005.
ECtHR, Monory v. Hungary, application no. 71099/01, 05 April 2005.
ECtHR, Bosphorushava Yollari Turizm ve Ticaret Anonim Sirketi v. Ireland, application no. 45036/98, 30 June 2005.
ECtHR, Sorensen and Rusmussen v. Denmark, application nos. 52562/99 and 52620/99, 11 January 2006.
ECtHR, Aristimuno Mendizabal v. France, application no. 51431/99, 17 January 2006.
ECtHR, Rodrigues Da Silva and Hoogkamer v. Netherlands, application no. 50435/99, 31 January 2006.
ECtHR, Weber and Saravia v. Germany, application no. 54934/00, 29 June 2006.
ECtHR, Keegan v. the United Kingdom, application no. 28867/03, 18 July 2006.
ECtHR, Uner v. the Netherlands, application no. 46410/99, 18 October 2006.
ECtHR, Ledyayeva, Dobrokhotova, Zolotareva and Romashina v. Russia, application nos. 53157/99, 53247/99, 56850/00 and 53695/00, 26 October 2006.
ECtHR, Sisojeva a.o. v. Latvia, application no. 60654/00, 15 January 2007.

ECtHR, Association for European Integration and Human Rights and Ekimdzhiev v. Bulgaria, application no. 62540/00, 08 June 2007.
ECtHR, Folgero a.o. v. Norway, application no. 15472/02, 29 June 2007.
ECtHR, Cebotari v. Moldova, application no. 35615/06, 13 November 2007.
ECtHR, Pfeifer v. Austria, application no. 12556/03, 15 November 2007.
ECtHR, Stefanov v. Bulgaria, applicaiton no. 65755/01, 22 May 2008.
ECtHR, Liberty and others v. the United Kingdom, application no. 58243/00, 01 July 2008.
ECtHR, Kart v. Turkey, application no. 8917/05, 08 July 2008.
ECtHR, Mancevschi v. Modova, application no. 33066/04, 07 October 2008.
ECtHR, Gulijev v. Lithuania, application no. 10425/30, 16 December 2008.
ECtHR, Iordachi and other v. Moldova, application no. 25198/02, 10 February 2009.
ECtHR, Duda v. France, application no. 37387/05, 17 March 2009.
ECtHR, Georgia v. Russia (I), application no. 13255/07, 30 June 2009.
ECtHR, Tanase v. Moldova, application no. 7/08, 27 April 2010.
ECtHR, Kennedy v. the United Kingdom, application no. 26839/05, 18 May 2010.
ECtHR, Aksu v. Turkey, application nos. 4149/04 and 41029/04, 27 July 2010.
ECtHR, Goranova-Karaeneva v. Bulgaria, application no. 12739/05, 08 March 2011.
ECtHR, Case of Association "21 December 1989" and others v. Romania, application nos. 33810/07 and 18817/08, 24 May 2011.
ECtHR, Diamante and Pelliccioni v. San Marino, application no. 32250/08, 27 September 2011.
ECtHR, Arvelo Apont v. the Netherlands, application no. 28770/05, 3 November 2011.
ECtHR, Georgia v. Russia (II), application no. 38263/08, 13 December 2011.
ECtHR, Kanagaratnam and others v. Belgium, application no. 15297/09, 13 December 2011.
ECtHR, Interdnestrcom v. Moldova, application no. 48814/06, 13 March 2012.
ECtHR, Colon v. the Netherlands, application no. 49458/06, 15 May 2012.
ECtHR (Grand Chamber), Aksu v. Turkey, application nos. 4149/04 and 41029/04, 15 March 2012.
ECtHR, Lutsenko v. Ukraine, application no. 6492/11, 03 July 2012.
ECtHR, Hadzhiev v. Bulgaria, applicaiton no. 22373/04, 23 October 2012.
ECtHR, M.M. v. the United Kingdom, application no. 24029/07, 13 November 2012.
ECtHR, Lenev v. Bulgaria, application no. 41452/07, 04 December 2012.
ECtHR, Michaud v. France, application no. 12323/33, 06 December 2012.
ECtHR, M.N. and F.Z. v. France and Greece, application nos. 59677/09 and 1453/10, 08 January 2013.
ECtHR, X. and others v. Austria, application no. 19010/07, 19 February 2013.
ECtHR, Animal Defenders International v. the United Kingdom, application no. 48876/08, 22 April 2013.
ECtHR, Tymoshenko v. Ukraine, application no. 49872/11, 30 April 2013.
ECtHR, Lunch and Whelan v. Ireland, application nos. 70495/10 and 74565/10, 18 June 2013.
ECtHR, Vassis and others v. France, application no. 62736/09, 27 June 2013.
ECtHR, Mikalauskas v. Malta, application no. 4458/10, 23 July 2013.
ECtHR, Delfi v. Estonia (first instance), application no. 64569/09, 10 October 2013.
ECtHR, Vallianatos and others v. Greece, application nos. 29381/09 and 32684, 07 November 2013.
ECtHR, Big Brother Watch and others v. the United Kingdom, application no. 58170/13, 07 January 2014.
ECtHR, Mateescu v. Romania, application no. 1944/10, 14 January 2014.
ECtHR, Avotins v. Latvia, application no. 17502/07, 25 February 2014.
ECtHR, Ilgar Mammadov v. Azerbaijan, application no. 15172/13, 22 May 2014.

ECtHR, Berger-Krall and others v. Slovenia, application no. 14717/04, 12 June 2014.
ECtHR, Ucar and others v. Turkey, application no. 4692/09, 24 June 2014.
ECtHR, S.A.S. v. France, application no. 43835/11, 01 July 2014.
ECtHR, Matelly v. France, application no. 10609/10, 02 October 2014.
ECtHR, Delta Pekarny A.S. v. Czech Republic, application no. 97/11, 02 October 2014.
ECtHR, Emars v. Latvia, application no. 22412/08, 18 November 2014.
ECtHR, Delfi v. Estonia (Grand Chamber), application no. 64569/09, 16 June 2015.
ECtHR, Roman Zakharov v. Russia, application no. 47143/06, 04 December 2015.
ECtHR, Szabó and Vissy v. Hungary, application no. 37138/14, 12 January 2016.

1.3. OTHER

A.H. Robertson, 'Collected edition of the 'travaux préparatoires' of the European Convention on Human Rights = Recueil des travaux préparatoires de la Convention Européenne des Droits de l'Homme. Vol. 1 Preparatory Commission of the Council of Europe Committee of Ministers, Consultative Assembly, 11 May-8 September 1949', The Hague, Nijhoff, 1975.

A.H. Robertson, 'Collected edition of the 'travaux préparatoires' of the European Convention on Human Rights = Recueil des travaux préparatoires de la Convention Européenne des Droits de l'Homme; Council of Europe. Vol. 2 Consultative Assembly, second session of the Committee of Ministers, Standing Committee of the Assembly, 10 August-18 November 1949', The Hague, Nijhoff, 1975.

A.H. Robertson, 'Collected edition of the 'travaux préparatoires' of the European Convention on Human Rights = Recueil des travaux préparatoires de la Convention Européenne des Droits de l'Homme. Council of Europe. Vol. 3 Committee of Experts, 2 February-10 March 1950', The Hague, Nijhoff, 1975.

A.H. Robertson, 'Collected edition of the 'travaux préparatoires' of the European Convention on Human Rights = Recueil des travaux préparatoires de la Convention Européenne des Droits de l'Homme; Council of Europe. Vol. 4 Committee of Experts, Committee of Ministers, Conference of Senior Officials, 30 March-June 1950', The Hague, Nijhoff, 1975.

A H Robertson, Collected edition of the 'travaux préparatoires' of the European Convention on Human Rights = Recueil des travaux préparatoires de la Convention Européenne des Droits de l'Homme; Council of Europe. Vol. 5 Legal Committee, Ad hoc Joint Committee, Committee of Ministers, Consultative Assembly, 23 June – 28 August 1950 (Nijhoff, 1975) 68.

A.H. Robertson, 'Collected edition of the 'travaux préparatoires' of the European Convention on Human Rights = Recueil des travaux préparatoires de la Convention Européenne des Droits de l'Homme. Council of Europe. Council of Europe. Vol. 6 / Consultative Assembly = Assemblee Consultative', The Hague, Nijhoff, 1975.

Council of Europe report: New technologies: a challenge to privacy protection? (1989). <www.coe.int/t/dghl/standardsetting/dataprotection/Reports/NewTechnologies_1989_en.pdf>.

Council of Europe, 'Freedom of expression in Europe: case-law concerning article 10 of the European Convention on Human Rights', Strasbourg, Council of Europe Publishing, 2007.

Recommendation CM/Rec(2010)13 of the Committee of Ministers to member states on the protection of individuals with regard to automatic processing of personal data in the context of profiling (Adopted by the Committee of Ministers on 23 November 2010 at the 1099th meeting of the Ministers' Deputies).

2. EUROPEAN UNION

2.1. OFFICIAL TEXTS

Directive 95/46/EC of the European Parliament and of the Council of 24 October 1995 on the protection of individuals with regard to the processing of personal data and on the free movement of such data.

Charter of Fundamental Rights of the European Union (2000/C 364/01). <www.europarl.europa.eu/charter/pdf/text_en.pdf>.

Directive 2000/31/EC of the European Parliament and of the Council of 8 June 2000 on certain legal aspects of information society services, in particular electronic commerce, in the Internal Market ('Directive on electronic commerce'), Official Journal L 178, 17/07/2000 P. 0001 – 0016.

The Principles Of European Contract Law <www.jus.uio.no/lm/eu.contract.principles.parts.1.to.3.2002/>.

Directive 2002/22/EC of the European Parliament and of the Council of 7 March 2002 on universal service and users' rights relating to electronic communications networks and services (Universal Service Directive).

Directive 2002/58/EC of the European Parliament and of the Council of 12 July 2002 concerning the processing of personal data and the protection of privacy in the electronic communications sector (Directive on privacy and electronic communications), Official Journal L 201, 31/07/2002 P. 0037 – 0047.

Directive 2003/98/EC of the European Parliament and of the Council of 17 November 2003 on the re-use of public sector information, L 345/90, 31 12 2003.

Directive 2004/48/EC of the European Parliament and of the Council on the enforcement of intellectual property rights, L 195/16.

Treaty of Lisbon amending the Treaty on European Union and the Treaty Establishing the European Community (2007/C 306/01).

Council Framework Decision 2008/977/JHA of 27 November 2008 on the protection of personal data processed in the framework of police and judicial cooperation in criminal matters, OJ L 350, 30 Dec. 2008.

Regulation (EU) 2016/679 of the European Parliament and of the Council of 27 April 2016 on the protection of natural persons with regard to the processing of personal data and on the free movement of such data, and repealing Directive 95/46/EC (General Data Protection Regulation).

Directive (EU) 2016/680 of the European Parliament and of the Council of 27 April 2016 on the protection of natural persons with regard to the processing of personal data by competent authorities for the purposes of the prevention, investigation, detection or prosecution of criminal offences or the execution of criminal penalties, and on the free movement of such data, and repealing Council Framework Decision 2008/977/JHA.

Directive (EU) 2016/681 of the European Parliament and of the Council of 27 April 2016 on the use of passenger name record (PNR) data for the prevention, detection, investigation and prosecution of terrorist offences and serious crime.

2.2. CASE LAW OF THE EUROPEAN COURT OF JUSTICE

European Court of Justice, Joined Cases C-465/00, C-138/01, and C-139/01, Rechnungshof and Österreichischer Rundfunk, Wirtschaftskammer Steiermark, Marktgemeinde Kaltenleutgeben, Land Niederösterreich, Österreichische Nationalbank, Stadt Wiener Neustadt, Austrian Airlines, Österreichische Luftverkehrs-AG, and between Christa Neukomm, Joseph Lauermann, and Österreichischer Rundfunk, 20 May 2003.
European Court of Justice, Case C-101/01 Bodil Lindqvist, 6 November 2003.
European Court of Justice, Grand Chamber, Case C-73/07 Tietosuojavaltuutettu v Satakunnan Markkinapörssi Oy, Satamedia Oy, 16 December 2008.
European Court of Justice (Grand Chamber), Case C-524/06 Heinz Huber v Bundesrepublik Deutschland, 16 December 2008.
European Court of Justice (Grand Chamber), Case C-518/07 European Commission, v Federal Republic of Germany, 9 March 2010.
European Court of Justice (Grand Chamber), Cases C-92/09 and C-93/09 Volker und Markus Schecke GbR and Hartmut Eifert v Land Hessen,, 9 November 2010.
European Court of Justice, L'Oréal SA, Lancôme parfums et beauté & Cie SNC, Laboratoire Garnier & Cie, L'Oréal (UK) Ltd v. eBay International AG, eBay Europe SARL, eBay (UK) Ltd, Stephen Potts, Tracy Ratchford, Marie Ormsby, James Clarke, Joanna Clarke, Glen Fox, Rukhsana Bi, Case C-324/09, 12 July 2011.
European Court of Justice (Third Chamber), Joined Cases C-468/10 and C-469/10 Asociación Nacional de Establecimientos Financieros de Crédito (ASNEF), Federación de Comercio Electrónico y Marketing Directo (FECEMD) v Administración del Estado, intervening parties: Unión General de Trabajadores (UGT), Telefónica de España SAU, France Telecom España SA, Telefónica Móviles de España SAU, Vodafone España SA, Asociación de Usuarios de la Comunicación, 24 November 2011.
European Court of Justice (Grand Chamber), Case C-614/10 European Commission v Republic of Austria, 16 October 2012.
European Court of Justice (Third Chamber), Case C-342/12 Worten – Equipamentos para o Lar SA v Autoridade para as Condições de Trabalho (ACT), 30 May 2013.
European Court of Justice, Digital Rights Ireland and Seitlinger and Others, Joined Cases C-293/12 and C-594/12, 8 April 2014.
European Court of Justice, Google Spain SL, Google Inc. v Agencia Española de Protección de Datos (AEPD), Mario Costeja González,, case C-131/12, 13 May 2014.
European Court of Justice, František Rynes v. Úřad pro ochranu osobních údajů, Case C-212/13, 11 December 2014.
European Court of Justice, Coty Germany GmbH v. Stadtsparkasse Magdeburg, Case C-580/13, 16 Juli 2015

2.3. OPINIONS

Article 29 Working Party, 'Opinion 4/2007 on the concept of personal data', 01248/07/EN, WP 136, Brussels, 20 June 2007.
Article 29 Data Protection Working, 'Opinion 8/2010 on applicable law', 0836–02/10/EN, WP 179, Brussels, 16 December 2010.

Article 29 Data Protection Working, 'Opinion 01/2012 on the data protection reform proposals', 00530/12/EN, WP 191, Brussels, 23 March 2012.

Article 29 Data Protection Working, Opinion 05/2012 on Cloud Computing, 01037/12/EN, WP 196, Brussels, 1 July 2012.

Article 29 Data Protection Working, Opinion 03/2013 on purpose limitation', WP 203, 00569/13/EN, Brussel, 2 April 2013.

Article 29 Data Protection Working, 'Opinion 06/2014 on the notion of legitimate interests of the data controller under Article 7 of Directive 95/46/EC', WP 217, 844/14/EN, Brussel, 9 April 2014.

Article 29 Data Protection Working Party, 'Opinion 05/2014 on Anonymisation Techniques', 0829/14/EN, WP216, Brussels, 10 April 2014.

European Data Protection Supervisor, 'Opinion of the European Data Protection Supervisor on the data protection reform package', Brussels, 7 March 2012.

Opinion of Advocate General Campos Sanchez-Bordona, Patrick Breyer v. Bundesrepublik Deutschland, Case C-582/14, 12 May 2016.

2.4. OTHER

European Commission, Proposal for a Council Directive concerning the protection of individuals in relation to the processing of personal data COM(90) 314 final – SYN 287 (Submitted by the Commission on 27 July 1990) (90/C 277/03).

Economic and Social Committee, Opinion on: the proposal for a Council Directive concerning the protection of individuals in relation to the processing of personal data, – the proposal for a Council Directive concerning the protection of personal data and privacy in the context of public digital telecommunications networks, in particular the integrated services digital network (ISDN) and public digital mobile networks, and – the proposal for a Council Decision in the field of information security. 17 June 1991 Official Journal of the European Communities No C 159/38–48.

No C94/181, Official Journal of the European Communities, 13 April 1992; Wednesday, 11 March 1992.

Commission of the European Communities, First report on the implementation of the Data Protection Directive (95/46/EC), COM(2003) 265 final, Brussels, 15 May 2003.

European Commission, 'Communication from the Commission to the European Parliament, the Council, the Economic and Social Committee and the Committee of the Regions. A comprehensive approach on personal data protection in the European Union', Brussels, 4 Nov. 2010, COM(2010) 609 final.

The Study on the economic benefits of privacy enhancing technologies, London Economics, July 2010. <http://ec.europa.eu/justice/policies/privacy/docs/studies/final_report_pets_16_07_10_en.pdf>.

European Commission, Proposal for a Regulation of the European Parliament and of the Council on the protection of individuals with regard to the processing of personal data and on the free movement of such data (General Data Protection Regulation). Version 56, (29/11/2011). <www.statewatch.org/news/2011/dec/eu-com-draft-dp-reg-inter-service-consultation.pdf>.

European Commission, Commission Staff Working Paper, 'Impact Assessment Accompanying the document Regulation of the European Parliament and of the Council on the protection of individuals with regard to the processing of personal data and on the free movement of such data (General Data Protection Regulation) and Directive of the European Parliament and of the Council on the protection of individuals with regard to the processing of personal data by competent authorities for the purposes of prevention, investigation, detection or prosecution of criminal offences or the execution of criminal penalties, and the free movement of such data', Brussels, 25 January 2012, { SEC(2012) 73 final}, COM(2012) 11 final.

European Commission, Proposal for a Regulation of the European Parliament and of the Council on the protection of individuals with regard to the processing of personal data and on the free movement of such data (General Data Protection Regulation), Brussels, 25 January 2012, {SEC(2012) 72 final}, COM(2012) 11 final, 2012/0011 (COD).

European Commission, Brussels, Proposal for a Directive of the European Parliament and of the Council on the protection of individuals with regard to the processing of personal data by competent authorities for the purposes of prevention, investigation, detection or prosecution of criminal offences or the execution of criminal penalties, and the free movement of such data, Brussels, 25 January 2012, COM(2012) 10 final, 2012/0010 (COD).
<http://eur-lex.europa.eu/LexUriServ/LexUriServ.do?uri=COM:2012:0010:FIN:EN:PDF>.

European Parliament, Draft European Parliament Legislative Resolution on the proposal for a regulation of the European Parliament and of the Council on the protection of individuals with regard to the processing of personal data and on the free movement of such data (General Data Protection Regulation), Brussel, 2013. <www.europarl.europa.eu/sides/getDoc.do?pubRef=-%2F%2FEP%2F%2FTEXT%2BREPORT%2BA7-2013-0402%2B0%2BDOC%2BXML%2BV0%2F%2FEN&language=EN>.

3. INTERNATIONAL LEGAL DOCUMENTS

African Charter on Human and Peoples' Rights.
    <www.achpr.org/instruments/achpr/>.
International Covenant on Civil and Political Rights.
    <www.ohchr.org/Documents/ProfessionalInterest/ccpr.pdf>.
International Conference of Data Protection and Privacy Commissioners, 'Resolution Big Data', Mauritius, 2014.
    <www.privacyconference2014.org/media/16602/Resolution-Big-Data.pdf>.
International Working Group on Data Protection in Telecommunications, 'Working Paper on Big Data and Privacy. Privacy principles under pressure in the age of Big Data analytics', 55th Meeting, Skopje, 5 – 6 May 2014.
Organisation for Economic Co-operation and Development, 'Policy issues in data protection and privacy: concepts and perspectives: proceedings of the OECD seminar, 24th to 26th June 1974', OECD, Paris, 1976.
OECD Guidelines on the Protection of Privacy and Transborder Flows of Personal Data <www.oecd.org/sti/ieconomy/oecdguidelinesontheprotectionofprivacyandtransborderflowsofpersonaldata.htm>.
OECD, 'Corporate Social Responsibility Partners for Progress', OECD Publishing, Paris, 2001.

Universal Declaration on Human Rights.
<www.un.org/en/universal-declaration-human-rights/>.
UN documents: E/HR/3.

4. NATIONAL LEGAL DOCUMENTS

4.1. GERMANY

Grundgesetz für die Bundesrepublik Deutschland.
<https://www.bundestag.de/grundgesetz>.

4.2. NETHERLANDS

Dutch Civil Code: < www.dutchcivillaw.com/civilcodegeneral.htm>.
Hoge Raad, Wilnisse Visser, NJ 1922, 473, 13 February 1922.
Rechtbank Den Haag, Burgers v. Plassterk, C/09/455237 / HA ZA 13–1325, 23-07-2014.
Rechtbank Den Haag, C/09/456689 / HA ZA 13–1396, 24 June 2015, ECLI:NL:RBDHA:2015:7145.

4.3. UNITED KINGDOM

House of Lords, A (FC) and others (FC) (Appellants) v. Secretary of State for the Home Department, UKHL 56, 2004.

4.4. UNITED STATES OF AMERICA

Supreme Court of the United States, Roe v. Wade, 410 U.S. 113, 1973.
Secretary's Advisory Committee on Automated Personal Data Systems, Records, Computers and the Rights of Citizens, 1973.
<https://www.hsdl.org/?view&did=479784>.
The Privacy Act of 1974, 5 U.S.C. §552a.
Privacy Protection Study Commission, Personal Privacy in an Information Society 1977.
Curlender v. Bio-Science Laboratories, Civ. No. 58192. Court of Appeals of California, Second Appellate District, Division One. June 11, 1980.
Federal Trade Commission, Privacy Online: A Report to Congress 1998.
Supreme Court of the United States, Riley v. California, No. 13–132. Argued April 29, 2014 – Decided June 25, 2014.
Privacy and Civil Liberties Oversight Board Report on the Surveillance Program Operated Pursuant to Sec7on 702 of the Foreign Intelligence Surveillance Act July 2, 2014.

5. LITERATURE

D. Acosta Arcarazo & C. C. Murphy, *EU Security and Justice Law: After Lisbon and Stockholm* (Hart Publishing 2014).

P. E. Agre & M. Rotenberg, *Technology and Privacy: The New Landscape* (MIT Press 2001).

M. M. Aid, *The Secret Sentry: The Untold History of the National Security Agency* (Bloomsbury Press 2009).

J.-F. Akandji-Kombe, 'Positive Obligations under the European Convention on Human Rights', Human Rights Handbooks, No. 7, 2007.

T. A. Aleinikoff, 'Constitutional Law in the Age of Balancing' (1987) 97(5) Yale Law Journal.

A. L. Allen, *Why Privacy Isn't Everything: Feminist Reflections on Personal Accountability* (Rowman & Littlefield 2003).

A. L. Allen, *Unpopular Privacy: What Must we Hide?* (Oxford University Press 2011).

B. van Alsenoy & M. Koekkoek, 'Internet and Jurisdiction after Google Spain: The Extraterritorial Reach of the 'Right to Be Delisted'' (2015) 5(2) International Data Privacy Law.

J. Altena-Davidsen, 'De reikwijdte van de plicht tot conforme interpretatie in het strafrecht tegen de achtergrond van de verhouding tussen de Europese en de nationale rechtsorde' (2012) 4 Ars Aequi.

J. Ambrose & M. Leta, 'Lessons from the Avalanche of Numbers: Big Data in Historical Context' (2015) I/S: A Journal of Law and Policy for the Information Society <http://ssrn.com/abstract=2486981>.

C. Anderson, 'The End of Theory: The Data Deluge Makes the Scientific Method Obsolete', (*Wired Magazine*, 16 July 2008) <www.uvm.edu/~cmplxsys/wordpress/wp-content/uploads/reading-group/pdfs/2008/anderson2008.pdf>.

M. Andrejevic, 'The Big Data Divide' (2014) 8 International Journal of Communication.

C. J. Angelopoulos, 'European Intermediary Liability in Copyright: A Tort-based Analysis' (2016) FdR: Instituut voor Informatierecht (IViR) <http://hdl.handle.net/11245/1.527223>.

J. Annas, *The Morality of Happiness* (Oxford University Press 1995).

J. Annas, *Intelligent Virtue* (Oxford University Press 2011).

T. Aquinas, *Summa Theologica* (First Published 1485, Benziger Bros 1948).

Y. Arai-Takahashi, *The Margin of Appreciation Doctrine and the Principle of Proportionality in the Jurisprudence of the ECHR* (Intersentia 2002).

H. Arendt, *The Human Condition* (University of Chicago Press 1958).

P. Ariès & G. Duby, *A History of Private Life* (Harvard University Press 1987).

Aristotle, *Nichomachean Ethics* (Clarendon Press 1925, Translation W.D. Ross)

E. Ascombe, 'Modern Moral Philosophy' (1958) 33 Philosophy.

A. Ashworth, L. Zedner & P. Tomlin, *Prevention and the Limits of the Criminal Law* (Oxford University Press 2013).

J. Austin, 'The Providence of Jurisprudence Determined. Being the first part of a series of lectures on jurisprudence, or, the philosophy of positive law. Lecture I'. <www.heinonline.org/HOL/Page?handle=hein.beal/profjdete0001&id=1>.

C. Bailliet, *Non-State Actors, Soft Law, and Protective Regimes: From the Margins* (Cambridge University Press 2012).

E. Barendt, *Freedom of Speech* (Oxford University Press 2007).

C. A. Bates, 'Law and the Rule of Law and Its Place Relative to Politeia in Aristotle's Politics'. In: L. Huppers-Cluysenaer & N.M.M.S. Coelho (eds), *Aristotle and the Philosophy of Law: Theory, Practice and Justice* (Springer 2013).

U. Beck, *Risk Society: Towards a New Modernity* (Sage 1992).

S. I. Benn, 'Privacy, Freedom, and Respect for Persons', in: F. Schoeman (ed.), *Philosophical Dimensions of Privacy: An Anthology* (Cambridge University Press 1984).

S. C. Bennett, 'The "Right to be Forgotten": Reconciling EU and US Perspectives' (2012) 30 Berkeley Journal of International Law.

J. Bentham, *Panopticon; or The Inspection-House* (1791).

P. Biasetti, 'Rights, Duties, and Moral Conflicts' (2014) 16(2) Ethics & Politics.

J. Biggs, *The Guilty Mind: Psychiatry and the Law of Homicide* (Harcourt Brace 1955).

J. Bikker, 'Disaster Victim Identification in the Information Age: The Use of Personal Data, Post-Mortem Privacy and the Rights of the Victim's Relatives' (2013) 10(1) *SCRIPTed*.

E. J. Bloustein, 'Privacy as an Aspect of Human Dignity: An Answer to Dean Prosser', 39 New York University Law Review 962.

E. J. Bloustein, *Individual & Group privacy* (Transaction Publishers 2004).

L. J. M. Boer, '"Echoes of Times Past": On the Paradoxical Nature of Article 2(4)' (2014) Journal of Conflict and Security Law.

U. Bojars, A. Passant, J.G. Breslin & S. Decker, 'Social network and data portability using semantic web technologies', < http://ceur-ws.org/Vol-333/saw1.pdf>.

D. Bollier, 'The Promise and Peril of Big Data' (2010) <www.emc.com/collateral/analyst-reports/10334-ar-promise-peril-of-big-data.pdf>.

D. Boyd & K. Crawford, 'Six Provocations for Big Data' (2011) <http://papers.ssrn.com/sol3/papers.cfm?abstract_id=1926431>.

D. Boyd & K. Crawford, 'Critical questions for big data: Provocations for a cultural, technological, and scholarly phenomenon' (2012) 5 Information, Communication & Society.

V. Bradley Lewis, 'Politeia kai Nomoi: On the Coherence of Plato's Political Philosophy' (1998) 31(2) Polity.

R. van Brakel, 'Pre-emptive Big Data Surveillance and its (Dis)Empowering Consequences: the Case of Predictive Policing', in: B. van der Sloot, D. Broeders & E. Schrijvers (eds.), *Exploring the Boundaries of Big Data* (Amsterdam University Press 2016).

M. Brinton Lykes, 'Human rights violations as structural violence', in: D. J. Christie, R. V. Wagner & D. A. Winter (eds), 'Peace, Conflict, and Violence: Peace Psychology for the 21st Century' (Prentice-Hall 2001).

D. Broeders, The New Digital Borders of Europe EU Databases and the Surveillance of Irregular Migrants' (2007) 22(1) International Sociology.

J. Brunnée & S. J. Toope, *Legitimacy and legality in international law: an interactional account* (Cambridge University Press 2010).

W. van der Burg, 'The Morality of Aspiration', in: W. J. Witteveen & W. Van der Burg (eds.), *Rediscovering Fuller. Essays on Implicit law and Institutional Design* (Amsterdam University Press 1999).

H. Burkert, *Freedom of Information and Data Protection* (Gesellschaft für Mathematik und Datenverarbeitung 1983).

L. Busch, 'A Dozen Ways to Get Lost in Translation: Inherent Challenges in Large Scale Data Sets' (2014) 8 International Journal of Communication.

L. A. Bygrave, 'Automated Profiling: Minding the machine: Article 15 of the EC Data Protection Directive and Automated Profiling' (2001) 17(1) Computer Law & Security Review.

T. Calders & S. Verwer, 'Three Naive Bayes Approaches for Discrimination-Free Classification' (2010) 21(2) Data Mining and Knowledge Discovery.

B. Cali, 'Balancing Human Rights? Methodological Problems with Weights, Scales and Proportions' (2007) 29(1) Human Rights Quarterly.

T. Campbell, *Beyond Smart cities: How Cities Network, Learn and Innovate* (Earthscan 2012).

P. Cane (ed.), *The Hart-Fuller Debate in the Twenty-First Century* (Hart 2010).

R. Card, A. R. N. Cross & P. A. Jones, *Criminal Law* (Oxford University Press 2006).

S. Carrera, 'The EU Border Management Strategy: FRONTEX and the Challenges of Irregular Immigration in the Canary Islands' (2007) CEPS Working Documents, SSRN.

J. Casey, *Pagan Virtue: An Essay in Ethics* (Clarendon Press 1990).

J. Castellino, *Global Minority Rights* (Burlington 2011).

S. Chesterman, *One Nation Under Surveillance: A New Social Contract To Defend Freedom Without Sacrificing Liberty* (Oxford University Press 2011).

R. P. Claude & Burns H. Weston, *Human Rights in the World Community: Issues And Action* (University of Pennsylvania Press 2006).

J. E. Cohen, *Configuring the Networked Self: Law, Code, and the Play of Everyday Practice* (Yale University Press 2012).

J. L. Cohen, *Regulating Intimacy: A New Legal Paradigm* (Princeton University Press 2002).

S. Cohen, 'Nudging and Informed Consent' (2013) 13(6) The American Journal of Bioethics.

J. L. Coleman, 'Negative and Positive Positivism' (1982) 11(1) The Journal of Legal Studies.

Committee on Homosexual Offences and Prostitution, 'Report of the Committee on Homosexual Offences and Prostitution. London: Her Majesty's Stationery Office', 1957.

T. M. Cooley, *A Treatise on the Law of Torts* (Callaghan 1888).

A. Corbin, 'Rights and Duties', Faculty Scholarship Series. Paper 2932, 1924.

N. Cox, 'Delfi AS v Estonia: The Liability of Secondary Internet Publishers for Violation of Reputational Rights under the European Convention on Human Rights' (2014) 77(4) The Modern Law Review.

T. Craig & M. E. Ludloff, *Privacy and Big Data: The Players, Regulators, and Stakeholders* (O'Reilly Media 2011).

K. Crawford & J. Schultz, *Big Data and Due Process: Toward a Framework to Redress Predictive Privacy Harms* (2014) 55 Boston College Law Review.

R. Crisp & M. Slote (eds.), *Virtue Ethics* (Oxford University Press 2007).

R. Cryer, H. Friman, D. Robinson & E. Wilmshurst, *An Introduction to International Criminal Law and Procedure* (Cambridge University Press 2014).

E. Curran, 'Hobbes's Theory of Rights – A Modern Interest Theory' (2002) 6(1) The Journal of Ethics.

H. J. Curzer, 'Aristotle's Much Maligned Megalopsychos' (1911) 69(2) Australasian Journal of Philosophy.

B. H. M. Custers, *The Power of Knowledge; Ethical, Legal, and Technological Aspects of Data Mining and Group Profiling in Epidemiology* (Wolf Legal Publishers 2004).

B. H. M. Custers and others (eds.), *Discrimination and Privacy in the Information Society. Data Mining and Profiling in Large Databases* (Springer 2012).

U. Dammann, O. Mallmann & S. Simitis (eds), *Data Protection Legislation: An International Documentation: Engl.-German: eine internationale Dokumentation = Die Gesetzgebung zum Datenschutz'* (Metzner 1977).

S. Darwall, *Virtue Ethics* (Blackwell Publishers 2003).

K. Davis & D. Patterson, *Ethics of Big Data: Balancing Risk and Innovation* (O' Reilly Media 2012). <www.commit-nl.nl/sites/default/files/Ethics%20of%20Big%20Data_0.pdf>.

J. W. DeCew, *In Pursuit of Privacy: Law, Ethics, and the Rise of Technology* (Cornell University Press 1997).

M. Depaul & L. Zagzebski, *Intellectual Virtue: Perspectives from Ethics and Epistemology* (Clarendon Press 2003).

R. Desgagne, 'Integrating Environmental Values into the European Convention on Human Rights' (1995) 89(2) *American Journal of International Law*.

P. Devlin, *The Enforcement of Morals* (Liberty Fund Indianapolis 2009).

N. Diakopoulos, 'Algorithmic Accountability Reporting: On the Investigation of Black Boxes', (*Tow Center for Digital Journalism*, December 2013) <http://towcenter.org/wp-content/uploads/2014/02/78524_Tow-Center-Report-web-1.pdf>.

P. van Dijk, F. van Hoof, A. van Rijk & L. Zwaak (eds.), *Theory and Practice of the European Convention on Human Rights* (Intersentia 2006).

C. Docksey, 'The European Court of Justice and the Decade of Surveillance', in: H. Hijmans & H. Kranenborg (eds.), *Data Protection anno 2014: How to Restore Trust? Contributions in honour of Peter Hustinx, European Data Protection Supervisor (2004–2014)* (International Specialized Book Services 2014).

J. Donnelly, 'How are rights and duties correlative?' (1982) 16(4) Journal of Value Inquiry.

M. Dreyfus & A. Patt, 'The European Commission White Paper on Adaptation: Appraising its Strategic Success as an Instrument of Soft Law' (2012) 17 Mitigation and Adaptation Strategies for Global Change.

K. Driscoll & S. Walker, 'Working Within a Black Box: Transparency in the Collection and Production of Big Twitter Data' (2014) 8 International Journal of Communication.

P.-L. Dusseault, 'Privacy and social media in the Age of Big Data: Report of the Standing Committee on Access to Information, Privacy and Ethics', <www.parl.gc.ca/content/hoc/Committee/411/ETHI/Reports/RP6094136/ethirp05/ethirp05-e.pdf>.

R. Dworkin, 'Rights as Trumps', in: Waldron, J. (ed.), *Theories of Rights* (Oxford University Press 1984).

D. Dyzenhaus, 'The Grudge Informer Case Revisited' (2007) 83 New York University Law *Review* 1000.

D. Dyzenhaus, 'The Morality of Legality', <www.law.berkeley.edu/files/The_Morality_of_Legality_DDyzenhaus.pdf>.

E. J. Eberle, 'Human Dignity, Privacy, and Personality in German and American Constitutional Law' (1997) *Utah Law Review* 963.

L. Edwards, 'Post Mortem Privacy' (2013) 10(1) SCRIPTed.

A. Eide & T. Swinehart, *The Universal Declaration of Human Rights: A Commentary* (Scandinavian University Press 1992).

N. A. N. M. van Eijk et al., 'Moving Towards Balance: A Study Into Duties of Care on the Internet', <www.ivir.nl/publicaties/download/679>.

W. N. Eskridge, 'Relationship between Obligations and Rights of Citizens' (2001) 69 *Fordham Law Review* 1721.

A. Etzioni, *The Limits of Privacy* (Basic Books 1999).

A. Etzioni & J. H. Marsh (eds.), *Rights vs. Public Safety after 9/11: America in the Age of Terrorism* (Lanham, Rowman & Littlefield Publishers 2003).

E. Etzioni-Halevy, 'Fragile Democracy: The Use and Abuse of Power in Western Societies', (Transaction 1989).

C. Evans, *Freedom of Religion under the European Convention on Human Rights* (Oxford University Press 2001).

J. Fairfield & C. Engel, 'Privacy as public good', <http://papers.ssrn.com/sol3/papers.cfm?abstract_id=2418445>.

F. Falcón y Tella, *Challenges for Human Rights* (Martinus Nijhoff Publishers 2007).

J. Feinberg, 'Duties, Rights, and Claims' (1966) 3(2) American Philosophical Quarterly.

- 'The nature and value of rights' (1970) Journal of Value Inquiry.
- 'Review'(1973) 70(9) The Journal of Philosophy.
- 'The Rights of Animals and Future Generations', in W. Blackstone (ed.), *Philosophy and Environmental Crisis* (University of Georgia Press 1974).
- *Harm to Others* (Oxford University Press 1984).
- *Offense to Others* (Oxford University Press 1985).
- *Harm to Self* (Oxford University Press 1986).
- *Harmless Wrongdoing* (Oxford University Press 1988).

E. W. Felten, 'Written Testimony of Edward W. Felten', 2013. <www.cs.princeton.edu/~felten/testimony-2013-10-02.pdf>.

L. Floridi, 'Big Data and their Epistemological Challenge' (2012) 25(4) Philosophy and Technology.

P. Foot, *Natural goodness* (Clarendon Press 2001).

P. Foot, *Virtues and Vices and Other Essays in Moral Philosophy* (Clarendon Press 2009).

M. Foucault, *Discipline and Punish: The Birth of the Prison* (Vintage Books 1995).

L. Foxhall & A. D. E. Lewis, *Greek law in its Political Setting: Justifications not Justice* (Oxford University Press 1996).

C. S. Frederiksen and others, *Corporate Social Responsibility and Governance Theory and Practice* (Springer 2015).

L. Friedman, 'In Defense of Corporate Criminal Liability' (2003) 23 Harvard Journal of Law & Public Policy 2000.

L. L. Fuller, 'Source Consideration and Form' (1941) 41(5) Columbia Law Review.

- 'American Legal Philosophy at Mid-Century: A Review of Edwin W. Patterson's Jurisprudence, Men and Ideas of the Law' (1954) 6 Journal of Legal Education 457.
- 'Freedom: A Suggested Analysis' (1955) 68(8) Harvard Law Review.
- 'The Philosophy of Codes of Ethics' (1955) 74(5) Electrical Engineering.
- 'Human Purpose and Natural Law' (1956) 53(22) The Journal of Philosophy.
- 'Positivism and Fidelity to Law: A Reply to Professor Hart' (1957) 71 Harvard Law Review 630.
- 'Government Secrecy and the Forms of Social Order', in: C. J. Friedrich (ed.), *Community* (The Liberal Arts Press 1959).
- 'Irrigation and Tyranny' (1965) 17(6) Stanford Law Review.
- 'Freedom as a Problem of Allocating Choice' (1968) 112(2) Proceedings of the American Philosophical Society.
- *The Morality of Law* (Yale University Press 1969).
- 'Human Interaction and the Law' (1969) 14(1) American Journal of Jurisprudence.

- *Anatomy of the Law* (Penguin Books 1971).
- 'Law as an Instrument of Social Control and Law as a Facilitation of Human Interaction' (1975) 89 Brigham Young University Law Review.
- 'Some Presuppositions Shaping the Concept of "Socialization"', in: J. L. Tapp & F. J. Levinne, *Law, Justice and the Individual in Society: Psychological and Legal issues* (Holt, Rinehart and Winston 1977).
- *The Principles of Social Order* (Duke University Press 1981).

A. Galetta & P. De Hert, 'Complementing the Surveillance Law Principles of the ECtHR with its Environmental Law Principles: An Integrated Technology Approach to a Human Rights Framework for Surveillance' (2014) 10(1) Utrecht Law Review.

D. García San José, *Environmental Protection and the European Convention on Human Rights* (Council of Europe Publishing 2005).

M. Gardiner (ed.), *Virtue Ethics Old and New* (Cornell University Press 2005).

S. Garfinkel, *Database Nation: The Death of Privacy in the 21st Century* (O'Reilly Media 2000).

R. Gavison, 'Privacy and the Limits of Law' (1980) 89 Yale Law Journal 455.

P. T. Geach, *The Virtues* (Cambridge University Press 1977).

S. Van der Geest, 'Toilets, Privacy and Perceptions of Dirt in Kwahu Tafo', in: S. Van der Geest and N. Obirih-Opareh (eds), *Toilets and Sanitation in Ghana: An Urgent Matter* (Accra Institute of Scientific and Technological Information 2001).

S. Van der Geest, 'The Toilet: Dignity, Privacy and Care of Elderly People in Kwahu, Ghana', in: S. Makoni & K. Stroeken (eds), *Ageing in Africa: Sociolinguistic and Anthropological Approaches* (Ashgate 2002).

J. Gerards, 'The Prism of Fundamental Rights' (2012) 8(2) European Constitutional Law Review.

F. Gilbert, 'EU Data Protection Overhaul: New Draft Regulation' (2012) 29(3) The Computer & Internet Lawyer.

J. Goldstein, A. M. Dershowitz & R. D. Schwartz, *Criminal Law: Theory and Process* (Collier Macmillan 1974).

N. Gotzmann, 'Legal Personality of the Corporation and International Criminal Law: Globalisation, Corporate Human Rights Abuses and the Rome Statute' (2008) 1(1) Queensland Law Student Review. <www.law.uq.edu.au/articles/qlsr/Gotzmann-QLSR.pdf>.

D. Gray & D. Citron, 'The Right to Quantitative Privacy' (2013) 101 Minnesota Law Review.

L. Green, 'Positivism and the Inseparability of Law and Morals' (2008) 83 New York University Law Review 1000.

S. Greer, *The Exceptions to Articles 8 to 11 of the European Convention on Human Rights* (Council of Europe 1997).

G. K. Greschbach, G. Kreitz & S. Buchegger, 'The Devil is in the Metadata – New Privacy Challenges in Decentralised Online Social Networks',<www.csc.kth.se/~bgre/pub/GreschbachKB12_MetadataPrivacyDecentralisedOnlineSocialNetworks.pdf>

H. Gross, *A Theory of Criminal Justice* (Oxford University Press 1979).

S. Guex, 'The Origins of the Swiss Banking Secrecy Law and Its Repercussions for Swiss Federal Policy' (2000) 74 Business History Review.

E. Guldix, *Personality Rights, Privacy and Private life in Relation to Each Other* (V.U. Brussel 1986). [E. Guldix, 'De Persoonlijkheidsrechten, de Persoonlijke Levenssfeer en het Privéleven in hun Onderling Verband' (V.U. Brussel 1986).]

L. J. Gurak, *Persuasion and Privacy in Cyberspace: Online Protests Over Lotus MarketPlace and the Clipper Chip* (Yale University Press 1999).

K. Guzik, 'Discrimination by Design: Data Mining in the United States' "War on Terrorism"' (2009) 7 Surveillance & Society.

J. Habermas, 'Über den internen Zusammenhang zwischen Rechtsstaat und Demokratie', in: Preuß, Ulrich K. (Hrsg.), *Zum Begriff der Verfassung. Die Ordnung des Politischen* (Fischer 1994).

J. Habermas, 'On the Internal Relation between the Rule of Law and Democracy' (1995) 3 European Journal of Philosophy.

R. Halwani, *Virtuous Liaisons: Care, Love, Sex, and Virtue Ethics* (Open Court 2003).

D. Hand, H. Mannila & P. Smyth, *Principles of Data Mining* (The MIT Press 2001).

E. Harbinja, 'Does the EU Data Protection Regime Protect Post-Mortem Privacy and What ould be the Potential Alternatives?' (2013) 10[1] *SCRIPTed*.

H. L.A. Hart, 'Are There any Natural Rights?', Philosophical Review, 64, 1955.

– 'Positivism and the Separation of Law and Morals' (1958) 71(4) *Harvard Law Review*.

– *Law, Liberty and Morality* (Stanford University Press 1963).

N. Helberger, 'Diversity by Design' (2011) 1 Journal of Information Policy 443.

E. Herlin-Karnell, 'EU Competence in Criminal Law after Lisbon', in: A. Biondi, P. Eeckhout & S. Ripley (eds.), *EU Law after Lisbon* (Oxford University Press 2012).

P. de Hert, 'Human Rights and Data Protection. European Case-Law 1995–1997', [Mensenrechten en bescherming van persoonsgegevens. Overzicht en synthese van de Europese rechtspraak 1955–1997), Jaarboek ICM 1997 (Maklu 1998).

P. De Hert & V. Papakonstantinou, 'The Proposed Data Protection Regulation Replacing Directive 95/46/EC: A Sound System for the Protection of Individuals' (2012) 28 Computer Law & Security Review.

H. Hijmans, 'The European Union as Guardian of Internet Privacy: The Story of Art 16 TFEU', Dordrecht, Springer International Publishing, 2016.

M. Hildebrandt & S. Gutwirth (eds), *Profiling the European Citizen Cross-Disciplinary Perspectives* (Springer 2008).

M. Hildebrandt, 'Who is Profiling Who? Invisible Visibility', in: S. Gutwirth, Y. Poullet, P. de Hert, C. de Terwagne & S. Nouwt (eds), *Reinventing Data Protection?* (Springer 2009).

– 'The Dawn of a Critical Transparency Right for the Profiling Era' (2012) Digital Enlightenment Yearbook.

– *Smart Technologies and the End(s) of Law. Novel Entanglements of Law and Technology* (Edward Elgar 2015).

M. F. H. Hirsch Ballin, *Anticipative Criminal Investigation: Theory and Counterterrorism Practice in the Netherlands and the United States* (T.M.C. Asser Press 2012).

T. Hobbes, *Leviathan* (First published 1651, Cambridge University Press 1996).

J. V. J. van Hoboken & N. Helberger, 'Little Brother Is Tagging You – Legal and Policy Implications of Amateur Data Controllers' (2010) 11(4) Computer Law International.

W. N. Hohfeld, *Fundamental Legal Conceptions* (Yale University Press 1966).

F. W. Hondius, *Emerging Data Protection in Europe* (1975).

C. J. Hoofnagle, 'How the Fair Credit Reporting Act Regulates Big Data'(*SSRN.com* 10 September 2013) <http://papers.ssrn.com/sol3/papers.cfm?abstract_id=2432955>.

G. Hornung, 'A General Data Protection Regulation for Europe? Light and Shade in the Commission's Draft of 25 January 2012' (2012) 74(1) SCRIPTed.

W. von Humboldt, *The Limits of State Action* (Cambridge University Press 1969).

D. Hume, *A Treatise on Human Nature: Being an Attempt to Introduce the Experimental Method of Reasoning into Moral Subjects, and Dialogues Concerning Natural Religion* (Longmans Green 1878).

– *An Enquiry Concerning the Principles of Morals* (First Published 1751, Clarendon Press 2010).

– *A Treatise of Human Nature* (First published 1738, San Bernardino 2014).

S. Humphreys, 'Law, custom and culture in Herodotus', <http://kainani.hpu.edu/sschwartz/HIST4911_Lectures/Humphreys1987.pdf>.

T. Hurka, *Virtue, Vice, and Value* (Oxford University Press 2001).

R. Hursthouse, *On Virtue Ethics* (Oxford University Press 1999).

R. Hursthouse, 'Virtue Ethics', in: E. N. Zalta (ed.), *The Stanford Encyclopedia of Philosophy* (Stanford University Press 2013).

F. Hutcheson, *An Inquiry into the Original of Our Ideas of Beauty and Virtue* (Robert & Andrew Foulis 1772).

J. C. Inness, *Privacy, Intimacy and Isolation* (Oxford University Press 1992).

J. P. A. Ioannidis, 'Why most published research findings are false' (2005) 2(8) PLoS Medicine <http://journals.plos.org/plosmedicine/article?id=10.1371/journal.pmed.0020124>.

M. G. Johnson & J. Symonides, *The Universal Declaration of Human Rights: A History of its Creation and Implementation, 1948–1998* (Unesco 1998).

I. Kant, *The Metaphysics of Morals* (First published 1785, Cambridge University Press 1996).

E. Kasket, 'Access to the Digital Self in Life and Death: Privacy in the Context of Posthumously Persistent Facebook Profiles' (2013) 10(1) SCRIPTed.

H. W. K. Kaspersen, 'Data Protection and E-Commerce', in A. R. Lodder and H. W. K. Kaspersen, *eDirectives: Guide to European Union Law on E-Commerce* (Kluwer Law International 2002).

L. Katz, *Bad Acts and Guilty Minds: Conundrums of the Criminal Law* (University of Chicago Press 1987).

I. Kerr & J. Earle, 'Prediction, Preemption, Presumption. How Big Data Threatens Big Picture Privacy' (2013) 66 Stanford Law Review Online.

R. Kitchin, *The Data Revolution: Big Data, Data Infrastructures & their Consequences* (Sage 2014).

R. Kitchin, 'Thinking Critically about and Researching Algorithms', The Programmable City Working Paper 5, 2014 <http://dx.doi.org/10.2139/ssrn.2515786>.

M. Klatt, 'Positive Obligations under the European Convention on Human Rights' (2011) 71 Zeitschrift für ausländisches öffentliches Recht und Völkerrecht.

J. Kokott & C. Sobotta, 'The Distinction between privacy and data protection in the jurisprudence of the CJEU and the ECtHR', in: H. Hijmans & H. Kranenborg (eds.), *Data Protection anno 2014: How to Restore Trust? Contributions in honour of Peter Hustinx, European Data Protection Supervisor (2004–2014)* (Intersentia, 2014).

M. R. Koot, *Measuring and Predicting Anonymity* (Universiteit van Amsterdam 2012).

S. C. J. J. Kortmann & B. C. J. Hamel, *Wrongful Birth en Wrongful Life* (Kluwer 2004).

P. Kuhn, 'Sex Discrimination in Labor Markets: The Role of Statistical Evidence' (1987) 77 The American Economic Review.

C. Kuner, *European Data Protection Law: Corporate Compliance and Regulation* (Oxford University Press 2007).

C. Kuner, 'The European Commission's Proposed Data Protection Regulation: A Copernican Revolution in European Data Protection Law' (2012) Privacy & Security Law Report, 2012.

M. Kuneva, 'European Consumer Commissioner, Keynote Speech' (Roundtable on Online Data Collection, Targeting and Profiling, Brussels, 31 March 2009).

M. LaCour-Little, 'Discrimination in Mortgage Lending: A Critical Review of the Literature' (1999) 7 Journal of Real Estate Literature.

J. Vande Lanotte & Y. Haeck, *Handboek EVRM. Dl.2 Artikelsgewijze commentaar*, Vol. 1, Antwerpen (Intersentia 2004).

J. Vande Lanotte & Y. Haeck, *Handboek EVRM. Dl.2 Artikelsgewijze commentaar*, Vol. 2 (Intersentia 2004).

R. Laperrière, 'Crossing the Borders of Privacy: Transborder Flows of Personal Data from Canada' (Canada Department of Justice Canada 1991).

LAPSI Policy Recommendation Nr. 4: Privacy and Personal Data Protection <https://ec.europa.eu/digital-agenda/en/news/lapsi-policy-recommendation-4-privacy-and-personal-data-protection>.

T. Laqueur, *Making Sex: Body and Gender from the Greeks to Freud* (Harvard University Press 1992).

D. T. Larose, *Data Mining Methods and Models* (John Wiley & Sons 2006).

L. Lazarus and others, 'The Relationship Between Rights and Responsibilities', University of Oxford, Ministry of Justice Research Series 18/09, December 2009. <https://www.matrixlaw.co.uk/uploads/other/21_08_2013_04_20_27_The%20relationship%20between%20rights%20and%20responsibities%20Ministry%20of%20Justice%20Research%20Series%20December%202009.pdf>.

D. Lazer and others, *Big Data. The Parable of Google Flu: Traps in Big Data Analysis* (Science 2014).

S. Léonard, 'EU Border Security and Migration into the European Union: FRONTEX and Securitisation through Practices' (2010) 19(2) European Security.

L. Lessig, *Code and Other Laws of Cyberspace* (Basic Books 1999).

A. Lever, 'Privacy and Democracy: What the Secret Ballot Reveals' (2015) 11(2) Law, Culture and Humanities.

J. Locke, *Two treatises of Government* (First published 1689, Cambridge University Press, 1988).

W. J. Long & M. P. Quek, 'Personal Data Privacy Protection in an Age of Globalization: The US-EU Safe Harbor Compromise' (2002) 9(3) Journal of European Public Policy.

J. P. Loof, 'Mensenrechten en Staatsveiligheid: Verenigbare Grootheden? Opschorting en Beperking van Mensenrechtenbescherming Tijdens Noodtoestanden en andere Situaties die de Staatsveiligheid Bedreigen (Wolf Legal Publishers 2005).

D. Lyons, 'Surveillance, Snowden, and Big Data: Capacities, Consequences, Critique' (2014) 1(13) Big Data & Society.

D. Lyons, 'The Correlativity of Rights and Duties' (1970) 4(1) Noûs.

D. Luban, 'The Rule of Law and Human Dignity: Reexamining Fuller's Canons' (2010) 2(29) Hague Journal of the Rule of Law.

T. Lukoianova & V. Rubin, 'Veracity Roadmap: Is Big Data Objective, Truthful and Credible?' (2014) 24(1) Advances in Classification Research Online.

T. R. Machan, *Human Rights and Human Liberties* (Nelson-Hall 1975).

A. MacIntyre, *After Virtue: A Study in Moral Theory* (Duckworth 1981).

A. MacIntyre, *Dependent Rational Animals: Why Human Beings Need the Virtues* (Open Court 1999).

S. Madden, 'From Databases to Big Data' (2012) 16(3) IEEE Internet Computing.

J. Malkan, 'Stolen Photographs: Personality, Publicity, and Privacy' (1975) 75 Texas Law Review 779.

A. Marthews & C. Tucker, 'Government Surveillance and Internet Search Behavior', <http://papers.ssrn.com/sol3/papers.cfm?abstract_id=2412564>.

L. May & Z. Hoskins, *International Criminal Law and Philosophy* (Cambridge University Press 2014).

V. Mayer-Schönberger & K. Cukier, 'Big Data: A Revolution that Will Transform How We Live, Work, and Think', Houghton Mifflin Harcourt, Boston, 2013.

A. McAfee & E. Brynjolfsson, 'Big Data: The Management Revolution' (2012) Harvard Business Review.

D. McCallig, 'Private But Eventually Public: Why Copyright in Unpublished Works Matters in the Digital Age' (2013) 10(1) SCRIPTed.

T. E. McGonagle, *Minority Rights, Freedom of Expression and of the Media: Dynamics and Dilemmas* (Intersentia 2011).

A. McHarg, 'Reconciling Human Rights and the Public Interest: Conceptual Problems and Doctrinal Uncertainty in the Jurisprudence of the European Court of Human Rights' (1999) 62(5) The Modern Law Review.

C. Mellors, 'Governments and the Individual – Their Secrecy and his Privacy', in: J. B. Yound (ed.), *Privacy* (John Wiley & Sons 1978).

T. Mertens, 'Radbruch and Hart on the Grudge Informer: A Reconsideration' (2002) 15 Ratio Juris 186.

H. K. Michael, 'The Role of Natural Law in Early American Constitutionalism: Did the Founders Contemplate Judicial Enforcement of 'Unwritten' Individual Rights?' (1991) 69 North Carolina Law Review 421.

S. Miettinen, *Criminal Law and Policy in the European Union* (Routledge 2013).

J. S. Mill, *On Liberty* (First published 1859, Norton 1975).

B. Miltner, 'Revisiting Extraterritoriality after Al-Skeini: The ECHR and Its Lessons' (2012) 33 Michigan Journal of International Law 693.

E. M. L. Moerel, *Binding Corporate Rules Corporate Self-Regulation of Global Data Transfers* (Oxford University Press 2012).

E. M. L. Moerel, 'How to Make the Draft EU Regulation on Data Protection Future Proof', 2014 <www.debrauw.com/wp-content/uploads/NEWS%20-%20PUBLICATIONS/Moerel_oratie.pdf>.

A. R. Mowbray, *The Development of Positive Obligations under the European Convention on Human Rights by the European Court of Human Rights* (Portland 2004).

T. Murphy & G. O'Cuinn, 'Work in progress. New technologies and the European Court of Human Rights' (2010) 10(4) Human Rights Law Review.

A. W. Neal, 'Securitization and Risk at the EU border: The Origins of FRONTEX' (2009) 47(2) Journal of Common Market studies.

R. Nehmelman, *The General Personality Right: A Comparative Study on the General Personality Right in Germany and the Netherlands* (Tjeenk Willink 2002). [R. Nehmelman, *Het Algemeen Persoonlijkheidsrecht: Een Rechtsvergelijkende Studie naar het Algemeen Persoonlijkheidsrecht in Duitsland en Nederland* (Tjeenk Willink 2002).]

B. C. Newell, 'The Massive Metadata Machine: Liberty, Power, and Secret Mass Surveillance in the U.S. and Europe' (2014) 10(2) /S: A Journal of Law and Policy.

B. C. Newell, 'Technopolicing, Surveillance, and Citizen Oversight: A Neorepublican Theory of Liberty and Information Control' (2014) 31 Government Information Quarterly 421.

A. Newman & D. Bach, 'Soft Law and the Diffusion of Global Financial Regulation' (2014) Journal of European Public Policy.

B. Niblett, *Data Protection Act 1984* (Oyez Longman 1984).

A. J. Nieuwenhuis, *Between Privacy and Personality Rights: A Constitutional and Comparative Study* (Ars Aequi Libri 2001). [A. J. Nieuwenhuis, *Tussen Privacy en Persoonlijkheidsrecht: Een Grondrechtelijk en Rechtsvergelijkend Onderzoek* (Ars Aequi Libri 2001).]

– *Regarding the Limits of the Freedom of Speech: Theory, Comparative Analysis, Discrimination, Pornography* (Ars Aequi Libri 2011). [A.J. Nieuwenhuis, 'Over de Grens van de Vrijheid van Meningsuiting: Theorie, Rechtsvergelijking, Discriminatie, Pornografie' (Ars Aequi Libri 2011).]

– 'The ECHR and the Development of Positive Obligations'. [A. Nieuwenhuis, 'Het EHRM en de Ontwikkeling van de Positieve Verplichtingen'.] In: A. Nieuwenhuis, J.-H. Reestman & C. Zoethout (red.), *Rechterlijk activisme: opstellen aangeboden aan prof. mr. J.A. Peters* (Ars Aequi Libri 2011).

– *Over de grens van de Vrijheid van Meningsuiting: Theorie, Rechtsvergelijking, Discriminatie, Pornografie* (Ars Aequi Libri 2015).

M. B. Nimmer, *Nimmer on Freedom of Speech: A Treatise on the Theory of the First Amendment* (Matthew Bender 1984).

H. Nissenbaum, *Privacy in Context: Technology, Policy, and the Integrity of Social Life* (Stanford University Press 2010).

S. Nouwt, B. R. de Vries & P. Balboni, *Reasonable Expectations of Privacy? Eleven Country Reports on Camera Surveillance and Workplace Privacy* (T.M.C. Asser Press 2005).

M. C. Nussbaum, 'Human Functioning and Social Justice: In Defense of Aristotelian Essentialism' (1992) 20(2) Political Theory.

– *Frontiers of Justice: Disability, Nationality, Species Membership* (Harvard University Press 2007).

P. Ohm, 'Broken Promises of Privacy: Responding to the Surprising Failure of Anonymisation' (2010) 57 UCLA Law Review 1701.

C. Ovey & R. C. A. White, *European Convention on Human Rights* (Oxford University Press 2002).

T. Paine, *The Rights of Man: For the Benefit of All Mankind* (Webster 1797).

E. Pariser, *The Filter bubble: What the Internet is Hiding From You* (Viking 2011).

F. A. Pasquale & D. K. Citron, 'Promoting innovation while preventing discrimination: Policy goals for the Scored Society' (2014) 89 Washington Law Review 1413–24 <http://ssrn.com/abstract=2552864>.

F. Pasquale, *The Black Box Society: The Secret Algorithms that Control Money and Information* (Harvard University Press 2015).

T. M. Payton & T. Claypoole, *Privacy in the Age of Big Data: Recognizing Threats, Defending your Rights, and Protecting your Family* (Rowman & Littlefield 2014).

S. Peers, 'The Directive on data protection and law enforcement: A Missed Opportunity?', 2012 <www.statewatch.org/analyses/no-176-leas-data%20protection.pdf>.

R. A. Posner, 'Privacy, Secrecy, and Reputation', 28 Buffalo Law Review 1978.

– *The Economics of Justice* (Harvard University Press 1981).
R. Pound, 'Interests of Personality' (1915) 28(4) Harvard Law Review.
C. Puschmann & J. Burgess, 'Metaphors of Big Data' (2014) 8 International Journal of Communication.
N. Purtova, *Property Rights in Personal Data: A European Perspective* (Kluwer Law International 2011).
W. Quinn, *Morality and Action* (Cambridge University Press 1993).
G. Radbruch, 'Statutory Lawlessness and *Supra*-Statutory Law (1946)' (2006) 26(1) Oxford Journal of Legal Studies.
W. H. Rehnquist, 'Is an Expanded Right of Privacy Consistent with Fair and Effective Law Enforcement? Or: Privacy, You've Come a Long Way, Baby' (1975) 23(1) University of Kansas Law Review.
T. Regan & P. Singer (eds.), *Animal Rights and Human Obligations'* (Englewood Cliffs 1976).
P. M. Regan, *Legislating Privacy: Technology, Social Values, and Public Policy* (University of North Carolina Press 1995).
W. N. Renke, 'Who Controls the Past Now Controls the Future: Counter-Terrorism, Data Mining and Privacy' (2006) 43 The Alberta Law Review.
N. M. Richards, 'The Dangers of Surveillance' (2013) 5 Harvard Law Review <http://harvardlawreview.org/2013/05/the-dangers-of-surveillance/>.
– & J. H. King, 'Three Paradoxes of Big Data' (2013) 66 Stanford Law Review Online 44.
– J. H. King, 'Big Data Ethics' (2014) 49 Wake Forest Law Review.
M. Ridley, *The Origins of Virtue* (Viking 1996).
N. Robinson, 'The Universal Declaration of Human Rights: Its Origin, Significance, Application, and Interpretation' (World Jewish Congress 1958).
B. Roessler, *The Value of Privacy* (Polity Press 2005).
– & D. Mokrosinska, 'Privacy and Social Interaction' *Philosophy Social Criticism* (19 July 2013).
J. Rosen, *The Unwanted Gaze: The Destruction of Privacy in America* (Vintage 2000).
I. Rubenstein, 'Big Data: The End of Privacy or a New Beginning?' (2013) 3(2) International Data Privacy Law.
K. Rundle, *Forms Liberate: Reclaiming the Jurisprudence of Lon L Fuller* (Hart Publishing 2012).
D. C. Russell, *Practical Intelligence and the Virtues* (Clarendon Press 2011).
T. S. N. Sastry, 'Introduction to Human Rights and Duties', <www.unipune.ac.in/pdf_files/Final%20Book_03042012.pdf>.
A. Satija & F. B. Hu, 'Big Data and Systematic Reviews in Nutritional Epidemiology' (2014) 72(1) Nutrition Reviews.
F. Schauer, 'Fear, Risk and the First Amendment: Unraveling the Chilling Effect' (1978) 58 Boston University Law Review 685.
B. W. Schermer, 'The Limits of Privacy in Automated Profiling and Data Mining' (2011) 7 Computer Law & Security Review.
B. Schneier, *Data and Goliath: The Hidden Battles to Collect Your Data and Control Your World* (W. W. Norton & Company 2015)
C. B. Schutte, 'The European Fundamental Right of Property: Article 1 of Protocol No. 1 to the European Convention on Human Rights: Its Origins, its Working and its Impact on National Legal Orders' (Kluwer 2004).
P. M. Schwartz & K.-N. Peifer, 'Prosser's Privacy and the German Right of Personality: Are Four Privacy Torts Better than One Unitary Concept?' (2010) 98 California Law Review 1925.

J. C. Scott, *Seeing Like a State: How Certain Schemes to Improve the Human Condition Have Failed* (Yale University Press 1998).

M. Shapiro, *Smart Cities: Quality of Life, Productivity, and the Growth Effects of Human Capital* (National Bureau of Economic Research 2005).

S. J. Shapiro, *Legality* (Harvard University Press 2011).

S. Shute & A.P. Simester (eds.), *Criminal Law Theory: Doctrines of the General Part* (Oxford University Press 2002).

A-L. Sibony & A. Alemanno (eds.), *Nudging and the Law – What can EU Law learn from Behavioural Sciences?* (Hart Publishing 2014).

S. S. Silbey, 'The Availability of Law Redux: The Correlation of Rights and Duties' (2014) 48(2) Law & Society Review.

S. Simitis, 'Reviewing Privacy in an Information Society' (1987) 135(3) University of Pennsylvania Law Review.

R. Sizer & P. Newman, *The Data Protection Act: A Practical Guide* (Gower 1984).

D. Skillicorn, *Knowledge Discovery for Counterterrorism and Law Enforcement* (CRC Press 2009).

B. van der Sloot, 'Public Sector Information & Data Protection: A Plea for Personal Privacy Settings for the Re-use of PSI' (2011) 1(2) Informatica e Diritto.

– 'Walking a Thin Line: The Regulation of EPGs' (2012) 3(2) JIPITEC.

– 'From Data Minimization to Data Minimummization', in: B. Custers, T. Calders, B. Schermer & T. Zarsky (eds.), *Discrimination and Privacy in the Information Society. Data Mining and Profiling in Large Databases* (Springer 2012).

– 'Between Fact and Fiction: An Analysis of the Case Law on Article 12 ECHR' (2014) 26(4) Child and Family Law Quarterly.

– 'Privacy in the Post-NSA Era: Time for a Fundamental Revision?' (2014) 5(1) JIPITEC.

– 'Privacy as Human Flourishing: Could a Shift Towards Virtue Ethics Strengthen Privacy Protection in the Age of Big Data?' (2014) 5(3) JIPITEC.

– 'Is All Fair in Love and War? An Analysis of the Case Law on Article 15 ECHR' (2014) 53(1) Military Law and the Law of War Review.

– 'Do Data Protection Rules Protect the Individual and Should They? An Assessment of the Proposed General Data Protection Regulation' (2014) 4(4) International Data Privacy Law.

– 'Delfi/Estland' (2014) 4(1) European Human Rights Cases.

– 'Do Privacy and Data Protection Rules Apply to Legal Persons and Should They? A Proposal for a Two-Tiered System' (2015) 31(1) Computer Law & Security Review.

– 'How to Assess Privacy Violations in the Age of Big Data? Analysing the Three Different Tests Developed by the ECtHR and Adding for a Fourth One' (2015) 24(1) Information & Communications Technology Law.

– 'Privacy as Personality Right: Why the ECtHR's Focus on Ulterior Interests Might Prove Indispensable in the Age of Big Data' (2015) 31(80) Utrecht Journal of International and European Law.

– 'The Individual in the Big Data Era: Moving Towards an Agent-Based Privacy Paradigm', in: B. van der Sloot & D. Broeders & E. Schrijvers (eds.), *Exploring the Boundaries of Big Data* (Amsterdam University Press 2016).

– 'Privacy as virtue: searching for a new privacy paradigm in the age of Big Data', in: M. Henning (ed.), *Räume und Kulturen des Privaten* (Springer 2016, forthcoming).

- 'Do Groups Have a Right to Privacy and Should They?', in: L. Taylor, L. Floridi & B. van der Sloot (eds.), *Group Privacy: New Challenges of Data Technologies*, Springer, Dordrecht, 2017.
- 'Legal Fundamentalism: Is Data Protection Really a Fundamental Right?', in: S. Gutwirth, R. Leenes & P. De Hert (eds.), *Data Protection and Privacy: (In)visibilities and Infrastructure* (Springer 2017, forthcoming).
- , D. Broeders & E. Schrijvers (eds.), *Exploring the boundaries of Big Data* (Amsterdam University Press 2016).
- & S. van Schendel, 'International and Comparative Legal Study on Big Data', WRR-rapport, working paper 20, 2016, <www.wrr.nl/publicaties/publicatie/article/international-and-comparative-legal-study-on-big-data/ >.

M. Slote, *From Morality to Virtue* (Oxford University Press 1992).
- *Morals from Motives* (Oxford University Press 2001).
- *Moral Sentimentalism* (Oxford University Press 2010).
- *The Impossibility of Perfection: Aristotle, Feminism, and the Complexities of Ethics* (Oxford University Press 2011).

D. J. Solove, 'Conceptualizing Privacy' (2002) 90 California Law Review 1087.
- *The Digital Person: Technology and Privacy in the Information Age* (New York University Press 2004).
- 'A Taxonomy of Privacy' (2006) 154 University of Pennsylvania Law Review 478.
- *The Future of Reputation: Gossip, Rumor, and Privacy on the Internet* (Yale University Press 2007).
- *Understanding Privacy* (Harvard University Press 2008).
- *Nothing to Hide: The False Tradeoff between Privacy and Security* (Yale University Press 2011).

G. D. Squires, 'Racial Profiling, Insurance Style: Insurance Redlining and the Uneven Development of Metropolitan Areas' (2003) 25(4) Journal of Urban Affairs.

O. Stefan, *Soft Law in Court: Competition Law, State Aid and the Court of Justice of the European Union* (Kluwer Law International 2013).

D. D. Stevenson & N. J. Wagoner, 'Bargaining in the Shadow of Big Data' (2014) 66(5) Florida Law Review.

S. Strömholm, 'Right of Privacy and Rights of the Personality: A Comparative Survey' (Nordic Conference on Privacy organized by the International Commission of Jurists, Stockholm, 1967).

T. W. Stone, 'Margin of Appreciation Gone Awry: The European Court of Human Rights' Implicit Use of the Precautionary Principle in Fretté v. France to Backtrack on Protection from Discrimination on the Basis of Sexual Orientation' (2003) 3(1) Connecticut Public Interest Law Journal.

R. S. Summers, *Lon L. Fuller* (Edward Arnold 1984).

M. Susi, 'Delfi AS v. Estonia' (2014) 108(2) The American Journal of International Law.

L. Sweeney, 'k-anonymity: A Model for Protecting Privacy' (2002) 10(5) International Journal of Uncertainty, Fuzziness and Knowledge-Based Systems.

I. Szekely, 'The Right to Forget, the Right to Be Forgotten: Personal Reflections on the Fate of Personal Data in the Information Society', in S. Gutwirth and others (eds), *European Data Protection: In Good Health?* (Springer 2012).

L. Taylor, L. Floridi & B. van der Sloot (eds.), *Group Privacy: New Challenges of Data Technologies*, Springer, Dordrecht, 2017.

H. T. Tavani, 'Genomic Research and Data-Mining Technology: Implications for Personal Privacy and Informed Consent' (2004) 6 Ethics and Information Technology.

O. Tene & J. Polonetsky, 'Privacy in the Age of Big Data: A Time for Big Decisions' (2012) 64 Stanford Law Review.

– & J. Polonetsky, 'Big Data For All: Privacy and User Control in the Age of Analytics' (2013) 11(5) Northwestern Journal of Technology and Intellectual Property.

– & J. Polonetsky, 'Taming The Golem: Challenges of Ethical Algorithmic Decision Making', working paper < https://fpf.org/wp-content/uploads/2016/05/Golem_May153–1.docx>.

L. Tessman, *Burdened Virtues: Virtue Ethics for Liberatory Struggles* (Oxford University Press 2005).

R. Thaler & C. Sunstein, *Nudge: Improving Decisions about Health, Wealth, and Happiness* (Penguin Books 2009).

J. J. Thomson, 'The Right to Privacy' (1975) 4(4) Philosophy & Public Affairs.

S. Toh & R. Platt, 'Big data in Epidemiology: Too Big to Fail?' (2013) 24(6) Epidemiology.

D. Tokmetzis, 'Over Five Eyes en Third Parties: Met Wie Werkt de NSA Samen?' (*De Correspondent* 2013) <https://decorrespondent.nl/525/Over-Five-Eyes-en-Third-Parties-met-wie-werkt-de-NSA-samen-/25565925-b5edb16e>.

H. Tomlinson, 'Positive Obligations under the European Convention on Human Rights', <http://bit.ly/17U9TDa>.

S. Tsakyrakis, 'Proportionality: An Assault on Human Rights?' (2009) 7(3) International Journal Constitutional Law.

K. Vasak, 'Human Rights: A Thirty-Year Struggle: The Sustained Efforts to give Force of law to the Universal Declaration of Human Rights' (1977) 30(11) UNESCO Courier.

A. Verdoodt, *Naissance et Signification de la Déclaration Universelle des Droits de L'Homme* (Warny 1964).

L. F. M. Verhey, *Horizontal Effect of Fundamental Rights, in Particular the Right to Privacy* (Tjeenk Willink 1992). [L. F. M. Verhey, *Horizontale Werking van Grondrechten, in het Bijzonder van het Recht op Privacy* (Tjeenk Willink 1992).]

E. Vetere & D. Pedro (eds.), 'Victims of Crime and Abuse of Power: Festschrift in Honour of Irene Melup' (11th UN Congress on Crime Prevention and Criminal Justice, Bangkok, April 2005).

T. M. Vinod Kumar (ed.), *E-Governance for Smart Cities* (Singapore 2015).

D. Voorhoof, 'Delfi AS v. Estonia: Grand Chamber Confirms Liability of Online News Portal for Offensive Comments Posted by its Readers' (*Strasbourg Observers* 18 June 2015) <https://strasbourgobservers.com/2015/06/18/delfi-as-v-estonia-grand-chamber-confirms-liability-of-online-news-portal-for-offensive-comments-posted-by-its-readers/>.

D. van der Vyver & J. Witte (ed.), *Religious Human Rights in Global Perspective* (Nijhoff 1996).

R. Wacks, *Personal Information: Privacy and the Law* (Oxford University Press 1989).

J. Waldron, 'How Law Protects Dignity', <www.pem.cam.ac.uk/wp-content/uploads/2012/07/1A-Waldron-article.pdf>.

C. Warren & B. Laslett, 'Privacy and Secrecy: A Conceptual Comparison' (1977) 33(3) Journal of Social Issues.

S. D. Warren & L. D. Brandeis, 'The Right to Privacy' (1890) 4(5) Harvard Law Review.

G. L. Weil, *The European Convention on Human Rights: Background, Development and Prospects* (Sijthoff 1963).

S. Weiss, 'Privacy Threat Model for Data Portability in Social Network Applications' (2009) 29 International Journal of Information Management.

J. Welchman, *The Practice of Virtue: Classic and Contemporary Readings in Virtue Ethics* (Hackett 2006).

E. Werna, R. Keivani & D. F. Murphy, *Corporate Social Responsibility and Urban Development: Lessons from the South* (Palgrave Macmillan 2009).

A. F. Westin, *Privacy and Freedom* (The Bodley Head 1970).

A. F. Westin & M. A. Baker, *Databanks in a Free Society: Computers, Record-keeping and Privacy* (Quadrangle 1972).

C. Westphal, *Data Mining for Intelligence, Fraud & Criminal Detection* (CRC Press 2009).

L. Westra, *Environmental Justice and the Rights of Unborn and Future Generations: "Law, Environmental Harm and the Right to Health"* (Routledge 2008).

J. Q. Whitman, 'The Two Western Cultures of Privacy: Dignity Versus Liberty' (2004) 113 The Yale Law Journal.

T. M. Wilkinson, 'Nudging and Manipulation' (2013) 61 Political Studies.

T. H. A. Wisman, 'Purpose and Function Creep by Design: Transforming the Face of Surveillance through the Internet of Things' (2013) 3(2) European Journal of Law and Technology.

W. J. Witteveen & W. van der Burg, *Rediscovering Fuller: Essays on Implicit law and Institutional Design* (Amsterdam University Press 1999).

WODC, Veiligheid in cyberspace' (2013) Jv, 2012 1 <https://www.wodc.nl/images/jv1201-volledige-tekst_tcm44-412407.pdf>.

L. Woods, 'The Delfi AS vs Estonia judgement explained' (*LSE Media Policy Project Blog* 6 June 2015) <http://blogs.lse.ac.uk/mediapolicyproject/2015/06/16/the-delfi-as-vs-estonia-judgement-explained/>.

WRR, 'iOverheid', 20111 < www.wrr.nl/fileadmin/nl/publicaties/PDF-Rapporten/I_Overheid.pdf>.

WRR, 'Met kennis van gedrag beleid maken', 2014 <www.wrr.nl/fileadmin/nl/publicaties/PDF-Rapporten/92_Met_kennis_van_gedrag_beleid_maken.pdf >.

WRR, *Big Data in een vrije en veilige samenleving*, WRR-rapport (Amsterdam University Press 2016).

G. Yaffe, *Attempts: In the Philosophy of Action and the Criminal Law* (Oxford University Press 2010).

S. D. Young, 'A "big data" approach to HIV epidemiology and prevention' (2015) 70 Preventive Medicine.

L. T. Zagzebski, *Virtues of the Mind: An Inquiry into the Nature of Virtue and the Ethical Foundations of Knowledge* (Cambridge University Press 1996).

– *Divine Motivation Theory* (Cambridge University Press 2004).

T. Zarsky, 'Mine your own business! Making the Case for the Implications of the Data Mining of Personal Information in the Forum of Public Opinion' (2003) 5(1) Yale Journal of Law and Technology.

– 'Transparent Predictions' (2013) 4 University of Illinois Law Review.

– 'Understanding Discrimination in the Scored Society' (2014) 89 Washington Law Review 1375.

– 'The Trouble with Algorithmic Decisions. An Analytic Road map to Examine Efficiency and Fairness in Automated and Opaque Decision Making' (2016) 41(1) Science, Technology, & Human Values.

F. Zuiderveen Borgesius, *Improving Privacy Protection in the Area of Behavioural Targeting* (Kluwer Law International 2015).
L. Zwaak, 'General Survey of the European Convention', in: P. van Dijk and others (eds), *Theory and Practice of the European Convention on Human Rights* (Intersentia 2006).
T. Zwart, *The Admissibility of Human Rights Petitions: The Case Law of the European Commission of Human Rights and the Human Rights Committee* (Nijhoff 1994).

6. WEBSITES

<www.csmcd.eu/downloads/Generations_of_Human_Rights.pdf>.
<https://decorrespondent.nl/525/over-five-eyes-en-third-parties-met-wie-werkt-de-nsa-samen/25565925-b5edb16e>.
<www.echr.coe.int/Documents/FS_Terrorism_ENG.pdf>.
<http://gadfly.igc.org/Rawls/2-RDP.PDF>.
<www.law.uq.edu.au/articles/qlsr/Gotzmann-QLSR.pdf>.
<www.law.louisville.edu/library/collections/brandeis/node/227>.
<http://legal.un.org/ilc/texts/instruments/english/draft%20articles/9_6_2001.pdf>.
<https://ndpr.nd.edu/news/23369-morals-from-motives/>.
<www.nrc.nl/nieuws/2013/10/31/dit-is-wat-we-nu-weten-over-de-nsa-de-onthullingen-op-een-rijtje-a1430205 >.
<www.nrc.nl/nieuws/2014/01/30/nsa-luisterde-landen-af-tijdens-klimaattop-kopenhagen-in-2009-a1427578 >.
<http://people.umass.edu/cox/NE_2.pdf>
<www.s-j-c.net/main/english/images/humanrightsfinal.pdf>.
<http://stanford.library.usyd.edu.au/entries/ethics-virtue/>.
<https://www.theguardian.com/us-news/the-nsa-files>.
<www.theguardian.com/world/2013/sep/09/nsa-spying-brazil-oil-petrobras>.
<www.tagesschau.de/thema/snowden/index.html>.
<www.thejakartapost.com/news/2006/09/04/fourth-generation-human-rights.html>.
<www.youtube.com/watch?v=mG9uwOhRUcE>.

School of Human Rights Research Series

The School of Human Rights Research is a joint effort by human rights researchers in the Netherlands. Its central research theme is the nature and meaning of international standards in the field of human rights, their application and promotion in the national legal order, their interplay with national standards, and the international supervision of such application. The School of Human Rights Research Series only includes English titles that contribute to a better understanding of the different aspects of human rights.

Editorial Board of the Series:
Prof. dr. J.E. Goldschmidt (Utrecht University), Prof. dr. D.A. Hellema (Utrecht University), Prof. dr. W.J.M. van Genugten (Tilburg University), Prof. dr. F. Coomans (Maastricht University), Prof. dr. P.A.M. Mevis (Erasmus University Rotterdam), Dr. J.-P. Loof (Leiden University) and Dr. O.M. Ribbelink (Asser Institute).

For previous volumes in the series, please visit http://shr.intersentia.com.

Published titles within the Series:
69. Stefanie Jansen-Wilhelm, *Accepting Assistance in the Aftermath of Disasters* ISBN 978-1-78068-329-4
70. Helen Beckmann-Hamzei, *The Child in ICC Proceedings* ISBN 978-1-78068-339-3
71. Karel De Meester, *The Investigation Phase in International Criminal Procedure: In Search of Common Rules* ISBN 978-17-806-8305-8
72. Nelleke Koffeman, *Morally Sensitive Issues and Cross-Border Movement in the EU* ISBN 978-1-78068-349-2
73. Roland Moerland, *The Killing of Death* ISBN 978-1-78068-351-5
74. Andrea Broderick, *The Long and Winding Road to Disability Equality and Inclusion* ISBN 978-1-78068-358-4
75. Christina Peristeridou, *The Principle of Legality in European Criminal Law* ISBN 978-1-78068-357-7
76. Emilie Kuijtk, *Humanitarian Assistance and State Sovereignty in International Law* ISBN 978-1-78068-366-9
77. Lize R. Glas *The Theory, Potential and Practice of Procedural Dialogue in the European Convention on Human Rights System* ISBN 978-1-78068-375-1
78. Paulien de Morree, *Rights and Wrongs under the ECHR* ISBN 978-1-78068-418-5
79. Malu Beijer, *The Limits of Fundamental Rights Protection by the EU* ISBN 978-1-78068-455-0
80. Marie Elske Gispen, *Human Rights and Drug Control* ISBN 978-1-78068-454-3

www.ingramcontent.com/pod-product-compliance
Ingram Content Group UK Ltd.
Pitfield, Milton Keynes, MK11 3LW, UK
UKHW051848210426
5322IPUK00024B/610